Robert P. Holley, PhD, MLS
Editor

Cataloger, Editor, and Scholar: Essays in Honor of Ruth C. Carter

Cataloger, Editor, and Scholar: Essays in Honor of Ruth C. Carter has been co-published simultaneously as *Cataloging & Classification Quarterly*, Volume 44, Numbers 1/2 and 3/4 2007.

Pre-publication REVIEWS, COMMENTARIES, EVALUATIONS . . .

"This far reaching group of essays is a fitting tribute to the distinguished career of the librarian whom it honors. . . . TRANSCENDS THE REALM OF TECHNICAL SERVICE OPERATIONS TODAY. Both traditional and cutting edge issues are explored in depth in a series of carefully researched articles. Like the milestones achieved by the person it honors, this work will prove a core resource in providing insights into where librarians need to be going in developing library services and automated systems. . . . A fitting tribute to Ruth Carter's distinguished career. . . . WILL SERVE AS A MAJOR RESOURCE for administrators and those interested in the ongoing development of technical services operations in these demanding times."

William A. Gosling, MLS, BA
Curator
Children's Literature Collection
Special Collections Library University Library
University of Michigan

Cataloger, Editor, and Scholar: Essays in Honor of Ruth C. Carter

Cataloger, Editor, and Scholar: Essays in Honor of Ruth C. Carter has been co-published simultaneously as *Cataloging & Classification Quarterly*, Volume 44, Numbers 1/2 and 3/4 2007.

> **Monographs from *Cataloging & Classification Quarterly*®**
>
> For additional information on these and other Haworth Press titles, including descriptions, tables of contents, reviews, and prices, use the QuickSearch catalog at http://www.HaworthPress.com.

1. ***The Future of the Union Catalogue: Proceedings of the International Symposium on the Future of the Union Catalogue,*** edited by C. Donald Cook (Vol. 2, No. 1/2, 1982). *Experts explore the current concepts and future prospects of the union catalogue.*

2. ***AACR2 and Serials: The American View,*** edited by Neal L. Edgar (Vol. 3, No. 2/3, 1983). *"This book will help any librarian or serials user concerned with the pitfalls and accomplishments of modern serials cataloging." (American Reference Books Annual)*

3. ***Computer Software Cataloging: Techniques and Examples,*** edited by Deanne Holzberlein, PhD, MLS (Vol. 6, No. 2, 1986). *"Detailed explanations of each of the essential fields in a cataloging record. Will help any librarian who is grappling with the complicated responsibility of cataloging computer software." (Public Libraries)*

4. ***The United States Newspaper Program: Cataloging Aspects,*** edited by Ruth C. Carter, PhD (Vol. 6, No. 4, 1986). *"Required reading for all who use newspapers for research (historians and librarians in particular), newspaper cataloguers, administrators of newspaper collections, and–most important–those who control the preservation pursestrings." (Australian Academic & Research Libraries)*

5. ***Education and Training for Catalogers and Classifiers,*** edited by Ruth C. Carter, PhD (Vol. 7, No. 4, 1987). *"Recommended for all students and members of the profession who possess an interest in cataloging." (RQ-Reference and Adult Services Division)*

6. ***National and International Bibliographic Databases: Trends and Prospects,*** edited by Michael Carpenter, PhD, MBA, MLS (Vol. 8, No. 3/4, 1988). *"A fascinating work, containing much of concern both to the general cataloger and to the language or area specialist as well. It is also highly recommended reading for all those interested in bibliographic databases, their development, or their history." (Library Resources & Technical Services)*

7. ***Cataloging Sound Recordings: A Manual with Examples,*** by Deanne Holzberlein, PhD, MLS (Supp. #1, 1988). *"A valuable, easy to read working tool which should be part of the standard equipment of all catalogers who handle sound recordings." (ALR)*

8. ***Authority Control in the Online Environment: Considerations and Practices,*** edited by Barbara B. Tillett, PhD (Vol. 9, No. 3, 1989). *"Marks an excellent addition to the field. . . . [It] is intended, as stated in the introduction, to 'offer background and inspiration for future thinking.' In achieving this goal, it has certainly succeeded." (Information Technology & Libraries)*

9. ***Subject Control in Online Catalogs,*** edited by Robert P. Holley, PhD, MLS (Vol. 10, No. 1/2, 1990). *"The authors demonstrate the reasons underlying some of the problems and how solutions may be sought. . . . Also included are some fine research studies where the researchers have sought to test the interaction of users with the catalogue, as well as looking at use by library practitioners." (Library Association Record)*

10. ***Library of Congress Subject Headings: Philosophy, Practice, and Prospects,*** by William E. Studwell, MSLS (Supp. #2, 1990). *"Plays an important role in any debate on subject cataloging and succeeds in focusing the reader on the possibilities and problems of using Library of Congress Subject Headings and of subject cataloging in the future." (Australian Academic & Research Libraries)*

11. ***Describing Archival Materials: The Use of the MARC AMC Format,*** edited by Richard P. Smiraglia, MLS (Vol. 11, No. 3/4, 1991). *"A valuable introduction to the use of the MARC AMC format and the principles of archival cataloging itself." (Library Resources & Technical Services)*

12. ***Enhancing Access to Information: Designing Catalogs for the 21st Century,*** edited by David A. Tyckoson (Vol. 13, No. 3/4, 1992). *"Its down-to-earth, nontechnical orientation should appeal to practitioners including administrators and public service librarians." (Library Resources & Technical Services)*

13. ***Retrospective Conversion Now in Paperback: History, Approaches, Considerations,*** edited by Brian Schottlaender, MLS (Vol. 14, No. 3/4, 1992). *"Fascinating insight into the ways and means of converting and updating manual catalogs to machine-readable format." (Library Association Record)*

14. ***Languages of the World: Cataloging Issues and Problems,*** edited by Martin D. Joachim (Vol. 17, No. 1/2, 1994). *"An excellent introduction to the problems libraries must face when cataloging materials not written in English. . . . should be read by every cataloger having to work with international materials, and it is recommended for all library schools. Nicely indexed." (Academic Library Book Review)*

15. ***Cooperative Cataloging: Past, Present and Future,*** edited by Barry B. Baker, MLS (Vol. 17, No. 3/4, 1994). *"The value of this collection lies in its historical perspective and analysis of past and present approaches to shared cataloging. . . . Recommended to library schools and large general collections needing materials on the history of library and information science." (Library Journal)*

16. ***Cataloging Government Publications Online,*** edited by Carolyn C. Sherayko, MLS (Vol. 18, No. 3/4, 1994). *"Presents a wealth of detailed information in a clear and digestible form, and reveals many of the practicalities involved in getting government publications collections onto online cataloging systems." (The Law Librarian)*

17. ***Classification: Options and Opportunities,*** edited by Alan R. Thomas, MA, FLA (Vol. 19, No. 3/4, 1995). *"There is much new and valuable insight to be found in all the chapters. . . . Timely in refreshing our confidence in the value of well-designed and applied classification in providing the best of service to the end-users." (Catalogue and Index)*

18. ***Cataloging and Classification Standards and Rules,*** edited by John J. Reimer, MLS (Vol. 21, No. 3/4, 1996). *"Includes chapters by a number of experts on many of our best loved library standards. . . . Recommended to those who want to understand the history and development of our library standards and to understand the issues at play in the development of new standards." (LASIE)*

19. ***Electronic Resources: Selection and Bibliographic Control,*** edited by Ling-yuh W. (Miko) Pattie, MSLS, and Bonnie Jean Cox, MSLS (Vol. 22, No. 3/4, 1996). *"Recommended for any reader who is searching for a thorough, well-rounded, inclusive compendium on the subject." (The Journal of Academic Librarianship)*

20. ***Cataloging and Classification: Trends, Transformations, Teaching, and Training,*** edited by James R. Shearer, MA, ALA, and Alan R. Thomas, MA, FLA (Vol. 24, No. 1/2, 1997). *"Offers a comprehensive retrospective and innovative projection for the future." (The Catholic Library Association)*

21. ***Portraits in Cataloging and Classification: Theorists, Educators, and Practitioners of the Late Twentieth Century,*** edited by Carolynne Myall, MA, CAS, and Ruth C. Carter, PhD (Vol. 25, No. 2/3/4, 1998). *"This delightful tome introduces us to a side of our profession that we rarely see: the human beings behind the philosophy, rules, and interpretations that have guided our professional lives over the past half century. No collection on cataloging would be complete without a copy of this work." (Walter M. High, PhD, Automation Librarian, North Carolina Supreme Court Library; Assistant Law Librarian for Technical Services, North Carolina University, Chapel Hill)*

22. ***Maps and Related Cartographic Materials: Cataloging, Classification, and Bibliographic Control,*** edited by Paige G. Andrew, MLS, and Mary Lynette Larsgaard, BA, MA (Vol. 27, No. 1/2/3/4, 1999). Discover how to catalog the major formats of cartographic materials, including sheet maps, early and contemporary atlases, remote-sensed images (i.e., aerial photographs and satellite images), globes, geologic sections, digital material, and items on CD-ROM.

23. ***The LCSH Century: One Hundred Years with the Library of Congress Subject Headings System,*** edited by Alva T. Stone, MLS (Vol. 29, No. 1/2, 2000). *Traces the 100-year history of the Library of Congress Subject Headings, from its beginning with the implementation of a dictionary catalog in 1898 to the present day, exploring the most significant changes in LCSH policies and practices, including a summary of other contributions celebrating the centennial of the world's most popular library subject heading language.*

24. ***Managing Cataloging and the Organization of Information: Philosophies, Practices and Challenges at the Onset of the 21st Century,*** edited by Ruth C. Carter, PhD, MS, MA (Vol. 30, No. 1/2/3, 2000). *"A fascinating series of practical, forthright accounts of national, academic, and special library cataloging operations in action. . . . Yields an abundance of practical solutions for shared problems, now and for the future. Highly recommended." (Laura Jizba, Head Cataloger, Portland State University Library, Oregon)*

25. ***The Audiovisual Cataloging Current,*** edited by Sandra K. Roe, MS (Vol. 31, No. 2/3/4, 2001). *"All the great writers, teachers, and lecturers are here: Olson, Fox, Intner, Weihs, Weitz, and Yee. This eclectic collection is sure to find a permanent place on many catalogers' bookshelves. . . . Something for everyone. . . . Explicit cataloging guidelines and AACR2R interpretations galore." (Verna Urbanski, MA, MLS, Chief Media Cataloger, University of North Florida, Jacksonville)*

26. ***Works as Entities for Information Retrieval,*** edited by Richard P. Smiraglia, PhD (Vol. 33, No. 3/4, 2002). *Examines domain-specific research about works and the problems inherent in their representation for information storage and retrieval.*

27. ***Education for Cataloging and the Organization of Information: Pitfalls and the Pendulum,*** edited by Janet Swan Hill, BA, MA (Vol. 34, No. 1/2/3, 2002). *Examines the history, context, present, and future of education for cataloging and bibliographic control.*

28. ***Historical Aspects of Cataloging and Classification,*** edited by Martin D. Joachim, MA (classical languages and literatures), MA (library science) (Vol. 35, No. 1/2, 2002 and Vol. 35, No. 3/4, 2003). *Traces the development of cataloging and classification in countries and institutions around the world.*

29. ***Electronic Cataloging: AACR2 and Metadata for Serials and Monographs,*** edited by Sheila S. Intner, DLS, MLS, BA, Sally C. Tseng, MLS, BA, and Mary Lynette Larsgaard, MA, BA (Vol. 36, No. 3/4, 2003). *"The twelve contributing authors represent some of the most important thinkers and practitioners in cataloging." (Peggy Johnson, MBA, MA, Associate University Librarian, University of Minnesota Libraries)*

30. ***Knowledge Organization and Classification in International Information Retrieval,*** edited by Nancy J. Williamson, PhD, and Clare Beghtol, PhD (Vol. 37, No. 1/2, 2003). *Examines the issues of information retrieval in relation to increased globalization of information and knowledge.*

31. ***The Thesaurus: Review, Renaissance, and Revision,*** edited by Sandra K. Roe, MS, and Alan R. Thomas, MA, FLA (Vol. 37, No. 3/4, 2004). *Examines the historical development of the thesaurus, and the standards employed for thesaurus construction, use, and evaluation.*

32. ***Authority Control in Organizing and Accessing Information: Definition and International Experience,*** edited by Arlene G. Taylor, PhD, MS, and Barbara B. Tillett, PhD, MLS (Vol. 38, No. 3/4, 2004 and Vol. 39, No. 1/2, 2004). *Presents international perspectives on authority control for names, works, and subject terminology in library, archival, museum, and other systems that provide access to information.*

33. ***Functional Requirements for Bibliographic Records (FRBR): Hype or Cure-All?*** edited by Patrick LeBoeuf (Vol. 39, No. 3/4, 2005). *Examines the origin, and theoretical and practical aspects of IFLA's Functional Requirements for Bibliographic Records.*

34. ***Metadata: A Cataloger's Primer,*** edited by Richard P. Smiraglia, PhD (Vol. 40, No. 3/4, 2005). *"A comprehensive overview of metadata written by experts in the field." (Michael Gorman, President-Elect, American Library Association)*

35. ***Education for Library Cataloging: International Perspectives,*** edited by Dajin D. Sun, MSLS, MA, and Ruth C. Carter, PhD, MS, MA (Vol. 41, No. 2, 2005 and Vol. 41, No. 3/4, 2006). *Library school faculty and professional librarians from more than 20 countries discuss the international development of educational programs for cataloging and classification.*

36. ***Moving Beyond the Presentation Layer: Content and Context in the Dewey Decimal Classification (DDC) System,*** edited by Joan S. Mitchell, MLS, BA, and Diane Vizine-Goetz, PhD, MLS, BA (Vol. 42, No. 3/4, 2006). *The authors, drawn broadly from the knowledge organization community, explore the Dewey Decimal Classification (DDC) system from a number of perspectives. In doing so, each peels away a bit of the "presentation layer"–the familiar linear notational sequence–to expose the content and context offered by the DDC.*

37. ***Knitting the Semantic Web,*** edited by Jane Greenberg, PhD, and Eva Méndez, PhD (Vol. 43, No. 3/4, 2007). *Leaders in library, information, and computer science explore developing and maintaining of the semantically rich and advantageous extension of the original Web, known as the Semantic Web.*

38. ***Cataloger, Editor, and Scholar: Essays in Honor of Ruth C. Carter,*** edited by Robert P. Holley, PhD, MLS (Vol. 44, No. 1/2/3/4, 2007). **Cataloger, Editor, and Scholar** *honors the work of Ruth C. Carter to mark her retirement as editor of* Cataloging & Classification Quarterly. *This unique collection features contributions from 22 authors, including many experts in the field, who recall the important aspects of Dr. Carter's life and career and present essays that celebrate her dedication to technical services, cataloging, history, and management. The book includes an interview with Dr. Carter and a review of* Cataloging & Classification Quarterly *during her 20 years as editor.*

ALL HAWORTH INFORMATION PRESS
BOOKS AND JOURNALS ARE PRINTED
ON CERTIFIED ACID-FREE PAPER

Cataloger, Editor, and Scholar: Essays in Honor of Ruth C. Carter

Robert P. Holley, PhD, MLS
Editor

Cataloger, Editor, and Scholar: Essays in Honor of Ruth C. Carter has been co-published simultaneously as *Cataloging & Classification Quarterly*, Volume 44, Numbers 1/2 and 3/4 2007.

The Haworth Information Press®
An Imprint of The Haworth Press, Inc.

www.HaworthPress.com

Published by

The Haworth Information Press®, 10 Alice Street, Binghamton, NY 13904-1580 USA

The Haworth Information Press® is an imprint of The Haworth Press, Inc., 10 Alice Street, Binghamton, NY 13904-1580 USA.

Cataloger, Editor, and Scholar: Essays in Honor of Ruth C. Carter has been co-published simultaneously as *Cataloging & Classification Quarterly*®, Volume 44, Numbers 1/2 & 3/4 2007.

© 2007 by The Haworth Press, Inc. All rights reserved. No part of this work may be reproduced or utilized in any form or by any means, electronic or mechanical, including photocopying, microfilm and recording, or by any information storage and retrieval system, without permission in writing from the publisher. Printed in the United States of America.

The development, preparation, and publication of this work has been undertaken with great care. However, the publisher, employees, editors, and agents of The Haworth Press and all imprints of The Haworth Press, Inc., including The Haworth Medical Press® and Pharmaceutical Products Press®, are not responsible for any errors contained herein or for consequences that may ensue from use of materials or information contained in this work. With regard to case studies, identities and circumstances of individuals discussed herein have been changed to protect confidentiality. Any resemblance to actual persons, living or dead, is entirely coincidental.

The Haworth Press is committed to the dissemination of ideas and information according to the highest standards of intellectual freedom and the free exchange of ideas. Statements made and opinions expressed in this publication do not necessarily reflect the views of the Publisher, Directors, management, or staff of The Haworth Press, Inc., or an endorsement by them.

Cover design by Kerry E. Mack.

Library of Congress Cataloging-in-Publication Data

Cataloger, editor, and scholar : essays in honor of Ruth C. Carter / Robert P. Holley, guest editor.
    p. cm.
    "Co-published simulataneously as Cataloging & classification quarterly, volume 44, numbers 1/2 & 3/4."
    Includes bibliographical references and index.
    ISBN-13: 978-0-7890-3622-3 (alk. paper)
    ISBN-10: 0-7890-36222-3 (alk. paper)
    1. Cataloging. 2. Technical services (Libraries) 3. Carter, Ruth C.–Career in library science. I. Holley, Robert P. II. Carter, Ruth C. III. Cataloging & classification quarterly.
Z693.C375 2007
025.3–dc22
                                        2006039107

The HAWORTH PRESS, Inc.
Abstracting, Indexing & Outward Linking
PRINT and ELECTRONIC BOOKS & JOURNALS

This section provides you with a list of major indexing & abstracting services and other tools for bibliographic access. That is to say, each service began covering this periodical during the year noted in the right column. Most Websites which are listed below have indicated that they will either post, disseminate, compile, archive, cite or alert their own Website users with research-based content from this work. (This list is as current as the copyright date of this publication.)

Abstracting, Website/Indexing Coverage . . . . Year When Coverage Began

- **Academic Search Premier (EBSCO)** <http://search.ebscohost.com> 2006
- **INSPEC (The Institution of Engineering and Technology)**
  <http://www.iee.org.uk/publish/> 1982
- **LISA: Library and Information Science Abstracts (ProQuest CSA)**
  <http://www.csa.com/factsheets/list-set-c.php> 1989
- **MasterFILE Premier (EBSCO)** <http://search.ebscohost.com> 2006
- *Academic Source Premier (EBSCO)* <http://search.ebscohost.com> 2007
- *Advanced Polymers Abstracts (Cambridge Scientific Abstracts)*
  <http://www.csa.com/factsheets/ema-polymers-set-c.php> 2006
- *Aluminum Industry Abstracts (Cambridge Scientific Abstracts)*
  <http://www.csa.com/factsheets/aia-set-c.php> 2006
- *Cabell's Directory of Publishing Opportunities in Educational Technology & Library Science* <http://www.cabells.com> 2006
- *Cambridge Scientific Abstracts* <http://www.csa.com> 2006
- *Ceramic Abstracts (Cambridge Scientific Abstracts)*
  <http://www.csa.com/factsheets/wca-set-c.php> 2006
- *Composites Industry Abstracts (Cambridge Scientific Abstracts)*
  <http://www.csa.com/factsheets/ema-composites-set-c.php> 2006
- *Computer & Control Abstracts (INSPEC–The Institution of Engineering and Technology)* <http://www.iee.org.uk/publish/> 2006
- *Computer and Information Systems Abstracts (Cambridge Scientific Abstracts)* <http://www.csa.com/factsheets/computer-set-c.php> 2004
- *Corrosion Abstracts (Cambridge Scientific Abstracts)*
  <http://www.csa.com/factsheets/corrosion-set-c.php> 2006

(continued)

- *CSA Engineering Research Database (Cambridge Scientific Abstracts)* <http://www.csa.com/factsheets/engineering-set-c.php>............... 2006
- *CSA High Technology Research Database with Aerospace (Cambridge Scientific Abstracts)* <http://www.csa.com/factsheets/hightech-set-c.php> .. 2006
- *CSA Technology Research Database (Cambridge Scientific Abstracts)* <http://www.csa.com/factsheets/techresearch-set-c.php> 2006
- *CSA/ASCE Civil Engineering Abstracts (Cambridge Scientific Abstracts)* <http://www.csa.com/factsheets/civil-set-c.php> 2006
- *Current Abstracts (EBSCO)* <http://search.ebscohost.com> 2007
- *Current Citations Express (EBSCO)* <http://search.ebscohost.com>........ 2007
- *EBSCOhost Electronic Journals Service (EJS)* <http://search.ebscohost.com>.................................. 2001
- *Education Research Complete (EBSCO)* <http://search.ebscohost.com> 2006
- *Education Research Index (EBSCO)* <http://search.ebscohost.com> 2007
- *Electrical & Electronics Abstracts (INSPEC–The Institution of Engineering and Technology)* <http://www.iee.org.uk/publish/>...... 2006
- *Electronic Collections Online (OCLC)* <http://www.oclc.org/electroniccollections/>.................... 2006
- *Electronics and Communications Abstracts (Cambridge Scientific Abstracts)* <http://www.csa.com/factsheets/electronics-set-c.php> 2006
- *Elsevier Eflow-I* 2006
- *Elsevier Scopus* <http://www.info.scopus.com> 2005
- *Engineered Materials Abstracts (Cambridge Scientific Abstracts)* <http://www.csa.com/factsheets/emaclust-set-c.php> 2006
- *Google* <http://www.google.com> 2004
- *Google Scholar* <http://scholar.google.com> 2004
- *Haworth Document Delivery Center* <http://www.HaworthPress.com/journals/dds.asp>.................. 1980
- *(IBR) International Bibliography of Book Reviews on the Humanities and Social Sciences (Thomson)* <http://www.saur.de> 2006
- *(IBZ) International Bibliography of Periodical Literature on the Humanities and Social Sciences (Thomson)* <http://www.saur.de> 1995
- *Index Guide to College Journals* 1999
- *Index to Periodical Articles Related to Law* <http://www.law.utexas.edu> ... 1989
- *Information Science & Technology Abstracts (EBSCO)* <http://search.ebscohost.com>.................................. 2007
- *Informed Librarian, The* <http://www.informedlibrarian.com>............ 1993
- *INIST-CNRS* <http://www.inist.fr>................................... 1999

(continued)

- *Internationale Bibliographie der geistes- und sozialwissenschaftlichen Zeitschriftenliteratur . . . See IBZ . . . . <http://www.saur.de> 1995*
- *Journal of Academic Librarianship: Guide to Professional Literature, The . . . 1997*
- *JournalSeek <http://www.journalseek.net> 2006*
- *Konyvtari Figyelo (Library Review). 1995*
- *Legal Information Management Index (LIMI) <http://www.legalinformationservices.com> 2007*
- *Library Literature & Information Science Index/Full Text (H. W. Wilson) <http://www.hwwilson.com> 1984*
- *Library, Information Science & Technology Abstracts (EBSCO) <http://search.ebscohost.com>. 2006*
- *Library, Information Science & Technology Abstracts with Full Text (EBSCO) <http://search.ebscohost.com>. 2007*
- *Links@Ovid (via CrossRef targeted DOI links) <http://www.ovid.com> 2005*
- *Materials Business File (Cambridge Scientific Abstracts) <http://www.csa.com/factsheets/mbf-set-c.php> 2006*
- *Materials Research Database with METADEX (Cambridge Scientific Abstracts) <http://www.csa.com/factsheets/materials-set-c.php> 2006*
- *Mechanical & Transportation Engineering Abstracts (Cambridge Scientific Abstracts) <http://www.csa.com/factsheets/mechtrans-set-c.php> 2006*
- *METADEX (Cambridge Scientific Abstracts) <http://www.csa.com/factsheets/metadex-set-c.php>. 2006*
- *NewJour (Electronic Journals & Newsletters) <http://gort.ucsd.edu/newjour/>. 2006*
- *OCLC ArticleFirst <http://www.oclc.org/services/databases/>. 2007*
- *Ovid Linksolver (OpenURL link resolver via CrossRef targeted DOI links) <http://www.linksolver.com> 2005*
- *Physics Abstracts (INSPEC–The Institution of Engineering and Technology) <http://www.iee.org.uk/publish/>. 2006*
- *Referativnyi Zhurnal (Abstracts Journal of the All-Russian Institute of Scientific and Technical Information–in Russian) <http://www.viniti.ru> 1992*
- *Scopus (see instead Elsevier Scopus) <http://www.info.scopus.com> 2005*
- *Solid State and Superconductivity Abstracts (Cambridge Scientific Abstracts) <http://www.csa.com/factsheets/solid-state-set-c.php> 2006*
- *Subject Index to Literature on Electronic Sources of Information <http://library2.usask.ca/~dworacze/SUB_INT.HTM>. 1996*
- *SwetsWise <http://www.swets.com>. 2001*
- *TOC Premier (EBSCO) <http://search.ebscohost.com>. 2007*
- *WilsonWeb <http://vnweb.hwwilsonweb.com/hww/Journals/> 2005*

(continued)

Bibliographic Access

- *Cabell's Directory of Publishing Opportunities in Educational Curriculum and Methods <http://www.cabells.com/>*

- *Magazines for Libraries (Katz)*

- *MediaFinder <http://www.mediafinder.com/>*

- *Ulrich's Periodicals Directory: The Global Source for Periodicals Information Since 1932 <http://www.bowkerlink.com>*

Special Bibliographic Notes related to special journal issues (separates) and indexing/abstracting:

- indexing/abstracting services in this list will also cover material in any "separate" that is co-published simultaneously with Haworth's special thematic journal issue or DocuSerial. Indexing/abstracting usually covers material at the article/chapter level.
- monographic co-editions are intended for either non-subscribers or libraries which intend to purchase a second copy for their circulating collections.
- monographic co-editions are reported to all jobbers/wholesalers/approval plans. The source journal is listed as the "series" to assist the prevention of duplicate purchasing in the same manner utilized for books-in-series.
- to facilitate user/access services all indexing/abstracting services are encouraged to utilize the co-indexing entry note indicated at the bottom of the first page of each article/chapter/contribution.
- this is intended to assist a library user of any reference tool (whether print, electronic, online, or CD-ROM) to locate the monographic version if the library has purchased this version but not a subscription to the source journal.
- individual articles/chapters in any Haworth publication are also available through the Haworth Document Delivery Service (HDDS).

As part of Haworth's continuing commitment to better serve our library patrons, we are proud to be working with the following electronic services:

AGGREGATOR SERVICES

EBSCOhost

Ingenta

J-Gate

Minerva

OCLC FirstSearch

Oxmill

SwetsWise

LINK RESOLVER SERVICES

1Cate (Openly Informatics)

ChemPort (American Chemical Society)

CrossRef

Gold Rush (Coalliance)

LinkOut (PubMed)

LINKplus (Atypon)

LinkSolver (Ovid)

LinkSource with A-to-Z (EBSCO)

Resource Linker (Ulrich)

SerialsSolutions (ProQuest)

SFX (Ex Libris)

Sirsi Resolver (SirsiDynix)

Tour (TDnet)

Vlink (Extensity, formerly Geac)

WebBridge (Innovative Interfaces)

Cataloger, Editor, and Scholar: Essays in Honor of Ruth C. Carter

CONTENTS

Introduction	1

PART I: IN HONOR OF DR. RUTH CARTER

The Story of Ruth: The Life and Contributions of Ruth C. Carter *Kathryn Luther Henderson*	7
An Interview with Ruth C. Carter *Ruth C. Carter* *Linda C. Ewbank*	19
Cataloging & Classification Quarterly, 1990-2006 *Sandra K. Roe* *Rebecca Culbertson* *Laurel Jizba*	39
In Honor of Ruth C. Carter *Sheila S. Intner*	53

PART II: HISTORICAL STUDIES

Books and Other Reading Materials in Early Monroe County, Indiana *Martin D. Joachim*	55
Annotation: A Lost Art in Cataloguing *J. H. Bowman*	95

Twenty-Five Years of Bibliographic Control Research
   at the University of Bradford   113
    F. H. Ayres
    J. M. Ridley

International Cataloguing Tradition and Italian Rules:
   Common Ground and Specific Features   131
    Carlo Bianchini
    Mauro Guerrini

PART III: RESEARCH STUDIES

Technical Services and Tenure: Impediments and Strategies   151
    Janet Swann Hill

The "Works" Phenomenon and Best Selling Books   179
    Richard P. Smiraglia

Measuring Typographical Errors' Impact on Retrieval
   in Bibliographic Databases   197
    Jeffrey Beall
    Karen Kafadar

Error Rates in Monograph Copy Cataloging Bibliographic
   Records Before and After Outsourcing at the University
   of Saskatchewan Library   213
    Vinh-The Lam

Meeting the Needs of Special Format Catalogers: Ideas
   for Professional Organizations, Library Schools,
   and Professional Catalogers   221
    Robert L. Bothmann

Copy Cataloging for Print and Video Monographs in Two
   Academic Libraries: A Case Study of Editing Required
   for Accuracy and Completeness   233
    Carolynne Myall
    Sydney Chambers

Are Technical Services Topics Underrepresented
   in the Contributed Papers at the ACRL National
   Conferences?   259
     Robert P. Holley

PART IV: POSITION PAPERS

Quo Vadis, Cataloging?   271
     Elizabeth N. Steinhagen
     Mary Ellen Hanson
     Sharon A. Moynahan

Principia Bibliographica? Balancing Principles, Practice,
   and Pragmatics in a Changing Digital Environment   281
     Dick R. Miller

Cataloging Compared to Descriptive Bibliography, Abstracting
   and Indexing Services, and Metadata   307
     Martha M. Yee

Knowledge Structures and the Internet: Progress and Prospects   329
     Nancy J. Williamson

Numbers to Identify Entities (ISADNs–International
   Standard Authority Data Numbers)   343
     Barbara B. Tillett

When You Come to a Fork in the Road, Pick It Up: A Case
   Study in Managing by Self-Responsibility   363
     Lyn Condron

Index   377

ABOUT THE EDITOR

Robert P. Holley, PhD, MLS, is Professor in the Library & Information Science Program, Wayne State University, Detroit, Michigan, where he teaches courses in collection development, management, academic libraries, and grant writing. Since his arrival at Wayne State University in 1988, he has also been Associate Dean, Director of the Library & Information Science Program, and Interim Dean of University Libraries. He was Assistant Director for Technical Services at the Marriott Library, the University of Utah from 1979-1988. He began his library career in the Sterling Memorial Library, Yale University (1971-1979) where he held positions of increasing responsibility in the Catalog Department. Dr. Holley has edited five books and authored many articles on diverse library topics. He was editor of *Resource Sharing & Information Networks* from 1989-2000. He is a past-president of ALCTS (1994-1995) and was a founding member of the IFLA Section on Classification (1981), which he chaired from 1985-1989.

Dr. Holley has a long association with *Cataloging & Classification Quarterly* and with Ruth Carter. Along with Robert Killheffer, he published "Is There an Answer to the Subject Access Crisis?" in the second issue of *Cataloging & Classification Quarterly* (Vol. 1, 2/3, 1982, pp. 125-133). He has been a member of its Editorial Board since 1987 and has served on four "Best of Volume XX Task Forces," including chairing three. In 1989, he edited a special issue of *CCQ* on *Subject Control in Online Catalogs*. Overall, Dr. Holley has published eight articles and five book reviews in *CCQ*. In addition, he frequently serves as a peer reviewer for the journal. He came to know Ruth Carter during their time together in ALCTS. They also attended several IFLA conferences together though their professional interests led to participation in different divisions.

Introduction

Ruth Carter has many friends! The number of contributions to this festschrift in honor of her stepping down as editor of *Cataloging & Classification Quarterly* is a strong testament to her high regard by leaders in the field. I accepted the invitation to edit this volume in April, 2005 because of my long association with Ruth and my wish to provide a fitting tribute to her years of service to the journal.

I developed the plan for the festschrift in consultation with Sandy Roe, the current editor of *CCQ*. I extended an invitation to contribute a paper to members of the editorial board, to the most frequent contributors to the journal, and to a few select leaders in cataloging. In addition, Sandy and I sought out several contributions that would deal with Ruth's professional career and the importance of the journal. Finally, Linda C. Ewbank interviewed Ruth to gain her perspective on her professional career and term as editor.

As can be seen from the number of articles, the response was enormous. Many others declined with regret. I did not assign topics to the contributors. When asked about possible subjects, I told the authors "to write an article that would make Ruth proud." This decision resulted in the somewhat eclectic nature of the festschrift as the various authors chose a wide variety of topics and methodologies.

I have grouped the contributions into the following categories:

- In honor of Dr. Ruth Carter
- Historical studies
- Research studies
- Position papers

All articles were peer reviewed. I wish to thank the following for their efforts and especially for their promptness in returning the articles with comments:

- Eastern Michigan University
  - Birong Ho
- Madison Public Library
  - Jon Muzall
- University of Colorado at Boulder
  - Christopher Cronin
  - Anna M. Ferris
  - M. Winslow Lundy
  - Paul Moeller
- Wayne State Univesity
  - Anaclare Evans
  - Richard Moritz

PART I: IN HONOR OF DR. RUTH CARTER

In "The Story of Ruth: The Life and Contributions of Ruth C. Carter," Kathryn Luther Henderson, her cataloging professor at the University of Illinois at Urbana-Champaign, recounts the amazing career of Ruth Carter as a librarian, researcher, editor, and active member of multiple professional associations. She stresses her multifaceted contributions in serials, technical services, and archives as well as her ability to draw the highest level of achievement from her colleagues.

Linda C. Ewbank interviewed Ruth Carter for the festschrift. In "An Interview with Ruth C. Carter," Ruth comments not only on her life but also on the key issues in cataloging at the beginning of the 21st century. She describes her experiences as the editor of *CCQ* and her role in professional organizations. She concludes by letting us know a bit about her interests outside of librarianship and her plans for the future.

In "*Cataloging & Classification Quarterly*, 1990-2006," Sandra K. Roe, Rebecca Culbertson, and Laurel Jizba analyze the contents of the journal by looking at contributors, article types, and changes in topics. Their results show that authorship has become more diverse and that topics have changed to reflect developments in cataloging, most frequently caused by advances in technology.

Sheila S. Intner has written a poem "In Honor of Ruth C. Carter."

PART II: HISTORICAL STUDIES

In a major study on the availability of "Books and Other Reading Materials in Early Monroe County, Indiana," Martin D. Joachim draws upon both published and unpublished sources to show that books were easy to acquire during Indiana's frontier period in the first half of the 19th century. He includes information about both library and private ownership of reading materials along with extensive documentation on holdings, including individual titles.

"Annotation: A Lost Art in Cataloguing" by J. H. Bowman traces the use of annotations in early 20th century Great Britain to clarify obscure titles or to provide further information about the subject-matter. Annotations started to disappear after World War I with the decline of the printed catalog. He draws parallels between annotations and current table-of-contents information.

F. H. Ayres and J. M. Ridley describe "Twenty-Five Years of Bibliographic Control Research at the University of Bradford." With the cooperation of the Department of Computing, the Bradford University Library has undertaken many creative projects including the Universal Standard Bibliographic Code; database merging, deduplication, and quality control; and the BOPAC project that creates faster and better access to library online catalogs.

The final paper in this section, "International Cataloguing Tradition and Italian Rules: Common Ground and Specific Features," authored by Carlo Bianchini and Mauro Guerrini, traces the history of the development of cataloging codes in Italy. The authors chronicle the effects of the tension between international standards and local tradition and the need to reconcile the two. They also emphasize the need to make the catalog easier to use.

PART III: RESEARCH STUDIES

Janet Swann Hill presents her findings on "Technical Services and Tenure: Impediments and Strategies." Tenure is a difficult issue for librarians because it is based on the faculty model of teaching and research. Through an examination of documents and a questionnaire, she examines whether technical services librarians, whose work most often does not include significant direct contact with users, face difficulties in achieving tenure that their public services colleagues do not. She concludes by discussing strategies to increase the likelihood for technical services librarians to obtain tenure.

In "The 'Works' Phenomenon and Best Selling Books," Richard P. Smiraglia empirically examines the instantiation of a sample of best selling works of the 20th century. His analysis of the bibliographic records in OCLC and RLIN and their instantiations on the World Wide Web found that many of these best selling books have large and complex networks. He concludes that solutions that worked for the catalog may need to be modified for the World Wide Web.

Jeffrey Beall and Karen Kafadar present their study on "Measuring Typographical Errors' Impact on Retrieval in Bibliographic Databases." They test the hypothesis that, with the prevalence of keyword searching, a typographical error may not have an impact on retrieval if the word is found correctly spelled elsewhere in the record. They discovered that the presence of a typo blocks access to a significant number of records (35% to 99%), depending upon the frequency of the word being searched and its likelihood of being misspelled.

In "Error Rates in Monograph Copy Cataloging Bibliographic Records Before and After Outsourcing at the University of Saskatchewan Library," Vinh-The Lam determines that, for monograph copy cataloging, outsourcing had no significant effect upon cataloging quality at the University of Saskatchewan Library and that the error rates were low and acceptable.

Robert L. Bothmann is concerned about "Meeting the Needs of Special Format Catalogers: Ideas for Professional Organizations, Library Schools, and Professional Catalogers." Through a voluntary online survey of special format catalogers, he learned that most of them learned their special skills on the job. They expressed a need for more training and for more attention within professional organizations to their concerns. He then offers suggestions for future steps, especially since 50% of the catalogers surveyed intend to retire within fifteen years.

The topic of Carolynne Myall's and Sydney Chambers' article is "Copy Cataloging for Print and Video Monographs in Two Academic Libraries: A Case Study of Editing Required for Accuracy and Completeness." By analyzing a sample of cataloging at two mid-sized academic libraries over a three-month period, they determined that video/DVD monographs require much more editing because national-level records are not available. They propose a cooperative program to create high quality records for these items.

Robert P. Holley poses the question "Are Technical Services Topics Underrepresented in the Contributed Papers at the ACRL National Conferences?" He examines the contributed papers from the twelve ACRL National Conferences for those with subjects of interest to members of ALCTS. Only 14.66% dealt with topics that are part of the charge of the units within ALCTS. In eliminating collection development topics, also of interest to public services librarians, the percentage dropped to 7.52%. His unexpected discovery is that the contributed papers have become much more holistic with the arrival of the Internet and electronic resources.

PART IV: POSITION PAPERS

Elizabeth N. Steinhagen, Mary Ellen Hanson, and Sharon A. Moynahan summarize the recent history of cataloging and speculate about future directions in "Quo Vadis, Cataloging?" They trace the path from the golden age of cataloging in the 1970s and 1980s through the economic retrenchment of the 1990s and early 2000s. They also consider the effects on technology including the rapid rise of search engines such as Google. They conclude with the advice that cataloging must move forward beyond replicating the old paper catalog card to focus on cataloging as part of the intellectual process of access for research.

Dick R. Miller studies the differences between the authority control offered by cataloging and the chaos on the World Wide Web in his "Principia Bibliographica? Balancing Principles, Practice, and Pragmatics in a Changing Digital Environment." Through a systematic examination of several different examples, he looks at the varying approaches and suggests ways to achieve the best of both worlds. He believes that catalogers should take a much more active role in the digital environment.

In "Cataloging Compared to Descriptive Bibliography, Abstracting and Indexing Services, and Metadata," Martha M. Yee deepens the understanding of cataloging by comparing it to descriptive bibliography, indexing and abstracting services, and metadata. She pays particular attention to providing a clearer sense of what metadata is. Yee feels that it is important not to overlook the differences among these various systems in the creation of new cataloging rules.

Nancy J. Williamson evaluates improvements in subject access since 1997 to materials on the Internet with her "Knowledge Structures and the Internet: Progress and Prospects." She looks at search engines; Web subject directories; thesauri; and gateways and portals. Williamson concludes that subject access for Internet materials has definitely improved but also that much remains to be done to assure that quality information rises to the top.

In "Numbers to Identify Entities (ISADNs–International Standard Authority Data Numbers)," Barbara B. Tillett considers whether it is advisable to develop a system of International Standard Authority Data Numbers. While she recognizes the appeal of unique identifiers, she concludes that the existing machine-generated control numbers from our authority records are adequate until we know better what future systems need.

The volume concludes with a management case study, "When You Come to a Fork in the Road, Pick It Up: A Case Study in Managing by Self-Responsibility." Lyn Condron strongly believes that the key to management success is initiating and supporting self-responsibility by the manager, by the individuals, and by the team as a group. She discusses the application of this principle to cataloging production; teams and meetings; competency management; the general work environment; and quality assurance.

Robert P. Holley

PART I: IN HONOR OF DR. RUTH CARTER

The Story of Ruth: The Life and Contributions of Ruth C. Carter

Kathryn Luther Henderson

SUMMARY. Ruth C. Carter's professional career has spanned over three decades of service as librarian, archivist, and editor. Specific aspects of that service are noted in this biographical sketch that commemorates her twenty years as editor of *Cataloging & Classification Quarterly*. doi:10.1300/J104v44n01_02 *[Article copies available for a fee from The Haworth Document Delivery Service: 1-800-HAWORTH. E-mail address: <docdelivery@haworthpress.com> Website: <http://www.HaworthPress.com> © 2007 by The Haworth Press, Inc. All rights reserved.]*

KEYWORDS. Ruth C. Carter, *Cataloging & Classification Quarterly*

Kathryn Luther Henderson is Professor, Graduate School of Library and Information Science, University of Illinois at Urbana-Champaign, 501 East Daniel Street, Champaign, IL 61820-6211 (E-mail: lutherk@uiuc.edu).

[Haworth co-indexing entry note]: "The Story of Ruth: The Life and Contributions of Ruth C. Carter." Henderson, Kathryn Luther. Co-published simultaneously in *Cataloging & Classification Quarterly* (The Haworth Information Press, an imprint of The Haworth Press, Inc.) Vol. 44, No. 1/2, 2007, pp. 7-17; and: *Cataloger, Editor, and Scholar: Essays in Honor of Ruth C. Carter* (ed: Robert P. Holley) The Haworth Information Press, an imprint of The Haworth Press, Inc., 2007, pp. 7-17. Single or multiple copies of this article are available for a fee from The Haworth Document Delivery Service [1-800-HAWORTH, 9:00 a.m. - 5:00 p.m. (EST). E-mail address: docdelivery@haworthpress.com].

Available online at http://ccq.haworthpress.com
© 2007 by The Haworth Press, Inc. All rights reserved.
doi:10.1300/J104v44n01_02

THE CINCINNATI YEARS

Ruth Carol Brill was born on December 13, 1937 to Raymond E. and Helen Jane Prophater Brill in Cincinnati, Ohio. Two years later, their second daughter, Mary, was born. Neither parent had received a great deal of formal education. In fact, neither of them had completed high school; they both, however, valued education. Mr. Brill was a detective with the Cincinnati Police Department; he especially enjoyed reading mystery stories and books on archaeology. Ruth remembers that both she and Mary were avid readers of Perry Mason mysteries. (Can we speculate that such a beginning might have helped Ruth develop her analytical mind and problem solving abilities?)

Ruth attended kindergarten, elementary, and secondary public schools in Cincinnati and continued the pattern of staying in Cincinnati for bachelor's and master's degrees. All of these educational experiences took place on the same street in Cincinnati within a mile and a half distance.

Ruth's Bachelor of Science degree from the University of Cincinnati in 1959 included a concentration in Education, and she began her first professional position as a teacher of history and geography at Greenhills High School, Greenhills, Ohio. Her students were seventh and eighth graders. This experience did not encourage her to actively continue a career in teaching, but later Ruth wrote that librarians are teachers in their roles as supervisors, trainers, and mentors in transmitting philosophical and practical aspects of the profession. Ruth fulfilled all of these teaching roles in her library career (Carter, 2001b, 1).

Rather than teaching students, Ruth returned to being a student. Now the first-generation college graduate in her family was pursuing a master's degree! While she had abandoned a teaching career, she did not abandon the subject matter. History was the discipline in which the Master of Arts degree from the University of Cincinnati was awarded in 1961. This led to her next professional position as Curator of Manuscripts and Reference Assistant at the Cincinnati Historical Society where she worked from 1961-1963.

The year 1963 was an important milestone in Ruth's life. On August 30, 1963, she married John L. Carter, whom she had met at the University of Cincinnati. Also in 1963, she received a good score on the Federal Service Entrance Exam and worked as a training officer in the Adjutant General's Office, United States Army, in Washington, D.C. (Perhaps the Education degree was at work here, too.) In the beginning days of the computer era, she was able to enroll in a six month's program in systems analysis and training that led to a two-year stint as a Computer Systems Analyst, Office of Chief of Staff, United States Army (Carter, 1998, 8).

MOVING WESTWARD: THE URBANA-CHAMPAIGN ERA

In 1966, John completed his doctorate in geology from the University of Cincinnati and accepted the position of Curator in the Geology Department at the University of Illinois at Urbana-Champaign (UIUC); so John and Ruth moved to Illinois. For the next several years, Ruth assisted John with the bibliographic and indexing work associated with the monograph, *Bibliography and Index of North American Carboniferous Brachiopods, 1898-1968*, which was published as Memoir 128 of the Geological Society of America in 1970.

During that time, Ruth also enrolled in and audited some courses in zoology at UIUC, but she also took the big step that resulted in the direction that would influence the next stages of her professional life; she enrolled in the University of Illinois at Urbana-Champaign, Graduate School of Library Science (later the name was changed to Graduate School of Library and Information Science) (GSLIS). She had been awarded a Title II-B HEA fellowship in Library Science.

In the fall semester of 1969, there were forty-seven students in the Cataloging and Classification I course that I taught at GSLIS. Although GSLIS had a few required core courses, this course was not one of them; but almost all students in the School realized the importance of cataloging courses and enrolled in at least this basic course regardless of their career goals. One of these students was Ruth C. Carter. Ruth had openly acknowledged to me that she had come to library school to learn what was necessary to become an excellent reference librarian. No doubt she was encouraged toward this goal by her experience answering reference questions at the Cincinnati Historical Society and her bibliographic and indexing work with John's monograph. To me, the type of student that I envision as a potentially successful cataloger is one who can analyze a situation, identify the problems, find alternative solutions, apply principles and rules, come up with viable solutions, and evaluate those solutions. (Is this not somewhat like a Perry Mason syndrome?) It did not take me long to place Ruth in that category of potentially successful catalogers. I was delighted when Ruth enrolled in the advanced cataloging class in the spring semester 1970. This introduced her to serials cataloging that later became an important aspect of her work.

If one studies Ruth's impressive resume, one notices that since 1970 no reference positions appear in that listing; but the resume is replete with a wide array of achievements in technical services. If I had anything to do with her change in specialization, I offer my apologies to the public service community; yet I know that Ruth has often stated that technical services are also user services and that the work that she has done in technical services has been to enable and enhance services to the users of libraries and archives.

Concerted efforts toward library automation were beginning in the late 1960s and early 1970s so that Ruth's early experience with computers in Washington served her well, not only in her library science courses but also in the positions that she later held in those early days of automation.

Ruth's first professional library position was at Parkland College located in Champaign, Illinois. Parkland had opened in 1967 as a community college covering the whole or parts of twelve counties in east central Illinois. Parkland had no dedicated campus as such in its early days and was located in scattered sites in downtown Champaign. Parkland's first library was in a former store in the center of the city; this became the site where Ruth held her first professional position. (Today, Parkland has an extensive dedicated campus, many programs, and over 11,000 students.)

When Parkland opened, the technical services position had been filled by one of my former students. As that individual left for a position in a university library, Parkland's library director asked me for suggestions of persons skilled in cataloging and automation. I suggested Ruth. She was hired; and, from 1970-1972, she was Head of Technical Services and Automation at Parkland College.

Our roles as teacher and student reversed in 1971 during my sabbatical leave when I worked with Ruth on an early acquisitions project that she had underway at Parkland College. An especially valuable lesson that I learned from Ruth involved a programmer with whom she was working. He insisted that a process she wanted applied could not possibly be implemented. Patiently and politely, Ruth, with her knowledge of systems analysis and programming, indicated that the process could be implemented. It might take a bit more time and effort to accomplish but it could be done–and it was.

During the first week of October 1971, OCLC went online for the first time to its constituent libraries in Ohio. Fred Kilgour had invited my husband and me, along with Ruth, to Columbus for this momentous event. While discussing automated acquisitions programs, Fred and Ruth discovered that they had devised rather similar early automated acquisitions programs at different institutions. Ruth's was the Parkland program mentioned above. This was Ruth's first encounter with OCLC, but it was not to be her last. From 1973-1996, she was involved in OCLC services and activities including serving on the OCLC Users Council as well as being a member of committees related to serials control and union listing.

THE PITTSBURGH ERA

In 1972, the Carters moved to Pittsburgh when John accepted a position at the Carnegie Museum of Natural History. Again Ruth's early background in computers was beneficial as she was first hired in a temporary position as a system analyst at the University of Pittsburgh Library. This led to a succession of increasingly responsible positions in the University of Pittsburgh Libraries, moving from Systems Librarian to Head, Serials Department to Head, Catalog Department to Technical Services Coordinator, and eventually to Assistant Director for Automation and Technical Services. These were important times for serials control activities, and Ruth's name became closely associated with serials, not only at the University of Pittsburgh but also through OCLC and other professional committees and task force groups. One of her particular interests was union listing. She served on the CONSER Policy Committee for over a decade in its formative years. She also served on committees of the Pennsylvania Newspaper Project that advanced this local component of the larger U.S. Newspaper Program and contributed to regional and national bibliographic control and preservation of newspapers.

From 1984-1987, she served as Chair-Elect, Chair, and Past Chair of the Serials Section of the Resources & Technical Services Division (RTSD) (predecessor of the Association for Library Collections and Technical Services (ALCTS)) of the American Library Association (ALA). Her service became international through her serving from 1991-1999 as the ALA representative to the International Federation of Library Associations and Institutions (IFLA) Standing Committee on Serial Publications.

In 1986, the profession, through ALA, honored Ruth Carter with the prestigious Bowker/Ulrich's Serials Librarianship Award given for distinguished contributions to serials librarianship through research, publication, management, and educational activities related to serials. This was only the second time that the award had been given.

RESEARCH AND PUBLICATION

Early on, Ruth realized that her role as a professional librarian included research and publication. Her numerous articles covering serials control, union listing, technical standards, online services, collection development, cataloging codes, systems analysis, and library automation have been published in respected refereed journals such as *Serials Librarian, Serials Review, Canadian Library Journal, Library Resources & Technical Services, Library HiTech, Technical Services Quarterly, Journal of Library Automation,* and *Library Trends* and in compilations such as the *Encyclopedia of Library and Information Science.*

With Scott Bruntjen, she authored the monograph *Data Conversion* (Knowledge Industry Publications, 1983). This publication provided guidance to many librarians who were engaged in retrospective conversion of their catalogs to the online format.

It was shortly after this in 1984 that Peter Gellatly, Senior Editor for The Haworth Press, Inc., approached Ruth about becoming editor of *Cataloging & Classification Quarterly* (*CCQ*). Since Peter's name was long associated with serials, we can conjecture that Ruth's work in serials and her authorship in that area had caught Peter's sharp eyes. Although Ruth admits that she "had never even dreamed of being an editor" (Carter, 1998, 7), the next important phase of her career and one that she would label "one of the major satisfactions" of her career (Carter, 1998, 7) began in the fall of 1985 with *CCQ*'s volume six and continued through volume forty-one. (Serialists will forever praise and bless her for keeping the same journal title throughout her editorship!)

She acknowledged that editing was an enormous challenge and responsibility. Two decades later, it is obvious that she has succeeded in both aspects. After two decades of rapid change, *CCQ* remains strong and is a highly respected journal in its specialty. Through *CCQ*, Ruth has continued to lead the profession into new philosophical and theoretical understandings of these areas as well as to include articles that documented the practical aspects of everyday work. Her knowledge of history allowed her to place the present within the context of the past and to project it into the future. Her perceptive editorial introductions to most issues set the tone of the articles that followed. Her choice of theme issues illustrated her ability to keep her finger on the pulse of the profession and to realize that a series of articles was sometimes necessary to cover especially important and timely subject areas. She chose experts in the subjects as guest editors of theme issues; but she edited or co-edited some of the theme issues herself, several of which became published monographs.

As librarians began to work with the cataloging and preservation of newspapers, she edited *The United States Newspaper Program: Cataloging Aspects* (Haworth, 1986). When librarians became increasingly concerned about the education of catalogers, she edited *Education and Training for Catalogers and Classifiers* (Haworth, 1987). As the twentieth century was coming to a close, she and Carolynne Myall edited *Portraits in Cataloging and Classification: Theorists, Educators and Practitioners of the Late Twentieth Century* (Haworth, 1998) so that some of the persons who had given guidance to that important period in history would be properly recognized. Realizing how catalogers had moved ever more from practitioners to managers, Ruth edited the three-part *Managing Cataloging and the Organization of Information: Philosophies, Practices and Challenges at the Onset of the 21st Century* (Haworth, 2000). In her first "Editorial" as editor, she acknowledged that *CCQ* was "intended to be an international forum in the field of cataloging and classification" (Carter, 1985, 1) so that it is fitting that her last theme issue as editor of *CCQ* should be *Education for Library Cataloging: International Perspectives* (Haworth, 2006), which she co-edited with Dajin Sun, a native of China, who began his professional cataloging career working with Ruth at Pittsburgh and is now Assistant Head of Cataloging at Yale.

Implementing Online Union Lists of Serials: The Pennsylvania Union List of Serials Experience (Haworth, 1989) was co-edited with James D. Hooks. With Linda C. Smith, she edited *Technical Services Management, 1965-1990: A Quarter Century of Change and a Look to the Future: Festschrift for Kathryn Luther Henderson* (Haworth, 1996), which chronicled events related to technical services for a period of great change in that area of librarianship.

Over the years, Haworth entrusted her with other editorial responsibilities. For a time, these included editorial responsibilities for the *Journal of Internet Cataloging* and the *Journal of Archival Information*. In 1990, she became editor of the Haworth Series in Cataloging and Classification; in 1999, she advanced to editor-in-chief of the Haworth Book Program in Library and Information Science and Executive Editor of the Haworth Information Press. In just a few short years, the "something different from anything I have done before," noted in her first "Editorial" in *CCQ*, had become a consuming part of her life (Carter, 1985, 1).

RELATIONSHIP WITH PEOPLE

Ruth has always acknowledged the importance of people in cataloging and classification. A sentence from one of her editorial introductions ("The Importance of People") (Carter, 2001a, 2) informed us that: "Without people there is not only no cataloging but there is no purpose to cataloging"; thus the user has remained her focus. In the fall 1985 issue of *CCQ*, she noted that she would choose an Editorial Board "composed of individuals with a variety of skills, backgrounds, and perspectives on the areas included within the scope of *Cataloging & Classification Quarterly*" (Carter, 1985, 1). Checking the original list of Board members against that of the last volume for which she would write an editorial introduction for a general issue, it can be seen that although Ruth added new Editorial Board members over time, eleven of the original twenty-one Board members in 1985 remained Board members in 2005 (*Cataloging & Classification Quarterly*, 2005, preliminary pages). Something about Ruth inspires loyalty; and, on June 24, 2005 during the ALA Annual Conference, many of these Editorial Board members gathered to honor Ruth. Over those twenty years, Ruth acknowledged working with many others including the Haworth staff members.

Countless now established authors and editors owe a debt to Ruth Carter for helping them become contributors to the literature of the profession while others have benefited from her mentoring as a supervisor or through mentoring experiences in library and information science courses. The "*CCQ* Interview" sections, which Ruth established, with Carolynne Myall as Interview Editor, have helped *CCQ* readers become better acquainted with many practitioners, theorists, and educators in the fields of cataloging and classification.

SERVICE THROUGH PROFESSIONAL ORGANIZATIONS AND CONSULTATIONS

Dr. Carter has also served the profession well through her extensive work in professional organizations, especially the Pennsylvania Library

Association and the American Library Association (ALA). She was chair of ALA's Library and Information Technology Association's (LITA) Technical Standards for Library Automation Committee. Her principal professional association service has been, however, through ALA's Association for Library Collections and Technical Services (ALCTS). She served on numerous committees culminating in her presidency of ALCTS in 1991. Among other accomplishments during her presidency was the initiation of the ALCTS online newsletter, *ALCTS Network News* (*AN2*), the first ALA division newsletter to be issued in electronic form. She also represented ALA and ALCTS at numerous IFLA conferences.

Ruth served as a consultant to many organizations at the local, state, and national level. Participation in programs and workshops found her speaking at many conferences and meetings on a variety of subjects. She served as Co-Project Director, University of Pittsburgh for three HEA Title II-C grants.

HONORS

In addition to the Bowker/Ulrich Serials Librarianship Award, Ruth was elected to the following honor societies: Beta Phi Mu (library and information science), Kappa Delta Pi (education), Phi Alpha Theta (history), and Sigma Delta Pi (Spanish). In 2000, she was the recipient of the Graduate School of Library and Information Science, University of Illinois at Urbana-Champaign, Library School Alumni Association Distinguished Alumna/Alumnus Award given for her many years of distinguished service to the library and information science profession.

BACK TO HISTORY AND ARCHIVES

While engaged in all these activities, Ruth still found time to pursue a Ph.D. in History at the University of Pittsburgh. The degree was awarded in 1993. The return to her early love of history also brought her back into the archival field. Her last position at the University of Pittsburgh was as Head, Archives Service Center and Curator of Historical Collections where she served from 1996 until her retirement in mid-1999. During that period, she was appointed to the Pennsylvania State Historical Records Advisory Board. Somehow she also found time to prepare another monograph, *For Honor, Glory, and Union: the*

Mexican and Civil War Letters of Brig. Gen. William Haines Lytle, which was published by the University Press of Kentucky in 1999.

IN PRAISE OF RUTH

When Suzanne Striedieck, as Chair, Serials Section Bowker/Ulrich's Serials Librarianship Award Committee, presented the Bowker/Ulrich Award to Ruth in 1986, she noted: "It is a challenge to pin down Ruth Carter's primary contributions since her activities are so extensive and wide ranging" (Striedieck, 1986, 428). It has been even more of a challenge to pin down her contributions two decades later as I have attempted to do in the above paragraphs. How does one characterize someone who has contributed so much locally, regionally, nationally, and internationally to the information profession? Perhaps we can turn to Ruth's own words, used in a different context.

When Ruth wrote the ALCTS Annual Report for the year of her presidency, she began with these words: "Energy! Outreach! Services! Vision! Enthusiasm! Teamwork! Building on our Past! Shaping Our Future!" to characterize the year in which ALCTS had reorganized and set new goals for its future. She saw these terms as words to convey "the fun, excitement, and opportunities of working with library collections and technical services" (Carter, 1991, 462). Ruth would be too modest to characterize her own career in these action words, but all her actions for well over three decades are evidence that they were (and still are) what has guided this outstanding librarian and archivist. What these words do not convey are the integrity, unselfishness, modesty, and graciousness with which Ruth has pursued all aspects of her career. And all the while, she *was* having fun!

For thirty-six years, I have carried in my own memory words that Ruth wrote as she completed one of my courses. "This course," she wrote, "got more out of me than I ever thought I could give." Ruth Carter has been giving more to the profession since then than she probably thought she could give or would be called upon to give–but give she did; and we who know her well have not been surprised by how much she has given. Thank you, Ruth, most of all for just being you. In the "Some Closing Thoughts" (Carter, 2005, 2) editorial for the last general issue that you would edit, you wrote that we would stay in both your "heart and head"; and so will you stay in ours. We anticipate that "The Story of Ruth" will continue in some way to enhance the profession even though the "chapter" as editor of *CCQ* has been completed.

WORKS CITED

The author expresses her gratitude to Ruth C. Carter for supplying some biographical details included in this biography.

Carter, Ruth C. 1991. "ALCTS Annual Reports, 1990-91" *Library Resources & Technical Services* 35(4):462.
Carter, Ruth C. 1985. "Editorial" *Cataloging & Classification Quarterly* 6(1):1.
Carter, Ruth C. 1998. "The Editors of *CCQ*" *Cataloging & Classification Quarterly* 28(2/3):7-9.
Carter, Ruth C. 2001a. "The Importance of People" *Cataloging & Classification Quarterly* 32(3):2.
Carter, Ruth C. 2005. "Some Closing Thoughts" *Cataloging & Classification Quarterly* 41(1):2.
Carter, Ruth C. 2001b. "Teachers" *Cataloging & Classification Quarterly* 33(1):1.
Cataloging & Classification Quarterly 2005. 41(1): Preliminary pages.
Striedieck, Suzanne. 1986. "Ruth Carter" *Library Resources & Technical Services* 39(4):428.

doi:10.1300/J104v44n01_02

An Interview with Ruth C. Carter

Ruth C. Carter
Linda C. Ewbank

SUMMARY. Ruth Carter discusses her career as a librarian, archivist, historian, and long-time editor of *CCQ* and other journals. Topics include her education, mentors, professional positions, work in library organizations, and interests outside of librarianship as well as trends in cataloging research, the future of cataloging, and the relations and connections among her areas of interest. doi:10.1300/J104v44n01_03 *[Article copies available for a fee from The Haworth Document Delivery Service: 1-800-HAWORTH. E-mail address: <docdelivery@haworthpress.com> Website: <http://www.HaworthPress.com> © 2007 by The Haworth Press, Inc. All rights reserved.]*

KEYWORDS. Ruth C. Carter, Kathryn Luther Henderson, Rolland E. Stevens, Edward K. Muller, history, archives, technical services, cataloging, editing, *CCQ*, ALCTS, IFLA

Ruth C. Carter is Editor Emeritus of *Cataloging & Classification Quarterly*. She can be reached at 1717 Blalock Street, Mt. Pleasant, SC 29466-7112 (E-mail: rccarter@nauticom.net or rccats3@yahoo.com). Linda C. Ewbank is Senior Cataloger, History and Literature Cataloging Division, Slavic Team, Library of Congress, 101 Independence Avenue, SE, Washington, DC 20540 (E-mail: lewb@loc.gov).

[Haworth co-indexing entry note]: "An Interview with Ruth C. Carter." Carter, Ruth C., and Linda C. Ewbank. Co-published simultaneously in *Cataloging & Classification Quarterly* (The Haworth Information Press, an imprint of The Haworth Press, Inc.) Vol. 44, No. 1/2, 2007, pp. 19-38; and: *Cataloger, Editor, and Scholar: Essays in Honor of Ruth C. Carter* (ed: Robert P. Holley) The Haworth Information Press, an imprint of The Haworth Press, Inc., 2007, pp. 19-38. Single or multiple copies of this article are available for a fee from The Haworth Document Delivery Service [1-800-HAWORTH, 9:00 a.m. - 5:00 p.m. (EST). E-mail address: docdelivery@haworthpress.com].

Available online at http://ccq.haworthpress.com
© 2007 by The Haworth Press, Inc. All rights reserved.
doi:10.1300/J104v44n01_03

Could you tell us about your educational background and career?

My first two degrees I received at the University of Cincinnati–a BS in Education and an MA in History. As a point of minor interest, I went from kindergarten through my first Master's degree on the same street (Clifton Avenue) in Cincinnati. Between the BS and the MA, I taught seventh and eighth grade social studies for one year. Following the Master's degree, I worked for two years as the Curator of Manuscripts and Reference Assistant at the Ohio Historical and Philosophical Society (OHPS) (now the Cincinnati Historical Society). At that time, the OHPS was located in the basement of the main library of the University of Cincinnati. Thus, it is reasonable to say that my library and archives career started simultaneously with the initial major emphasis on archival work.

When I left the historical society, I took a civilian job as a training officer with the Department of the Army and worked in the Pentagon. This was partly because I was young and wanted to try something different but probably, in truth, mostly because my future husband was working in DC at the Smithsonian. While I was at the Pentagon in the early 1960s, there was an effort to test both civilian staff and GIs for computer programming aptitude as this predated university computer curricula. I took the test, did very well, and was selected for a six-month data processing training program. At the end of the program, I became a Systems Analyst for the Army and did that for slightly over two years. This was an interesting experience as it was in the very early days of the Vietnam War, and I got to work with data related to the 5-year plans and learned as early as 1965 that even some army officers were unhappy with the war. But leaving that aside, the time came when my husband completed his PhD work and took a position at the University of Illinois.

After helping my husband with a major bibliographic project that ultimately became a Memoir of the Geological Society of America, I entered the library science program at the University of Illinois. There I took many excellent courses, two of which were Kathryn Luther Henderson's cataloging courses. They persuaded me to shift my library interest from reference and systems to technical services and systems.

When I completed my MS in Library Science, I took a job for two years as Head of Technical Services at Parkland Junior College in Champaign, Illinois. At the end of that time, my husband took a job at the Carnegie Museum of Natural History in Pittsburgh. My first job in

Pittsburgh was a temporary one as a Systems Analyst in the University of Pittsburgh Library. Over several years, I worked into a permanent faculty-librarian stream position at Pitt, first as Head of Serials and then as Head of Cataloging. This led eventually to becoming Assistant Director of Technical Services and for a time my assistant director responsibilities also included Automation.

My final degree is a PhD in History from the University of Pittsburgh. I undertook doctoral work part time while I was an Assistant Director. I did it for fun, never thinking that it would factor into my career. But when the director wanted to downsize Technical Services, it worked out that I would become head of Archives and Curator of Historical Collections. A history PhD was actually valuable there and enhanced my interactions with both the History faculty and donors to the Archives.

How did you become interested in librarianship and archival work?

I think my interest in both librarianship and archival work is an outgrowth of my love of history. When I was in the 4th grade, my mother gave me a wonderful book called *Colonial Twins of Virginia*; and I've been hooked on history ever since. As I mentioned already, after I received my MA in History, I worked for two years at the Cincinnati Historical Society as the Curator of Manuscripts. This was my introduction to archival work. I really enjoyed organizing collections and providing access for them and for individual manuscripts. I learned a lot. I must add though that the librarian nearly discouraged me from finding it an appropriate field. She told me that, because "you like to read too much," I was the worst type of person to become a librarian. Apparently, if I needed a break for a few minutes, it was a bad thing to start reading the books on our ready reference shelves!

When we moved to Illinois in 1966, I didn't try to find work but rather helped my husband on a massive bibliographic project covering 70 years of geological literature in his field of paleontology. I examined over 2,000 sources, in many different languages, of which at least 200 were borrowed on interlibrary loan. After a couple of years when it became clear that I needed to work and after spending three years as an intensive library user, I realized that I enjoyed being involved with books and libraries more than I enjoyed computers. So I applied for library school at Illinois; and the rest, as they say, is history.

Most of my library career, however, has combined my knowledge of computers with my passion for libraries. Technical services, including cataloging, was the perfect area to meld my two interests and backgrounds. Later, toward the end of my career; I was able to work in archives and be directly involved with historical resources again. In a sense, my career came full circle.

Who are the people who have had the most important influence on your work or who have served as your role models or mentors?

I think the people who have been most influential in a positive way in my work have been three educators rather than people for whom I worked.

Two of the faculty at the University of Illinois when I was in library school, Kathryn Luther Henderson and Rolland E. Stevens, were particularly influential, particularly in creating enthusiasm for my chosen profession. Of these, I have seldom mentioned Professor Stevens before because his influence on my overall career was less direct than that of Mrs. Henderson (whom I affectionately know as Kathie). Before I talk more about Mrs. Henderson and her influence on me, I would like to mention that I took two excellent courses from Dr. Stevens. They were Resources of American Research Libraries and History of Books and Libraries. The former provided an overview of issues confronting research libraries from cooperative acquisitions, storage, equipment, and many other topics. Since I spent the large majority of my library career in a research library, his course was very useful. It also played into my interest in history through the term project in which each student had to choose a discipline and then evaluate the University of Illinois's holdings and compare it to the holdings of other research libraries with strong collections in the same field. I chose American History from roughly 1789 to the Civil War. Interestingly enough, two decades later this became my area of concentration when I did my history doctoral work. The History of Books and Libraries course required two research papers. One of those I later enhanced and published in Martin Joachim's *CCQ* theme issue on historical aspects of cataloging and classification. My paper was on the topic of three book collectors in imperial Spain and included information on their catalogs.

Kathryn Luther Henderson is without question the major influence in my professional career and the person I consider my mentor. By luck, she became my advisor when I entered library school. Although at the time I did not intend to pursue cataloging or technical services, I signed up for her cataloging course because it seemed important to get well grounded in the basics of librarianship. The first semester of cataloging quickly proved challenging, and consequently I then took advanced cataloging with her the following semester. By that time, I knew that my interests lay in technical services and systems. My first position after I received my MS was as the Head of Technical Services at Parkland College in Champaign, Illinois. Parkland was eager (this was 1970) to automate some library functions; and I wrote the specifications for programs to produce orders, maintain on-order lists, and the like. The programmer we hired completed work in a timely fashion; and, by the fall 1971, we were in production. Then, I began work on specifications for using our automated information to support some reference work. Mrs. Henderson at this time had a sabbatical so that she and I did some of this work together. It was also in this period that I first visited OCLC when Kathie and her husband, William T. Henderson invited me along on a trip they made. Thus, I first got to OCLC when it was still housed on the Ohio State Campus and had a staff of only a handful of people.

After my husband and I moved to Pittsburgh in 1972, Kathie and I kept in touch. When I decided to take on the editorship of *CCQ*, she was the first person I contacted about being on the editorial board and to get her suggestions for other members. Later, Kathie recommended Sandy Roe to me when *CCQ* needed a new News Column Editor. Sandy worked out so well that I recommended Sandy as my successor as editor. I've also had the pleasure of working with a number of catalogers who were Kathie's students. It has also been a pleasure to stay in contact with library school students through my service as a mentor in the technical services course taught by the Kathie and her husband William T. Henderson. Throughout it all, Kathie has been an inspiration, a role model, and a provider of advice and encouragement while she also worked hard on *CCQ* with manuscript reviews and many suggestions for articles and topics.

I would be remiss in discussing influential people in my professional life and education if I did not mention Edward K. Muller, my dissertation advisor in the University of Pittsburgh's Department of History. Little did I guess when I first met Ted while serving together on the University of Pittsburgh Senate Committee on Commonwealth Relations that he would turn out to be my dissertation advisor. I also did not guess when I first started doctoral work that it would be a factor in my career. Being a graduate student in history at age 50 was something I did just for pleasure. Although there are many satisfactions in being an Assistant Director, there is also a lot of paperwork, personnel issues, and process. Immersing myself in historical research and studies gave me a different kind of challenge. Three years after I completed my PhD, circumstances in the University of Pittsburgh Library System offered me the opportunity to become head of archives and curator of historical collections. Considering that Technical Services at Pitt was undergoing a major downsizing, I was fortunate to be able to turn my energies to archives that the director wanted to reinvigorate. Professor Muller is a major user of the extensive Pitt archives that include a large social and political focus on ethnic and industrial Pittsburgh, especially late 19th and 20th centuries. We collaborated on several projects for the archives, one of which was the establishment of a State and Local Government program. In conjunction with a colleague from the Institute of Politics, we submitted a successful grant proposal for an oral history project.

It is also been my pleasure to work with many dedicated, talented, and creative people in both technical services and archives. There are too many people to name individually, but hopefully they know who they are. In general, I have enjoyed my career most when I have worked closely with people or resources as opposed to pushing paperwork.

Your career has been unusually multi-faceted–systems, technical services, archives, editing journals, doing historical research; what interrelationships and interactions have these different areas had with each other?

In my mind, most of these areas, although seemingly disparate in some respects, are closely interrelated.

First, systems and technology are the means to an end whether making possible an online catalog, doing statistical analysis of historical data, or making more widely accessible archival data such as photographs and finding aids. I do see systems as a tool. It can be complicated; but, even back in the 1960s when I was first involved in data processing and systems, it was found that catalogers tested very well for programming skills. There is a similarity in mind set as both cataloging and programming involve attention to detail and a logical, analytical mind. These same characteristics also apply to work with serials and to historical research. When I did my master's degree in history in the early 1960s, there was little or no use of statistical analysis. One of the big changes I found in the late 1980s and early 1990s when I did doctoral work was the extensive use of statistics in history as an academic discipline. History had swung from individual and narrative history to statistical analysis whether economic or social data and to much less emphasis on individual people or events. More recently, there is something of a return to the bigger picture and the value of narrative. Nonetheless, statistics and computers remain tools in history, just as systems are essential to much of librarianship including reference databases and the huge online catalogs and the ability to interconnect these catalogs not just nationally but globally.

Archives in a way bridge history and libraries. Archives involve the collection of mostly unique historical resources and their organization and preservation as well as providing reference services. All the basic library functions–acquisition, organization, provision of access, preservation, and reference services–are part of archives. As recently as twenty or thirty years ago, a researcher for the most part had to visit the repositories that potentially had relevant holdings to a project. Today, the inclusion of archival finding aids and sometimes images of manuscripts, photographs, and other archival holdings online is a great boon for historical researchers whether they are scholars or someone researching family history.

Editing journals has always seemed a natural outgrowth of my interest in both technical services and systems and my historical predilection. When we publish, we both share with the present and document for the future. I was never in an institution that had tenure for librarians so that there was no premium placed on publishing. Rather, I felt that publishing was a responsibility to communicate with other professionals and to share whatever newer developments I participated in. There are many people who do interesting new things in their work; many of those new techniques, etc., would be useful learning experiences for others. However, not enough people take the time to write. I think that just as we benefit from the experiences of others, we have a responsibility, if not obligation, to share our experiences. I fully realize that there are many demands placed on library professionals including those in cataloging and technical services and that time is a precious and scarce resource. Still, I hope that most people publish at least a couple of times in the course of their careers.

I'd also like to observe that one of the benefits to me as a part time doctoral student and full time librarian/library administrator in technical services was that it forced me to become a library user. I suspect there were times that I wasn't too popular when I was reporting problems with broken down microfilm readers or improperly cataloged items, to name just a few. In short, all the areas you mentioned are really part of a continuum of library services, of their users, and of creators of published resources so that I feel that there was a rather seamless interface between all of the areas you asked about.

What are some similarities and differences between library cataloging and archival organization?

There are, as you suggest by your question, both similarities and differences between library cataloging and archival organization.

One difference is that by definition most archival materials are unique whereas many library resources (I'm talking about physical materials here) are available in multiple locations and copies. That more than one library holds the same library resource makes possible shared or copy cataloging. Archival materials on the other hand are often found in large collections that must be organized and given access by the archives that hold them. Even single or few item holdings such as manuscripts, diaries, etc., that are not part of larger collections are uniquely held. One of the challenges of archives is how to organize and give sufficient access to large collections that often cannot receive detailed piece-by-piece treatment.

Archival collections are often stored in boxes with many items per box. They are virtually never in open stack collections where a user can go directly to the shelves. Thus, classification, while used in archives, is less important than in libraries where users may directly browse at least some portion of a collection.

Because archival collections are unique, the researcher does need sufficient information about a collection to know whether or not to visit a collection, to request a copy of a finding aid, or to seek out other remote access. Archives often photocopy resources, but this is only viable once a fairly specific request can be made. While non-rare library resources are routinely available via interlibrary loan, this is not the case with archives. Consequently, archival finding aids are of critical importance. They often list individual items including the "to and from" of letters, some subject information, and the like. In recent years, finding aids have been a priority to include online; and they are often made accessible through Encoded Archival Description.

If the electronic era has revolutionized library catalogs through international participation and access, it has perhaps even more dramatically revolutionized access to archives. This occurs in two ways–one is placing many finding aids online; the second is often placing images of archival resources online. Initially many archival resources were digitized as a means of preserving these often-fragile resources. But a byproduct has been widespread access to materials formerly able to be examined at one location only. The Library of Congress American Memory Project, which includes many digitized photographs, is one example. The availability of the papers of Senator John Heinz held at Carnegie Mellon University is another example. In this case, more than one million items have been digitized and are available online. Of course, organization of these materials for user-friendly navigation has been critical.

Despite various differences between library cataloging and archival organization, there is a basic similarity in the desire to provide access by those elements most likely to be used in a search whether that is a title, responsible person or body, dates (whether a single publication date or date range for a collection), and some content/subject information. Both library cataloging and archival organization have made major strides in transitioning to the electronic era for access and will continue to improve the user's ability to connect with desired information. I would note that one of my most humbling and informing experiences was to go back to the Cincinnati Historical Society as a user when I was working on my dissertation that was based in large part on a large collection of papers of the Lytle Family in the 19th century. I had actually organized about two thirds of the collection and prepared its finding aid when I worked at the Society in the early 1960s. You can imagine my shock when I tried to use the finding aid and rapidly became aware of its deficiencies. In fact, one of the advantages of having computerized finding aids is that the initial organization by, let us say, letter writer or date of letter is not so critical because the computer facilitates multiple access methods. On the other hand, being able to browse a paper copy does have some advantages over trying to browse online. What's good is being able to use the two together, at least for finding aids of large collections. Alternatively, I have to say online catalogs for library resources seem to stand mostly unchallenged by card catalogs.

What should we be doing now to ensure that historians of the future have access to all the research materials they need (both primary and secondary sources, and both physical and intellectual access)?

This is a really important question, and there is no one answer. First, we have to be sure that some library or archival repository acquires all the research materials. Even for secondary resources, this is not necessarily easy. Many libraries with dependence on approval plans are collecting more and more of the same titles, especially books. There are also more resources in more forms than ever before. It is expensive to acquire, store, and preserve resources as well as to provide access to them. It is important to be able to meet a large proportion of an institution's user needs locally, but it is also important to have diversity in collections whether this is regional or national. Over the years, there have been many different attempts to insure that most items are held somewhere; but many smaller press or local publications, for example, may not be selected.

The acquisition of archival materials is not a passive process. Although, for instance, some resources may come in more or less automatically through institutional policies or ongoing agreements with organizations or associations, many primary resources require conscious collecting. Archival gems are often found in leaking basements, attics, business closings, and the like. They can be generated by local ethnic, religious, labor, political, or social groups to name a few. Sometimes a donor may initiate contact with an archives; other times the acquisition is dependent upon an archivist convincing an organization or other entity that its records are valuable for future historians.

Once resources, regardless of whether they are primary or secondary, are acquired, they need to be organized and described. They also need to be preserved. One of the great benefits of the electronic environment is that more and more resources are digitized. This makes them available not only to onsite users but to those in remote locations. Still, the level of detail often is a critical factor. For example, a historian's dream may be to be able to search on the full text of every manuscript in all theoretically relevant collections for a particular person; but the likelihood of having full text search at that level is unlikely to ever happen for many reasons. Still, enormous progress has been made toward that goal. It is a very exciting time to be a user of libraries and archives.

Do you think there is a fundamental difference between the kinds of organization, description, and access required by Internet resources and physical library materials? Can traditional methods of bibliographic control be applied effectively to Internet resources, or is a different approach required? Conversely, are new methods needed for library cataloging?

I have to admit I haven't thought a lot specifically about the differences between Internet resources and physical library materials in terms of organization, description, and access. But, if one assumes that both physical and Internet resources will be intermingled in online catalogs, then some commonality of approach in at least description and access is required. Of course, this could also mean that resource type is even more important as a basic qualifier.

A user still needs to locate either a known item or items pertinent to a particular inquiry. Thus, both entries that identify a particular item as well as those that provide subject access are necessary. This need is the same regardless of the type of resource. What may be different is that a user may or may not be concerned with whether or not a resource is local–in physical form that can be browsed quickly onsite–or borrowed and examined. If a resource is an Internet resource, can it be accessed locally and perhaps printed; or are constraints in place?

As far as organization is concerned, that can pertain to how items are displayed in a catalog as well as how physical items are stored. For archives, how is a collection arranged internally? While physical items, such as an archival collection and its finding aid, for example, may have a unilateral arrangement and organization, once there is electronic access, there can be multiple access points. Even Internet resources are stored once but accessed often.

I'm not sure what else I can say here as there are many great minds in our profession that are committed to furthering the theoretical basis of bibliographic control and the provision of access to resources.

During your time as head of cataloging and later head of technical services in the University of Pittsburgh Library, were there aspects of the work of the department and the division that you took a particular interest in, directions in which you tried to move, or goals that you considered particularly important?

Because I started out in serials, I probably have always held serials in general close in my thoughts. Even there, though, I gravitated toward more direct involvement in the bibliographic control aspects of serials including union list activities and the introduction of true cataloging for serials, which had not happened earlier at Pitt. This led to national cooperative cataloging and CONSER participation as I can explain further.

Basically, the University of Pittsburgh got into CONSER and other cooperative cataloging programs because of Pitt's union list and its hosting union list work for the Pittsburgh Regional Library Center (PRLC). In the early days of building a database for serials check-in on OCLC, OCLC sought to add bibliographic data for a large number of serial titles quickly. Since Pitt and PRLC had large machine readable union lists, these were acquired by OCLC in about 1975 (I don't remember the exact date). and added to its online database. However, it soon became apparent that the bibliographic data did not meet cataloging standards. Consequently, we were able to join CONSER in order to be able to upgrade records for titles we held. This eventually led to our full and enthusiastic participation not just in CONSER but in NACO and OCLC's Enhance program. The staff and librarians valued doing quality work at the national level. It certainly enhanced my job to participate in the CONSER Policy Committee as well as the jobs of the catalogers to contribute cataloging records at the highest level. I think most of us felt it was an important contribution to national, even international, bibliographic control and a factor in job satisfaction.

Over the years, I also spent time developing diverse grant proposals with various colleagues with some success including one to catalog a Bolivian pamphlet collection and the Nietz collection of early American school textbooks. My union list related activities also included a grant proposal under the auspices of PRLC for the Pennsylvania Union List of Serials (PaULS). This led to a nearly five-year project to build a statewide online union list on OCLC. It involved travel in Pennsylvania and also West Virginia including close work with the State Library of Pennsylvania. Several of my own early articles documented the development of the PaULS.

Binding, preservation, subscriptions, serial check-in, acquisitions, processing, catalog maintenance, and all aspects of cataloging were in my purview at various times. All had interesting facets, and most involved working closely with automation planning and implementation. Still, I would have to confess to a particular interest in the cooperative cataloging programs and statewide/network large-scale projects. I also cared about the people with whom I worked closely or for whom I had some responsibility and did try, at least I would like to think so, to support each individual's strengths.

It seems to me that cataloging is in a strange situation right now. On the one hand, a great deal of thought-provoking and potentially useful theoretical work is being done (for example, the development of FRBR); but, on the other, there is a tendency for library administrators to devalue and deprofessionalize cataloging or even to claim that it is unnecessary. Where does this leave working catalogers, and what kind of future might result from these developments?

Yes, I too wonder about cataloging and bibliographic control in terms of the advanced theoretical work taking place and the practicalities of online searching via keyword and the various search engines whether

Google or other options. Being a person who has always valued "balance" it is hard to say that one or the other is not valuable.

Presumably, theory can inform search engine design as well as the design of more traditional catalog records. Meanwhile, I think some of the challenges lie in the area of serving users of many languages with single bibliographic records. If the descriptive (metadata) part of records reflects the title, author, and other concrete data about an item regardless of format in the language(s) in which it was issued, then perhaps subject access may be more critical in terms of access via additional languages. Also, the possibility of limiting searches is terribly important whether by date, year, or country of origin–just to name a few.

Perhaps one of the ongoing roles of catalogers will be to provide links to facilitate retrieving records in various languages or to structure searches by format, date, or other things that are part of an item's metadata. As more items are digitized either initially or retrospectively, the metadata become more critical. In addition, there are still many local, small press publications and other items such as pamphlets, manuscripts, and various media such as maps, music, and realia that require cataloging beyond what is done once and copied by many. It has been my experience, now dated somewhat, that for some time, say back into the 1980s or very early 1990s, that cataloging related work has been assigned so that the tasks are handled by paraprofessionals and other staff where possible. Librarians have more often dealt with original cataloging, complex titles, subject analysis, revision, and problem solving. Even works requiring language and or subject expertise are often drafted by paraprofessionals and then reviewed/revised by librarians. Catalogers are often called on to be managers of workflow including outsourced materials.

While I don't pretend to be a theorist about cataloging, I do know that in order to advance the organization of information and the systems and catalogs supporting it, there must be those who understand both the bibliographic data and the relationships between the various data elements, the systems including search engines and catalogs that present the data to users, and the potential access points wanted and needed by users. In many ways, I believe that catalogers are the necessary link between users and the systems (catalogs) from which information is sought and that, thereby, catalogers or those who organize information for use are truly the intellectual keystone of libraries and lead the way for others involved in organizing and presenting information.

Unfortunately, as you allude to, library administrators often are eager to pare down what they see as a labor-intensive part of any individual library. Moreover, I do understand the need to be efficient in terms of the use of human resources and that the ideal is not always practical. Still, I think that cooperative cataloging, digitization programs, or the like are important. It is hard to argue with the idea that, to the extent possible, the intellectual work of description and subject analysis should be done once and then used many times. I think that our digital/electronic world has made possible a shift of emphasis within individual libraries and the formation of different partnerships including those with vendors to provide more bibliographic data along with the materials they supply.

I don't see catalogers being eliminated. They may be called something else; they may work in different units such as a digital resource unit, metadata services, or whatever. But catalogers, under whatever name–both the hands on catalogers and the theorists–will always be needed. Formats may change, but the basic functions remain.

During your twenty years as editor of CCQ, what changes have you observed in the types of topics that people research and write about, or in the methods and approaches applied to topics of scholarly inquiry? What topics and issues do you think will be most prominent and important in the future?

After I had completed 10 volumes of *CCQ*, Marie Kascus and I did a special issue that included an index by Marie and some statistical analysis that tracked changes in the content, both subject and geographic, of *CCQ* since its inception. Even at that early date, I think this covered through volume 15, it was clear that *CCQ* was increasingly international in content and that many more people outside the United States and Canada were submitting papers. In the 26 volumes (of 36 total) under my editorship since then (through v. 41), internationalization of the authors and contents is the most dominant single trend. In fact, the last issues (41(2) and 41(3/4)) for which I hold responsibility have only international authors by design.

In the early days of my editorship, quite a few articles were proposals for subject heading revisions and for new or revised classification schemes. Although this type of article may still occasionally appear, it is much rarer. Subject analysis has probably grown overall in proportion, but there is still considerable diversity in content. Description, authority control, management/workflow, education, user issues, and special formats are all represented in *CCQ*. The fact that *CCQ* now normally publishes two volumes per year allows for more representation of all topics and is a sign of the vigor of the field.

Two other changes over the years have been the increased use of columns and frequent theme issues. The columns have served to document current issues such as through the "News Column," provide reviews of new literature relative to cataloging and classification, explore new developments and the people who have influenced the profession through interviews, and, most recently, topics related to electronic resource cataloging. *CCQ* was also the first library journal (as far as I know) to develop its own home page.

Both theory and practice will continue to be important in the future. *CCQ* is valued by those working in libraries as well as by educators and researchers. Thus, I think it will continue to cover what is happening in libraries from workflow to training as well as providing clarification and guidance on new rules and concepts. I certainly expect it to keep an international audience as not only are catalogs now used around the world but there is increasing acknowledgement of the effectiveness of shared standards for cataloging or for what will in the future be known as resource description and access. I also look for a continuation of theme issues. The general issues are interesting because they usually treat a number of different topics and allow for unsolicited manuscripts whereas the theme issues provide a chance to offer in-depth coverage on a particular subject whether it be audio-visual cataloging, authority control, management of cataloging, metadata or education, to name a few recent topics. Because we live in an increasingly electronic world, that facet will continue to be reflected in articles as new technologies evolve and catalogers adapt what they do to take advantage of new opportunities.

Overall, I have often felt amazement at the strength, vitality, and diversity of the cataloging community as reflected in the literature and fully expect that to continue. I suppose that ideally it would be fun to do a systematic analysis of the content of and contributors to *CCQ* as was done after volume 15, but it will have to be by someone other than me. Perhaps this is a good class project at some point as it is always useful to track a profession over time through its literature.

How did you view your role as an editor, and what was it about editing these journals that sustained your interest through twenty years?

I viewed my role as editor in a number of ways. It was part coordinator and facilitator, part educator, part entrepreneur, some leadership and, I hope, inspiration, and partly contributing to the scholarly world through publication. Different editors no doubt have different strengths; and I was always most interested in getting good contributions and contributors, as opposed to say, the details of editing manuscripts. Most of the years that I was editor, I did the majority of the work at home on evenings and weekends so that by the time I logged in manuscripts, sent out manuscripts for review, followed up with both authors and reviewers, and put the issues together including writing editorials, there was not a lot of time left to do a lot of rewriting for grammar or other detail items. This is probably both good and bad. I sometimes had to choose between trying to get the journal out in a reasonably timely fashion rather than having a beautifully written paper. All in all, the content was the most important factor to me. Of course, when time permitted or a paper badly needed help, then some attention had to be given to writing style.

As editor I strove for balance between the theoretical or research articles and those that were applied and conveyed actual experience. *CCQ*, for example, has readers who find case studies useful when considering something for their own institutions. It also has many who want to keep up with the latest research and theoretical developments. In addition, I tried to never impose my own opinion on the contents of an article if it was controversial. I did not think it was an editor's job to publish only points of view with which I agreed.

I mentioned education as a role of a journal editor. Education involves, of course, the content of the journal as it is received by the readers; but it also involves interacting with authors. The review process is very important, and most authors are grateful for suggestions made by reviewers. First time authors often benefit very much from constructive comments on how to improve their work.

Most of the time being editor was fun! I couldn't have sustained more than 20 years if I didn't enjoy it at least most of the time. Naturally, I didn't like telling people I couldn't accept their manuscripts; but, for the most part, they were very understanding and learned from the experience. Writing editorials was also an opportunity to highlight some of the positives of catalogers and cataloging.

I especially enjoyed seeing *CCQ* grow internationally. It was always exciting to get the mail–one never knew from which country the next manuscript would originate. In my early days as editor, it was postal mail. In more recent years it has often been via e-mail attached files. Certainly having e-mail has made it easier to work with authors both in the United States and internationally.

Meetings with the editorial board members and columnists and dialog both by e-mail, telephone, or other in person venues with the members of *CCQ* and the various journals' editorial board members also added to my pleasure in being editor. I don't think I could have sustained being an editor if I didn't like the people with whom I worked on a regular basis. This also includes Bill Cohen, the Haworth Press publisher, and the many other fine people at the press who helped turn *Cataloging & Classification Quarterly*, the *Journal of Internet Cataloging (JIC)*, and the *Journal of Archival Organization (JAO)* into reality. Roger Brisson and Thomas J. Frusciano were founding co-editors of *JIC* and *JAO* respectively, and neither journal would have been possible without their expertise and commitment to the importance of publishing.

I guess the bottom line is that I always felt *CCQ* and the other journals were worthwhile. In my opinion, they contribute to current members and students of the profession(s) and also provide documentation for future generations of what we are doing now. Exchanging information through publication is a very important aspect of scholarly communication, and I am proud to have been part of that process. I am also honored that many people with whom I worked closely on *CCQ* are contributing to this Festschrift. My appreciation goes to everyone who is part of this Festschrift effort as well as others who have made so many important contributions to *CCQ* in so many ways over the years.

Could you tell us about your work in library organizations, especially ALCTS and IFLA?

It's probably obvious that I believe in the value of professional organizations. Although many librarians are not required to publish, it is still valuable, even necessary, to exchange information and to "network." Professional organizations in both the archival and library fields perform a valuable function. I think it is important to share what one is doing in one's own institution, to meet others doing similar work in other institutions, and to hear presentations on current developments at all levels including implementations in individual libraries. These are probably the most valuable parts of being involved in organizations whether local, state, national, or international.

I was privileged to serve as President of the Association for Library Collections and Technical Services (ALCTS) after many years of activity in the Serials Section. Some of my closest friendships were formed as a result of my involvement in ALA, mostly ALCTS but also LITA. During the three year commitment as President, Vice-President, and Past President of ALCTS, it is worth noting that it meant a shift in involvement to mostly the process involved in keeping the organization going and moving away from "content." But an organization requires multiple people to participate in the procedural parts of its existence in order to provide the forum for all the substantive knowledge opportunities that it provides. I always felt that if one wanted to benefit from the opportunities presented that it was only reasonable to contribute to the process components also.

In IFLA, I was a member of the Section on Serial Publications as an ALA representative. It was interesting to get to meet and work with librarians from many countries. I also belonged to IFLA's Round Table for Editors of Library Journals. One of the highlights of being in IFLA occurred during the conference in Moscow in 1991. As some may remember, August 1991 was the coup in the Soviet Union and for three days tanks lined the streets of Moscow. They surrounded the Hotel Rossiia next to Red Square where I and some other U.S. librarians were staying. It was truly exciting to be in Moscow during these turbulent days and have an experience that no amount of money could have bought. The putsch was over the Wednesday of the conference, and there was a conference wide party that night as scheduled. There really was dancing in the hall, and everyone celebrated. In this way, one of the most exciting experiences of my life happened at IFLA. A few years later, in 1994, IFLA was in Cuba during one of the boat people periods; and it was rather amazing to watch the news on CNN and be in Cuba where the news was being made. It was also quite moving to learn how much Cuban librarians wanted to be part of the international community and to exchange information.

I also participated in the Pennsylvania Library Association and later in the Mid Atlantic Regional Archives Conference (MARAC) when that became appropriate to my job. I found MARAC to be very valuable with many substantive presentations, and thus I recommend the regional and national archives associations highly for those in the archival field.

What are your major interests outside of librarianship?

I've always loved history; we've already talked a bit about that. In conjunction with history, I would have to admit to being a bit of a "political junkie." Since I first heard election returns as a pre-teen on the radio when Truman and Dewey ran in 1948, I have been fascinated by politics and have followed every presidential election since and the off-year elections as well. This ties in to my interest in foreign affairs and international travel. Over the past 35 years, I've been fortunate enough to make quite a few international trips. These have often been in conjunction with either my or my husband's professional meetings but not always. Ironically, now when I have more time to travel, neither my husband nor I feel up to any big trips out of the country. I won't say never, but at this point major international travel is probably not on my agenda.

I also enjoy reading and do a lot, especially history, mysteries, and cookbooks plus two newspapers a day and various news and cooking magazines. My mother was a good baker; and I still like to bake a lot, particularly pies, cookies, and breads. Again, though, there is the problem of getting older so that one has to be careful not to over indulge!

We don't have children, but we stay close to my sister and John's sister and their children. Also, we have had three generations of cats over the past 35 plus years. They never fail to keep us company and amuse us, and I would have to say our cats have been and are one of the major pleasures in my life. I've also been lucky to have long term friends, and they too are important. I have yet to have a boring minute since I retired. There is so much to enjoy and to learn. Even now it is interesting to get to know a different region of the country as we have lived half the year near Charleston, South Carolina for the past three winters and expect to retire here permanently by the end of 2006.

What are your plans for the future?

I've already mentioned that we plan to move permanently to South Carolina by the end of 2006. When we go back to Pennsylvania in May, my husband and I will have to get our house ready to sell and dispose of many possessions. We started a bit during 2005; but, after more than 30 years in one house, it is a monumental job, especially as we both have lots of books and seem to be "pack rats" in general.

After we are settled fulltime in South Carolina, we hope to relax, take it easy, and enjoy each other, the sunshine, warmer winters, and great food. I hope that we won't have to spend too much time worrying about hurricanes, but they are always a risk where we live as we are just a couple of miles from the ocean.

I expect to pursue my hobbies such as reading and baking and keeping up on the news. I'll also enjoy my cats and try to keep up with friends and family including my many wonderful *CCQ* colleagues.

On an academic note, there are still several history projects I would like to pursue if circumstances permit. Most of them are off shoots one way or another of my dissertation. For example, I published *For Honor, Glory and Union: the Mexican and Civil War Letters of Brig. Gen. William Haines Lytle* (Univ. Press of Kentucky, 1999). Gen. Lytle was a member of the third generation of the 19th century Cincinnati family that I covered in my dissertation. His first Civil War regiment, the 10th Ohio Volunteer Infantry, has never had a regimental history; and I have collected a good bit of information related to the 10th Ohio. My dissertation, covering about the first 65 years of the 19th century as lived by a prominent, politically active, Ohio family with ties to the Mid-Atlantic and Kentucky, was topically organized. I still have hopes of following through with some of those topics, for example, travel and communication. But before I even think about pursuing serious historical projects, I need to get moved from Pennsylvania to South Carolina; and, then depending on other factors such as my health, energy, and that of my husband, I will see what is reasonable to tackle. One way or another, I sure won't be bored and will have more of interest to do than there is time.

That all sounds like fun; thank you very much, and best wishes for a happy and productive retirement!

doi:10.1300/J104v44n01_03

Cataloging & Classification Quarterly, 1990-2006

Sandra K. Roe
Rebecca Culbertson
Laurel Jizba

SUMMARY. The authors review the contents of *Cataloging & Classification Quarterly* and provide an examination of the contributors, article types, and changes in emphasis in topics. doi:10.1300/J104v44n01_04 *[Article copies available for a fee from The Haworth Document Delivery Service: 1-800-HAWORTH. E-mail address: <docdelivery@haworthpress.com> Website: <http://www.HaworthPress.com> © 2007 by The Haworth Press, Inc. All rights reserved.]*

KEYWORDS. *Cataloging & Classification Quarterly*

Cataloging & Classification Quarterly (*CCQ*) began publication in 1980 under the editorial leadership of C. Donald Cook. George E. Gibbs followed Cook and edited volumes 3 through 5.[1] This festschrift honors

---

Sandra K. Roe is Bibliographic Services Librarian, Milner Library, Illinois State University, Normal, IL 61790-8900 (E-mail: skroe@ilstu.edu). Rebecca Culbertson is Electronic Resources Cataloging Librarian, Metadata Services Department, University of California, San Diego Libraries (E-mail: becky@library.ucsd.edu). Laurel Jizba is an Independent Cataloging Consultant and Trainer (E-mail: jizbalaurel@yahoo.com).

[Haworth co-indexing entry note]: "*Cataloging & Classification Quarterly*, 1990-2006." Roe, Sandra K., Rebecca Culbertson, and Laurel Jizba. Co-published simultaneously in *Cataloging & Classification Quarterly* (The Haworth Information Press, an imprint of The Haworth Press, Inc.) Vol. 44, No. 1/2, 2007, pp. 39-52; and: *Cataloger, Editor, and Scholar: Essays in Honor of Ruth C. Carter* (ed: Robert P. Holley) The Haworth Information Press, an imprint of The Haworth Press, Inc., 2007, pp. 39-52. Single or multiple copies of this article are available for a fee from The Haworth Document Delivery Service [1-800-HAWORTH, 9:00 a.m. - 5:00 p.m. (EST). E-mail address: docdelivery@haworthpress.com].

Available online at http://ccq.haworthpress.com
© 2007 by The Haworth Press, Inc. All rights reserved.
doi:10.1300/J104v44n01_04

Ruth C. Carter who served as editor of *CCQ* for the incredible span of more than twenty years–from volume 6, published in 1985 but begun earlier, of course, through volume 41, published in 2006.

In 1991, Carter and Kascus marked *CCQ*'s tenth anniversary by analyzing the contents of its first ten volumes.[2] That article presented a statistical analysis of the contributors, editors, and changes in emphasis of topics in *CCQ*. That study is replicated here in part and encompasses the broader period of Dr. Carter's editorship. Generally, the results are reported in ten volume sets.[3]

CONTRIBUTORS

The country provided or implied by the address of the senior or first named author was recorded for each of the 990 articles published in *CCQ* from volume 1 (1980) through volume 41 (2006). Those things other than full length articles, such as editorials, reports, news columns, book reviews, and letters to the editor, were not included in this analysis. Table 1 lists each country alphabetically and provides the number of articles published from each country both by volume range and in total. The majority of articles overall have originated in the United States (731), followed in frequency by Canada (61), the United Kingdom (36), Italy (27), Australia and Germany (both with 14), and France (10). Table 2 collapses these countries into regions to provide a more concise snapshot of this same geographic distribution by volume range and in total.

These data reflect the growing number of international contributions throughout *CCQ*'s publication history and demonstrate that Carter and Kascus' earlier finding–a "discernable trend . . . toward the internationalization of *CCQ*"–has continued throughout the 15 years since their study was published.[4] The variety in the number of countries of origin for authors has grown from 12 for volumes 1-10 to 33 for volumes 31-41, while the percentage of contributions from the United States has decreased from 84.7% for volumes 1-10 to 54% for volumes 31-41.

THEME ISSUES

Thematic issues have been interspersed with general issues throughout *CCQ*'s history. During Cook's editorship, two issues were devoted to single topic. These were the Library of Congress subject headings in

TABLE 1. Country of First Named Author

Country of Origin	v.1-10	v.11-20	v.21-30	v.31-41	Total
Argentina			1	2	3
Australia		2	4	8	14
Barbados	1				1
Botswana			1	2	3
Brazil			1		1
Canada	20	7	16	18	61
China		1	3	4	8
Costa Rica				1	1
Croatia			1	1	2
Denmark		1	1	2	4
Egypt					1
Ethiopia		1			1
Finland			1		1
France	1	1	2	6	10
Germany	2		4	8	14
Greece			1	1	2
Hong Kong				1	1
India				6	6
Iran		1		6	7
Ireland		1			1
Israel	1	2		2	5
Italy	1		1	25	27
Japan	1		1	4	6
Korea		1		1	2
Malaysia			1		1
Mexico			4	3	7
Netherlands			2		2
Nigeria	2			2	4
Norway	1			1	2
Papua New Guinea	3				3
Peru				1	1
Poland				1	1
Portugal				2	2
Romania				1	1
Saudi Arabia		1		3	4
Slovenia		1		2	3
South Africa		1	1	2	4
Spain			1	2	3
Sweden				1	1
Switzerland				2	2
United Kingdom	4	5	18	9	36
USA	205	204	168	154	731
Total	**242**	**230**	**233**	**285**	**990**

TABLE 2. Region of First Named Author

Region of Origin	v.1-10	Percent	v.11-20	Percent	v.21-30	Percent	v.31-41	Percent	Total
North America	225	93.0	211	91.7	188	80.7	175	61.4	799
USA	205	84.7	204	88.7	168	72.1	154	54.0	731
Canada	20	8.3	7	3.0	16	6.9	18	6.3	61
Mexico	0	--	0	--	4	1.7	3	1.1	7
Europe	9	3.7	9	3.9	32	13.7	64	22.5	114
UK	4	1.7	5	2.2	18	7.7	9	3.2	36
Italy	1	.4	0	--	1	.4	25	8.8	27
Germany	2	.8	0	--	4	1.7	8	2.8	14
France	1	.4	1	.4	2	.9	6	2.1	10
Other	1	.4	3	1.3	7	3.0	16	5.6	27
Asia/Oceania	4	1.7	4	1.8	9	3.8	24	8.4	41
Middle East/ Africa	3	1.2	6	2.6	2	.9	18	6.3	29
South/ Central Amer.	1	.4	0	--	2	.9	4	1.4	7
Total	242		230		233		285		990

volume 1, no. 2/3 and "The Future of the Union Catalogue" in volume 2, no. 1/2. "AACR2 and Serials: The American View" appeared in volume 3, no. 2/3 with Neal L. Edgar as Guest Editor. Another issue on a single topic, this one entirely authored by Deanne Holzberlein, "Computer Software Cataloging: Technique and Examples," was published as volume 6, no. 2. From volume 6 forward, theme issues were published regularly, typically one per volume. All other issues of *CCQ* are general issues and include articles on a variety of topics.

Table 3 is a complete list of all *CCQ* theme issues and includes the year of publication, title, guest editor(s), subject(s), volume and issue number(s), and the number of articles for each. Thirty-eight theme issues containing 550 articles were published between volume 1 (1980) and volume 42 (2006). This represents 54.3% of all articles published in

TABLE 3. Between 1980 and 2006, 38 individual or combined issues were devoted to a single theme. This table provides the year of publication, title, guest editor(s), subject(s), volume and issue number(s), and the number of articles for each.

Pub. Date	Theme issue title	Guest Editor(s)	Subject	Vol./No.	No. of articles
1982	Library of Congress Subject Headings		LCSH	1(2/3)	6
1982	The Future of the union catalog: Proceedings of the International Symposium on the Future of the Union Catalogue, University of Toronto, May 21-22, 1981		Union catalogs	2(1/2)	9
1982/1983	AACR2 and Serials: The American View	Edgar	Serial publications/Cataloging	3(2/3)	17
1986	Computer Software Cataloging: Techniques and Examples		Computer software/Cataloging	6(2)	7
1986	The United States Newspaper Program: Cataloging Aspects		Newspapers/Cataloging	6(4)	7
1987	Education and Training for Catalogers and Classifiers	Carter	Catalogers/Teaching	7(4)	12
1988	National and International Bibliographic Databases: Trends and Prospects	Carpenter	Bibliography, National	8(3/4)	16
1989	Authority Control in the Online Environment: Considerations and Practices	Tillett	Personal names	9(3)	10
1989	Subject Control in Online Catalogs	Holley	Online catalogs, Evaluation	10(1/2)	15
1990	Classification as an Enhancement of Intellectual Access to Information in an Online Environment	Speller, Jr.	Classification/Systems	11(1)	9
1990	Describing Archival Materials: The Use of the MARC AMC Format	Smiraglia	Archives/Cataloging	11(3/4)	9
1991	Enhancing Access to Information: Designing Catalogs for the 21st Century	Tyckoson	Online catalogs	13(3/4)	13

43

TABLE 3 (continued)

Pub. Date	Theme issue title	Guest Editor(s)	Subject	Vol./No.	No. of articles
1992	Retrospective Conversion: History, Approaches, Considerations	Schottlaender	Retrospective conversion	14(3/4)	8
1993	Education for Technical Services: Putting Theory into Practice for the 1990's	McAllister-Harper & Speller	Catalogers/Education	16(3)	12
1993	Languages of the World: Cataloging Issues and Problems	Joachim	Foreign language materials/Cataloging, Transliteration	17(1/2)	18
1993	Cooperative Cataloging: Past, Present, and Future	Baker	Cataloging, Cooperative	17(3/4)	10
1994	Cataloging Government Publications Online	Sherayko	United States/Government Printing Office	18(3/4)	14
1995	Classification: Options and Opportunities	Thomas	Classification/Systems	19(3/4)	16
1995	New Roles for Classification in Libraries and Information Networks: Presentations and Reports, from the Thirty-Sixth Allerton Institute, October 23-25, 1994 (Pauline Atherton Cochrane, Institute Organizer)	Carter	Classification/Systems, Classification/Aims and objectives	21(2)	13
1996	Cataloging and Classification Standards and Rules	Riemer	Standardization of bibliographic records	21(3/4)	11
1996	Electronic Resources: Selection and Bibliographic Control	Pattie & Cox	Internet/Cataloging	22(3/4)	12
1997	Cataloging and Classification: Trends, Transformations, Teaching, and Training	Shearer & Thomas	Cataloging/Automation	24(1/2)	12
1998	Portraits in Cataloging and Classification: Theorists, Educators, and Practitioners of the Late Twentieth Century	Myall & Carter	Catalogers, Cataloging/Teaching	25(2/3, 4)	18
1999	Maps and Related Cartographic Materials: Cataloging, Classification, and Bibliographic Control	Andrew & Larsgaard	Maps/Cataloging	27(1/2, 3/4)	21

2000	The LCSH Century: One Hundred Years with the *Library of Congress Subject Headings System*	Stone	LCSH, LCSH/Evaluation	29(1/2)	15
2000	Managing Cataloging and the Organization of Information: Philosophies, Practices and Challenges at the Onset of the 21st Century.	Carter	Cataloging/Administration	30 (1, 2/3)	22
2001	The Audiovisual Cataloging Current	Roe	Audiovisual materials/Cataloging	31 (2, 3/4)	15
2002	Works as Entities for Information Retrieval	Smiraglia	Bibliographic control	33(3/4)	11
2002	Education for Cataloging and the Organization of Information: Pitfalls and Pendulum	Swan Hill	Cataloging/Teaching	34(1/2, 3)	24
2002/2003	Historical Aspects of Cataloging and Classification	Joachim	Cataloging/History	35(1/2, 3/4)	27
2003	Electronic Cataloging: AACR2 and Metadata for Serials and Monographs	Intner *et al.*	Metadata	36(3/4)	11
2003	Knowledge Organization and Classification in International Information Retrieval	Williamson & Beghtol	Classification/Systems	37(1/2)	14
2004	The Thesaurus: Review, Renaissance, and Revision	Roe & Thomas	Thesauri	37(3/4)	10
2004	Authority Control in Organizing and Accessing Information: Definition and International Experience	Taylor & Tillett	Authority control	38(3/4), 39(1/2)	46
2005	Functional Requirements for Bibliographic Records (FRBR): Hype or Cure-All?	Le Boeuf	Standardization of bibliographic records	39(3/4)	17
2005	Metadata: A Cataloger's Primer	Smiraglia	Metadata	40(3/4)	11
2005	Education for Library Cataloging: International Perspectives	Sun & Carter	Cataloging/Teaching	41(2, 3/4)	22
2006	Moving Beyond the Presentation Layer: Content and Context in the Dewey Decimal Classification (DDC) System	Mitchell & Vizine-Goetz	Classification/Systems/Dewey decimal	42(3/4)	10

CCQ during this period. The subjects that appear in Table 3 are those subject terms that were assigned most frequently to the individual articles that make up each theme issue by H. W. Wilson in their database, Library Literature & Information Science Full Text.

TYPES

CCQ has a long tradition of providing content that includes both the historical and the contemporary and both theoretical/scholarly research and practical application. Like the Carter and Kascus analysis before us, we identified each article as historical, research, theoretical, applied, opinion, or futuristic.[5] This process was somewhat arbitrary; and others than the authors would have perhaps assigned the types differently. Table 4 presents these article types by volume range and percentages from volume 11-41. These data reveal an increase in the frequency of all article types with the exception of applied and futuristic. The percentage of applied articles dropped from 51.7% in volumes 11-20 to 27.4% in volumes 31-41, and futuristic articles decreased very slightly from .8% to .4%. Overall, the most frequently occurring type is applied or practice-oriented articles with 296, followed by research and theoretical articles with 144 and 140 respectively.

TOPICS

The subject indexing used for this study was drawn from the H. W. Wilson database, Library Literature & Information Science Full Text. H. W. Wilson began including indexing for *CCQ* in this database with volume 5, no. 2 (1984). The subject terms assigned come from the Wilson subject thesaurus. The final issue indexed at the time of this study was volume 40, no. 3-4 (2005). Multiple subject terms were assigned to 86.8% of these articles. The most subject terms assigned to any one article was nine.

Since the topical data was very rich in terms of both specific headings and patterns in heading assignments, we determined that there was more than one way to examine the data and conducted more than one style of topical analysis. Only the 708 full length articles published in volume 11 (1990) through volume 40 (2005) were included in these topical analyses. Editorials, columns, book reviews, letters to the editor, and so forth were not included in these analyses.

TABLE 4. Analysis by Article Type

Article Type	v.11-20	Percent	v.21-30	Percent	v.31-41	Percent	Total
Historical	16	7.0	17	7.3	40	14.0	73
Research	39	17.0	34	14.6	71	24.9	144
Theoretical	42	18.3	39	16.7	59	20.7	140
Applied	119	51.7	99	42.5	78	27.4	296
Opinion	12	5.2	40	17.2	36	12.6	88
Futuristic	2	.8	4	1.7	1	.4	7
Total	230	100.0	233	100.0	285	100.0	748

Topical Analysis 1

Our first statistical examination by topic was to look at the topics using specifically named headings. In each of the three groups by decade, headings clustered at a frequency of 12 or more occurrences. There was a very broad scatter of headings that appeared less frequently; these have not been included.

Six hundred and seventy-nine headings were assigned to 219 articles published in volumes 11-20. Those that were assigned most frequently (>12 times) to this group of articles were:

Cataloging	56
Classification	42
Online catalogs	41
College and university libraries	29
Authority control	23
Library of Congress Subject Headings	22
OCLC, Inc./Applications	16
Cataloging, Cooperative	14
Anglo-American Cataloguing Rules	14

Six hundred and seventy-five headings were assigned to 233 articles published in volumes 21-30. Those that were assigned most frequently (>12 times) to this group of articles were:

Cataloging	69
College and university libraries	44
Classification	34
Catalogers	21
Library of Congress Subject Headings	20
Online catalogs	19
Maps	18
MARC System	16
Internet	13

Seven hundred and thirty-three headings were assigned to 256 articles published in the latest issues, volumes 31-40. Those that were assigned most frequently (>12 times) to this group of articles were:

Cataloging	76
Authority control	52
Standardization of bibliographic records	35
Classification	28
Metadata	20
Anglo-American Cataloguing Rules	17
College and university libraries	16
Library of Congress Subject Headings	13
MARC System	13
Online catalogs	12

Topical Analysis 2

Our second statistical examination was to look at the topics by examining heading patterns mixed in with some of the more heavily used specifically named headings. For this analysis, we looked only at the last and first sets of volumes: at the earliest, volumes 11-20, and then at the latest, volumes 31-40, again using the terms assigned in the H. W. Wilson database.

Those heading patterns assigned most frequently (> 12 times) to this first group of articles in volumes 11-20 were, in order of greatest usage, this time measured in the number of instances found among all of the assigned headings (Table 5).

Next we looked at the same heading patterns assigned most frequently to the latest group of articles found in volumes 31-40. This time we also measured the number of instances found among all of the assigned headings. These results were then compared with the headings assigned in the earliest group of headings (Table 6).

In this second topical analysis comparing the earlier sets of volumes with the later sets of volumes, there have been some changes in the topic

TABLE 5. Frequently Assigned Subject Headings, v. 11-20

Subject terms	v.11-20
Cataloging [as a term alone or with other terms or in any phrase] Includes: College and university libraries/Cataloging; [Format or genre noun)]/Cataloging; [National or ethnic group (adjective)]; [Nation or ethnic group (adjective) literature/Cataloging; Cataloging, Cooperative; Cataloging/Administration; Cataloging/Author entry; and other variations. Does not include Anglo-American Cataloguing Rules.	200
Subject [as a term alone or with other terms or in any phrase] Includes: Library of Congress subject headings, Subject headings, Subject access, Subject cataloging/Evaluation, Subject Cataloging Commercial, Subject Cataloging/Case studies, Subject cataloging/Policy analysis, Subject headings [by type or genre], Standardization/Subject headings, and other variations	50
Classification [as a term alone or with other terms or in any phrase] Includes: Classification/Automation, Newspapers/Classification, Standardization/Classification, Classification [by country], Classification/Systems/[name of specific system, i.e., Library of Congress, Bliss, Universal Decimal, Dewey], [name of] literature/Classification, Use studies/Classification, Classification/Evaluation, Reader interest classification, Classification/Bibliography, Public Libraries/Classification, and other variations	44
Online catalogs	41
College and university libraries/Cataloging	40
[Proper name of a specific library]	29
[Format or genre (noun)]/Cataloging Includes: Academic dissertations, Archives, Audiovisual materials, Cartographic materials, Computer software, Motion pictures, Microforms, Newspapers, Pictures, Recorded sound archives, Recordings, Scores, Serial publications, Textbooks, Videorecordings	28
[Nation or ethnic group (adjective)] literature/Cataloging Includes: African, Asian, Canadian, Chinese, Danish, Icelandic, Indian, Ethiopian, Greek, Middle Eastern, North American Indian, Portuguese, Slavic	28
Authority control	23
Library of Congress subject headings	21
OCLC, Inc.	16
Cataloging, Cooperative	14
Anglo-American Cataloguing Rules	14
Databases [as a term alone or with other terms or in any phrase]	12

TABLE 6. Frequently Assigned Subject Headings, v. 31-40

Subject terms	v.31-40	% increase or decrease
Cataloging [as a term alone or with other terms or in any phrase] Includes: College and university libraries/Cataloging; [Format or genre noun)]/Cataloging; [National or ethnic group (adjective)]; [Nation or ethnic group (adjective) literature/Cataloging; Cataloging, Cooperative; Cataloging/Administration; Cataloging/Author entry; and other variations. Does not include Anglo-American Cataloguing Rules.	179	−10.0%
Subject [as a term alone or with other terms or in any phrase] Includes: Library of Congress subject headings, Subject headings, Subject access, Subject cataloging/Evaluation, Subject Cataloging Commercial, Subject Cataloging/Case studies, Subject cataloging/Policy analysis, Subject headings [by type or genre], Standardization/Subject headings, and other variations	27	−47.0%
Classification [as a term alone or with other terms or in any phrase] Includes: Classification/Automation, Newspapers/Classification, Standardization/ Classification, Classification [by country], Classification/Systems/[name of specific system, i.e., Library of Congress, Bliss, Universal Decimal, Dewey], [name of] literature/Classification, Use studies/Classification, Classification/Evaluation, Reader interest classification, Classification/Bibliography, Public Libraries/Classification, and other variations	34	−23.0%
Online catalogs	12	−72.0%
College and university libraries/Cataloging	13	−55.0%
[Proper name of a specific library]	16	−45.0%
[Format or genre (noun)]/Cataloging Includes: Academic dissertations, Archives, Audiovisual materials, Cartographic materials, Computer software, Motion pictures, Microforms, Newspapers, Pictures, Recorded sound archives, Recordings, Scores, Serial publications, Textbooks, Videorecordings	45	+45.0%
[Nation or ethnic group (adjective)] literature/Cataloging Includes: African, Asian, Canadian, Chinese, Danish, Icelandic, Indian, Ethiopian, Greek, Middle Eastern, North American Indian, Portuguese, Slavic	29	marginal increase
Authority control	64	+178.0%
Library of Congress subject headings	11	−47.0%
OCLC, Inc.	9	−44.0%
Cataloging, Cooperative	3	−78.0%
Anglo-American Cataloguing Rules	15	marginal increase
Databases [as a term alone or with other terms or in any phrase]	1	−92.0%

assignment and therefore in the nature of the articles over the period examined. These modifications reflect changes taking place within the cataloging profession and the world at large.

Decreases in uses of "cataloging," "subject," and "classification" [used as a term alone or with other terms or in any phrase], of the term "online catalogs," and of the pattern "[proper name of a specific library]" are apparent in the table above. That said, certainly these terms continued to serve as the largest group of terms assigned to the aggregated articles in volumes 31-40.

Increases for the same periods in which assigned topical terms were compared are seen in the use of the term "authority control" (a 145% increase) as well as in the roughly three times greater assignment of headings assigned to articles that reflect the topics of cataloger education or the teaching of cataloging. Also, more discourse in the journal took place surrounding specific types of cataloging as there was a 45% growth in assigning the pattern [Format or genre (noun)]/Cataloging.

New terms that did not show up in the first group of volumes analyzed include "metadata" (18 instances), "semantic web" (1 instance), "XML (computer language)" (7 instances), "Data mining" (2 instances), and "Web portals" and "CDS/ISIS (computer language)" (1 instance each). The general term "software" was not used at all, even though it had appeared in volumes 11-20, yielding instead to more specific names of software. This trend may be said to reflect the larger scope of Internet-based concepts in which library cataloging has come to reside and a more widespread understanding of the role of specific types of software deployment.

Further, an increase in the use of "thesauri" (5 instances) could be seen in the latest group of volumes, including assignment of thesauri with subdivisions, as in: "thesauri/evaluation," "thesauri/history," and "thesauri/bibliography." "Indexing" also received more attention than in the past as did "audiovisual materials/cataloging," which more than doubled from three to eight assigned instances.

CONCLUSION

In summary, our examinations showed that, given the data at hand, there are many ways in which the articles published in *CCQ* have reflected changes in discourse within the library profession, within cataloging in particular, and within society at large by encompassing an increased diversity in authorship, by embracing longstanding philosophical and practical issues as well as changing technologies–and by always presenting new ways of considering issues of cataloging and classification.

NOTES

1. Ruth C. Carter, "The Editors of CCQ," *Cataloging & Classification Quarterly* 25, no. 2/3 (1998): 5-9.
2. Ruth C. Carter and Marie A. Kascus, "*Cataloging & Classification Quarterly*, 1980-1990: Content, Change, and Trends," *Cataloging & Classification Quarterly* 12, no. 3/4 (1991): 69-79.
3. Dr. Carter was Editor-in-Chief through v.41(3/4), as well as for v.42(3/4), and so data for v.41 have been included when available, stretching the most recent 10-volume group to 11 volumes, and the theme issue published as v.42(3/4) has been included in Table 4.
4. Carter and Kascus: 73.
5. Carter and Kascus: 71.

doi:10.1300/J104v44n01_04

In Honor of Ruth C. Carter

Sheila S. Intner

If ever one doubts some are destined to serve with no thought of self,
A glance at technical services dispels it without delay;
Though patrons might think books spring, fully cataloged, from a library's shelf,
We know how much work it takes to get them that way.

Ruth knows all about this, because tech services is her beat,
And her library is one of our leaders.
She's seen all the changes, first hand, from cards to the 'Net,
And helped us morph from paper to screen readers.

Of all technical services tasks, those that afford the least of the glory,
Are done by the head as she follows her mission,
To argue with vendors, smooth out the problems, and fight for the money,
To provide for her staff the best working conditions.

Ruth did that and more, we know from staff members,
Making OPAC music under her baton;

Sheila S. Intner is Professor Emerita, Simmons GSLIS at Mount Holyoke College. She may be reached c/o Carol I. Henry, 4008 Cleveland Street, Kensington, MD 20895 (E-mail: Shemat@aol.com).

[Haworth co-indexing entry note]: "In Honor of Ruth C. Carter." Intner, Sheila S. Co-published simultaneously in *Cataloging & Classification Quarterly* (The Haworth Information Press, an imprint of The Haworth Press, Inc.) Vol. 44, No. 1/2, 2007, pp. 53-54; and: *Cataloger, Editor, and Scholar: Essays in Honor of Ruth C. Carter* (ed: Robert P. Holley) The Haworth Information Press, an imprint of The Haworth Press, Inc., 2007, pp. 53-54. Single or multiple copies of this article are available for a fee from The Haworth Document Delivery Service [1-800-HAWORTH, 9:00 a.m. - 5:00 p.m. (EST). E-mail address: docdelivery@haworthpress.com].

Available online at http://ccq.haworthpress.com
© 2007 by The Haworth Press, Inc. All rights reserved.
doi:10.1300/J104v44n01_05

She toiled aplenty for heaps of Januarys to Decembers,
To ensure the department rolled on.

How proper that Ruth, schooled as a tech services head,
Embraced scholarly work for added fulfillment.
And to a journal editorship allowed her leisure to be wed,
Sacrificing fun and frolic to that commitment.

Now gathering authors; now thinking up themes; now doing markups of the editorial sort;
Now starting new features and a new journal, too;
Creating professional materials we can't do without.
Can you imagine a world without *CCQ*?

Can you imagine a world in which JOIC fails to provoke,
Metadiscussions and metadebates?
Not our world, for sure! For to it Ruth gave and all of us took,
A legacy of intellectual weight.

Step forward, Ruth Carter, and accept what you've earned,
Plaudits, kudos, and thanks!
Wear them with pride in the new corner you've turned,
You'll ever be part of our ranks.

PART II: HISTORICAL STUDIES

Books and Other Reading Materials in Early Monroe County, Indiana

Martin D. Joachim

SUMMARY. This paper analyzes the availability of books and other reading materials in Monroe County, Indiana, through 1850. It examines both unpublished and published primary sources as well as secondary sources to reveal that books and reading were part of life on the western frontier. doi:10.1300/J104v44n01_06 *[Article copies available for a fee from The Haworth Document Delivery Service: 1-800-HAWORTH. E-mail address: <docdelivery@haworthpress.com> Website: <http://www.HaworthPress.com> © 2007 by The Haworth Press, Inc. All rights reserved.]*

KEYWORDS. Monroe County (Ind.), Monroe County (Ind.) Library, Indiana University, library history, history of the book, book ownership, will and probate records

---

Martin D. Joachim is retired Principal Cataloger, Indiana University Libraries, Bloomington, IN 47405 (E-mail: joachimm@indiana.edu).

[Haworth co-indexing entry note]: "Books and Other Reading Materials in Early Monroe County, Indiana." Joachim, Martin D. Co-published simultaneously in *Cataloging & Classification Quarterly* (The Haworth Information Press, an imprint of The Haworth Press, Inc.) Vol. 44, No. 1/2, 2007, pp. 55-93; and: *Cataloger, Editor, and Scholar: Essays in Honor of Ruth C. Carter* (ed: Robert P. Holley) The Haworth Information Press, an imprint of The Haworth Press, Inc., 2007, pp. 55-93. Single or multiple copies of this article are available for a fee from The Haworth Document Delivery Service [1-800-HAWORTH, 9:00 a.m. - 5:00 p.m. (EST). E-mail address: docdelivery@haworthpress.com].

Available online at http://ccq.haworthpress.com
© 2007 by The Haworth Press, Inc. All rights reserved.
doi:10.1300/J104v44n01_06

INTRODUCTION

An examination of early Monroe County, Indiana, records and newspapers reveals that books and other reading materials were easily available in the county in the first half of the nineteenth century. The libraries of Indiana University and Monroe County had sizeable collections by mid-century. A number of newspapers and journals appeared during the early history of the county. What has not been evident, however, is the extent to which individuals owned books.[1] This paper will analyze many of the available primary sources from Monroe County through 1850 and will attempt to determine the general availability of books in the county, the extent of private book ownership, the kind of people who owned books, and the reading interests of the population.

INDIANA UNIVERSITY LIBRARY

Although the claim of Charles Pering that "I do not believe there is an institution in the West, which contains so many rare and sterling works of merit,"[2] may be debatable, the number of volumes in the Indiana University Library[3] in Bloomington grew to 5,000 by the middle of the nineteenth century. According to the report of the Board of Trustees, in 1829 the library had 235 volumes, "so assorted as to embrace History, Geography, Belles Lettres, and treatises on Chemistry, and mental and moral philosophy."[4] *The American Almanac for 1832* indicates that there were 182 volumes in the college library with an additional 50 in student libraries.[5] By 1834, according to the Board of Trustees report, there were between 400 and 500 volumes in the library.[6] *The American Almanac for 1835* notes 400 volumes in the college library and 200 in student libraries.[7] Six hundred volumes in the university library with an additional 400 in student libraries existed by 1840.[8] R. Carlyle Buley claims that such figures from *The American Almanac for 1840* are "probably mere guesses . . . and practically meaningless."[9] A catalogue published in 1842, however, classifies the holdings of the university library and lists 1,445 titles.[10] By the middle of the century, the Indiana University Library contained some 5,000 volumes and embraced "a choice collection of Greek, Latin, French, and English classics, the best standard works on history, biography, and the sciences, together with a selected variety of miscellaneous literature."[11] The figure of 5,000 includes the several hundred volumes in each of the university's two literary societies and in the Law School Library.

In addition to the books in the university library, students also owned books; the books they possessed, however, were not likely to be owned by most other inhabitants of Monroe County. A notice for the State Seminary, for example, announced that:

> the institution will for the present be strictly classical, and each scholar will be required to furnish himself with a supply of classical books, of which the following are recommended, and will be needed from term to term:
>
> Ross's Latin grammar, latest edition[12]
> Colloquies of Corderius[13]
> Selectae e Veteri[14]
> Selectae e Profania[15]
> Caesar
> Virgil, and Mairs introduction[16]
> Volpys Grammar–latest edition[17]
> Testament
> Graeca minora[18]
>
> ... The choice of Lexicon in either language is left discretionary with the student: Ainsworth's in Latin[19] and Schrevelius' in Greek[20] are however recommended ... [21]

Because students usually lived in private homes, they "were in close touch with the life of the community about them."[22] The types of classical books listed above were, therefore, at least accessible in some homes in Monroe County. The number of homes was small since there were only fifteen students enrolled in the Seminary in 1825.[23] By 1850, the university was no longer restricted to the study of Greek and Latin. There were 163 students, down from 197 in 1849.[24] Thus by then, contact with students meant that the opportunity was greater for access to a wider variety of books than in 1825.

MONROE COUNTY LIBRARY

A library for Monroe County was authorized with legislative organization of the county in an act approved January 14, 1818. Section 6 of the act indicates an early awareness of the importance of books and libraries:

The agent to be appointed for the county of Monroe, shall reserve in his hands ten per centum out of the nett [sic] proceeds of the sales of lots which may be made at the seat of justice of said county for the use of a county library.[25]

In 1821, a few dozen standard works were purchased, "not cheap yellow-covered books."[26] There is discrepancy in the sources as to the number of volumes in the Monroe County Library. By July 1830, according to Charles Blanchard, the library had about 800 volumes.[27] *The Bloomington Post* of March 15, 1839 lists the books contained in the Monroe County Library; 152 titles in about 500 volumes are itemized.[28] The Monroe County Public Library still has in its possession a manuscript "Catalogue of Books in the Monroe County Library." The catalog, dating from about 1850, lists 832 titles acquired since 1821. Jewett's figure of 4,000 volumes[29] by 1850, therefore, appears to be a much inflated number. Blanchard, furthermore, notes that there were over 2,000 volumes in the library at the time his book was published in 1884. This discrepancy cannot be credited to a loss by fire since "this same old library, now comprising over 200 volumes of standard works, is yet [in 1884] in the same old office that was built during the twenties."[30] The variance in figures may be explained in part by inadequate records of purchases and additions to the library. Many early records were lost in a fire on February 26, 1838. Dr. C. G. Ballard was treasurer of the Monroe County Library at the time; the library's account books and other papers were in his medical office that was completely destroyed by the fire.[31] Regardless of actual library holdings, however, it seems evident that there was concern early in the history of Monroe County to build a valuable library.

Additional information about private book ownership appears in the Record of the trustee meetings of the Monroe County Library.[32] The first entry in the ledger of the meetings is dated March 31, 1820. The minutes through 1850 indicate only one instance of a book being presented to the library as a gift from an individual. "*The Christian System*, 1 volume, was presented to the Library by Mr. D. Batterton."[33] Batterton had served as a trustee of the library.[34]

The Record documents the sale of three works by the Monroe County Library. The following entry identifies one of these works:

Ordered by the board of Trustees that the Treasurer Call on Joseph A. Wright and take his note with good & Sufficient Security for the Sum of eighteen dollars with Interest thereon from date thereof. The above Sum is in value for Nicholsons encyclopedia Sold to Said J. A. Wright.[35]

A later entry reveals that Wright also purchased the other two works:

Ordered that Blackstone's Commentary, and 'Chitty's Pleadings' be sold to the highest bidder provided they bring the amount of the original cost.

Ordered that Joseph A. Wright (having purchased the above books) execute his note with approved security on a credit of twelve months for thirty-two dollars, to the Treasurer of the Library, of which sum fifteen dollars is to draw interest from the date the last sum being for Chitty's Pleadings.[36]

Certain entries in the Record might be construed to mean that librarians of Monroe County often took books with them when they left office. The following, for example, refers to Joseph A. Wright and William Lowe:

On motion ordered [by the trustees] that the present librarian be and he is hereby authorized to call on Joseph A. Wright a former librarian for the following books, To Wit, Chataubriands Travels one vol, Salmagundi first vol, Miltons Work one vol, Shakespeair 2nd vol, and if Said Wright will not Deliver up Said Books, the Present Librarian is hereby Authorised to bring Suit and Collect the amount of Said books in money from Said Wright.

Ordered that the Librarian proceed in the same manner with Wm. Lowe a former Librarian for Volnie's Ruins.[37]

Settling accounts with former librarians seems to have been a frequent responsibility of current librarians. Wright himself was:

authorized to call on Addison Smith the former librarian for the Vicar of Wakefield 1 volume or the price of said book, also to call on John Bowland former Librarian for the following books (to wit) Blairs Lectures 1 volume, Chittys Pleadings 3 volumes, Lewis & Clarks travels, 1st volume & Lyric Poems 1 vol or for the price of said books & on failure to return the same the present Librarian is further empowered to prosecute a suit therefore.[38]

These entries in the Record do not, however, mean that these librarians had unlawfully taken books from the library when they left office. Early librarians, in fact, were often fiscally responsible for all the books in their libraries. If books were missing for any reason whatsoever, the librarians were financially responsible for them. Thus, entries in the Record authorizing current librarians to retrieve books from former librarians indicate a means of settling accounts on missing books and do not necessarily mean that the former librarians had taken the missing books.

The Record also indicates the problems that the library board had in securing compensation for library books borrowed by David A. Killough, who had served as treasurer of the trustees of the Monroe County Library. At the time of his death at age 44 on August 5, 1836, he was also serving as a justice of the peace.[39] It is unclear whether or not Killough had kept these books unlawfully; his estate eventually did pay the cost of certain library materials. The treasurer of the trustees was ordered to "call upon the administrator of David Killough Deceased former Treasurer, to deliver up to him all Books, papers and moneys or any other thing belonging or In any wise appertaining to said County Library."[40] The settlement of this matter spread over many years. It was "ordered by the Board that a committee be appointed to settle with the Administrator of the Estate of David Killough . . . and if they can not be settle[d] the same to take the same to the Probate Court for adjustment."[41] Allowed from Killough's estate "to Monroe County Library as per receipt . . . [was] $50.00."[42] An entry in the Record almost four years later "ordered that the Treasurer take such steps as may be necessary for securing the balance of the sum due to Library from the Estate of David Killough."[43] And still, five years later, the Record shows that a member of the board "had made a partial examine [sic] of the probate docket and found a balance of about twenty five dollars with interest from about 1841, due to the library."[44]

The Record indirectly indicates that books were sometimes taken illegally from the Monroe County Library. An occasional newspaper announcement, however, is more to the point in offering evidence that librarians have long had to deal with the problem of stolen and lost books:

> LOST BOOK: Previous to my taking charge of the Monroe County Library the 3d vol. of Christian's Blackston was taken out and not

returned by some person unknown to me; whoever may have the same in their possession or can give any information thereof will confer a special favor by so doing not only on the public, but also to B. M. Ewing, Lib'n.[45]

THE COUNTY PRESS

In addition to the books available in the university and county libraries, other reading materials were available in Monroe County. Newspapers published in the county before 1851 included the *Indiana Gazette, Democrat, Bloomington Equator, Bloomington Herald, Independent Whig, Indiana Globe, Indiana Tribune and Monroe County Farmer, Bloomington Post, Bloomington Reporter, Bloomington Republican,* and *Bloomington Progress.*[46] Blanchard also mentions two other papers published in Monroe County in the first half of the century: *The Far West* and *Ben Franklin.*[47] All these newspapers were published in Bloomington, with the earliest being the *Indiana Gazette* beginning in 1824 and ceasing publication on April 1, 1826. Buley also notes the *Indiana Gazette and Literary Advocate*, which died shortly after it began publication in 1826.[48]

Although newspapers represented the majority of the output of the county press, there was also some periodicals published in Monroe County. The *Literary Register*, a college literary magazine, was published in 1832; the *Budget of Fun* in 1835; and the *Equator of the Weekly Press and Gazette of Our Family, School, and Church Interests* in 1840. *The Yellow Jacket*, also in 1840, "was so caustic as to have to be printed out of town."[49] *The Madison Museum*, 1832-1833, was devoted to news, literature, and amusement.[50] In 1847 the Bloomington *Medical Investigator* was published, intended as the organ of the Botanico-Medicals, a minor division of the Botanics.[51] In the 1840s, there also appeared a monthly entitled *The Christian Record*, published "in the interests of the Christian Church."[52]

PRIVATE BOOK OWNERSHIP

It is clear that there was much reading material available in Monroe County in the first half of the nineteenth century. But how many individuals owned books? As noted above, university students owned books. The Record of the Monroe County Library through 1850 offers only one example of a gift from an individual to the library, that from a member of the board, and three examples of books sold by the library to an individual, those purchased by a librarian. This source, then, offers limited information about the extent of private book ownership.

"There were," says Buley, "relatively few books among the early settlers" in the Old Northwest.[53] "Personal libraries of significance were not numerous, though here and there, even in the small towns, were exceptional individuals with libraries of several hundred volumes."[54]

To determine whether any of these exceptional individuals lived in Monroe County, several source materials were examined. Will and probate records in the Monroe County Courthouse yielded information about bequests of books, inventories of estates, and sales of estates including books. Selected early newspapers from Monroe County were inspected to locate information about the relationship of the people of the county to books. Indiana University's Lilly Library contains a number of account books and day books of early Monroe County merchants. These ledgers itemize frequent sales of books. Other sources, such as the records of the Monroe County Bible Society, were also examined in order to find materials about the availability of books in the county.

Early will records are small in number with only eighty-five having been filed through 1850. Some of these wills indicate, however, that the testators were aware of the value of books and education. In his will dated August 1, 1825, James Smith, for example, provides for his wife "to dispose of all or any land of said Estate for her benefit . . . and Education of my Dear children."[55] Samuel Dunn's will, dated December 8, 1838, shows his desire for "three years schooling and the necessary books and clothing for my son Benjamin."[56] John Childers, whose will, dated September 2, 1850, shows that he also had two daughters, stipulates only "that my son have a liberal education if my division of property will allow it given to him."[57]

Whereas nine of the eighty-five wills examined mention education or schooling, only two specify bequests of books. John Owens's will, dated October 2, 1840, provides for the disposal of "all beds and beddings, tables, chairs, table linens, books and other papers and documents."[58] Owens was a successful merchant, farmer, and moneylender in Monroe County from about 1816; he identifies himself in his will as a "Farmer of Monroe County."[59] None is as specific in its mention of books and private libraries as that of Nathan B. Derrow, a Presbyterian clergyman sent into Indiana by the Connecticut Missionary Society in 1816. He bequeaths:

> to my true and loving wife Laura L. Derrow one half of my libra[ry] such books as she shall select–And to the Theological and Literary Institution or college of the Connecticut Western Reserve the other half of my books.[60]

Although the number of volumes in Derrow's personal library is not stipulated, it may be inferred that it was large. What was a large library for a clergyman? Harris discusses the library of the Reverend Andrew Fulton of Jefferson County; it contained over 200 titles in about 400 volumes and was the largest personal library that Harris encountered in his study.[61] Most clergy, however, had small personal libraries. Harris states that:

> it must be remembered that many of the early ministers in Indiana were "itinerants"; they moved about constantly, and a few books were all that could be carried with them though they might desire many more. The largest theological libraries . . . belonged to clergy who for one reason or another did not travel a circuit.[62]

Derrow was an educated man who knew the value of books. He "was perhaps more deeply conscious of the need of schools and teachers among the early pioneers than was any other evangel of the gospel in all the Hoosier Backwoods."[63] When Derrow came to Indiana in 1816, "there was alarming and woeful ignorance to be relieved."[64] He found many families with no books at all and inability to read the tracts that were presented to them.

Of the eighty-five wills filed in Monroe County through 1850, Nathan B. Derrow's in the most explicit in the mention of books and private libraries. The unanswered questions, however, remain. Did he have his books with him in Monroe County? Why are his will and the Trumbull County, Ohio, record of his death filed among the will records of Monroe County, Indiana?

The probate books of Monroe County contain a variety of records; for this study inventory lists and records of sales of estates are the major sources for information about books.[65] The earliest inventory list that mentions books is that dealing with the estate of James Sheffield.[66] Undated, it falls between records dated December 28, 1818 and October 2, 1820. According to Blanchard, letters of administration were granted on

Sheffield's estate between the August 1818 and March 1819 terms of the Probate Court.[67] The inventory states simply "Books" and assigns a value of $.75; the entire estate was valued as $628.66 1/2.[68]

Bartlet Woodward's estate,[69] valued at $1331.44, included "1 lot of books"[70] worth $6.00. Two inventory lists, dated December 11, 1821 and January 2, 1822, appear. Included in a list of expenses filed on March 20, 1824 by his widow and administratrix for the care of his infant heirs was one school book worth $.75.[71] Woodward was an early settler in Monroe County and "became a prominent citizen, and was elected one of the first County Commissioners of the county in 1818."[72]

The next inventory to include books is of the estate of William Berry.[73] The inventory is undated but was filed about the middle of 1823. It lists two books worth $.50 out of property valued at $496.12 1/2.[74] Although his estate included only two books, Berry's will, which he signed September 7, 1822, indicates an interest in the education of his children: "I also injoin on my daughter Hannah, my sons William & Green to whom I gave my plantation to give all my children as much schooling as they conveniently can."[75]

For the three books in the inventory of the estate of Andrew Christy,[76] no value is given; nor is a value given to the entire estate. Christy's will, dated April 22, 1822,[77] makes no specific bequests of books; the inventory is dated September 2, 1822. A list of the sale of property of the estate of Edward Cox is dated November 1, 1823. There is no indication that there were books other than the one that was sold for $.37 1/2; a total of $72.62¾ was made from the sale.[78]

A seller of whiskey and a tavern owner, William Hardin, also owned books. The inventory of his estate lists one Bible and hymn book at $.75 and twenty-one pamphlets at $.50. The estate was valued at $278.64.[79] The sale record of the estate on March 18, 1825 shows a total number of books not equaling the number in the inventory. Seven books were sold for 6 1/2¢ each, eight for 20¢, sixteen for 34¢, one for 7¢, and one for 3¢.[80] Included in the list of items selected by Hardin's widow as her share of the estate were the Bible and hymn book.[81] Hardin had the first store in Bloomington; he opened it in June 1818 and sold mainly whiskey.[82]

The next inventory to mention books is that of the estate of one Joseph Smith. Dated November 22, 1825, the list mentions "Books" at a value of $3.00 out of a total estate valued at $433.00.[83] Smith's will, dated August 1, 1825, does not specifically mention books; but Smith does state that "it is my will to have and dispose of all or any land of said

Estate for her [i.e., his wife's] benefit and support and Education of my Dear Children."[84]

The June 22, 1826 inventory of William Hamilton Gray's estate lists a "chest of books" valued at $19.00 and a total estate of $120.50.[85] Gray's will, dated March 7, 1826, does not specifically bequeath his books; but he does provide for the purchase of books after the settlement of the expenses of his estate:

> Should any of this money remain after these charges, I will and bequeath it to the Blue Spring Community. I also will and bequeath unto the Blue Spring Community the first instalment [sic] of payment of a note of of [sic] hand, One Hundred and fifty Dollars. . . . These moneys I desire to be appropriated in purchasing books, or other useful means for educating the Children of said Community or any other Charitable purposes which the Community may think proper.[86]

Gray himself was apparently a member of the community, but his name does not appear among the twenty-seven whose signatures appear on the community's constitution. A newspaper obituary states that Gray died on the 27th of March 1826 at age 24 in East Harmony and notes that he "commenced his Academical studies, when he was very young. While at school, he was the diligent scholar, and the bosom friend of all his calss [sic] mates. Before he had entirely finished his litery [sic] pursuits, he espoused the cause of Christianity . . ."[87] Because of his studies, perhaps, he acquired an interest that resulted in the "chest of books" inventoried in his estate.

The first inventory to list a specific title, except for the Bible, is for the estate of Marmaduke Potter, a stone worker. The inventory of March 5, 1827 includes Walker's *Pocket Dictionary*[88] valued at $.75.[89] The inventory includes statements of money which was owed to Potter for stone work done on the courthouse and for various jobs of hauling and quarrying.

The July 18, 1827, inventory of Daniel Rawlins[90] includes several titles:

1 old family Bible	1.00
The Reformer Reformed[91]	.50
Fletcher's *Life & Appeal*[92]	.50
Fletcher's *Checks* (4 vols.)[93]	1.00
Wesley's Life[94]	1.00

Island of Great Britain (4 vols.)[95]   1.50
Family Advisor[96]   .25
Life of Mr. Fletcher[97]   .25
Saints Everlasting Rest[98]   .50
Methodist Discipline[99]   .25

In an estate valued at $1817.97¾, the books total $6.75. The record of Rawlins's widow's share of the estate indicates that she selected no books, not even the family Bible.[100] It is clear from the titles of the books that Rawlins owned that he was a Methodist; he was, in fact, among the first Methodists in Monroe County.[101] Rawlins also served as a trustee of the Monroe County Library.[102]

The next inventory to itemize books is for the estate of Joseph Smith. The November 18, 1828, inventory lists "old books."[103] The assigned value was $1.00 in a total estate worth $107.00.

The only book itemized in the July 16, 1829 inventory of the estate of Allen Rea[104] is a Bible at $3.00.[105] The sale bill of the estate shows that the Bible sold for $3.77 and that $138.14¼ worth of personal property was sold.[106]

A "parcel of books" appears in the inventory of Jeremiah Kirby's estate.[107] Dated August 19, 1829, the inventory values the books at $3.62 1/2 and the estate at $688.18¾. Selected by his widow for her share of the estate was one large Bible valued at $1.75.[108]

Moses Williams, who was among the earliest settlers in Bloomington,[109] had "one lot of books"[110] in the inventory of his estate of June 1, 1830. The books were valued at $.50 and the estate at $115.75.[111]

Probate Order Book A includes records for the administration of forty-seven estates. Thirty-one of these records include inventories or sales records of the estates, and fourteen of those specifically mention books. The information available in Probate Order Books B-F is less than Book A by itself. There are records in Books B-F showing the administration of 501 estates through 1850. Only eleven inventories or records of sales appear; and, in these inventories, a single one specifies books.

Not until the inventory entry of May 30, 1849 for the estate of William Tribble is there further mention of books. Valued at $978.90, the estate included a book case at $3.00 and a "lot of books" at $3.00.[112] The sale bill for the estate discloses that the book case sold for $3.25.[113] It also specifies the following books:

View of the wor[l]d[114]	2.60
Revised statutes of 31[115]	.12 1/2
1 book	.25
1 lot of books	.12 1/2

The books itemized in the wills and probate records can be categorized as follows:

Bibles, religion, etc.	**11**
Bibles	3
The Reformer Reformed	1
Fletcher's *Checks*	1
Fletcher's *Life & Appeal*	1
Wesley's Life	1
Life of Mr. Fletcher	1
Saints' Everlasting Rest	1
Methodist Discipline	1
Hymn book	1
Law, etc.	**1**
Revised Statutes of 31	
Miscellaneous	**5**
School books	1
Walker's *Pocket Dictionary*	1
Island of Great Britain	1
Family Adviser	1
View of the World	1
Unidentified books	**40**
	Total 57

In addition to these items are other collections identified by such phrases as "chest of books," "one lot of books," "old books," "parcel of books," or simply by the word "books."

BUYING AND SELLING OF BOOKS

Many of the books listed in the wills and probate records discussed above were undoubtedly purchased at Monroe County's general stores. It was, in fact, the general or country store from which most pioneers on the Western frontier obtained their books. Virtually all frontier stores sold books, and they often carried large varieties of books.[116] The fact that books were readily available may at first seem surprising. Peckham notes that "the general verdict about the dearth of books in frontier society is deceptively logical. We have assumed that in a rude society which had little time for reading there was no incentive to acquire books, and thus the exceptional frontierman who might wish to read found it difficult to obtain reading matter."[117] In addition to farmers, of course, there were also teachers, doctors, merchants, clergymen, and craftsmen who settled the frontier towns. The country stores were able to provide books to satisfy the reading needs of their customers.

The general stores of Monroe County also sold books right along with whiskey, tobacco, cloth, kerosene, farm implements, food, and the many other items that they stocked. F. T. Butler's general store in Ellettsville, for example, advertised dry goods, hardware, groceries, window glass, medicine, saddlery, boots and shoes, stationery, and books for sale.[118] Since account books or daybooks of several of Monroe County's stores are in the Manuscripts Division of Indiana University's Lilly Library, they were examined to determine book sales in the first half of the nineteenth century. Merchants who stocked and sold books in Monroe County and whose records were examined include James Hemphill, Joshua Howe, John Wright, Thomas McCalla, and H. D. Woodward.

The records of the store of James Knox Hemphill, 1801-1837, include his accounts, those of his estate, and later accounts of an unidentified merchant. The accounts cover the period from May 15, 1835, to August 1865. The following books are itemized as having been sold through 1850:

Books	*Number Sold*
Bibles	11
Testaments	6
Psalm books	2
Spelling books	18
Primers	6
Readers	12
Music books	6
Almanacs	1
Arithmetics	1
Pike's Arithmetic[119]	3
Life of Marion[120]	1

Books	Number Sold
History of Marion↑	1
Unidentified books	9

The daybook of John Wright, a Bloomington merchant, covers the period from December 30, 1837 to September 29, 1838. In these nine months, Wright's store sold the following books:

Books	*Number Sold*
Almanacs	8
Primers	1
Spelling books	41
Dictionaries	1
Arithmetics	1
Readers	2
Hymn books	1
Life of Washington[121]	1
Smith's Grammar[122]	2
Gunn's Medicine[123]	2
Parley's Reader[124]	1

The daybook of the general store of Thomas McCalla is in two volumes with entries from June 15 to December 27, 1839, and from May 23, 1845 to April 25, 1846. The records show that McCalla stocked a wide variety of books. Books sold include the following:

Books	*Number Sold*
Spelling books	109
Drill books	2
Dictionaries	3
Primers	18
Arithmetics	2
Psalm books	2
Hymn books	1
Bibles	7
Webster's *Dictionary*	1
English rule	1
Plays	12
Catechisms	5
Almanacs	15
Unidentified books	7

Geography and atlas	6
English grammar	1
(illegible) *Mechanics*	1
Herschel's *Astronomy*[125]	15
Ainsworth's *Dictionary*[126]	1
Colburn's *Algebra*[127]	2
Ross' Latin *Grammar*[128]	2
Kirkham's *Grammar*[129]	1
Eberle's *Therapeutics*[130]	1
Bourdon's *Algebra*[131]	1
Missouri *Harmony*[132]	1
Brown's *Catechism*[133]	1
Brown's *Psalms*[134]	1
Dupuy's *Hymns*[135]	1
Davies' *Arithmetic*[136]	15
Davies' Legendre[137]	6
Morse's *Geography*[138]	1
Smith's *Grammar*[139]	6
Goodrich's *2nd Reader*[140]	3
Goodrich's *3rd Reader*↑	3
1st Reader↑	3
Fourth Reader↑	6
Smith's *Basic Syntax*[141]	11
Whately's *Logic*[142]	1
Pike's *Arithmetic*[143]	5
Eclectic Reader no. 1[144]	3
Eclectic Reader no. 2↑	4
Eclectic Reader no. 3↑	8
Eclectic Readers↑	11
Oliver Twist[145]	1

Three additional account books in the Lilly Library offer little or no information about the sale of books through 1850. The account book of H. D. Woodward covers the period from January 19, 1849 to January 10, 1853. In June 1850, Woodward records the sale of twenty-three unidentified books; there is no other entry for book sales through the end of 1850. The account book of Joshua O. Howe[146] does not list sales by item sold. Finally, there is an account book of the Graham general store in Ellettsville. The ledger is fragmentary in that it covers the period from May 10, 1844 to June 24, 1852. In the scant twelve pages; there is no mention of books.[147]

An itemization of book sales in the ledgers and account books of Hemphill, Wright, McCalla, and Woodward is summarized as follows:

Almanacs	**24**
Arithmetics, etc.	**37**
Arithmetics	4
Bourdon's *Algebra*	1
Colburn's Algebra	2
Davies' *Arithmetic*	15
Davies' Legendre	6
Pike's *Arithmetic*	9
Bibles, religion, etc.	**39**
Bibles	18
Brown's *Catechism*	1
Brown's *Psalms*	1
Catechisms	5
Dupuy's *Hymns*	1
Hymn books	2
Psalm books	4
Testaments	6
Missouri Harmony	1
Language, readers, etc.	**261**
Dictionaries	4
Ainsworth's *Dictionary*	1
Webster's *Dictionary*	1
Drill books	2
English grammar	1
English rule	1
Kirkham's *Grammar*	1
Smith's *Basic Syntax*	2
Smith's *Grammar*	8
Spelling books	168
Ross' *Latin Grammar*	2
Primers	25
Readers	14
Eclectic Readers	2
Eclectic Reader no. 1	3
Eclectic Reader no. 2	4

Eclectic Reader no. 3	8
Goodrich's *1st Reader*	6
Goodrich's *2nd Reader*	3
Goodrich's *3rd Reader*	3
Goodrich's *4th Reader*	1
Parley's *Reader*	1
Science, medicine, etc.	**25**
Geography & atlas	6
Morse's *Geography*	1
Herschel's *Astronomy*	14
Eberle's *Therapeutics*	1
Gunn's *Medicine*	2
(illegible) *Mechanics*	1
Music	**7**
Music books	6
Singing books	1
History, biography, etc.	**3**
History of Marion	1
Life of Marion	1
Life of Washington	1
Philosophy	**1**
Whately's *Logic*	1
Literature	**13**
Plays	12
Oliver Twist	1
Unidentified books	**39**
	Total 448

The records analyzed here represent only a small part of the businesses in Monroe County in the first half of the nineteenth century. There were, according to Blanchard, over sixty merchants in the city of Bloomington alone up to 1850.[148] It is likely that most of these merchants stocked books in their stores.

Early Bloomington newspapers also yield information about the availability of books in Monroe County and show that citizens could acquire books by ordering them as well as by purchasing them at local stores. Booksellers' lists were prominent in early newspapers. In fact, they occupied more column space than any other advertisements except those for land sales.[149]

The American Sunday School Union maintained a depository in Cincinnati for its publications and advertised their availability in Monroe County. The categories of books that could be ordered included the Bible, Scripture illustrations, juvenile biography, picture books for small children, missionary biography, and books about the martyrs, natural history, temperance, and the lives of pious persons. It was "believed that editors of religious Periodicals in the West would confer a very acceptable favor on the community" if they advertised the availability of such books from the American Sunday School Union.[150] The appearance of this notice in *The Post* indicates that the Union's agents sought out more than "religious Periodicals" for the inclusion of its announcements.

In an announcement dated August 27, 1838, Joseph Huber, a book agent from Louisville, advertised that "a depository of Bibles, Testaments and sundry Schoolbooks have been established at Louisville . . . which will be sold at cost."[151]

Newspapers on the frontier carried frequent announcements of the availability of books. Following is one such example:

> NEW BOOKS: The subscribers have received a quantity of valuable books, and will continue to keep on hand, such books as may be wanted, the public are requested to call and examine our stock. N.B. We request all those whose accounts have been of long standing to call and settle the same, as money is greatly needed.[152]

This announcement was made by the establishment of Nichols, Alexander & Carter. Blanchard identifies these three as merchants.[153] Their business was not a bookstore. Harris notes, in fact, that there were few real bookstores in the West in the early part of the nineteenth century since there was not enough of a market to deal exclusively in books.[154]

There was a book bindery in Bloomington; but it probably specialized in the binding of ledgers, account books, and the like. An announcement, for example, advises that "Clerks, Merchants and Magistrates, can have blank books cheap."[155]

INDIVIDUAL READING TASTES

The relatively low number of Bibles listed in wills and probate records should not be surprising since Bibles were often family heirlooms or genealogical record books. They were no doubt often passed on to family members when their owners' deaths seemed near at hand.[156] The Bible was probably the most readily available book in Monroe County. The Monroe County Bible Society, on September 18, 1837, "resolved that this Society undertake to supply the destitute families of the County with a Bible by the first of April next."[157] The treasurer's report of the Society, furthermore, regularly includes an accounting of the number of Bibles bought and sold.

Newspapers regularly carried advertisements announcing the availability of Bibles. A prospectus from a C. L. M'Gee offers the public for one dollar:

> the New Testament of Our Lord and Saviour Jesus Christ; with an introduction, giving an account of Jewish, and other sects; with prefatory remarks to each epistle of said Testament; and also, notes illustrative of obscure passages, and explaining obsolete words and phrases; for the use of Schools, Academies, and private families; by J. A. Cummins, author of Ancient and Modern Geography.[158]

Polyglot Bibles were available on subscription from Z. Williams.[159] As mentioned above, the American Sunday-School Union in Cincinnati and Joseph Huber in Louisville offered Bibles for sale; and, of course, Bibles could be purchased at the various general stores of Monroe County.

It is clear from examining the summary of books sold in the general stores and typical newspaper advertisement for books that practical or inspirational books were most often owned by Monroe County residents in the first half of the nineteenth century. Readers and books on language and science were, according to the sources examined, most frequently purchased.

Literature, on the other hand, is rarely cited in the general store account books. Aside from a vague designation of "plays," only one specifically mentioned literary works is itemized, that being *Oliver Twist*. The will and probate records do not specify even one literary title. In fact, it was generally considered a waste of time, if not downright immoral, for one to read works of fiction. This attitude is evident, for example, in a letter to the editor, pseudonymously signed by Alpheus:

> Mr. Editor:—Since my earliest recollection I have been delighted with tales of romance, and since I learned to read, I have been accustomed to pursue the works of fiction, and thus have whiled

away many hours of weary time. I will not endeavour to maintain the *utility* of such writings, for it is well known to a large majority of our *enlightened* citizens, nor is it opposed by any except those termed the *moral* part of our community.[160]

This letter was written in praise of the author of *Victor Desaix*.[161] Alpheus does not identify the author except to note that he is a native of Bloomington whose "towering genius will render his name immortal and raise the standard of literature here in the 'far off west.'"[162]

A list of books contained in the Monroe County Library in 1839[163] also reveals that non-fiction works represented most of the library's holdings at that time. There were, however, some literary works; novels of Sir Walter Scott and Frederick Marryat, for example, are listed.

CONCLUSION

In total, only 548 estates appear in the probate records through 1850. One might infer from the population of Monroe County that more than 548 estates would be probated. From a figure of 2,679 in 1820,[164] the population of the county rose to 6,577 in 1830,[165] to 10,143 in 1840,[166] and 11,286 in 1850.[167] Perhaps the attitude of William Lowe, 1736-1840, the first clerk of Monroe County from 1818-1820 and one of the first trustees of the Indiana Seminary from 1820-1826 and in 1828, was common among the citizenry. His will, dated July 11, 1833, includes the following statement:

> It is my will that no inventory be taken of my estate which will dispense with the necessity of settling the estate in the Probate Court except the Recording of this will as it has been my object while liveing to shun all courts (especially the Probate Court) therefore I do not want my estate to be settled in this way.[168]

The inventories of estates that do appear include lists of varying length and thus of varying utility for analyzing which books were privately owned in Monroe County. The estate of William Hamilton Gray, for example, has only four entries: "1 Watch, Sundry Articles of Clothing, bed & bedding, Chest of Books."[169] On the other hand, the itemization of Bartlett Woodward's estate goes on for five pages.[170] Included in that list is "1 lot of books." Since only fifteen inventories or sales bills of estates specifically mention books, however, these probate records by themselves give only a superficial view of privately owned books. Although vague expressions such as "chest of books" or "parcel of books" do appear, it is unlikely that these represented sizeable collections since the value assigned to them was relatively small. There is, of course, no reason to suppose that the many estates that were not specifically itemized would not have included books.

Although it is impossible to know exactly how many individuals owned books, it is certain that far more did than the probate and will records indicate. Many personal libraries were lost or destroyed by fire. It is known, for example, that a fire on February 26, 1838, completely destroyed the personal medical library of Doctors Foster and Ballard.[171]

The ledgers and account books of Monroe County general stores analyzed in this study do reveal that books were available, and the sale records frequently list the persons to whom these items were sold and show that many people purchased books. The account books examined represent only a small part of the actual business conducted in Monroe County. If complete records were available for all the merchants in Monroe County through 1850, these records would likely show that books were bought and sold in large numbers. Harris concludes that a sizeable part of the population of southern Indiana in the first half of the nineteenth century owned books and that the collections were small.[172] There is no indication that Monroe County was an exception in regard to the size of private libraries. On the basis of sources analyzed, however, there does appear to be a difference in the type of books that the people of Monroe County acquired. Harris's study concludes that the 500 collections that he analyzed were basically religious in nature.[173] Such does not appear to have been the case in Monroe County. The summaries of book sales in the ledgers of Hemphill, Wright, McCalla, and Woodward show that less than nine percent of the books itemized are religious; and the books of a religious nature mentioned in the wills and probate records total about eighteen percent.

The provision of books and religious literature to the West was, however, supported enthusiastically by Christians in the East. The Missionary Society of Connecticut, for example, reported in 1818 that it had up to that time sent nearly 42,000 books and tracts to the frontier.[174] These books and pamphlets included such titles as Richard Cecil's *A Friendly Visit to the House of Mourning*, Richard Baxter's *A Call to the Unconverted* and *The Saints' Everlasting Rest*, and Legh Richmond's *The Dairyman's Daughter*.[175]

Available sources from Monroe County have shown that books were easy to acquire and that individuals did own them in the first half of the nineteenth century. The records show that Nathan B. Derrow possibly had a large library although its actual size is not known.[176] There is no other indication that there were in Monroe County any of the "exceptional individuals with libraries of several hundred volumes"[177] that Buley mentions. In addition to clergymen, however, those who did own books were farmers, merchants, doctors, librarians, students, and laborers. Books were a part of life on the western frontier.

NOTES

1. In his doctoral dissertation, "The Availability of Books and the Nature of Book Ownership on the Southern Indiana Frontier, 1800-1850" (Indiana University, 1971), Michael H. Harris discusses books and book ownership in Indiana but does not include an analysis of available records of Monroe County. The dissertation deals with the counties of Bartholomew, Daviess, Dubois, Franklin, Gibson, Harrison, Jefferson, Jennings, Johnson, Knox, Lawrence, Owen, Rush, Vanderburgh, Vigo, and Warrick.

2. The Bloomington Post, February 23, 1838, p. 3. Charles Pering of the Bloomington Female Academy was a strong supporter of the book purchases of Indiana University president Andrew Wylie in 1838. Wylie had come under considerable attack for spending $1500 for books. See Thomas D. Clark's discussion of this incident in "Building Libraries in the Early Ohio Valley," *The Journal of Library History* 6 (1971), p. 108-109.

3. Indiana University was chartered in 1820 as a State Seminary, became Indiana College in 1828 and Indiana University in 1838.

4. "Report of the Board of Trustees of the Indiana College, Oct. 28, 1830," Journal of the House of Representatives of the State of Indiana, Being the Fifteenth Session of the General Assembly . . . 1830 (Indianapolis: George Smith, State Printer, 1830), p. 43.

5. *The American Almanac for the Year 1832* (Boston: Gray and Bowen, 1831), p. 165.

6. "Annual Report of the Board of Trustees of Indiana College, Sept. 30, 1834," *Journal of the Senate of the State of Indiana during the Nineteenth Session of the General Assembly . . . 1834* (Indianapolis: Printed by Morrison and Bolton, 1834), p. 41.

7. *The American Almanac for the Year 1835* (Boston: Charles Brown, 1834), p. 239.

8. *The American Almanac for the Year 1840* (Boston: David H. Williams, 1839), p. 189.

9. R. Carlyle Buley, *The Old Northwest: Pioneer Period, 1815-1840* (Indianapolis: Indiana Historical Society, 1950), v. 2, p. 12.

10. *Catalogue of the Library of Indiana State University* (Bloomington: M. L. Deal, 1842). Marcus L. Deal, the publisher of this work, was also editor and publisher of *The Bloomington Post*; with Jesse Brandon he also published *The Far West*, a newspaper reflecting a pro-Whig sentiment.

11. Charles C. Jewett, *Notices of Public Libraries in the United States of America* (Washington: Printed for the House of Representatives, 1851), p. 120.

12. The American Latin Grammar, or, A Complete Introduction to the Latin Tongue, by Robert Ross.

13. Mathurin Cordier's *Colloquia Scholastica*, a Latin conversation and phrase book.

14. *Selectae e Veteri Testamento*, Old Testament selections in Latin.

15. Probably Jean Heuzet's Latin reader entitled *Selectae e Profanis Scriptoribus Historiae*.

16. John Mair's best-known work was probably *An Introduction to Latin Syntax*, which was published in many editions.

17. "Volpy" is Richard Valpy whose *Elements of Greek Grammar* and *Elements of Latin Grammar* were published in many editions.

18. Andrew Dalzel's *Collectanea Graeca Minora*, a Greek reader.

19. Robert Ainsworth's Thesaurus Linguae Latinae Compendarius, or, A Compendious Dictionary of the Latin Tongue; published also in many abridged editions.

20. Cornelis Schrevel's *Greek Lexicon*.

21. Indiana Gazette, January 8, 1825, p. 3.

22. Buley, v. 2, p. 412.

23. Mildred Hawksworth Lowell, "Indiana University Libraries, 1829-1942" (Ph.D. dissertation, University of Chicago, 1957), p. 402.

24. *Ibid.*

25. Indiana General Assembly, Special Acts Passed and Published at the Second Session of the General Assembly of the State of Indiana (Corydon: Printed and Published by A. & J. Brandon, 1818), p. 16.

26. History of Lawrence and Monroe Counties: Their People, Industries, and Institutions (Indianapolis: B. F. Bowen, 1914), p. 245.

27. Charles Blanchard, Counties of Morgan, Monroe, and Brown, Indiana: Historical and Biographical (Chicago: F. A. Battey, 1884), p. 374.

28. See Appendix II.

29. Jewett, p. 120.

30. Blanchard, p. 401.

31. *The Bloomington Post*, March 2, 1838, p. 3.

32. Monroe County Library. Record of Trustees. This document will hereafter be referred to as Record.

33. Record, June 16, 1840. The work donated is Alexander Campbell's The Christian System in Reference to the Union of Christians and a Restoration of Primitive Christianity as Pleaded by the Current Reformation; first published in 1835.

34. Record, September 2, 1839. Batterton's election as trustee is documented in this entry.

35. Record, May 21, 1828. The work purchased by Wright is William Nicholson's British Encyclopedia, or, Dictionary of Arts and Sciences Comprising an Accurate and Popular View of the Present Improved State of Human Knowledge or one of the American editions published under the title American Edition of the British Encyclopedia, or, Dictionary of Arts and Sciences.

36. Record, February 25, 1830. Sir William Blackstone's *Commentaries on the Laws of England* was the most popular book among Indiana's first lawyers and, within a short time of its publication, became the standard reference source on English common law and the basic student textbook. Joseph Chitty's *Treatise on Pleading and Par-*

ties to Actions was also a common feature of private law libraries. Cf. Harris's "The Availability of Books and the Nature of Book Ownership on the Southern Indiana Frontier, 1800-1850," p. 170-181.

Wright had been elected Monroe County librarian on December 3, 1827, and resigned that position on February 25, 1830. (Record, December 3, 1827; February 25, 1830) Joseph A. Wright later served as governor of Indiana from 1849-1857. His position as librarian was the first public office of a fledgling politician whose career would ultimately include service as a member of both the Indiana and United States Houses of Representatives and Senates, as governor, and as United States minister to Prussia. For further information on Wright's career as librarian, see Martin D. Joachim, "Joseph A. Wright, Librarian," *Indiana Magazine of History* 78:3 (Sept. 1982): 242-248.

37. Record, February 25, 1830.
38. Record, December 3, 1827.
39. *The Post* (Bloomington), August 12, 1836, p. 3.
40. Record, August 29, 1836.
41. Record, July 19, 1837.
42. Probate Order Book C, p. 174.
43. Record, October 7, 1844.
44. Record, November 22, 1849.
45. *The Bloomington Post,* January 27, 1837, p. 3.
46. Winifred Gregory, American Newspapers, 1821-1936: a Union List of Files Available in the United States and Canada (New York: H. W. Wilson, 1937), p. 145-146.
47. Blanchard, p. 401-402.
48. Buley, v. 2, p. 493.
49. *Ibid.*, v. 2, p. 533.
50. *Ibid.*, v. 2, p. 532-533.
51. *Ibid.*, v. 1, p. 288.
52. Blanchard, p. 402.
53. Buley, v. 2, p. 565.
54. *Ibid.*, v. 2, p. 569.
55. Monroe County, Indiana. Will Record, Book I, p. 25-26. Hereafter this document will be referred to as Will Record.
56. Will Record, Book II, p. 117-118.
57. Will Record, Book II, p. 136.
58. Will Record, Book II, p. 12.
59. Will Record, Book II, p. 11.
60. Will Record, Book I, p. 38. The college of the Connecticut Western Reserve is today Case Western Reserve University, chartered as a college at Hudson, Ohio, in 1826. C. H. Cramer discusses "a petition . . . on the part of 'sundry citizens of Portage and Huron Counties,' for permission to incorporate a Literary and Theological Institution to be located in Hudson" in his book *Case Western Reserve: a History of the University, 1826-1976* (Boston: Little, Brown, 1976), p. 8. Discussion of this Literary and Theological Institution can also be found in Frederick Clayton White, *Western Reserve University, the Hudson Era: a History of Western Reserve College and Academy at Hudson, Ohio, from 1826 to 1882* (Cleveland: Western Reserve University Press, 1943), pp. 45ff.

What is puzzling about Derrow's will is that it appears at all in the will records of Monroe County since it is signed and dated in Trumbull County, Ohio. Derrow owned land in Ohio, Indiana, and Illinois, the disposition of which he provided in his will. Land in Indiana included "a quarter section of land lying in Indiana about thirty miles from the great Ohio falls," "one hundred acres of land contiguous to Honey Creek Preraire [sic] in Indiana," and "twenty five acres of land, it being the place of my former residence" in Vigo County. See Will Record, Book I, p. 37-38. *Minutes of the General Assembly... A.D. 1829* of the General Assembly of the Presbyterian Church in the United States of America (Philadelphia: Published by the Stated Clerk of the Assembly, 1829), p. 417, gives Derrow's name in a list of deceased without specific mention of a place of death. In "The Records of the Middle Association of Congregational Churches of the State of New York, 1806-1810," *Journal of the Presbyterian Historical Society* 10 (1919-1920), p. 221, it states only that he died in Ohio. It can be inferred that he died in Trumbull County. The Monroe County Will Record (Book I, p. 38-40) includes a copy of his will, dated November 3, 1828, with George Parsons, Trumbull County clerk, attesting. Letters of administration of his estate are dated November 27, 1828; once again George Parsons signs the document as county clerk.

61. Harris, p. 189.
62. Ibid., p. 187.
63. Lucien V. Rule, Forerunners of Lincoln in the Ohio Valley (Louisville: Brand & Fowler, 1927), p. 167.
64. James Albert Woodburn, "Pioneer Presbyterianism," Indiana Magazine of History 22 (1926), p. 365.
65. Monroe County, Indiana. Probate Order Books. Probate Order Books A-E and the first 160 pages of Book F cover the period through 1850 in over 2600 pages. Hereafter this source will be referred to as Probate Order Book. The Probate Order Books contain inventories of estates, records of sales of estates, petitions for guardianship, claims for funds by guardians of decedents' heirs, claims against estates, orders to sell real estate, filing of applications and letters of administration of estates, and petitions attesting to service during the Revolutionary War.
66. Probate Order Book A, p. 6-8.
67. Blanchard, p. 378.
68. Probate Order Book A, p. 6.
69. Probate Order Book A, p. 11-20.
70. Probate Order Book A, p. 15.
71. Probate Order Book A, p. 38.
72. Blanchard, p. 522.
73. Probate Order Book A, p. 31-33.
74. Probate Order Book A, p. 32.
75. Will Record, Book I, p. 9.
76. Probate Order Book A, p.
77. Will Record, Book I, p. 6-7.
78. Probate Order Book A, p. 55.
79. Probate Order Book A, p. 60.
80. Probate Order Book A, p. 68.
81. Probate Order Book A, p. 70.
82. Blanchard, p. 455. An advertisement in the *Indiana Gazette* of October 30, 1824, p. 3, appeared under the heading "Wm. Hardin–Entertainment." In advertising his tavern, Hardin "respectfully informs the public, and particularly his former friends and customers, that he still continues to occupy his old stand immediately opposite the courthouse, at the sign of the RISING SUN, as a house of entertainment. This adver-

tisement appeared in subsequent issues of the *Gazette* under the name of William Hardin until being replaced by one signed Elizabeth Hardin on December 28, 1824.

83. Probate Order Book A, p. 86.

84. Will Record, Book I, p. 25.

85. Probate Order Book A, p. 102.

86. Will Record, Book I, p. 28. The Blue Spring Community was a socialistic experiment of the 1820s. Its official name according to its constitution filed in Deed Record Book "B," p. 136-142, in the Monroe County Recorder's Office, was Blue Spring Community for the Promotion of Science and Industry. The community sprang up in 1826 in a place that was called Harmony "for the purpose of increasing the sources of a better system of education and morals than was afforded by the denominational and educational organizations of that day." (Blanchard, p. 513) The community lasted about one year.

87. *Indiana Gazette*, April 1, 1826, p. 2.

88. John Walker, 1732-1807, was an English actor, philologist, and lexicographer whose principal work, *A Critical Pronouncing Dictionary and Expositor of the English Language,* was published in 1791 and was subsequently published in various editions and abridgements.

89. Probate Order Book A, p. 152.

90. Probate Order Book A, p. 156, gives the name as Daniel Rawlings. There is disagreement about the form of name. The Record of the Monroe County Library for September 17, 1825, indicates the presence of a Daniel Rawlins at the meeting; and again, on p. 33, the spelling Rawlins appears. Blanchard also mentions Daniel Rawlins (p. 480). The *Indiana Gazette* of March 12, 1825, p. 2, on the other hand, includes a public notice by Daniel Rawlings. A probate notice in the *Bloomington Republican and Indiana Gazette* of September 22, 1827, p. 4, indicates letters of administration on the estate of Daniel Rawlings taken out by his administratrix, Rebecca Rawlings, on July 28, 1827.

91. The Reformer Reformed, or, A Second Part of the Errors of Hopkinsianism Detected and Refuted, by Nathan Bangs; published 1816.

92. This entry refers probably to two works: a biography of John William Fletcher, 1729-1785, and his *An Appeal to Matter of Fact and Common Sense, or, A Rational Demonstration of Man's Corrupt and Lost Estate.* The *Life* might be John Wesley's *A Short Account of the Life and Death of the Rev. John Fletcher*, 1786; Joseph Benson's *The Life of the Rev. John William de la Flechere* [i.e., Fletcher] *Compiled from the Narratives of the Rev. Mr. Wesley*, 4th ed. published in 1817; or Robert Cox's *The Life of the Rev. John William Fletcher, Late Vicar of Madeley, Shropshire*, editions published in 1822 and 1825.

93. The third American edition of Fletcher's *Checks to Antinomianism* was published in four volumes in 1820.

94. Perhaps *The Life of Wesley and the Rise and Progress of Methodism*, by Robert Southey, published in 1820, or *The Life of the Rev. John Wesley*, by John Whitehead, published in two volumes, 1793-1796.

95. Perhaps Daniel Defoe's Tour thro' the Whole Island of Great Britain.

96. Probably The Family Adviser, or, A Plain and Modern Practice of Physic, by Henry Wilkins; published in 1793 with John Wesley's Primitive Physic.

97. See above, note 92.

98. The Saints' Everlasting Rest, or, A Treatise of the Blessed State of Saints in Their Enjoyment of God in Glory, by Richard Baxter; published in 1650 and issued frequently thereafter.
99. The Doctrines and Discipline of the Methodist Episcopal Church in America.
100. Probate Order Book B, p. 45-46.
101. Blanchard, p. 480.
102. Record, May 22, 1826. It is noted that Rawlins had taken the oath of office required by law to serve as trustee.
103. Probate Order Book A, p. 183.
104. This name is also variously spelled Ray or Rhea in the probate records.
105. Probate Order Book A, p. 186.
106. Probate Order Book A, p. 187.
107. Probate Order Book A, p. 196.
108. Probate Order Book A, p. 198.
109. Blanchard, p. 455.
110. Probate Order Book A, p. 238.
111. Probate Order Book A, p. 239.
112. Probate Order Book E, p. 379.
113. Probate Order Book E, p. 383.
114. *A View of the World as Exhibited in the Manners, Costumes, & Characteristics of All Nations*, originally written by Jehoshaphat Aspin and later adapted for the use of American schools by John L. Blake; published in 1835.
115. Most likely The Revised Laws of Indiana, in Which are Comprised All Such Acts of a General Nature as are in Force in Said State; published in 1831.
116. Lewis E. Atherton, *The Pioneer Merchant in Mid-America*, University of Missouri Studies: a Quarterly of Research, v. 14, no. 2 (Columbia, Mo.: University of Missouri, 1939), p. 20.
117. Howard H. Peckham, "Books and Reading on the Ohio Valley Frontier," *The Mississippi Valley Historical Review* 44 (1957-58), p. 649.
118. *The Post* (Bloomington), August 5, 1836, p. 2.
119. Nicholas Pike's A New and Complete System of Arithmetic Composed for the Use of Citizens of the United States, published in 1788 and issued in many subsequent editions, or his Abridgement of the New and Complete System of Arithmetick..., first published in 1793.
120. The Life of Gen. Francis Marion, a Celebrated Partisan Officer in the Revolutionary War Against the British and the Tories in South Carolina and Georgia, by Mason Locke Weems and Peter Horry; first published in 1809. It is assumed that History of Marion refers to the same work.
121. Because of the popularity of George Washington as a biographical subject, this work could not be specifically identified from this title.
122. Perhaps Roswell Chamberlain Smith's English Grammar on the Productive System: a Method of Instruction Recently Adopted in Germany and Switzerland; published in 1831 and in many subsequent editions.
123. Gunn's Domestic Medicine, or, Poor Man's Friend in the Hours of Affliction, Pain, and Sickness, by John C. Gunn; 1st edition, 1830.
124. Peter Parley is the pseudonym of Samuel Griswold Goodrich, 1793-1860. In his *Recollections of a Lifetime, or, Men and Things I Have Seen* (New York: Miller, Orton, and Mulligan, 1857, v. 2, p. 537-544). Goodrich lists all his works. He states (p. 543):

"I thus stand before the public as the author and editor of about one hundred and seventy volumes–one hundred and sixteen bearing the name of Peter Parley." He also includes a list of spurious Parley books and notes that "the name of Parley has been supplied to several works of which I am not the author" (p. 549). It is unclear which of Parley's works–or spurious works–that Wright cites in his account book as Parley's *Reader.*

125. *Astronomy*, by Sir John Frederick William Herschel; published in 1833.

126. See above, note 19.

127. *An Introduction to Algebra upon the Inductive Method of Instruction*, by Warren Colburn; published in 1825 and in many subsequent editions.

128. See above, note 12.

129. By Samuel Kirkham. Published in 1823 as A Compendium of English Grammar Accompanied by an Appendix in Familiar Lectures and in subsequent editions as English Grammar in Familiar Lectures.

130. A Treatise of the Materia Medica and Therapeutics, by John Eberle; first edition, 1822.

131. Louis Pierre Marie Bourdon's *The Elements of Algebra,* translated from the French; first published in 1828.

132. The Missouri Harmony, or, A Choice Collection of Psalms, Tunes, Hymns, and Anthems, compiled by Allen D. Carden; first published in 1820.

133. Perhaps either *A Short Catechism for Young Children*, several editions of which were published in the first half of the nineteenth century by John Brown, 1722-1787, or *A Catechism in Three Parts Designed for the Use of Children*, by Clark Brown, published in 1797.

134. Perhaps *The Psalms of David in Metre* . . . , with notes by John Brown, 1722-1787.

135. *Hymns and Spiritual Songs*, compiled by Starke Dupuy.

136. Arithmetic Designed for Academies and Schools, by Charles Davies; published in 1841.

137. *Elements of Geometry and Trigonometry*, by Adrien Marie Legendre, translated by David Brewster and revised and adapted to the course of mathematical instruction in the United States by Charles Davies.

138. Jedidiah Morse's *Geography Made Easy*; published in 1784 and issued in many subsequent editions.

139. See above, note 122.

140. Readers by Samuel Griswold Goodrich. It is assumed that the first and fourth readers itemized in McCalla's account book are those of Goodrich since all were published in the same year. There is, however, a question about the publication date. Goodrich, in his *Recollections of a Lifetime* (see above note 117), indicates that the first through fifth readers were all published in 1846. As early as September 27, 1845, McCalla's ledger itemizes "1 Goodrichs 2d Reader."

141. This work was not identified.

142. *Elements of Logic*, by Richard Whately; published in 1826 and in many subsequent editions.

143. See above, note 119.

144. McGuffey's famous readers. The first two were published in 1836, the third and fourth in 1837, and the fifth in 1844.

145. Dickens's work was first published in 1838.

146. Howe, 1784-1868, served also as a member of the Board of Trustees of Indiana University from 1821 to 1825 and from 1832 to 1840. He opened his store on the west side of the courthouse square about 1819. The account book of his store covers the period from December 19, 1836, to September 20, 1841.

147. The Lilly Library also has an account book for the store of John Owens, a merchant, farmer, and moneylender and one of the earliest settlers of Monroe County. In four volumes totaling over 2,300 pages, this account book covers the period from September 17, 1827, to August 1, 1831; the entries are so faded that they are often illegible.

148. Blanchard, p. 457-459.

149. James M. Miller, *The Genesis of Western Culture: the Upper Ohio Valley, 1800-1825*, Ohio Historical Collections, vol. 8 (Columbus: Ohio State Archaeological and Historical Society, 1938), p. 147.

150. *The Post* (Bloomington), August 12, 1836, p. 1.

151. *The Bloomington Post*, August 31, 1838, p. 3.

152. *The Bloomington Post*, February 9, 1838, p. 3.

153. Blanchard, p. 458-459.

154. Harris, p. 104.

155. Bloomington Republican and Indiana Gazette, September 15, 1827, p. 4.

156. Harris, p. 158.

157. Monroe County Bible Society, Minutes, September 18, 1837. These records are located in the Lilly Library, Indiana University.

158. Bloomington Republican and Indiana Gazette, September 27, 1827, p. 4.

159. *The Bloomington Post*, June 3, 1836, p. 2.

160. *Ibid.*, July 21, 1837, p. 3.

161. The author of this work could not be identified.

162. *The Bloomington Post*, July 21, 1837, p. 3.

163. See Appendix II.

164. United States Census Bureau, *Census for 1820* (Washington: Printed by Gales & Seaton, 1821), p. 39*.

165. United States Census Bureau, *Fifth Census or Enumeration of the Inhabitants of the United States, 1830* (Washington: Printed by Duff Green, 1832), p. 145.

166. United States Census Bureau, *Sixth Census, or Enumeration of the Inhabitants of the United States... in 1840* (Washington: Printed by Blair and Rives, 1841), p. 359.

167. United States Census Bureau, *The Seventh Census of the United States, 1850* (Washington: Robert Armstrong, Public Printer, 1853), p. 770.

168. Will Record, Book II, p. 50.

169. Probate Order Book A, p. 102.

170. Probate Order Book A, p. 13-17.

171. *The Bloomington Post*, March 2, 1838, p. 3. Cf. above note 18.

172. Harris, p. 210.

173. *Ibid.*

174. Missionary Society of Connecticut, *Nineteenth Annual Narrative of Missionary Services* (Hartford, 1818), p. 23-24.

175. Colin Brummitt Goodykoontz, *Home Missions on the American Frontier* (Caldwell, Idaho: Caxton Printers, 1939), p. 131.

176. See above, p. 8-9.

177. See above, note 54.

BIBLIOGRAPHY

Primary Sources: Unpublished

Account Books of General Stores
   Robertson Graham (Ellettsville)
   James Hemphill (Bloomington)
   Thomas McCalla (Bloomington)
   H. D. Woodward (Bloomington)
   John Wright (Bloomington)
      (Located in Lilly Library, Indiana University)
Monroe County, Indiana
   Deed Record Book
   Probate Order Book
   Will Record
      (Located in Monroe County Courthouse)
Monroe County Bible Society
   Minutes
      (Located in Lilly Library, Indiana University)
Monroe County Library
   Record of Trustees
      (Located in Monroe County Public Library)

Primary Sources: Published

Newspapers
   Bloomington Republican and Indiana Gazette
   Indiana Gazette
   The Post (Bloomington)
      (Became *The Bloomington Post* with v. 2, no. 1, Nov. 11, 1836)

Indiana. General Assembly. *Special Acts Passed and Published at the Second Session of the General Assembly of the State of Indiana.* Corydon: Printed & Published by A. & J. Brandon, 1818.

Indiana. General Assembly. House of Representatives. "Report of the Board of Trustees of the Indiana College, Oct. 28, 1830." *Journal of the House of Representatives of the State of Indiana, Being the Fifteenth Session of the General Assembly . . . 1830.* Indianapolis: George Smith, State Printer, 1830: 41-45.

Indiana. General Assembly. Senate. "Annual Report of the Board of Trustees of Indiana College, Sept. 30, 1834." *Journal of the Senate of the State of Indiana during the Nineteenth Session of the General Assembly. . . 1834.*

Indiana University. *Catalogue of the Library of Indiana State University.* Bloomington: M. L. Deal, 1842.

Middle Association of Congregational Churches of the State of New York. "The Records of the Middle Association of Congregational Churches of the State of New York, 1806-1810." *Journal of the Presbyterian Historical Society* 10 (1919-1920): 217-229, 258-284; 11 (1921-1923): 20-38, 49-68.

Presbyterian Church in the United States of America. General Assembly. *Minutes . . . A.D. 1825*. Philadelphia: William Bradford, 1825.
_____. *Minutes . . . A.D. 1828*. Philadelphia: Printed by Lydia R. Bailey, 1828.
_____. *Minutes . . . A.D. 1829*. Philadelphia: Published by the Stated Clerk of the Assembly, 1829.
United States. Census Bureau. *Census for 1820*. Washington: Printed by Gales & Seaton, 1821.
_____. *Fifth Census or Enumeration of the Inhabitants of the United States, 1830*. Washington: Printed by Duff Green, 1832.
_____. *The Seventh Census of the United States, 1850*. Washington: Robert Armstrong, 1853.
_____. *Sixth Census or Enumeration of the Inhabitants of the United States . . . in 1840*. Washington: Printed by Blair and Rives, 1841.

Secondary Sources

Atherton, Lewis E. *The Pioneer Merchant in Mid-America*. University of Missouri Studies: a Quarterly of Research, v. 14, no. 2. Columbia, Mo.: University of Missouri, 1939.
Barnard, J. H. "Sketch of Early Presbyterian Church in Indiana." *Indiana Magazine of History* 21 (1925): 300-310.
A Biographical Directory of the Indiana General Assembly. vol. 1: 1816-1899. Indianapolis: Select Committee on the Centennial History of the Indiana General Assembly, 1980.
A Biographical History of Eminent and Self-Made Men of the State of Indiana. 2 vols. Cincinnati: Western Biographical Publishing Co., 1880.
Blanchard, Charles. *Counties of Morgan, Monroe, and Brown, Indiana: Historical and Biographical*. Chicago: F.A. Battey, 1884.
Buley, R. Carlyle. *The Old Northwest: Pioneer Period, 1815-1840*. 2 vols. Indianapolis: Indiana Historical Society, 1950.
Clark, Thomas D. "Building Libraries in the Early Ohio Valley." *The Journal of Library History* 6 (1971): 101-119.
_____. *Indiana University: Midwestern Pioneer*. Vol. 1: "The Early Years"; vol. 4: "Historical Documents since 1816." Bloomington: Indiana University Press, 1970-1977.
Cramer, C. H. *Case Western Reserve: a History of the University, 1826-1976*. Boston: Little, Brown, 1976.
Crane, Philip M. "Governor Jo Wright: Hoosier Conservative." Ph.D. dissertation, Indiana University, 1963.
Dunn, Jacob P. *Indiana and Indianans*. 5 vols. Chicago: American Historical Society, 1919.
Edson, Hanford A. *Contributions to the Early History of the Presbyterian Church in Indiana*. Cincinnati: Winona Publishing Co., 1898.
Edwards, Edward. "A Statistical View of the Principal Public Libraries in Europe and the United States of America." *Journal of the Statistical Society of London* 11 (1848): 250-281.
Goodykoontz, Colin Brummitt. *Home Missions on the American Frontier*. Caldwell, Idaho: Caxton Printers, 1939.

Gregory, Winifred. *American Newspapers, 1821-1936: a Union List of Files Available in the United States and Canada*. New York: H. W. Wilson, 1937.

Harris, Michael H. "The Availability of Books and the Nature of Book Ownership on the Southern Indiana Frontier, 1800-1850." Ph.D. dissertation, Indiana University, 1971.

History of Lawrence and Monroe Counties of Indiana: Their People, Industries, and Institutions. Indianapolis: B. F. Bowen, 1914.

Jewett, Charles C. *Notices of Public Libraries in the United States of America*. Washington: Printed for the House of Representatives, 1851.

Lowell, Mildred Hawksworth. "Indiana Univeristy Libraries, 1829-1942." Ph.D. dissertation, University of Chicago, 1957.

McMullen, Haynes. "Libraries in the Ohio Valley Before 1850." In *Reader in American Library History*, pp. 57-63. Edited by Michael H. Harris. Reader Series in Library and Information Science. Washington: NCR Microcard Editions, 1971.

Miller, James H. *The Genesis of Western Culture: the Upper Ohio Valley*, 1800-1825. Ohio Historical Collections, vol. 8. Columbus: Ohio State Archaeological and Historical Society, 1951.

Myers, Burton Dorr. *Trustees and Officers of Indiana University*, 1820 to 1950. Bloomington: Indiana University, 1951.

Peckham, Howard H. "Books and Reading on the Ohio Valley Frontier." *The Mississippi Valley Historical Review* 44 (1957-1958): 649-663.

The Prominent Facts Connected with the History of the Presbyterian Church in Rising Sun, Indiana. Rising Sun: The Session, 1851.

Rule, Lucien V. *Forerunners of Lincoln in the Ohio Valley*. Louisville: Brandt & Fowler, 1927.

Sweet, William Warren. *The Congregationalists: a Collection of Source Materials*. Religion on the American Frontier, 1783-1850, v. 3. Chicago: University of Chicago Press, 1939.

White, Frederick Clayton. *Western Reserve University, the Hudson Era: a History of Western Reserve College and Academy at Hudson, Ohio, from 1826 to 1882*. Cleveland: Western Reserve University Press, 1943.

Woodburn, James Albert. "Pioneer Presbyterianism." *Indiana Magazine of History* 22 (1926): 335-370.

Woollen, WilliamWesley. *Biographical and Historical Sketches of Early Indiana*. Indianapolis: Hammond, 1883.

doi:10.1300/J104v44n01_06

APPENDIX I. Specific Authors and/or Titles Mentioned in Unpublished Primary Sources*

Ainsworth, Robert. *Thesaurus Linguae Latinae Compendarius, or, A Compendious Dictionary of the Latin Tongue.*
Aspin, Jehoshaphat. *A View of the World as Exhibited in the Manners, Costumes & Characteristics of All Nations.*
Bangs, Nathan. *The Reformer Reformed, or, A Second Part of the Errors of Hopkinsianism Detected and Refuted.*
Baxter, Richard. *The Saints' Everlasting Rest, or, A Treatise of the Blessed State of Saints in Their Enjoyment of God in Glory.*
Benson, Joseph. *The Life of the Rev. John W. de la Flechere.*
Bible.
Bible. Old Testament. *Selectae e Veteri Testamento.*
Blackstone, Sir William. *Commentaries on the Laws of England.*
Bourdon, Louis Pierre Marie. *The Elements of Algebra.*
Brown, Clark. *A Catechism in Three Parts Designed for the Use of Children.*
Brown, John. *A Short Catechism for Young Children.*
Caesar.
Campbell, Alexander. *The Christian System in Reference to the Union of Christians and a Restoration of Primitive Christianity as Pleaded by the Current Reformation.*
Carden, Allen D., compiler. *The Missouri Harmony, or, A Choice Collection of Psalms, Hymns, and Anthems.*
Chitty, Joseph. *Treatise on Pleading and Parties to Actions.*
Colburn, Warren. *An Introduction to Algebra upon the Inductive Method of Instruction.*
Cordier, Mathurin. *Colloquia Scholastica.*
Cox, Robert. *The Life of the Rev. John William Fletcher.*
Dalzel, Andrew. *Collectanea Graeca Minora.*
Davies, Charles. *Arithmetic Designed for Academies and Schools.*
Defoe, Daniel. *Tour thro' the Whole Island of Great Britain.*
Dickens, Charles. *Oliver Twist.*
Dupuy, Starke. *Hymns and Spiritual Songs.*
Eberle, John. *A Treatise of the Materia Medica and Therapeutics.*
Fletcher, John William. *An Appeal to Matter of Fact and Common Sense, or, A National Demonstration of Man's Corrupt and Lost Estate.*
_____. *Checks to Antinomianism.*
Goodrich, Samuel Griswold. *Readers.*
Gunn, John C. *Gunn's Domestic Medicine, or, Poor Man's Friend in the Hours of Affliction, Pain, and Sickness.*

Herschel, Sir John Frederick William. *Astronomy*.
Heuzet, Jean. *Selectae e Profanis Scriptoribus Historiae*.
Indiana. *The Revised Laws of Indiana, in Which are Comprised All Such Acts of a General Nature as are in Force in Said State*.
Kirkham, Samuel. *A Compendium of English Grammar Accompanied by an Appendix in Familiar Lectures*.
Legendre, Adrien Marie. *Elements of Geometry and Trigonometry*.
McGuffey, William Holmes. *Eclectic Readers*.
Methodist Episcopal Church. *The Doctrines and Discipline of the Methodist Episcopal Church in America*.
Morse, Jedidiah. *Geography Made Easy*.
Nicholson, William. *British Encyclopedia, or, Dictionary of Arts and Sciences Comprising an Accurate and Popular View of the Present Improved State of Human Knowledge*.
Parley, Peter (pseud. of Samuel Griswold Goodrich). *Reader*.
Pike, Nicholas. *A New and Complete System of Arithmetic Composed for the Use of the Citizens of the United States*.
Ross, Robert. *The American Latin Grammar, or, A Complete Introduction to the Latin Tongue*.
Schrevel, Cornelis. *Greek Lexicon*.
Smith, Roswell Chamberlain. *English Grammar on the Productive System: a Method of Instruction Recently Adopted in Germany and Switzerland*.
Southey, Robert. *The Life of John Wesley*.
Valpy, Richard. *Elements of Greek Grammar*.
_____. *Elements of Latin Grammar*.
Virgil.
Walker, John. *A Critical Pronouncing Dictionary and Expositor of the English Language*.
Webster, Noah. *Dictionary*.
Weems, Mason Locke. *The Life of Gen. Francis Marion, a Celebrated Partisan Officer in the Revolutionary War Against the British and the Tories In south Carolina and Georgia*.
Wesley, John. *A Short Account of the Life and Death of the Rev. John Fletcher*.
Whately, Richard. *Elements of Logic*.
Whitehead, John. *The Life of the Rev. John Wesley*.
Wilkins, Henry. *The Family Adviser, or, A Plain and Modern Practice of Physic*.

*Included here are those authors and works that could be identified with some degree of certainty or possibility.

APPENDIX II. List of Books in the Monroe County Library*

Title	Volumes
State Papers	12
Milton's Works	1
Jefferson's Notes	1
Don Quixote	4
Pope's Works	5
Josephus	4
Hume's History of England	9
Franklin's Works	6
Plutarch's Lives	8
Ramsey's Universal History	12
Locke's Essays	1
Ree's Encyclopedia	41
Books of Plates	24
Goldsmith's An. Nature	5
Constitution United States	1
Beaty's Moral Science	2
Life of Washington	5
Clark's Ancient Israelites	1
Lass Casses Journal	4
Church History	4
Furguson's Rome	3
Buck's Theological Dictionary	1
Beaty on Truth	1
Furguson's Astronomy	2
Cuvier's Theory	1
Botanic Garden	1
Zoonomia	2
Volnie's Ruins	1
Shakespeare	10
Bonnycastle's South America	1
Park's Travels	1
Cook's Voyages	2
History of the Late War	1
Smith's Sermons	2
Rights of Man	1
Pradeaux Connexions	3
Com'al. Regulations	1
Clark's Commentaries	-

American Revolution	2
Blair's Lectures	1
Blackston	4
Cowper's Task	1
Curran's Speeches	2
Elements of Philosophy	2
Ewing's N. Philosophy	1
Federalist	1
Gibbon's Roman Empire	8
Goldsmith's Works	4
Johnston's Dictionary	1
Lewis and Clark's Travels	2
Life of Henry	1
Lyric Poems	1
Manners and Customs	2
Life of Marion	1
Philadelphia Agricultural Society	3
Modern Europe	3
Olive Branch	1
Ossian's Poems	2
Read's Works	4
Charles the V	3
Rollin's Ancient History	8
Salmegundi	2
Saurin's Sermons	7
Scottish Chiefs	3
Smiley's Philosophy	1
Solitude Sweetened	1
Spectator	8
Thompson's Seasons	1
Travels of Anacharsis	4
Vattel's Laws of Nations	1
Wealth of Nations	2
Paley's Philosophy	1
Brown's Philosophy	2
Montesquieu's Spirit of Law	2
Political Economy	2
Cooper's Novels	13
History of France	1
Irving's Columbus	2
Irving's Works	4

APPENDIX II (continued)

History of Ireland	5
Scott's Scotland	2
History of Greece	1
Biographical Dictionary	2
Herodotus	1
Burl's Spirit of Laws	2
Edgeworth's Tales	3
Whelp's Compend	1
Conversations on Chemistry	1
Jefferson's Manual	1
Life of Jackson	1
Duncan's Logic	1
Watts on the Mind	1
Scott's Novels	-
Weems' Washington	1
Seneca's Morals	1
French Revolution	1
Campbell's Poems	1
Barlow's Columbiad	1
Homer's Iliad	2
Homer's Odyssey	2
Dryden's Virgil	2
France's Horace	1
Disowned	1
Pelham	1
Devereanaux	1
Darnley	1
Chemical Philosophy	1
Agricultural Chemistry	1
Masonry	1
Dialogue of Devils	1
Eugene Aram	1
England and the English	2
Paul Clifford	2
Ross' Voyage	1
Sales Coram	4
Jonston's Works	2
Demosthenes' Speeches	1
Port Admiral	3

Insurgents	2
Calavan	2
S's. Phrenology	2
McKensie's Receipts	1
Reynold's Voyage	1
Allen Breck	2
Eben Erskin	2
Stanley Buxton	2
National Calendar	1
Steward's Philosophy	3
Burke's Works	3
Marryatt's Novels	12
Cruise of the Midge	-
Declaration of Independence	5
Swallow Barn and Horse Shoe Robison	4
Guy Revers & Infidel	4
Richeleau	-
Henry Masterton	2
Life of J. M. Hall	2
Mary of Burgundy	2
Tennessee	2
Polish Chiefs	2
Cavaliers of Virginia	2
Three Years in the Pacific	1
The Buccaneer	2
Cicero	2
Water Witch	-
Family Library	72
Staff Officer	2
Conquest of Grenada	2
Last Days of Pompei	2

*This list appeared in *The Bloomington Post* on March 15, 1839. These works are listed as they appeared in the newspaper article; no attempt has been made to identify the works cited.

Annotation:
A Lost Art in Cataloguing

J. H. Bowman

SUMMARY. Public library catalogues in early twentieth-century Britain frequently included annotations, either to clarify obscure titles or to provide further information about the subject-matter of the books they described. Two manuals giving instruction on how to do this were published at that time. Following World War I, with the decline of the printed catalogue, this kind of annotation became rarer, and was almost confined to bulletins of new books. The early issues of the *British National Bibliography* included some annotations in exceptional cases. Parallels are drawn with the provision of table-of-contents information in present-day OPACs. doi:10.1300/J104v44n01_07 *[Article copies available for a fee from The Haworth Document Delivery Service: 1-800-HAWORTH. E-mail address: <docdelivery@haworthpress.com> Website: <http://www.HaworthPress.com> © 2007 by The Haworth Press, Inc. All rights reserved.]*

KEYWORDS. Annotation, summaries, printed catalogues, table-of-contents

---

J. H. Bowman is Lecturer and Programme Director for Library and Information Studies, School of Library, Archive & Information Studies, University College London, Gower Street, London, WC1E 6BT, England (E-mail: j.bowman@ucl.ac.uk).

[Haworth co-indexing entry note]: "Annotation: A Lost Art in Cataloguing." Bowman, J. H. Co-published simultaneously in *Cataloging & Classification Quarterly* (The Haworth Information Press, an imprint of The Haworth Press, Inc.) Vol. 44, No. 1/2, 2007, pp. 95-111; and: *Cataloger, Editor, and Scholar: Essays in Honor of Ruth C. Carter* (ed: Robert P. Holley) The Haworth Information Press, an imprint of The Haworth Press, Inc., 2007, pp. 95-111. Single or multiple copies of this article are available for a fee from The Haworth Document Delivery Service [1-800-HAWORTH, 9:00 a.m. - 5:00 p.m. (EST). E-mail address: docdelivery@haworthpress.com].

Available online at http://ccq.haworthpress.com
© 2007 by The Haworth Press, Inc. All rights reserved.
doi:10.1300/J104v44n01_07

A little over a hundred years ago, some of Britain's public librarians began to include in catalogue entries some additional information that went beyond the bare bibliographic description. As most public libraries operated a closed access system at this time and readers could not therefore examine the books for themselves before choosing, these annotations, as they were called, were perceived as being useful to readers in assisting them in their selection. Nowadays, such annotations would be very rare indeed. The purpose of this paper is to examine the rise and fall of annotation. The discussion is confined chiefly to Britain, though it is clear that it was not purely a British phenomenon.

In an early article that includes reference to annotation, Brown and Jast say that, by its annotations, "a catalogue is lifted from a mere list of books to something approaching a 'guide, philosopher, and friend.'"[1] Annotations are intended to add to the reader's knowledge of the book and in particular to explain titles whose meaning is not clear. The authors criticize a few examples from actual catalogues and then go on to suggest annotations for certain rather obscure titles. Sometimes these do no more than translate foreign words:

BROWN. Horae subsecivae. ("Leisure Hours.")

CARLYLE. Sartor resartus. ("The Tailor Patched.")

In other cases, an obscure allusion or fanciful expression may be explained:

SMITH, *Mrs.* L. T. Water Gipsies. (Canal boatmen.)

TOWNSEND. Sea-Kings of the Mediterranean. (Knights-Hospitallers.)

Further examples follow, such as the level of assumed knowledge in a science textbook and very brief subject words for fiction.

Clearly this paper was not the start of annotation, but it may well have been the first attempt at a systematic exposition of its requirements. Brown and Jast were soon answered by Robert K. Dent, librarian of Aston Manor (now part of Birmingham), who felt that their suggestions were not particularly helpful and that simple explanations of the kind suggested were not enough to inform the reader about the contents of a book.[2] Much more would be needed, and this was more a matter for literary history than for cataloguers In short, if the author did not see fit to describe a book adequately in its title, it would be better not to make annotations. A subsequent note reveals that Dent had few supporters; several other librarians had written in support of annotation, which was clearly becoming quite widespread by this time.[3] Examples were submitted by Archibald Sparke of Kidderminster:

Dream of the sea [Poems].

In an enchanted island [Cyprus].

Ashes to ashes [Cremation].

Iron bound city [Paris].

An English hero [Cobden].

The editor describes Kent's view as being "hopelessly antiquated and out of sympathy with present-day movements in favour of improvement all round." Annotated catalogues were "slowly but surely making headway." In the same year, Brown reviewed the 1896 catalogue of a branch of Lewisham Public Libraries and stated that he believed this to be the first dictionary catalogue "in which annotations have been systematically added to every obscure title."[4] He refers to only a couple of earlier catalogues as having had annotations at all. Quinn gives several examples from (unnamed) actual catalogues, referring to their "immense value" and saying that "they are not as often inserted as they might be."[5] The novelty of annotation is further evidenced by Jast, by now librarian of Croydon, who writing in 1902 referred to "the new cataloguing," meaning "annotating and evaluing."[6] He contrasted the situation with that of 1883 when the original Library Association cataloguing rules had been drawn up, the implication being that annotation was unknown then. Examination of those rules shows that this was not entirely true, for they included the following two rules:

> 8. Contents of volumes are to be given when expedient, and in smaller type.
>
> 9. Notes explanatory or illustrative, or descriptive of bibliographical or other peculiarities, including imperfections, to be subjoined when necessary; tables of contents and notes to be in smaller type.[7]

Either of these rules could have permitted the kind of annotation discussed here.

We should perhaps pause at this point to consider how much detail there was in the catalogue records before the annotation was added. Most British public libraries at this time still had printed catalogues, which were usually in "dictionary" form, that is, with author, subject, and some title entries all interfiled in one sequence. Because of the expense of production, it was customary to keep the entries as short as possible; and indeed such catalogues were known as "title-a-liners."[8] It was therefore rare to find more after the entry point than the title; date of publication; and, in some cases, a note about illustrations or the book's size. Place of publication and name of publisher were almost unknown. It is therefore to this scanty description that we need to think of the annotation as being appended. We have already seen some examples where the annotation was merely added in square brackets at the end of the title. In other cases, particularly for longer annotations, it would appear in a separate paragraph, usually in smaller type, below the rest of the entry.

As the years passed, interest in annotation increased. One aspect, which was quite controversial, was the extent to which the annotator should evaluate ("evalue" in the language of the day) the books. This practice seems to have arisen in the United States and then made its way to Britain, but in a modified form. Whereas in the United States evaluative lists tended to be freestanding bibliographies, in Britain evaluation came to be attached to general public library catalogues.[9] This was not universally approved of because a librarian could hardly be an expert on all subjects and was scarcely in a position to evaluate books about them.

An article in the *Library World* gave examples of how to do the two different kinds of annotation for four novels issued in 1901 and 1902 by Newnes Ltd.[10] There is not room here to reproduce all eight annotations, but a comparison of two is instructive:

Critical evaluation:

>WELLS, H.G. The First Men in the Moon. Illust. 1901.
>
>A *voyage imaginaire* by this well-known exponent of the pseudo-scientific phantasy. It recounts with a Defoe-like *vraisemblance* a voyage to the moon. Mr. Wells' early training has enabled him to make effective use of a medley of economics and entomology. The

book ends somewhat weakly with an anticlimax in which farce and Hertzian radiation *à la* Marconi are ingeniously combined. The book is less satisfactory than some of its author's other efforts in the same *genre*.

Descriptive evaluation:

WELLS, H.G. The First Men in the Moon. Illust. 1901.

An inventor discovers a substance which overcomes the force of gravitation, and from it constructs a machine which enables the moon to be reached. The inhabitants (or Selenites) are discovered to be a highly organised community of mechanical experts, dwelling in the interior of the moon, ruled by a monarch and regulated by a minute system of expert specialism. In some respects this idea of a great community living in the interior of a planet has been anticipated by Holberg, in his "Niels Klim" (1741), in which a similar community is discovered in the interior of the earth, with a corresponding inaction of gravitation, as a subsidiary episode.

It is difficult quite to know what to make of these, specially written as they both are. The first appears to have gratuitously introduced as many French phrases as possible, presumably to poke fun at this style of annotation, while the other devotes more than a third of its space to demonstrating its erudition by referring to another work which its readers would not have heard of. Each in its different way seems to go beyond the requirements of simple annotation.

At around the same time, Brown gave some brief guidelines on annotation in saying that "the craze for critical 'evaluation' or 'appraisal' which has arisen within recent years should not be extended to catalogues of books issued at the public expense."[11] Stevenson reported on an American symposium entitled "The Appraisal of Literature."[12] Evaluation was at this time clearly widespread in the United States to the extent that few of the contributors felt the need to justify it. There were, however, several eminent librarians who disagreed with it, chiefly on the ground that it was not the function of a library. One suggested that it was really only appropriate for reference books.

The dissenters were followed in Britain by Ernest A. Savage, who was the first to set out what he saw as the *principles* of annotation. He defines an annotation as "an abstract of the character and individuality of the book catalogued";[13] there should be nothing that is not explanatory, "thus excluding judgment." He states that it is impossible to have regard to the reader when writing annotations because readers vary so much in their needs. The chief requirement is to show the character of the book and its relation to other books on the same subject. The qualifications of the author to write the book should be stated, followed by a brief summary of the subject matter. He works through an example illustrating how this is to be done. It is important to avoid criticism, as it is likely to lead to ridicule, or, if a book is misleading or otherwise unsatisfactory, to questions as to why it was bought. Savage states that most current annotation is "weak, anaemic" but that time and expense make any sort of annotation very difficult. He concludes with an appendix giving the instructions on annotation used at his library, Bromley.

Baker proposed that librarians should themselves undertake the task of providing efficient guides to literature and suggested that in Britain they had been held back by the dispute as to whether the annotations should be merely descriptive or evaluative.[14] He criticizes Savage for suggesting that annotation should "exclude judgment." Later he marvels at Savage's statement that he "cannot produce notes of six or ten lines apiece at a faster rate than nine notes an hour" (which is not exactly what Savage said), contrasting this with his own having sometimes taken more than nine hours on a single note.[15] The provision of annotated guides should be undertaken co-operatively because librarians would thereby be much less likely to lay themselves open to criticism for errors of judgment.

In 1906, W. E. Doubleday, Chief Librarian of Hampstead, published a new *Descriptive Catalogue of the Books in the Lending Department of the Central Library* that was reviewed by Savage.[16] It was a dictionary catalogue, which meant that most books would have more than one entry; and the annotations were placed under the subject entries. Savage has a few adverse comments, but on the whole he admires the way the annotation has been done and concludes with the statement that it is "undoubtedly the best general catalogue published in England for several years past."

It is significant that it was in a paper dealing with class-lists that Brown and Jast referred to annotation. The point is made later in an anonymous review that the nature of a dictionary catalogue "makes it unsuitable as a vehicle for the display of annotations" because in order to make the annotations useful the bulk of the catalogue would be greatly increased.[17] A class-list would be a different matter because it would normally cover only a section of the library.

Quinn in his new work makes a similar point.[18] He describes explanatory notes and other annotations as "a most commendable feature of modern cataloguing," but he also says that they are chiefly to be found in catalogues of additions. In a full dictionary catalogue, it is difficult to know which entry should include the annotation. Nevertheless, he refers to some "fully annotated" dictionary catalogues, namely those of the Bishopsgate Institute and of Hampstead Public Library. These must, however, have been rather exceptional; and, in any case, we have already seen that Hampstead's contained annotations only at the subject entries. It is very difficult to get an impression of how widespread detailed annotation was because there is no central collection of printed catalogues and few of them survive. An examination of the author's own collection (about twenty catalogues) reveals relatively few annotations, and these are chiefly confined to the elucidation of otherwise obscure titles.

The heyday of annotation was probably the first decade of the twentieth century; it was then that Savage's book was written that gives the most detailed treatment of the subject.[19] He makes it clear at the outset that what he recommends applies "only to popular libraries"[20] as opposed to those intended for scholars, and it seems always to have been the case that annotation was confined to public libraries. His book is divided into two parts: Part I "General considerations and practical work" and Part II "A code of annotation." A large number of definitions of terms are provided. That a change in practice had taken place is again shown by his reference to Cutter's dictum that only the best books should receive annotations; this "is not now generally accepted."[21]

Savage states that annotated entries induce people to read books that they would never have thought of reading, thus potentially tempting librarians to avoid annotating fiction and so reduce the amount read.[22] (There had been a long debate in the latter part of the nineteenth century about how far librarians ought to encourage or discourage the reading of fiction.)[23] Savage's view was that guidance on choosing fiction was just as important as for non-fiction, and he particularly commends the historical novel as a vehicle for imparting knowledge of history. Of great importance, of course, is to write the annotation without disclosing the whole plot or the ending.

Another aspect of annotation was that of recommending a course of reading on a subject. This could be done at a main class heading and was particularly appropriate for class-lists. Savage quotes the following example from Peterborough Public Library's class list 3, Science and the Arts (1898):[24]

ELECTRICITY AND MAGNETISM

Course of reading. Begin with JENKIN, or the fuller introduction of THOMPSON. Then read NOAD. MAXWELL is 'elementary' in name only. The nature of electricity if discussed in the philosophic treatise of LODGE. For a short popular exposition, treated historically, read MENDENHALL.

If this kind of annotation was widely practised, it must have taken a great deal of time to compile as well as becoming rapidly out of date. The author's collection contains no examples, and it was probably not very widespread.

An interesting feature of Savage's book is that he includes practical instruction on how to carry out annotation and suggests that in larger libraries it may be done by the assistants under the supervision of the librarian. Libraries with enough staff can divide the work of cataloguing and annotation among several different members, on different grades, who will prepare the bulk of the entry before passing it to the chief librarian. In order to prevent omissions, Savage advocates the use of a "Cataloguing process slip," which would accompany a batch of books as they go through the various processes and would act as a reminder for the assistants, who would check each point in relation to every book. The form contains the following information:[25]

Cataloguing process slip.

1. Biographees' names.

2. Biographees' notes.

3. Authors' names.

4. Authors' qualifications.

5. Previous editions.

6. Illustrations:

> Illus.

> Maps.

Plans.

Portraits.

Diagrams.

Facsimiles.

7. Series abbreviations.

8. Reviews.

9. Bibliographies.

10. Glossaries.

(Perhaps the term "Series abbreviations" needs explanation. In a printed catalogue, space was at a premium; and it was customary to abbreviate any series statements immensely, often to the extent that the abbreviation was unintelligible without a key. This point on the checklist would ensure that the correct abbreviation was used.)

In addition to this, each "senior" who was involved in annotation was provided with a "memory table" that gave reminders of the kinds of detail that should be included. (See Figure 1.)[26] At all points, the utmost brevity is urged on the annotator. Savage reckons that a senior and a junior together can annotate about twenty non-fiction books in an hour. In the next chapter, he describes the methods of instruction in use at the New York State Library School and at the Pratt Institute Library School, Brooklyn, N.Y.; the former includes many exercises in annotation. Part II of Savage's book consists of a set of rules for descriptive annotation of books and includes much detail.

The only other separately published work devoted to annotation was the pamphlet by Sayers.[27] A search of the Library of Congress catalogue does not retrieve any obvious parallels to either Savage or Sayers, which may indicate that less importance was attached to the subject in the United States. Sayers distinguishes between British and American practice by saying that the prevalent idea in America is that annotation means appraisal, whereas in Britain it is rather elucidation.[28] His definition of it is thus: "A descriptive extension of the title-page of a book in which the qualifications of the author, and the scope, purpose and place of the book are indicated."[29]

FIGURE 1. "Memory Table" from Earnest A. Savage, *Manual of Descriptive Annotation for Library Catalogues* (London: Library Supply Co., 1906), p. 57

> 1. AUTHOR (ed., compiler, ed. board): Qualifications; original research.
> 2. SUBJECT: Scope, theory; purpose; special features.
> 3. TREATMENT: Standpoint, bias; readers held in view; preparation necessary, copious notes, language of book, difficulty of foreign books, limits or novelty of treatment.
> 4. RELATION TO OTHER BOOKS: Effect of book, if important; cognate books, continuations, sequels.
> 5. EDITING: Plan, arrangement, changes in new ed., absence of index, whereabouts of index to set of a periodical.
> 6. BIBLIOGRAPHICAL: Date and manner of original publication, first books, source or basis, bibliographies, illustrations, unusual features in format or printing, numbered copies, changes of titles, binder's titles differing from real title, original titles of translated works, changes in periodical publications.
> 7. LITERATURE OF POWER: Environment, period, principal characters, historical personages introduced, theme, motive, dialect, presence of autobiographical material.
> 8. JUVENILES: Address annotations to books for children under ten to adults, those to books for children over ten to children, making language of annotations match language of book.
> 9. NOTE: Arrange matter as numbered 1 to 6 above. Acknowledge quotations. Give date of *critical* quotations. Explain obscure terms. Give call-marks of books referred to. BE CONCISE.

THE INTER-WAR YEARS

Because of rising prices, there was a rapid decline in printed catalogues after the First World War. Most libraries switched to cards, but nevertheless annotation continued to be of some importance. In the revised edition of his pamphlet in 1932, Sayers added a note saying that he was "assured that it was still of interest to students of cataloguing"; but it is unclear how much it was altered from the original 1918 edition. Certainly, the examples do not include any more recent books; and the impression conveyed is that it was still very much the same publication. He mentions the question of expense, evidently on the assumption that most public libraries would still have a printed catalogue; and this too seems to imply that the pamphlet was very much the same as in 1918.

The argument over the nature of annotation continued sporadically. For example, an adverse review of an annotation in a catalogue issued by Sheffield Public Libraries sparked an acrimonious correspondence in the *Library Assistant* and culminated in a short article by Snaith.[30] Harrison alluded to it in referring to evaluation with specific reference to library magazines.[31] Without evaluation, he says, it is impossible to write "an appetizing note." There is perhaps a slight implication that annotation was in decline at this time, but it is hard to be sure.

Sharp, writing in 1937, stated that there had been a shift in the nature of annotation. "The older sort of annotation was definitely informative; the modern sort is partly that and partly an attempt to persuade people into reading books they would otherwise pass by."[32] He felt it was doubtful whether 2% of public library users were interested in annotations. A survey in America in 1934 (unfortunately he gives no details) had revealed that opinion was just as divided there as in Britain, but there had been a general agreement that notes were desirable and useful. In the days of the printed catalogue, economy meant that annotations, if any, had to be brief. Sharp also draws a useful distinction between the note that might be used in a bulletin of new books and the one that would be included in a permanent catalogue. He includes three examples taken from recent bulletins, and it is clear from the level of detail that this extent of annotation would be very costly to include in the catalogue itself. Sayers, when he revised Brown's textbook, greatly reduced the amount of space given to annotation though he evidently expected it to continue to be carried out.[33]

That annotation was still being included as part of the students' cataloguing examination is shown by Collison who gives some advice.[34] Students were expected to write thirty words. Collison contrasts the two styles, which he refers to as Croydon-Savage (an odd mixed term but meaning that Sayers, Librarian of Croydon, agreed with Savage) and Bethnal Green. The former starts by giving the qualifications of the author and then summarizes the content. The latter is intended much more for promotional purposes, and the style is that of "introduction, evaluation, and enthusiasm."[35]

THE POST-WAR YEARS

After the Second World War, annotation seems to have declined even further in British public libraries. Taylor gives some brief guidance and states that any attempt to evaluate a book is "outside the province of the catalogue."[36] She makes the interesting point that an evaluation recorded in 1936 may be completely out of date when it is read ten years later and that no library can afford to revise its annotations. In another textbook, Norris writes as though annotation has had its day in general catalogues; she summarizes the advice of Savage and Sayers but says that it "serves very little purpose" in an open access library.[37] Only in bulletins and class lists is it useful; indeed they would be of little use without annotations. The subject does not appear in Piggott's symposium on cataloguing practice.[38] When the *British National Bibliography* (*BNB*) began publication in 1950, however, it included a small number of annotations of this kind, amplifying the subject matter of the title. Figure 2 shows a typical example.

A late attempt to arouse interest in annotation was made in 1961 by Philip Ward, who conducted a survey of 90 municipal and county libraries.[39] His enquiry asked: (1) whether the libraries annotated any of the entries in their adult non-fiction catalogue; (2) for three recent specimen entries that included annotations; and (3) about three specific recent books that had featured annotations in the *British National Bibliography* (*BNB*). It is clear from his examples that the kind of annotation he had in mind was the kind we have been examining here, chiefly additional information about subject matter rather than notes about previous editions and the like. He received 58 replies, of which 31 used annotation; 25 of these were municipal and 6 county libraries. Some of the county libraries did not provide any public catalogue at all. He noted that, of those libraries that used annotation, ten used only the annotations that appeared on *BNB* cards.

Many libraries did not feel that annotation was cost-effective, especially in view of the low use of the catalogue by members of the public. Battersea was one of the exceptions; nearly all books in their adult non-fiction catalogue were annotated. At Chelmsford, most of the annotations consisted of quotations from reviews. At Bethnal Green, it was felt important to avoid anything that might amount to appraisal. Several libraries suggested that more annotations should be included in the *BNB* and on *BNB* cards, and Ward obtained a statement on annotation policy from the editor of the *BNB*. Most of the categories were of the biblio-

FIGURE 2. Example of Annotation in *British National Bibliography 1950*, p. 525

```
            940.542—SPECIAL CAMPAIGNS OF THE WAR
940.542
Butler, Ewan, and Bradford, J          Selby
        Keep the memory green : the first of the many, France 1939-40.
     Hutchinson, 12/6. May [1950]. 180p. front., plates. 22cm.
                                                         (50-4568)
        The story of the British Expeditionary Force, 1939-40, and the evacua-
     tion from Dunkirk.
```

Reprinted with permission.

graphical kind such as would nowadays be included by most libraries following AACR2, but there were some others including:

- Indication of subjects included in a book but not represented in the class number chosen;
- Information not included in title transcript;
- The casts of plays.

The editor felt that the addition of feature headings against class-numbers obviated almost all the need for subject annotation, but Ward disagreed with this.[40] The more *BNB* cards came into use, the more important he felt it was that they should be annotated. The final part of his article consists of a proposed code for annotation in public libraries that started with a definition: "annotation is the compilation of notes on a book's history, subject and intention." He called for immediate standardization, which would be particularly beneficial in London in view of the impending local government reorganization. (This took place in 1965 and caused the merger of some boroughs.) There is no evidence that any action was taken, and it looks as though Ward was a lone voice. Far from increasing annotation, although it is difficult to find out when the *BNB* stopped adding this kind of annotation, they become very hard to find after this period.[41]

Maltby and Duxbury carried out a survey of annotation involving four municipal and four academic libraries.[42] Rather oddly, they made a contrast between "description" and "annotation" and asked the users which they would prefer, tacitly assuming that only one was possible. In view of the vagueness of the definition of annotation in this survey, it is difficult to make much of the results; but even the users of university libraries (where presumably such notes were relatively uncommon) seem to have felt that contents notes would be useful. This is one of the kinds of note that were probably provided in such catalogues anyway.

THE SITUATION TODAY

AACR2 now provides for many kinds of notes, and no doubt many of these would potentially come under the old category of annotation. Most of them, however, are bibliographical in some way; and it is unlikely that the old printed catalogues, under pressure for space, would have included this kind of information. The exceptions are rules 1.7B1

Nature, scope, or artistic form, 1.7B14 Audience, 1.7B17 Summary, and 1.7B18 Contents. These to some extent correspond to the kind of annotation that was encouraged and practised in the early twentieth century. Contents notes are still relatively common in cases where the publication includes several separate works, but the others have almost fallen into disuse. This is not surprising in view of the fact that AACR2 does not otherwise cover subject matter or the subject approach to retrieval at all. Cataloguers who do not also classify have no reason to examine the subject matter of the materials they deal with. The decline of annotation is borne out by a late reference to it by Bob Duckett as one of the "lost arts of cataloguing."[43] As for noting the qualifications of an author to write on the subject, this would be quite unheard of now.

ELECTRONIC CONTENTS INFORMATION

Although annotation in the old sense has died out, there is some indication that it could still be seen to have its uses. In a not entirely serious article, Hitchcock makes some suggestions for lengthy annotations to catalogue entries in his library.[44] Moreover, there has for some years now been discussion of how to improve the amount of information about a work that a user can obtain from the catalogue and the ways in which it can be retrieved. In the mid-1970s, Cochrane conducted the Subject Access Project, which proposed adding to catalogue records words from indexes and tables of contents.[45] This did not immediately bear fruit, largely because enriching records in this way would be very expensive and because there was considerable debate about whether users really needed it. As Van Orden pointed out in a summary of research up to 1990, there was a danger of overloading users with information.[46] It was likely that recall would be improved at the expense of precision. Nevertheless, there was some evidence that users wanted contents, summaries, or indexes included in catalogues.[47] In the early 1990s, it seemed unlikely that this would happen because it would be too expensive; but, by the middle of the decade, such contents information had become available commercially from external suppliers. Blackwell's, for example, began to offer such a service for American and Canadian titles in 1992 and for British in 1995.[48] Their service also allows the inclusion of authors' affiliations, very like the "qualifications" of the author previously referred to. Several library management systems now provide the facility to include contents information though it is unclear how widely it has been taken up. The purpose of including this information has been partly to give readers a better idea of the contents of resources but chiefly to improve retrieval by allowing them to perform keyword searches that include the content information. It could therefore be said that the desire to help readers by including additional information has resurfaced in a new guise and that the hoped for cooperation in providing such information has been fulfilled in the sense that it can be obtained from external sources. It is perhaps too early to estimate the utility of electronic contents, and there is certainly a danger of overwhelming the user by providing too much information. There is, however, some evidence that it increases awareness of stock that might otherwise have been ignored.[49] We can therefore conclude by saying that although the art of annotation in the old sense is dead, the cataloguers who performed it were really pioneers.

NOTES

1. James D. Brown and L. Stanley Jast, "The Compilation of Class Lists," *The Library* 9 (1897): 45-69, p. 61.

2. Robert K. Dent, "The New Cataloguer and Some of his Ways," *The Library* 9 (1897): 173-178.

3. *Library* 9 (1897): 357-358.

4. James D. Brown, "Lewisham Public Libraries. Catalogue of books contained in the lending department of the Perry Hill Branch Library. . . 1896," *The Library* 9 (1897): 117-118. By "J.D.B."

5. J. Henry Quinn, *Manual of Library Cataloguing* (London: Library Supply Co., 1899), p. 25.

6. L. Stanley Jast, "The Library Association Cataloguing Rules," *Library Association Record* 4 (1902): 578-582, at p. 579.

7. Library Association, *Cataloguing Rules of the Library Association of the United Kingdom (as revised at the Liverpool Meeting, 1883)*. [London: Library Association, 1883]. These rules were printed in some volumes of the Library Association Year-book during the succeeding years.

8. See Ernest A. Savage, *A Librarian's Memories: portraits & reflections* (London: Grafton, 1952), p. 98.

9. See 'Every Librarian his own Critic,' *Library World* 4 (1901/02): 121-124, at pp. 122-123.

10. "Appraisal or Description? Some examples," *Library World* 4 (1901/02): 264-267.

11. James Duff Brown, *Manual of Library Economy* (London: Scott, Greenwood, 1903), p. 280.

12. Robert Stevenson, "Appraisal versus Description: American testimony," *Library World* 6 (1903/04): 11-14.

13. Ernest A. Savage, "The Principles of Annotation," *Library Association Record* 6 (1904): 576-590.

14. Ernest A. Baker, "Co-operative Annotation and Guides," *Library Association Record* 7 (1905): 272-283.
15. Ibid., p. 282.
16. Ernest A. Savage, "The New Hampstead Catalogue," *Library World* 8 (1905/06): 321-322.
17. "The Annotation of Historical Books," *Library World* 3 (1900/01): 183-186. Possibly by Brown himself.
18. J. Henry Quinn, *Library Cataloguing* (London: Truslove & Hanson, 1913), p. 209.
19. Ernest A. Savage, *Manual of Descriptive Annotation for Library Catalogues*. With chapter on evaluation and historical note by Ernest A. Baker (London: Library Supply Co., 1906).
20. Ibid., p. iv.
21. Ibid., p. 5.
22. Ibid., p. 19.
23. See Paul Sturges and Alison Barr, "'The Fiction Nuisance' in Nineteenth-Century British Public Libraries," *Journal of Librarianship and Information Science* 24 (1992): 23-32.
24. Savage, Manual, p. 39.
25. Ibid., p. 52.
26. Ibid., p. 57.
27. W. C. Berwick Sayers, *First Steps in Annotation in Catalogues* (London: Association of Assistant Librarians, 1918). It has not been possible to locate a copy of this edition so that references have had to be made to the 2nd edition of 1932.
28. Ibid., p. 3-4.
29. Ibid., p. 4-5.
30. Stanley Snaith, "The Philosophy of Annotation: A Reply to Mr. Cranshaw," *Library Assistant* 23 (1930): 81-822. See also *Library Assistant* 23 (1930): 38-39 for correspondence.
31. K. C. Harrison, "Reflections on Annotation," *Library Assistant* 30, no. 449 (1937): 96-99.
32. Henry A. Sharp, *Cataloguing: A Textbook for Use in Libraries*, 2nd ed. (London: Grafton, 1937), p. 138.
33. James Duff Brown, *Manual of Library Economy*. 5th ed., by W. C. Berwick Sayers (London: Grafton, 1937).
34. R. L. W. Collison, "Annotation for the Student," *Library Assistant* 32, no. 6 (1939): 137-142.
35. Ibid., p. 138.
36. Margaret S. Taylor, *Fundamentals of Practical Cataloguing* (London: Allen & Unwin, 1948), p. 99.
37. Dorothy M. Norris, *A Primer of Cataloguing* (London: Association of Assistant Librarians, 1952), pp. 119-122.
38. Mary Piggott (ed.), *Cataloguing Principles and Practice: An Inquiry* (London: Library Association, 1954).
39. Philip Ward, "Annotation in Public Library Catalogues: British Practice and Policy," *Library Association Record* 64 (1962): 208-212.
40. Ibid., p. 211.
41. I have not been able to find any published statement of a change of policy.

42. A. Maltby and A. Duxbury, "Description and Annotation in Catalogues: Reader Requirements," *New Library World* 73 (1971/72): 260-262 and 273.

43. Bob Duckett, "Do Users Matter?" *Catalogue & Index* 111 (spring 1994): 1-8, at p. 6.

44. Leonard A. Hitchcock, 'Enriching the Record,' *Journal of Academic Librarianship* 26, no. 5 (2000): 359-363.

45. Pauline Atherton Cochrane, *Books are for Use: Final Report of the Subject Access Project to the Council on Library Resources* (Syracuse, N.Y.: Syracuse University School of Information Studies, 1978).

46. Richard Van Orden, "Content-Enriched Access to Electronic Information: Summaries of Selected Research," *Library Hi Tech* 8, no. 3 (1990): 27-32, p. 27.

47. Ibid., p. 29.

48. See Program 29, no. 4 (1995): 462. Information about Blackwell's Book Services Table of Contents (TOC) Enrichment Service is available at: http://www.blackwell.com/pdf/TOC2Brochure.pdf [accessed 31 August 2005]. See also Robert P. Holley, "Blackwell North America's Table of Contents Service," ISBN Review 15 (1994): 55-66 and Marty Crowe, *Table-of-contents Enhancement of the Catalog*. [Cornell University Library], 1997. Available at: http://www.library.cornell.edu/cts/martyrep.htm [accessed 31 August 2005].

49. See Ruth C. Morris, "Online Tables of Contents for Books: Effects on Usage," *Bulletin of the Medical Library Association* 89, no. 1 (2001): 29-36.

doi:10.1300/J104v44n01_07

Twenty-Five Years of Bibliographic Control Research at the University of Bradford

F. H. Ayres
J. M. Ridley

SUMMARY. This article describes cooperation between Bradford University Library and the Department of Computing that has resulted in nine research projects over a twenty-five year period on various aspects of bibliographic control. It recounts the origins of the Universal Standard Bibliographic Code (USBC) and its development for the identification of both books and non-book material. It then describes various aspects of the projects including simulating the merging necessary to set up a national database, the cleaning of a database, its use in inter-library lending, and its application together with expert systems for the quality control of databases. The final project is BOPAC that has used modern technology to create faster and better access to a number of li-

---

F. H. Ayres is former University Librarian at Bradford University and now Bibliographic Consultant, Department of Computing, 3 High Close, Tranmere Park, Guiseley, Leeds, LS20 8JG, England (E-mail: fayres@britishlibrary.net). J. M. Ridley is Lecturer and Chair of Undergraduate Programmes, Department of Computing, University of Bradford BD7 1DP, UK (E-mail: M.J.Ridley@bradford.ac.uk).

[Haworth co-indexing entry note]: "Twenty-Five Years of Bibliographic Control Research at the University of Bradford." Ayres, F. H., and J. M. Ridley. Co-published simultaneously in *Cataloging & Classification Quarterly* (The Haworth Information Press, an imprint of The Haworth Press, Inc.) Vol. 44, No. 1/2, 2007, pp. 113-130; and: *Cataloger, Editor, and Scholar: Essays in Honor of Ruth C. Carter* (ed: Robert P. Holley) The Haworth Information Press, an imprint of The Haworth Press, Inc., 2007, pp. 113-130. Single or multiple copies of this article are available for a fee from The Haworth Document Delivery Service [1-800-HAWORTH, 9:00 a.m. - 5:00 p.m. (EST). E-mail address: docdelivery@haworthpress.com].

Available online at http://ccq.haworthpress.com
© 2007 by The Haworth Press, Inc. All rights reserved.
doi:10.1300/J104v44n01_08

brary catalogues worldwide and has demonstrated that authority control in its present form is not effective. doi:10.1300/J104v44n01_08 *[Article copies available for a fee from The Haworth Document Delivery Service: 1-800-HAWORTH. E-mail address: <docdelivery@haworthpress.com> Website: <http://www.HaworthPress.com> © 2007 by The Haworth Press, Inc. All rights reserved.]*

KEYWORDS. Universal Standard Bibliographic Code (USBC), database merging, duplicate detection, interlending, BOPAC, authority control

USBC: THE FIRST INITIAL CONCEPT

Bibliographic control research started with the concept of a computer produced alternative to the International Standard Book Number. The ISBN is now widely accepted throughout the world and is used by publishers, booksellers, and libraries. In spite of its success, it has certain structural disadvantages. The most important of these is that it is an allocated code; the publisher number is allocated by the Standard Book Numbering Agency and the book number itself by the publisher. Because it is an allocated number, it is subject to human error; and, even with strict control procedures by the publisher, duplicate numbers are created. This means that the same book may be allocated more than one number, and two books may be allocated the same number. Another major disadvantage is that it cannot be supplied retrospectively to out-of-print material although some publishers have allocated numbers to older material that is still in print.

It was because of these problems that the idea of a code that was derived automatically from the bibliographic record and that was standardised and universal was suggested. This concept was first put forward in a paper in *Program* in 1974[1] and was based mainly on a method of coding that used the frequency distribution of the alphabetical letters of English text material. It used nine different elements of the bibliographic record to construct the code. At that time, it was visualised that the code could be obtained both manually and automatically and that it would be a numeric code. However, it soon became clear that manual application was both impractical and unnecessary. In time, it also became obvious that a mixed alphanumeric code would be more effective. Because of this, the USBN (Universal Standard Book Number) became the USBC (Universal Standard Bibliographic Code). Further research showed that the Code had an added advantage as it could be used just as effectively for material other than books.

Building on these promising results, work was continued at the University of Bradford to test the USBC[2] and to suggest ways to improve it. This paper also included a suggestion of the way in which the USBC would work if it were adopted as a universal standard. The publisher's computer would generate the USBC as soon as firm publication details became available. When the final record reached the National Centre, the USBC would be generated again and compared with the publisher's version. Any discrepancy would mean that the publication details had been changed. The authenticated USBC would then be compared against a master file of USBCs. In a very small number of cases, this would reveal that the new number was already on file. The computer would then change the number using a special element that was reserved for this purpose. This scenario, although it was put forward nearly twenty years ago, still remains valid.

THE FIRST EXTENSIVE TESTING

The first testing of the idea of a USBC outside Bradford was almost immediately carried out by Professor Lynch at the University of Sheffield. Beale and Lynch[3] tested the original code on two one-year cumulations of BNB MARC files. They found that the USBC created unique codes for 91% of the records in the files. They then carried out some alterations to the original code and tested the revised code on the same files. The revised Code was an improvement and created unique codes for 96% of the records.

The next stage in the development of the USBC owes much to Yannakoudakis in his work towards his PhD.[4] During his studies, he examined in depth the potential of automatic coding for bibliographical record control. However, the USBC was the focus of his research; and he covered it both theoretically and empirically. In his testing, he used over 135,000 records from three different databases. With good quality databases like BNB MARC, he was able to achieve success rates in excess of 99%. Dr Huggill, a senior lecturer in the Department of Computing, supervised Dr Yannakoudakis doctorate; and both worked on various USBC projects until the former retired and the latter took up a post with the Athens University of Economics and Business where he is now Head of Informatics.

THE FIRST RESEARCH PROJECT

Even with so much evidence on the feasibility of the concept of the USBC, the first application for funding in 1974 was turned down. This was probably because the concept of a derived code was new. Today it is universally used for establishing the identity and thus the file location from the first line of the address and the postcode. Then it was considered crude and unworkable. This meant that it was difficult to obtain research funding for the USBC. We then approached a number of senior librarians for their opinion. We argued that a universal machine-generated book code could facilitate the building of large national and regional databases and would make it much easier for individual libraries to use these databases. Lists of numbers held by one database could be compared with those of another, and the unique records in each could then shared. In this way, the piecemeal conversion of catalogue records that was now taking place in databases throughout the world would become simpler. Encouraged by the response, we tried a second time for funding.

The second application was successful, and we were awarded a three-year research project by the British Library Research and Development Department.[5] The first objective of the project was to develop and improve the USBC as a control code for the bibliographic record and to widen its scope to include non-book material and foreign language works. Two further objectives were important because they sought to test the value of the USBC in areas that were vital in the development of bibliographic control. The first of these was to test the effectiveness of the USBC for duplicate detection within a database. The second was to apply it to the merging of different databases.

The results of the first objective gave a much-improved code. This improved form of the code, tested on two BNB one-year MARC files, gave a coding failure rate that was brought down first from 0.03%, then to 0.02%, and finally to 0.1%.

The Code was also tested on non-book material, periodicals, and foreign language material with some success. From these results, it was possible to claim that:

(a) The USBC had reached a stage where it could be applied as a machine generated control code to bibliographical records catalogued to a good standard;

(b) The USBC could be applied to new bibliographic items at source provided certain safeguards were used; and

(c) The USBC is too sensitive to apply to files containing records catalogued to widely different standards. However, once "cleaned," these files would be suitable for USBC processing.

The failures of the USBC on good quality databases were lower than failures that could be attributed to those caused by human error as, for example, spelling errors, incorrect ISBNs, and bad cataloguing. Nevertheless, in order to reduce the error rate still further, a larger and more complex code was developed to deal with the small number of failures. This code, as its name JUMBO implied, was a very long one. Its main purpose was for use on sets of putative duplicates brought to light by the USBC and to check whether they were true duplicates. The first results of the new code were very promising, but it was later dropped in favour of an expert system approach that was more flexible. For example, the rules of the expert system can be changed more easily than reprocessing a whole database to change a JUMBO code. Another reason is that an expert system can look in great detail at a small set known to be of interest.

A case study illustrates how successful the USBC was in coding a file that was catalogued to high standards. As an example, the following results were achieved on the 1975 UK MARC File. Unique codes were created for all but seventy-five of the 31,369 records in the file. This residue consisted of six pairs of exact duplicates, seven pairs of hardback/paperback duplicates, and nine pairs of quasi-duplicates. The latter were all British Government publications where the differences were small but important, e.g., the difference between a treaty being ratified and not ratified. Most of these duplicates were not detected and appeared in the 1975 British National Bibliography that was produced from the UK MARC File.

Tests on the effectiveness of the USBC for merging databases were carried out by simulating the creation of a national database on a small scale using four BNB files and one from BLCMP for about 135,000 records in all. These records were given USBC's, and the resulting file of USBC's tested for overlap. An analysis of this file showed that the method gave an accurate picture of the overlap between the databases. However, a certain number of mismatches occurred mainly through variations in the cataloguing and the incorrect use of the MARC Format. The results were encouraging but showed the need for further work in this area. An unexpected finding was a small amount of overlap between the four BNB files. As well as the work on the simulation of a national database, a small-scale experiment was carried out on merging the periodical lists of the Universities of Bradford and Leeds. Neither of the databases had standardised formats; during the time allocated, it proved possible only to uncover the problems and indicate the kind of solutions that might be effective. This work was carried further in the two DOCMATCH Projects.

The use of the USBC for duplicate detection in a database proved to be the most challenging aspect of the work and to impinge on both the other objectives. Most duplicates in a database are unchallengeable duplicates, but a small minority are duplicates according to interpretation while others have been treated as duplicates because the bibliographical relationships between two records have not been shown correctly in the cataloguing. An example is the quite common placing of edition information in the notes field. Although the USBC is very effective in duplicate detection on files catalogued to dependable standards, on others it is necessary to have additional techniques for filtering out true duplicates from a set of putative duplicates. For this reason, the JUMBO Code and methods of weighting were developed. Tests showed that the principles worked out had a sound basis in practice but needed some modification.

MERGING:
SIMULATING THE SETTING UP
OF A NATIONAL DATABASE

Towards the end of the first research project, proposals to set up a national bibliographic database, UKLDS (United Kingdom Library Database System), were being considered. In order to set up the database, it would be necessary to establish a method of merging machine-readable files and for detecting duplicates within the files and between the files. Since Bradford University had demonstrated that this could be done using the USBC, the British Library Bibliographic Services Division commissioned a project to examine the potential for doing this for the UKLDS.[6]

The aims of the project were to:

- Determine the feasibility of using the USBC to create a merged retrospective database of MARC and non-MARC records and at the same time to eliminate duplicates with a high level of confidence.
- Provide data on which to estimate the cost of carrying out a full-scale merge of BL and cooperative retrospective files.
- Identify any characteristics of the retrospective files that may reduce the effectiveness of the merge process.
- Provide a fuller assessment than is at present available of the overlap between the respective files.
- Provide a corpus of records that occur in two or more files to be used to develop and test algorithms for taking a single record into the merged database.

In order to provide a large representative sample for the project, records for 1976 and 1981 from the following databases were supplied: UK MARC, Department of Printed Books, London University, SCOLCAP, Library of Congress, BLCMP, SWALCAP, and LASER. The total number or records processed was 661,725 although 23,861 of these were rejected for various reasons.

The procedure that was adopted was as follows:

- For each record in each file, a USBC was generated.
- Internal duplicates were identified for each file.
- Internal duplicates were manually analysed, and results were produced for each file.
- Using UK MARC as a starting base, each file was successfully merged. Records with unique USBCs were added to the base file, and a chain of duplicates was associated with each USBC.
- A sample of the duplicate chains from the final merged file was manually analysed.
- Statistical analyses of duplicate chains and overlap between the files were carried out.
- In order to test the effectiveness of the USBC, the records with an ISBN from the London University file and the BLCMP file were tested for an overlap to provide a partial comparison.
- Costing estimates were produced.

The results of the project showed that the USBC could be used successfully to set up a national database. The setting up process could be carried out very quickly, and overlap between the databases could be detected at the merge stage. Manual analysis of overlap items by cataloguers would ensure that the record accepted into the national database would be the record with the highest quality of cataloguing. The JUMBO Code, which was developed in the earlier research project, would enable the duplicate bibliographic records to be analysed automatically and in different ways. From this analysis, it would be possible to work out which record from a set of duplicates had a higher probability of being incorrect. It was also felt that these techniques could be developed into an integral part of the quality control in a national database.

During the course of the project, the working group set up to steer the national database decided not to proceed with UKLDS as it was originally envisaged but to seek to achieve the same objectives by means of a series of bilateral agreements. This was never done; and now, eleven years later, the original concept is being discussed again.

THE DOCMATCH PROJECTS: USING THE USBC WITH PERIODICAL ARTICLES

Shortly after the conclusion of the work on UKLDS, Bradford University was approached by the British Library Document Supply Centre to join them in a joint project that the EEC had agreed to fund.[7] The aim of the project was to investigate the problem of linkage between bibliographic databases and full text databases held by document suppliers and to develop algorithms for matching bibliographic references for documents ordered by users with references stored in electronic document delivery systems.

However, there had been a new development since the first project. A consortium of publishers had developed the ADONIS system that was a database of the full texts of over two hundred biomedical periodicals. Because of this development, it was felt by both EEC and the Document Supply Centre that the main aim of a new project should be the implementation of the USBC matching algorithm as proposed in DOCMATCH I and its development into a working system. ADONIS already used an allocated document identifier, the ADONIS number, to identify each article. The new project, to be called DOCMATCH II,[8] would be developed to act as a front end to ADONIS by accepting requests from existing document ordering systems and filtering out those not on ADONIS. This would be done by using a master index linking USBC's to ADONIS numbers. USBC's created for incoming citations would be matched against the master index. In many ways, the new project could be seen as a narrower study than DOCMATCH I since it involved only one document supplier and only one type of document, articles from journals. It may also be seen as a more in-depth study since it aimed to use a file of over 100,000 records compared with the much smaller files used in the earlier project.

CLEANING A DATABASE: WORK WITH BLCMP

An opportunity to test the expert system approach came when BLCMP, a cooperative cataloguing organisation, awarded the University of Bradford a contract to apply the Bradford techniques, including the expert system, to their database.[9] At this time, the BLCMP database consisted of some two and a half million records. The aim of the project was, therefore, to test and fine-tune the Bradford software on a sample of the BLCMP database and then develop this software so that it could be used on the BLCMP computer. Tests were carried out on a sample of 100,000 records after agreement had been reached on a form of the USBC suitable for the BLCMP database. USBC's were created for all the records in the sample; the sets of putative duplicates that resulted were examined; and, from the examination, a suitable expert system was constructed.[10]

In the end, the system was never implemented for a number of reasons. The USBC FORTRAN programs were more difficult to convert to the PL/1 programming language that was required by BLCMP than had been anticipated. It was difficult for BLCMP to schedule time on their computer to create USBCs for all the records in their database. However, the main reason that caused BLCMP to withdraw from the project was that there was no absolute guarantee that the expert system would not delete a very small number of duplicates that some clients would claim were not true duplicates. This was a pity because the use of the USBC would have eliminated tens of thousands of true duplicates from the BLCMP database.

THE QUALCAT PROJECT: USING USBCS AND EXPERT SYSTEMS FOR QUALITY CONTROL

The principal aims of the project were to:

- Set up a large bibliographic database integrating records covering a range of material from a number of different databases by using USBC technology for merging, cleaning, and control.
- Develop an expert system to select the best record from a number of duplicate records.
- Develop an expert system to link databases and centralised authority control.
- Develop a fully automated quality control package for day-to-day operation.
- Investigate interface problems for cataloguers using the systems.

The database assembled at Bradford consisted of records created during 1985 from BNB, HSS, and MARS from the British Library. It had been hoped to include other records from other databases, but this had not proved possible because the Bradford computing facilities were in process of being changed and could handle only 140,000 records. This was, however, large enough to test the aims of the project. All these records were merged into one relational database. This form of database was chosen because it provided powerful search facilities to analyse where information is held in a sample of MARC records. Before being able to assess which is the best record from a number of alternatives, the duplicate items for any record had to be assembled. This was done by using the USBC to gather sets of putative duplicates that were then examined by the expert system. Where ISBNs were present, they were used in the same way as the USBC to gather sets of putative duplicates.

At the same time as the database was set up at Bradford, another one was set up consisting of the records created during 1985 from the University of Bath database. This meant that Bath was then able to use the expert system to compare their database with the main database and select the best record. This attempt at integrating access to local and remote databases predated what is now becoming more common via the use of Z39.50/SR technology. This part of the project relied heavily on co-operation with the Centre for Bibliographic Management at the University of Bath.[11]

An important element of quality control is of course the use of an authority control file. In order to examine this function, a test file was set up consisting of the British Library Name Authority File. It never became part of QUALCAT because it was felt that it was not always possible to make automatic use of the information in the file.

Although the expert system approach was very successful, it could not be guaranteed always to work because of structural faults in the MARC format and in AACR2. These could be avoided if the MARC format were revised to ensure that no notes field was used to give manifestation information and that a clearer line were drawn between the functions of the collation and the notes field. This could be reinforced if AACR was revised to ensure that bibliographic relationship information was always given in the same place.

Overall the project showed that automation in the form of an expert system could be built into a system to extract duplicates from a database and to exercise quality control over records for the same work from a number of different databases.[12]

The project owed much to the advice and interest of Philip Bryant, Director of the Centre of Bibliographic Management at the University of Bath.

THE USE OF THE USBC IN INTER-LIBRARY LENDING

The Document Supply Centre (DSC), where the work described below was done, was receiving over four million requests a year of which two and a quarter million arrived in electronic form. In order to handle this volume of traffic, the DSC has installed an automated request processing system of which the key element is AUTOMATCH. This system takes each electronic request in turn and identifies whether it is a book, a serial, or a conference proceeding. If the item is a serial, AUTOMATCH is able to identify exactly what the serial is and then allocate the appropriate DSC shelf mark. It is not, however, able to do the same for books and conference proceedings. In addition, it has a failure rate of about five percent. Together these account for nearly half a million requests a year that cannot be fully integrated into the core automated request system.

Most of this residue consists of requests for books. In order to investigate whether the USBC technology available at Bradford could perform the same function for books that AUTOMATCH did for serials, the DSC asked Bradford to carry out a small feasibility study.[13]

The study used one week's supply of request data from the monograph stream output by AUTOMATCH. All the requests for 1992 material were then filtered out and coded with a form of the USBC. The next stage was to download all the 1992 records from the CD-ROM version of Books at Boston Spa. The restriction to 1992 was necessary because it was impractical in the short time scale to download all 700,000 records with the access/search software available on the CD-ROM. These records were then coded with the same form of USBC as the requests. Comparing codes from the requests with those from Books at Boston Spa enabled a match to be made and a stock number to be obtained.

The next stage was to produce an output. This consisted of the contents of each record together with three additional fields:

- the identified stock number
- publication date
- monograph title.

From this output, it was possible to establish three categories:

- correct matches
- mismatches
- failures to match at all.

These three categories were then manually examined with three different objectives. For the correct matches, a check was made to ensure that they were indeed correct. If they were not, the possibility of some change to the form of the USBC was considered. In the case of mismatches, an attempt to establish the reason for the mismatch was made. Finally, the failures to match at all were sorted into those that were failures of the system, those that were fractured references, and finally those that were not held by DSC.

After some fine-tuning, the programs were run again; and the results were sent to DSC who carried out their own independent manual check. This final check confirmed that the results were well within the success rates that had been set by the DSC at the start of the project. Bradford then cooperated with the DSC to incorporate the USBC into their core automated request system. The core of the system produced by Bradford in 1996 is still running and has now processed several million requests.

GREEK BIBLIOGRAPHIC DATABASE WORK: THE HELEN PROJECT

Project Helen[14] was an investigation into Greek language transliteration problems. The project was funded by the EEC and was a joint project between University of Bradford, University of Crete, and King's College, London. It investigated a number of issues related to conversion between the Latin and Greek alphabet and the representation of the Greek character set with an emphasis on conversion of bibliographic data. A major part of the project's work was the development of software for automated transliteration. The main emphasis of this was on retransliteration of Greek text that had been romanized so that it is available in its correct form in Greek.

Historically, most computer systems have been able to store and display only the Latin alphabet. Therefore, Greek words have been stored in transliterated form. That is, each Greek letter has been substituted by one or more Latin letters, possibly with accents. This has meant that an approximation, which may be pronounced roughly correctly, is kept. This approximation is also an unnatural form for Greek readers who would like to use the Greek script. In this respect, OPACs have been a step backwards from card catalogues that may well have had the correct Greek forms as well as transliterated text. A project questionnaire showed that twelve different transliteration schemes were in use in libraries.

In order to deal with this problem, the project developed software that will convert transliterated text back into Greek. Where reconversion cannot be made, possible alternatives were suggested. A range of different transliteration schemes can be used; and, if the transliteration scheme is unknown, the program attempts to determine automatically which scheme to use. The software can also access a database of names and other terms that are to be converted exceptionally.

Modular software was designed with an internal program interface that allows the development of a large common core of software. The specialised parts are the input and output functions of the software where the use of a particular character set come into play. The bulk of the conversion from Latin text to Greek is handled by the common parts of the software. This is achieved by the use of an internal abstract notion of Greek characters that is not tied to any particular character set. This allows most of the software's manipulation of the text to take place in the common modules of the programs. A number of versions have been developed and are available from the project in an effort to make the project's software available in suitable formats for as large an audience as possible. Core modules developed at Bradford were integrated into a library environment in Crete so that, for example, transliterated MARC records could be converted to their correct script.

The project was successful in the two broad areas of developing software for automated transliteration and of publicising the issues of transliteration. As is perhaps inevitable with any research project a number of further questions have been raised and avenues opened for more work.

BOPAC: A NEW GENERATION OF OPAC

There were two BOPAC Projects: BOPAC1 and BOPAC2. Building on the findings of the first project,[15] the second project set up an operational OPAC on the Internet. A major change since the first project has been the growth of the Internet in general and the World Wide Web in particular. These developments meant that the potential advantages we had seen with BOPAC1 could be delivered to any desktop (not just the Windows based PC used in BOPAC1). However, many emerging Web based interfaces to OPACs (and other information systems) did not seem to be making the most of the Web's possibilities. The result was BOPAC2 that was demonstrated at the Toronto Conference on the Future of AACR2 that laid the foundations for many of the current developments in areas such as the Functional Requirements for Bibliographical Records. In the intervening years, many OPAC's have appeared on the Web. However, they have not fundamentally changed. Some navigation is easier thanks to hyperlinks, but they still do not offer the personalisation, organisation, and above all the speed that BOPAC does.

It has three distinct elements:

- A WWW–Z39.50 gateway that provides access to catalogues and bibliographic databases through the Z39.50 protocol. The Gateway used was Europagate that was set up as the result of a European Research Project and is in the public domain.
- The Z39.50 server libraries and bibliographic databases. BOPAC2 now covers a wide range of targets.
- The Java applet. This is the program that gives BOPAC2 its power and versatility once a retrieval has been downloaded.

The most important of these developments is the advent of Java. This is vital because it has enabled OPACs like BOPAC2 to be designed with searching and display facilities not available to commercial OPACs in use today. It allows large retrievals to be downloaded with broad-based search criteria. The retrieval can then be analysed and organised very quickly using these new facilities in ways that were not possible with traditional OPACs. The records once downloaded and held in the computer's memory can be sorted or selected by many criteria while movement between them is very fast. At present, the list of libraries that BOPAC2 is able to access, providing the Z39.50 server is available, either singly or as a group, is about thirty, mainly British but including the Library of Congress and MELVYL.

One search screen covers all available search options, and the user chooses the size of the retrieval from a menu offering a number of options. It is simple to use without having the complexities and obligatory search commands of most library OPACs.

The first impression of BOPAC2 is its speed, and the second is the wide range of options. The discerning user will note how a large retrieval can be quickly tailored to meet a particular requirement. One of the major frustrations for most OPAC users is that only one screen can be viewed at a time. In BOPAC2, all retrievals and any selections can be scrolled through without the interruption of obtaining another screen.[16]

In spite of its obvious improvements over existing OPACs, several applications for funding to further develop BOPAC were turned down. However, there is still little evidence that any great improvement in library OPACs has occurred.

As far as we are aware, no other OPAC has the range of facilities or the speed of operation of BOPAC2. It has opened up new and far more effective ways for OPAC display.

Once the retrieval has been downloaded and the Java applet comes into operation, it is very fast–several orders of magnitude faster than in conventional OPACs.

With development support, we could move BOPAC2 from being a research project to an established service that would allow researchers unified access to an unparalleled collection of resources.

AUTHORITY CONTROL

BOPAC was probably our most successful research project. It also had an important spin off as it enabled us to carry out probably the first known test on how effective authority control was in practise. This we were able to do because it was possible to measure how related headings, both author and subject, were used. The LC OPAC was chosen for the tests because it was felt that, if anyone had got authority control right, it would be LC. We also assumed that a cross reference structure including "see also" was in place. Authority control to work properly should ensure that a search produces all the relevant material held by the library and that the results are displayed in an organised way.

Once a search has been downloaded, the BOPAC JAVA applet takes over and the movement between a number of display options takes seconds or less. The most important of these display options are author, title, and subject.

This paper is already too long to give details of the procedure to be followed, but it has been carefully detailed in the *Cataloging and Classification Quarterly* paper. It is possible to repeat the examples given in the paper by using BOPAC.

The techniques briefly described above have been fully documented in the *Cataloging and Classification Quarterly*.[17,18,19] It was also discussed more fully in postings to the AUTOCAT discussion list. In addition, we have had a large amount of email correspondence with senior people in the bibliographic control area.

We repeatedly asked our critics to test what we were claiming for BOPAC using BOPAC to do so. None of them appeared to have done so although some of them seemed to have assumed that we were involved in some form of bibliographic black magic. These were extreme cases. There is still, however, a disturbing lack of appreciation of modern database management and its potential for the improvement of our OPACs. For example, it is time to forget the card catalogue to make our OPACs faster and to work on the assumption that the cross reference function is not to tell you where to go but to take you there.

CONCLUSIONS

BOPAC has been available on the Internet for nearly ten years; and, during that time, it has had steady but not spectacular use. It is now receiving three to four thousand visits a year. We will try to keep it operational, but it may not be possible without further funding.

Librarianship and cataloguing face an uncertain future. Neither will survive until they use the technology that is available more effectively. They have been quick to criticise the search engines for their lack of organisation without demonstrating that what they offer is more effective. Unlike the search engines, they have a powerful knowledge database consisting of the OPACs of the world's major libraries, the major classification schemes, and finally the major authority control databases. The size of the final database would not be a problem since several search engines are operating with databases measured in billions. However, the problems of integrating them and extracting knowledge from them through this integration would need a major research effort.

ACKNOWLEDGEMENTS

The USBC work was fortunate in having a number of high calibre research assistants working on the various projects; we are grateful to the hard work of D. Ellis, E. Flokas, J. Cullen, Ms C. Gierl, and L. Nielson.

We were fortunate in receiving funding from a number of different organisations in particular the BL R & D Department who not only supported us financially but also provided a number of very helpful project officers. We are also grateful for funding from the British Library, Bibliographic Services Division; the EEC; the British Library Document Supply Centre; and BLCMP.

Finally we are grateful to those organisations who allowed us to use parts of their databases in our research: The British National Bibliography; the various divisions of the British Library; the Universities of Bradford, Leeds, Bath, and London; the Library of Congress; OCLC; LASER; SWALCAP; SCOLCAP; and BLCMP.

REFERENCES

1. Ayres, F. H. The Universal Standard Book Number (USBN): a New Method for the Construction of Control Numbers for Bibliographical Records. *Program*, 8, 166-173, 1974.

2. Ayres, F. H. The Universal Standard Book Number (USBN): Why, How and a Progress Report. *Program*, 10, 75-80, 1976.

3. Beale, D.D. and Lynch, M. F. An Evaluation of, and Improvement on, Ayres' Universal Standard Book Number. *Program*, 9, 34-45, 1975.

4. Yannakoudakis, E. J. *Automatic Coding for Bibliographic Record Control*. PhD Thesis. University of Bradford. 1979.

5. Ayres, F. H., Ellis, D., Huggill, J. A. W. and Yannakoudakis, E. J. *USBC (Universal Standard Book Code)–Its Development and Use as a Method of Bibliographic Control*. (British Library R & D Report No. 5817). University of Bradford. 1984.

6. Ayres, F. H., Ellis, D., Huggill, J. A. W. and Yannakoudakis, E. J. *USBC (Universal Standard Book Code): Its Use for Union File Creation*. British Library, Bibliographic Services Division. 1984.

7. Ayres, F. H., Ellis, D, Huggill, J. A. W., Line, M. B., Long, A. B., Millson, D. R., Russon, D. and Yannakoudakis, E. J. *DOCMATCH 1: Final Report*. British Library. 1986. Also published as EUR 10677 EN *Electronic Document Delivery -IX, The Link-*

age Between Bibliographic and Full-text Databases–a Feasibility Study. Commission of the European Communities. 1987.

8. Ayres, F. H., Huggill, J. A. W., Ridley, M. J. and Yannakoudakis, E. J. *DOCMATCH II; Report of Work Undertaken at the University of Bradford.* British Library, Document Supply Centre. 1990.

9. Ayres, F., Flokas, E., Huggill, J. A. W. and Yannakoudakis, E. J. *An Expert System for Duplicate Control. Report to the British Library R & D Department.* (Project no. SI/G/747). Department of Computing, University of Bradford. 1987.

10. Ayres, F. H., Flokas, E., Huggill, J. A. W. and Yannakoudakis, E. J. *Project Report: The Detection and Elimination of Duplicates from the BLCMP Database.* Department of Computing, University of Bradford. 1989.

11. Ayres, F. H., Cullen, J., Gierl, C., Huggill, J. A. W., Ridley, M. J. and Torsun, I. *QUALCAT: Automation of Quality Control in Cataloguing. Final Report.* (BLR&D Rep. 6068). Department of Computing, University of Bradford. 1991.

12. Ridley, M. An Expert System for Quality Control and Duplicate Detection in Bibliographic Databases. *Program*, 26, 1-18,1992.

13. Ayres, F. H., Nielsen, L. and Ridley, M. *Report on Study into Monograph Request Matching.* Department of Computing, University of Bradford. 1995.

14. E.Cornell, A. Hatjievgenidau, M.J. Ridley, ' Searching for Non Roman Script Terms,' Electronic Library and Visual Information Research (ELVIRA 2), *Aslib*, 1995, pp. 144-150.

15. FH Ayres, LPS Nielsen, MJ Ridley, Bibliographic Management: a New Approach Using the Manifestations concept and the Bradford OPAC, *Cataloging & Classification Quarterly* 22(1), 3-28, 1996.

16. FH Ayres, LPS Nielsen, MJ Ridley, 'BOPAC2: a New Concept in OPAC Design and Bibliographic Control,' *Cataloging & Classification Quarterly* 28(2),17-44, 1999.

17. FH Ayres, Authority Control Simply Does Not Work, *Cataloging & Classification Quarterly* 32(2), 49-59, 2001.

18. D CannCasciato, J Hopkins, J. McRee Elrod and W Schupbach. Response to (17) *Cataloging & Classification Quarterly* 34(2), 99-106, 2002.

19. FH Ayres, Response to (18) *Cataloging & Classification Quarterly* 34(2), 106-110, 2002.

doi:10.1300/J104v44n01_08

International Cataloguing Tradition and Italian Rules: Common Ground and Specific Features

Carlo Bianchini
Mauro Guerrini

SUMMARY. Many current cataloguing codes have their roots in a common tradition started by the 1961 Paris International Conference on Cataloguing Principles–ICCP. Since 1961, the construction of new national codes had been based on the sharing of cataloguing principles, on agreements for international cooperation, and on a common tradition. The new technological and international environment suggests, more and more, a redesign of those principles to include more suitable features and to assert firmly that the highest principle is the convenience of the users of the catalogue. Within this framework, the authors analyze the

---

Carlo Bianchini is Librarian, Natural History Museum of Udine, Via Lionello 1, I-33100 Udine, Italy (E-mail: c.bianchini@iol.it). Mauro Guerrini is Professor, Library and Information Science, Università degli Studi di Firenze (Florence University, Italy), Dipartimento di Studi sul Medioevo e Rinascimento, Piazza Brunelleschi, 6, I-50121 Firenze, Italy (E-mail: m.guerrini@leonet.it; Home page: http://www.meri.unifi.it/meri/guerrini.html).

The article was planned together by both authors who are in agreement on its total contents. Nevertheless, Carlo Bianchini is more responsible for Section 1 while Mauro Guerrini is more responsible for Section 2.

[Haworth co-indexing entry note]: "International Cataloguing Tradition and Italian Rules: Common Ground and Specific Features." Bianchini, Carlo, and Mauro Guerrini. Co-published simultaneously in *Cataloging & Classification Quarterly* (The Haworth Information Press, an imprint of The Haworth Press, Inc.) Vol. 44, No. 1/2, 2007, pp. 131-150; and: *Cataloger, Editor, and Scholar: Essays in Honor of Ruth C. Carter* (ed: Robert P. Holley) The Haworth Information Press, an imprint of The Haworth Press, Inc., 2007, pp. 131-150. Single or multiple copies of this article are available for a fee from The Haworth Document Delivery Service [1-800-HAWORTH, 9:00 a.m. - 5:00 p.m. (EST). E-mail address: docdelivery@haworthpress.com].

Available online at http://ccq.haworthpress.com
© 2007 by The Haworth Press, Inc. All rights reserved.
doi:10.1300/J104v44n01_09

Italian cataloguing tradition and its relationships with the international tradition and recount the main activities towards a revision of the present Italian code–Regole italiane di catalogazione per autori RICA. The paper shows that, since the first Italian rules written by Fumagalli, special attention has been paid to the international tradition (in particular toward Panizzi's rules). After describing the relationships among the international trends and the Italian codes of 1922, 1956, and 1979, the paper deals with the recent works of the new Commission that, since 1997, has started to revise RICA. The paper concludes by reflecting on the Italian position in the debate first on the ISBD and then on the new entity-relationship models. doi:10.1300/J104v44n01_09 *[Article copies available for a fee from The Haworth Document Delivery Service: 1-800-HAWORTH. E-mail address: <docdelivery@haworthpress.com> Website: <http://www.HaworthPress.com> © 2007 by The Haworth Press, Inc. All rights reserved.]*

KEYWORDS. Italian cataloguing rules, RICA, cataloguing history, Paris Principles, international cooperation

FOREWORD

Several countries that believe in international cooperation have long ago taken to sharing their cataloguing principles, re-examined their national traditions, and tried to harmonise their codes. This tradition, started by the 1961 Paris International Conference on Cataloguing Principles (ICCP), first with its *Statement of Principles*, then with the construction of new national codes, continues to become stronger and stricter. Many feel that there is a current need to redesign those principles with features more suitable to the new technological advances and to the international environment. Many also assert firmly that the highest principle is the convenience of the catalogue users.

This paper will present briefly the main activities aimed at a revision of the Italian code–*Regole italiane di catalogazione per autori* (RICA)– and how the international debate has influenced this code.

THE ITALIAN TRADITION

In 1869, soon after the unification of Italy, the Commissione Cibrario[1] recommended in its final report that every library have a general inventory, an author/title catalogue, and a subject catalogue. It also suggested that:

> in order to insure [. . .] uniformity in the construction of these catalogues, each librarian will state special rules to be followed by the staff assigned to compiling and copying them. For the fulfilment of this task, it recommends librarians to consult Panizzi's rules for the printed catalogue of the British Museum, *Letture di Bibliologia* by Tommaso Gar, the handbooks on librarianship by Petzholdt, Seizinger, and Edwards as well as the most important printed catalogues by Brunet, Graesse, etc.[2]

The first complete Italian code of rules was written by Giuseppe Fumagalli, based on his own experience and on the in-house code at the National Library in Florence. Published in *Cataloghi di biblioteca e indici bibliografici*,[3] it was awarded a prize by the Ministry. The gratifying verdict voiced by the judging committee is confirmed by the later debate in which this work is considered an irreproachable touchstone.[4] Fumagalli wrote: "The alphabetical author catalogue [. . .] is no doubt the most useful one in a library [. . . because] it informs, as quickly as possible, *if a given book is in the library* and where it is; but it also provides the materials for studies in bio-bibliography; that is, it tells us *which works the library has by a given author and which editions of a given book*."[5] The excerpt shows that Fumagalli had learned well Cutter's lesson so much so that he fixes the principles of the author/title catalogue in the same terms in which they will be stated, over seventy-five years later, in the Paris Principles.[6]

The first Italian rules as a national standard for descriptive cataloguing go back to 1922 when a special commission was established whose members were the heads of two honoured libraries (Guido Biagi, chair, and Giuliano Bonazzi), a supervisor from the ministry, and a university professor; its task was to analyze the rules in use in many Italian libraries and to construct a code, with the similar Anglo-American code as model, to be used in all Italian state libraries. When the special commission ended its work, a decree ratified and promulgated the first national cataloguing code *Regole per la compilazione del catalogo alfabetico* (Roma: Nardecchia, 1922). The code mirrored the need for uniformity at the national level of the alphabetical catalogue and for an end to the numerous local solutions, mainly of a practical nature. Its success is proved by its widespread application even beyond the state libraries for which it was devised.[7]

The 1922 rules, when put to use under the supervision of Giuliano Bonazzi in the retrospective cataloguing of the bibliographic materials in the Rome library "Vittorio Emanuele II," showed gaps stemming from two classes of problems: (1) some rules allowed for subjective interpretation; (2) some bibliographic cases were not to be found in any of the rules.

As far back as 1940, these shortcomings suggested the need for a revision or even a remaking of the 1922 rules so that a Commission of experts was appointed; but its work was interrupted by World War II.

In January 1951, with the spur of the recently started union catalogue of Italian libraries, a new commission[8] resumed the revision with two basic objectives:

1. to attune, as far as possible, the Italian rules to a type of international entry that would allow a foreigner to find easily the books searched in the alphabetical list of our catalogues;
2. "to rid the code of the dissimilarities and contradictions already found in it, to search for other ones, to broaden the rules according to a number of case studies greatly increased in twenty years of usage, in some cases to modify the form of the rules in order to make them less concise and more comprehensive and expansive, and, most of all, to increase the number of examples making them fit for current times."

During its deliberations, the Commission kept in mind the 1949 ALA Code, the rules adopted in Belgian and German libraries, and the 1939 rules of the Vatican Library. It noted, "sometimes with real satisfaction, that the construction of some of these rules adopted in foreign countries was motivated by the corresponding rules in the Italian code."[9]

The new cataloguing code, though it changed the rules in the 1922 code in many points, retained its structure;[10] in fact it neither increased nor decreased the number of rules. When we compare it to the 1922 code, the most relevant changes are:

1. works written even by two authors only, each one of whom wrote a clearly distinct and openly stated part, are to be entered as anonymous works with analytical entries for both authors (rule 18);
2. in publications for weddings, graduations, veil-takings, etc., refer from the names of the persons being celebrated (rule 19);

3. for works accompanied by a critical essay with its own title and sometimes in a separate volume, an analytical entry is made from the critical essay (rule 28);
4. for opera librettos refer from the title and the musician (rule 32);
5. for collections of writings taken from works by two or three authors, the main entry is made for the first; and analytical entries or reference entries are made for the others (rule 33);
6. a collection of inscriptions made by an author as a single and limited work that later becomes the starting point for a large collective publication must have a separate entry under its collection title (rule 34);
7. translations from various authors are treated according to the individual case, like collections or like works by different authors (rule 36);
8. rules and examples have been introduced for antipopes and patriarchs (rule 44) and for the wives of sovereigns (rule 45);
9. the rule for sovereigns who wrote in various languages has been changed, or rather inverted; the entries for the works by heads of state in the Renaissance and by Roman emperors have been regulated (rule 45).[11]

One last important change concerns the rules for corporate bodies: "the various forms of the name of academies and societies appear each one under its own denomination and not all under the last name; the various denominations are gathered in a chronological order in a general explanatory entry located before the group of entries with the last denomination" (rule 65).[12]

To note a peculiar detail, the code contains the use, ahead of the Paris Principles, of the phrase "main entry" for the entry with a full definition of the work. This "main entry" consists of, besides the entry word, four elements: (1) title; (2) imprint; (3) bibliographical notes; and (4) special notes.[13]

The element of change introduced by the 1961 Paris Conference was no doubt the main reason behind the revision leading to the publication of RICA in 1979. When the Italian delegation to Paris came back to Italy, it was convinced that the 1956 text had to be revised. Diego Maltese, from the National Central Library in Florence, backed the importance of an overall rethinking of the Italian code to bring it to a "consistent system of basic, clearly stated principles."[14] The Italian code–though with a tradition going back to Cutter[15] and enriched with contributions by Fumagalli, Chilovi, and Biagi–needed a complete harmonization of the rules, that is, a close examination of each rule (according to Lubetzky's model) that could relate the rule to a principle justifying its presence.

In 1962 at the XIX Congress of the Italian Library Association, "the suitability of drawing up a new edition of the rules" founded on the Paris Principles was recognized. After a debate in the library journals, a ministerial Commission was appointed in 1968.[16]

The theoretical foundations of the new cataloguing code had been stated earlier by Maltese in 1965 with the publication of "Principi di catalogazione e regole italiane" and then in 1966 in the work "Elementi di catalogazione per autori. Scelta e forma dell'intestazione."[17] Reviewing the former, Carlo Revelli, co-leader in the debate on the new principles and on the revision of the Italian rules, wrote: " In Italy the times are ripe for a radical revision of the rules for descriptive cataloguing [. . . bringing us in line] with the revision movement taking place almost everywhere. [. . .] I can't see any better starting point than this work by Maltese that deserves due consideration."[18]

The latter contribution by Maltese stressed the need to separate the problems linked with the choice of headings and the ones linked with the form of it, thus setting the basis for a division that would represent the structural innovation of the new code.

Maltese's commitment to the design of the new code based on the Paris Principles and his "on principle" plan appeared in a letter he wrote to A. H. Chaplin after the publication of the provisional edition of the comments on the Paris Principles. Maltese remembered:

> as early as the Rome session of the IFLA council [. . .], I voiced my doubts about the expediency of an "official" comment to the Paris Principles; from experience, I also advised against the unavoidable fallacy of examples [. . .]. I don't want to say that the Anglo-American code will not carry considerable weight in cataloguing practices all over the world (the ALA code carried it too), but what use was it, then, constructing principles, what use our thinking in preparation for them, let's say, from Osborn to Lubetzky (and to Chaplin), if certain compromising, perhaps inevitable, solutions take their place and are fully sanctioned?

Arthur Hugh Chaplin reaffirmed the concept that principles are international but that languages are national; principles must be suited to the culture and to the national language, that is, to local realities.

The *ad hoc* ministerial Rules Commission was created in 1968.[19] Since its members had their work obligations, they met only when possible. Much of the work was carried out by mail. Maltese, who was the chairman, shouldered the burden of collecting and abstracting the papers so that they could discuss matters more efficiently when they met. In April 1969, to confirm the strictly theoretical plan intended for the work, Revelli wrote to Maltese: "Dropping rules based on individual cases in favour of rules based on general principles forces the cataloguer to give up a *forma mentis* that tends to subdivide works by category of publication with the outcome that, with the growth of categories, solutions become more and more entangled." The proposal tended to get rid of adherence to laws and cases in keeping with the suggestions made by Osborn and Lubetzky even though this implied a conflict at every step between adherence to the Italian rules and obedience to the Paris Principles. The most strongly debated issues were:

1. *Choice and form of headings.* The rules introduced the division between choice and form of heading (not of entry word) that was already, but not systematically, present in the 1956 rules.
2. *Name of author.* The Commission introduced a break in the Italian tradition that carefully searched for the author's register name; it also considered and accepted the name on the document since it is the one looked for and preferred by the reader or at least by some readers.
3. *Jurisdictions.* The rules dropped the heading under bodies that are organs of governing-territorial jurisdictions in favour of a heading directly under the superior body of which they are organs. The rules kept the headings under those bodies–universities and libraries–that are not decentralized or peripheral organs of jurisdictions.
4. *Description.* The Commission gave much prominence to description–that is one of the great innovations in the new code–even more so than the rules for choice and form of heading that have always been issues treated in rules on author cataloguing. Description has a specific chapter, analogous with the space allotted to this subject by the 1967 AACR. The Commission took its start from a previous, rather generic, normative situation but could rely on the experience at BNI that provided an in-house descriptive code borrowed from the Library of Congress praxis (use of paragraphs, tracings, etc.)."[20]

In its research and synthesis, the Commission "paid particular attention to developments and new solutions to cataloguing issues world-wide. First the Anglo-American cataloguing rules, then the German ones were carefully studied but perhaps the Commission appreciated best the documents from the work of the IFLA Cataloguing Committee, especially *ISBD (M) International Standard Bibliographic Description for Monographic Publications*, the standard for descriptive rules. The Commission did not, however, forget the Italian tradition."[21]

Besides a general reorganisation of the structure of the code ("as a distribution of the discipline according to old criteria looked unfeasible"[22]), a first relevant innovation introduced by RICA was the concept of *the author presented as the main one*, that is, the author presented on the title page as prominent above the other authors in collective works. The rule implied that in these cases the choice of heading falls on a given entity, not by means of an analysis of the relationship between the entity and the work, but on merely formal criteria (or rather the form in which the information appears in the *manifestation*). Another change introduced–also regarding the choice of heading–was the suppression of paragraph 18, comma 3: "according to it a work written jointly was always entered under the title when the parts of the single authors appeared separate even if the authors were fewer than four. This rule, anyway, was a much debated innovation if compared with the 1921 rules."[23]

The decision to prefer entry under title for collections of texts by various authors was an attempt to reconcile the Paris Principles and the Italian tradition by thus reading in a more limiting sense the words in section 10.3 of the Principles. The analysis of the concept of work and of its logical and consistent use in RICA made by Alberto Petrucciani pointed out that the terms work, publication, and edition are used inaccurately as quasi-synonyms although they are not at all such.[24]

The most interesting paragraphs on choice of heading were the ones about works by corporate bodies. The Paris Principles talked about "entries under corporate bodies," a wording, adopted in spite of opposition to entry under corporate bodies strongly voiced by some participants. Avoiding calling them "authors" was done to satisfy these critics. In the RICA introductory *Report*, the treatment of corporate bodies was defined as "the most sensitive of all issues in descriptive cataloguing." The 1956 rules, according to the Commission, were especially unsatisfactory because they accepted the principle of corporate bodies as authors but lacked a definition for corporate body and for body as author "so that every cataloguer had a personal idea of what collective authorship under a corporate body might mean."[25]

The Italian tradition stood out for its appeal to the concept of "corporate body author," already used by the in-house rules in use in 1881 at the National Central Library in Florence. Retaining the concept of "corporate body author," RICA moved away from the content of the Paris Principles. "Therefore, the solution in RICA is outside the choice mandated by the Paris Principles about the treatment of corporate bodies even though the prescriptions look consistent and reaffirm the tradition recorded within the in-house rule at the National in Florence since 1881 and rule 49 in *Cataloghi di biblioteche e indici bibliografici* by Giuseppe Fumagalli."[26]

Regarding the form of heading, the need to ensure that an author is uniformly identified and qualified when it is strictly necessary to distinguish him/her from another author suggested as a general rule to make the form of heading match "the one chosen by the author for his/her own publications or the one by which the author is best known." This solution for the problem follows the principle of adopting a uniform heading; that is, to fix the unique and univocal form of name and of title so that all manifestations of an author's works are collocated in one point in the catalogue (the second function of the catalogue, stated at 2.2a of the Paris Principles). The problem was divided into three points:

1. which name or which title to use;
2. which form of the name or which form of the title to use, choosing either a fuller or a less complete form;
3. for personal authors with a name made up of more than one word, which entry word to adopt; that is, which access element to put first, choosing either a direct form or some inversion or rotation of terms.[27]

The general criterion proposed at point 7 of the Paris Principles pointed to the name (or form of name) or title most frequently used in the original editions of the works or, if this principle cannot be applied, in references to them in accepted authorities. From a full reading of points 7 and 8 of the Paris Principles, we can infer that the choice must fall on "*the name most frequently used in the original language* of the catalogued works." This solution implied collating the editions in the original language of the works–not directly, of course, but by means of accepted authorities–to establish and adopt the most recurrent form with the possibility of adopting a form based on translations only if the original language is not used in the catalogue.

Point 8.21 introduced yet another exception–the form that has become established in general usage–which makes for three criteria, not always in agreement but rather often antithetical, for adopting a uniform heading:

1. the form by which the author is most frequently identified in editions of his works even though this is difficult to establish so that the principle may vary from one library to another;
2. the form most frequently occuring in critical and reference works; and
3. the form established in general usage.

Almost forty-five years after the *Paris Principles*, we note that the results were positive about the choice of heading but not about its form; for the latter, each code followed its own particular course, mostly retaining local tradition.[28]

Going back to RICA, the Commission, although in its closing session, voiced the wish that "others will go on and construct rules for special materials and that a commentary will be started on the rules themselves that might become a useful aid." A commission to revise and update RICA was delayed until 1996 when the October 1996 decree officially appointed the "Commission for updating and eventually simplifying the rules for constructing the alphabetic catalogue in Italian libraries," a title that echoes the words for the 1956 rules, not for the 1979 ones.

THE ACTIVITIES OF THE COMMISSIONE RICA AND THE DEBATE IN ITALY BETWEEN INTERNATIONAL PERSPECTIVES

The Commission–commonly called Commissione RICA–was appointed in order to "re-examine analytically the text of the Italian rules for descriptive cataloguing and to check, over twenty years after publication, whether they actually conform to the evolution of cataloguing praxis around the world, to the electronic environment in which we now work, and to the new types of materials ever more present in our libraries."[29] Therefore, it is clear that the activities of the Commission would take place on two levels, though proceeding simultaneously: on an international level and on a national level, with a constant eye on conformity to the electronic environment. The Commission stated its target to be a thorough study of: (1) the rationale for a possible re-writing of the code; (2) the effectiveness of the Paris Principles; (3) the need to update terminology and examples; (4) whether RICA can be used for other types of materials."[30]

The Commission began an analysis, ended in 1997, according to which it considered substantially valid the Paris Principles that are the foundation of RICA. It also saw fit to broaden and develop the text of RICA by taking into account standards and documents produced internationally: ISBD, *Guidelines for Authority Records and References*, FRBR, FRANAR/FRAR, and ISO norms. The paramount aim of the revision was to harmonize the rules to the changed context in the organization of the catalogue, to the use of electronic technology, to the presence of new physical formats and different access modes, to the development of shared cataloguing, and to the implementation of cataloguing levels of varying complexity. After a first pause for evaluation offered by the workshop *La catalogazione verso il futuro*,[31] the Commission stated that the Paris Principles were still the basic principles although, as early as 1998, various cataloguing agencies had spoken in favour of replacing them and in the same year IFLA published FRBR, *Functional Requirements for Bibliographic Records*, that offered a new approach to the analysis of the bibliographic record. The direction has not changed in the two last years. ICCU took part officially in the Frankfurt IME ICC meeting and translated the text of the International Cataloguing Principles that began focusing on the need to go beyond the Paris Principles and to replace them with new principles:

> Over forty years later, having a common set of international cataloguing principles has become even more desirable as cataloguers and their clients use OPACs (Online Public Access Catalogues) around the world. Now, at the beginning of the 21st century, an effort has been made by IFLA to adapt the Paris Principles to objectives that are applicable to online library catalogues and beyond. The first of these objectives is to serve the convenience of the users of the catalogue. The new principles replace and broaden the Paris Principles and form an entry to all aspects of the bibliographic and authority records used in library catalogue.[32]

On the assumption that the Paris Principles were still valid, the Commissione RICA deemed it necessary to make gradual changes in the codes that may tend to harmonize rather than to re-write. The codes should envisage the possibility of "varying levels of cataloguing, even if a minimum amount of data and needed information must be retained,"[33] and should provide explanations on controversial issues: treatment of corporate bodies, form of transliterated names, the concept of intellectual responsibility, retrieval function versus bibliographic function, form of access, terminology, and abbreviations. In 2004, the Commissione RICA, on the basis of these guidelines, published a document on the form of heading for personal authors. A draft was distributed at the beginning of 2004 for preliminary verification and to gather the opinions of the library community on the proposed text. On November 13, 2004, an important response was prepared by the AIB Commission on Cataloguing and Indexing. A new version, updated to December 21, 2004, was published by ICCU; it looked more substantial and better defined (available at http://www.iccu.sbn.it/PDF/Forma_intestazione_Autore_personale.pdf (accessed February 15, 2006)).

The Commission stuck to the principle of establishing the rules in a logical, progressive, and consistent order by putting first a general rule on uniform heading followed by the rules on personal names and names of corporate bodies.

The main controversial issues in this draft dealt with: (1) separate "bibliographic identities" for the same person, (2) the preference between the original forms and forms in the language of the catalogue, and (3) keeping or dropping rules on categories and traditional exceptions.[34] On point 1, the Commissione RICA decided to retain the solution of the Paris Principles adopted by RICA; according to it, "a person, even when he/she changes name or uses different names in diverse occasions or for works of different genre, is always represented by one heading."[35] The Commission considered bibliographic identities unfeasible and decided that, theoretically, the concept of separate "bibliographic identities" seemed inconsistent."[36]

Point 2 in the proposed draft "restated the solution adopted by the Paris Principles and RICA: according to it, a uniform heading is normally based on the original form of the name, the one used in the publications in the original language rather than in translations or adaptations that may exist in the language of the catalogue or in a preferred "common" language. (Latin for the ancient and medieval world, English in some cases nowadays.)" The Commission, although it recognized the choice selected, even after the Paris Principles, by AACR and by the Spanish code as well as "the trend to give preference to translated or adapted forms that may seem more convenient for readers who have the use of translations, [. . .], also noticed that the trend towards a multicultural and intercultural society and the increasing global availability online of bibliographic data should purport an increased preference for the original form." On point 3, the goal has been to reduce exceptions or "to drop minor exceptions and to gather similar issues so as to get a simpler, clearer, and more consistent picture."[37]

Besides the workshop on "Cataloguing towards the future," there were two other important occasions for a debate on cataloguing rules: the AIB meetings in Genoa (1998) and Rome (1999). The Genoa Meeting represented a turning point. In a session openly devoted to *Il codice desiderato* [*The wished for code*],[38] several scholars declared their wish to modify RICA because the code needed updating, as asked for and hoped for by the Commission itself at the end of its sessions, in order to make it more adequate to the new evolving national and international context. In Rome, a full session was devoted to *La revisione dei codici di catalogazione: un punto di vista europeo* [*The revision of the cataloguing codes: a European point of view*][39] with the objective of discussing a question that is fundamental, as it also is for many European countries especially the ones in central Europe, on the threefold options for the revision of the Italian code:

1. to construct a new code (but, on what principles?);
2. to translate the Anglo-American code (and to adopt it *sic et sempliciter*?);
3. to graft the national tradition, if it exists, on to the roots of AACR2 (as the Spaniards did in 1995).[40]

The debate on the revision of the various national codes and the attention paid to the international situation has never lagged in Italy; on the contrary, some clues might make us see a sort of international parallel tradition that began in the eighties. In those years, AIB promoted the translation and dissemination of ISBD, *International Standard of Bibliographic Description*;[41] the standard largely took root in our libraries thanks to the great number of training courses carried out during that period. The widespread knowledge of ISBD caused the progressive but inevitable substitution (*de facto*, never officially admitted) of RICA *Parte III. Descrizione* by the appropriate ISBD.[42]

In 1997, AACR2R was translated into Italian.[43] At the same time, cataloguing terminology was studied carefully, most of all when translating IFLA standards and Dewey, so that new concepts could be rendered correctly in Italian. These efforts have brought important, innovative changes into the Italian professional vocabulary. This fact brings to light a relevant part of the history of library science yet to be analyzed and described. In recent years, Italy has constantly taken part in international meetings and has shown a slow, tireless, and qualified increase in its contribution to the theoretical debate with a twofold aspect: (1) direct participation in international events with papers presented at IFLA meetings and essays published in scholarly journals like the *Cataloging & Classification Quarterly*–a journal that recently published the proceedings of the 2003 conference on authority control in Florence;[44] and (2) the debate on the same issues in meetings organized by universities, ICCU, AIB, and other institutions with the participation of Italian scholars in the preparation of the draft and then in the revision of the text of the international cataloguing principles (IME ICC).

After the publication of FRBR, for instance, the AIB study group on cataloguing published an important contribution[45] that was highly valued at an international level. The Commissione RICA published a study: *L'applicazione del modello FRBR ai cataloghi: problemi generali e di impiego normativo.*[46] The essay by Isa De Pinedo and Alberto Petrucciani, titled *Un approccio all'applicazione del modello FRBR alle regole di catalogazione italiane: problemi e possibili soluzioni*, started a national debate on the possible use of FRBR in the construction of the Italian code. Several Italian scholars took part in this debate.[47]

The prompt dissemination of the new model provided by FRBR was due both to the translation of the *Report* by ICCU and to the presence of a favourable climate open to new solutions, no doubt thanks to the diffusion all over Italy of SBN (the National Library Service) in which the entity/relationship model was developed from the start in a consistent and convincing way. AIB has contributed to moving in this direction; its cataloguing and indexing section has produced a document that studied the draft handed out by the Commissione RICAn.[48] The document presented some important general observations followed by specific comments on each proposed rule. The AIB Cataloguing and Indexing Section pointed out a serious critical problem in the general structure of the study by the Commissione RICAn. The draft on the form of personal name cited FRBR and the revision work by IME ICC; however, the continuous, repeated reference to the Paris Principles, motivated by the RICA tradition, did not make clear what the relationship is between the layout of the future Italian code and the principles being completed at the international level. Since IME ICC is preparing a document that, according to its editors, will fully replace the Paris Principles, it is not clear what the relationship will be between the draft by the Commissione RICA and the construction of the new principles.

In other words, there is a risk that the new Italian code, when published, will be already outdated and obsolete because of its "unwavering" foundation on the Paris Principles if its editors do not take into due consideration the replacement of the Paris Principles by the ones that will be probably be titled IFLA Cataloguing Principles. Furthermore, the new Italian code should better study the distinctive features of the electronic catalogue and the online environment in which catalogues operate nowadays. It should also take care in regards to the recognition of the electronic medium as the preferred form for the creation of catalogues as well as the relationship between entities and the resulting structure of data.

Of course, the fact that we are dealing with a draft, that up to now the analysis has been limited to a single feature–uniform heading for persons–that the layout of the code may follow a structure that makes it insert the general purpose rules at the beginning, suggests a temporary softening of the authors' judgment about the substantial distance from the international context. It may be advisable to delay final evaluation until the complete draft is available. In any case, we want to highlight at least two far from irrelevant issues:

1. The stance taken by the Commissione RICA on "multiple bibliographic identities" can be fully accepted, particularly in the light of the Italian bibliographic tradition. Yet, we cannot hide the fact that the principle contradicts itself in the case of collective pseudonyms (the *see* reference from the personal name to the collective pseudonym for co-authored works is a *de facto* recognition of a different bibliographic identity);
2. With regard to the form of name, there are two possible approaches that are antithetical but forced to coexist: the original form of name and common usage. RICA, AACR2, and other codes show that they had the same problem in mind during code creation. According to the AIB Cataloguing and Indexing Commission, it must be admitted that "the original form is, on the whole, to be preferred because it seems philologically the most correct solution and because, for modern authors, it widely corresponds to the linguistic usage prevailing in Western countries (it is the name by which the author is known in the language of the bibliographic agency). Yet it may be inappropriate to make the use of the original form absolutely mandatory by enlarging its range to

cases in which it does not correspond to linguistic usage." In fact, if we consider only one approach to form, we risk creating solutions hard to share, like suggesting as original form a transliterated form or forcing the user to know the original form of Confucius or Averhoës in old Chinese or in Arabic.

Even more so, where will someone look for a work published not only in Japan or in Egypt, but also in Norway or Denmark, if it has been indexed under its original name? Under what name are geographical areas indexed since an authority record is the same in a search by author and in one by subject? We must not forget, with regard to this, the work by IFLA–not so far back in time as to deserve oblivion–on names of corporate bodies (*Form and Structure of Corporate Headings*–FSCH, 1980) and on names of persons (*Names of Persons*): "The activity for names of persons is carried out with a totally different point of view. IFLA decides not to normalize or, rather, not to give general guidelines on how to treat names of persons in the cataloguing rules, but to collect and codify the [existing] bibliographic custom." The outcome is that two publications "have similar objectives but are carried out following different notions. *Form and Structure of Corporate Headings* (FSCH) represents an international agreement edited by experts in the field. *Names of persons* enumerates national practices regarding the structure of personal names. Both methods can be justified, but obviously the results are not uniform."[49]

The document by the AIB Cataloguing and Indexing Commission goes on to state:

> In the choice between original form and linguistic usage, adopting the latter as preferred standard would lead, in many cases, to the use of the original form as preferred form but it would offer the advantage of avoiding the use of made-up or artificial forms (like the transliterated ones, particularly from non-alphabetic scripts, e.g., Japanese), or wholly imputed to a very specialized context, therefore alien to the linguistic and literary habits of most users of the catalogue.[50]

On the other hand, the founding element of the new principles is to serve the convenience of the user who speaks the vernacular and in whose favour it seems not only useful but also proper to give preference to common usage rather than to the original form.

CONCLUSIONS

In conclusion, we note that, overall, the development of the Italian rules follows a long tradition that has been able to sum up both international achievements and local specificity, albeit with a few contradictions. After the publication of RICA (1979), the lack of a permanent committee lead to a break in code revision as the need arose; we are now trying to make up for this break, a process that is not without delays and gaps. The objective is a code that can fit into the deep and safe channel of international cooperation and reconcile the local tradition with the need to harmonize with the international code of reference represented by AACR2. We consider the solution by the Spanish rules a very good one; before them, only Eva Verona with the Slavic code had succeeded in such a harmonization.

NOTES

1. The article was planned together by both authors who are in agreement on its total contents. Nevertheless, Carlo Bianchini is more responsible for Section 1 while Mauro Guerrini is more responsible for Section 2.

2. The Commissione Cibrario, officially known as "Commission on the scientific and disciplinary reorganization of the libraries in the kingdom," was instituted by the Ministry for Learning by the 20 July 1869 decree. Its task was to investigate the state of library services in Italy and to write a report whose outcome was the 24 November Royal Decree that, among other things, reorganized library services, established a new staff, classified libraries, and fixed the rules for admission to the training schools for librarians as well as the subjects in the curricula." See Attilio Mauro Caproni, "Virginia Carini Dainotti e il tema della formazione dei bibliotecari" in *Bollettino AIB*, vol. 39, n. 4 (dec. 1999), p. 436-442.

3. Giovanni Galli, *Regole italiane di catalogazione per autori tra Ottocento e Novecento*, Milano, Editrice Bibliografica, 1989, p. 49.

4. Giuseppe Fumagalli, *Cataloghi di biblioteca e indici bibliografici. Memoria di Giuseppe Fumagalli [. . .] premiata dal Ministero della istruzione pubblica nel 1° Concorso bibliografico*, Firenze, Sansoni, 1887.

5. Giovanni Galli, *Regole . . .* , cit., p. 59.

6. Giuseppe Fumagalli, *Cataloghi di biblioteca . . .* , cit., p. 116-117.

7. Galli remarks on the work of the famous Italian librarian: "*Cataloghi di biblioteca* is much more than a code to construct catalogues. If we agree that this activity is the heart of librarianship, we can state that the work by Fumagalli represents the start of the Italian librarianship not for its prescriptive content but for the way it organizes issues for its overall view of the object." (Giovanni Galli, *Regole . . .* , cit., p. 75).

8. The rules were organized as follows: Chapter I. On the catalogue and the entries; Chapter II. Entry word; Chapter III. The content of the entry; Chapter IV. Spelling and conventional signs. Appendix I. Incunabula.

9. The commission is made up of: Ettore Apollonj, chair; Nella Santovito Vichi, referent; Fernanda Ascarelli, Francesco Barberi, Marcella Bozza Mariani, Maria Marchetti, Emerenziana Vaccaro Sofia.

10. *Regole per la compilazione del catalogo alfabetico per autori nelle biblioteche italiane*, Roma, Fratelli Palombi, 1956, p. XI [from now onwards 1965]. The rules are signed by the commission members: Ettore Apollonj, chair; Nella Santovito Vichi, referent; Fernanda Ascarelli, Francesco Barberi, Marcella Bozza Mariani, Maria Marchetti, Emerenziana Vaccaro Sofia.

11. However, some appendices were added to the 1922 index: Appendix II. Geographical prints. Appendix III. Prints and Engravings. Appendix IV. Music. Appendix V. Transliterations. Appendix VI Abbreviations. Appendix VII Entry Arrangement. Analytical Index.

12. 1956 Rules, p. XII-XIII.

13. Ibid.

14. The 1956 Rules have a *Chapter I On the catalogue and the entries* that was a sort of glossary since it gave definitions for the basic concepts in the code. (i.e. Catalogue, alphabetical author catalogue, entry, entry word, author, anonymous works, title, etc.). The entries were classified as *main entries*, "the ones with a full description of a work"; *analytical entries*, "the ones for writings joined to another work or inside polygraphic collections"; see also references, "the ones that link a secondary author or title to the author or title in the main entry"; *see references* "the ones that simply refer from the form of an entry word to another." See the 1956 Rules, p. 1 and 2. See also RICA 139.

15. See Diego Maltese, "Contributo alla revisione delle Regole italiane di catalogazione per autori" in *Accademie e biblioteche d'Itala*, year 33, n. 4-5 (July-Oct. 1965), p. 283.

16. See Diego Maltese, "I principi internazionali di catalogazione" in *Accademie e biblioteche d'Italia*, year 30, n. 5-6 (Sept.-Dec. 1962), p. 258-269, particularly p. 268-269.

17. The events taking place between the approval of the Paris Principles and RICA are presented in Mauro Guerrini, "Il dibattito in Italia sulle norme di catalogazione per autore dalla Conferenza di Parigi alle RICA" in Id., *Riflessioni su principi, standard, regole e applicazioni. Saggi di storia, teoria e tecnica della catalogazione*, Udine, Forum, 1999, p. 45-92.

18. Diego Maltese, "Elementi di catalogazione per autori. Scelta e forma dell'intestazione" in *Accademie e biblioteche d'Italia*, year 34, n. 4 (July-Aug. 1966), p. 209-223. ID., *Principi di catalogazione e regole italiane*, Firenze, Olschki, 1965.

19. Carlo Revelli, Review in *Bollettino d'informazioni. Associazione italiana biblioteche*, year 6, n. 1 (Jan..-Feb. 1966), p. 23-32.

20. The Commission members are Francesco Barberi (chair), Diego Maltese (referent), Carola Ferrari, Carlo Revelli, Maria Valenti, Angela Vinay, and Giovannella Golisano (secretary); later two non-specialist university and library members were added: Maria Califano and Simonetta Nicolini.

21. Mauro Guerrini, "Il dibattito in Italia . . .," cit., p. 70.

22. *Regole italiane di catalogazione per autori*, Roma, ICCU, 1979, [from now onwards RICA], p. VIII.

23. RICA, p. IX.

24. RICA, p. XI.

25. Alberto Petrucciani, *Struttura delle norme di scelta dell'intestazione: le RICA e i nuovi modelli di analisi*, 2002, available on line at: http://www.iccu.sbn.it/ (accessed February 15, 2006).

26. RICA, p. XII.

27. Mauro Guerrini, "Ente autore? Un concetto assente dai Principi di Parigi," box inside ID., "Il trattamento catalografico degli enti collettivi dalla Conferenza di Parigi (1961) al First IFLA Meeting of Experts on an International Cataloguing Code (2003)," collaboration by Pino Buizza and Lucia Sardo, in *Biblioteche oggi*, year 21, n. 10 (Dec. 2003), p. 40; the full essay is on pages 37-53.

28. Mauro Guerrini, Pino Buizza, "Il controllo del punto di accesso alla registrazione per autore e titolo. Riflessioni sul comportamento delle principali agenzie bibliografiche nazionali a quarant'anni dai Principi di Parigi"; Paper presented at the workshop sponsored by ICCU, "Catalogazione e controllo di autorità, Giornate di studio," Rome, 21-22 novembre 2002. published in English as background paper, available on line at the IME ICC site: http://www.ddb.de/news/ilfa_conf_index.htm; presented in Spanish too at the 2004 Buenos Aires IME ICC2.

29. Mauro Guerrini, "La lingua del catalogo. Sulla forma del nome degli autori greci, latini, dell'oriente antico, del periodo medievale e umanistico, dei papi e dei santi," in Id., *Il catalogo di qualità*, Firenze, Regione Toscana Giunta Regionale, Pagnini e Martinelli, 2002, p. 51-85.

30. See http://www.iccu.sbn.it/ricacom.html (accessed February 15, 2006).

31. Ibid.

32. ICCU, *La catalogazione verso il futuro : normative, accessi, costi : Atti del seminario Roma, 13 marzo 1998*, Roma, ICCU, 1998.

33. See the Italian translation at the ICCU site: http://www.iccu.sbn.it/PDF/Traduzione_Principi.pdf (accessed February 15, 2006).

34. Cristina Magliano, "La Commissione RICA e la sua attività," 21 November 2002, available on line at: http://www.iccu.sbn.it/ricaaf.html (accessed February 15, 2006).

35. These themes had been dealt with and debated critically in Mauro Guerrini, *Riflessioni su principi, standard, regole e applicazioni*, cit, and in Id., *Il catalogo di qualità*, cit., two collections of essays previously published in several journals.

36. Commissione RICA, *Intestazione uniforme – Persone (testo aggiornato al 21 dicembre 2004)*, p. 1, available online at: http://www.iccu.sbn.it/PDF/Forma_intestazione_Autore_personale.pdf (accessed February 15, 2006).

37. Mauro Guerrini, Pino Buizza, "Il controllo del punto di accesso alla registrazione per autore e titolo," cit. hold the same opinion.

38. Ibid.

39. See MAURO GUERRINI, "Il codice desiderato. Verso RICA2? : evoluzione o rivoluzione?," in: *AIB 98. Atti del XLIV Congresso nazionale dell'Associazione italiana biblioteche, Genova, 28-30 aprile 1998*, by Fernanda Canepa and Graziano Ruffini, Roma, Associazione italiana biblioteche, 2001, p. 216-218; also vailable on line at: http://www.aib.it/aib/congr/co98rica.htm (accessed February 15, 2006).

40. See *AIB 99. Atti del XLV Congresso nazionale dell'Associazione italiana biblioteche, Roma, 16-19 maggio 1999*, by Enzo Frustaci and Mauro Guerrini, Roma, Associazione italiana biblioteche, 2001; also available online at: http://www.aib.it/aib/congr/co99index.htm (accessed February 15, 2006).

41. Mauro Guerrini, "La revisione dei codici di catalogazione: un punto di vista europeo. Nota introduttiva," in: *AIB 99* , cit., p. 82-83; also available on line at: http://www.aib.it/aib/congr/co99guerrini.htm (accessed February 15, 2006).

42. For ISBD translated into Italian, by AIB and later by ICCU, see http://www.ifla.org/VI/3/nd1/isbdital.htm (accessed February 15, 2006).

43. See Istituto centrale per il catalogo unico delle biblioteche italiane e per le informazioni bibliografiche, *Guida alla catalogazione nell'ambito del Servizio bibliotecario nazionale*, Roma, ICCU, 1987. The 1995 second edition is titled: *Guida alla catalogazione in SBN. Pubblicazioni monografiche, pubblicazioni in serie*. See the other guides published by ICCU and by other institutions.

44. *Regole di catalogazione angloamericane : seconda edizione, revisione del 1988*, redatte sotto la direzione del Joint steering committee for revision of AACR: the American Library Association, the Australian Committee on Cataloguing, the British Library, the Canadian Committee on Cataloguing, the Library Association, the Library of Congress, a cura di Michael Gorman e Paul W. Winkler. Edizione italiana a cura di Rossella Dini e Luigi Crocetti, Milano, Editrice Bibliografica, [1997].

45. *Authority control in organizing and accessing information: definition and international experience*. Part I [and] Part II, Arlene G. Taylor, Barbara B. Tillett, guest editors, with the assistance of Mauro Guerrini and Murtha Baca, in "Cataloging & classification quarterly," vol. 38, nos. 3-4 (2004); vol. 39, nos. 1-2 (2004); also published as a monograph: New York, The Haworth Information Press, [2004]; the Italian version is edited by Mauro Guerrini and Barbara B. Tillett, with cooperation by Lucia Sardo, [Firenze], Firenze University Press; [Roma], Associazione italiana biblioteche, 2003).

46. AIB. Gruppo di studio sulla catalogazione, "Osservazioni su Functional requirements for bibliographic records : final report," *Bollettino AIB*, vol. 39, n. 3 (Sept. 1999), p. 303-311.

47. Cfr. http://www.iccu.sbn.it/PDF/rica-frbr.pdf [sic] (accessed February 15, 2006).

48. See Carlo Ghilli, Mauro Guerrini, Antonella Novelli, "FRBR: analisi del record e nuovi codici di catalogazione," *Bollettino AIB*, 43 (2002), 2 (June), p. 145-159.

49. See http://www.aib.it/aib/commiss/catal/rica01.htm (accessed February 15, 2006).

50. Mauro Guerrini, Lucia Sardo, *Authority control*, Roma, Associazione italiana biblioteche, 2003, p. 38.

51. Commissione, p. 3.

doi:10.1300/J104v44n01_09

PART III: RESEARCH STUDIES

Technical Services and Tenure: Impediments and Strategies

Janet Swann Hill

SUMMARY. Although the appropriateness of faculty status for technical services librarians serving in academic libraries is often debated, these librarians usually share the same personnel status as other librarians in the same institution. The success of technical services librarians in achieving tenure is explored, along with perceptions about the relative ease with which they may attain it. Possible impediments to success are identified, with special focus on the portrayal and evaluation of the practice of librarianship, as distinct from scholarly or service pursuits. Strategies for countering these impediments are suggested. doi:10.1300/J104v44n03_01 *[Article copies available for a fee from The Haworth Document Delivery Service: 1-800-HAWORTH. E-mail address: <docdelivery@haworthpress.com> Website: <http://www.HaworthPress.com> © 2007 by The Haworth Press, Inc. All rights reserved.]*

Janet Swann Hill is Professor and Associate Director for Technical Services, University of Colorado Libraries, CB 184, Boulder, CO 80309 (E-mail: Janet.hill@colorado.edu).

[Haworth co-indexing entry note]: "Technical Services and Tenure: Impediments and Strategies." Hill, Janet Swann. Co-published simultaneously in *Cataloging & Classification Quarterly* (The Haworth Information Press, an imprint of The Haworth Press, Inc.) Vol. 44, No. 3/4, 2007, pp. 151-178; and: *Cataloger, Editor, and Scholar: Essays in Honor of Ruth C. Carter* (ed: Robert P. Holley) The Haworth Information Press, an imprint of The Haworth Press, Inc., 2007, pp. 151-178. Single or multiple copies of this article are available for a fee from The Haworth Document Delivery Service [1-800-HAWORTH, 9:00 a.m. - 5:00 p.m. (EST). E-mail address: docdelivery@haworthpress.com].

Available online at http://ccq.haworthpress.com
© 2007 by The Haworth Press, Inc. All rights reserved.
doi:10.1300/J104v44n03_01

KEYWORDS. Tenure, faculty status, technical services, evaluation, catalogers

INTRODUCTION

Faculty status for academic librarians has been a topic of discussion in the United States for nearly a century, but the first official endorsement of the concept by a professional association (the American Library Association Committee on the Classification of Library Personnel) did not come until 1929; the University of Illinois became the first major academic institution to grant faculty status to librarians in 1944.[1,2] Fifteen more years passed before the Association of College & Research Libraries (ACRL) endorsed faculty status as a right of academic librarians; and, in 1971, a formal statement was issued jointly by ACRL, the American Association of University Professors, and the Association of American Colleges.[3]

The ACRL standard has been revised and updated over the years, most recently in 2001; but its provisions have remained essentially the same. The basic rationale for faculty status is that:

> The academic librarian makes unique contributions to the academic community and to higher education itself. These contributions range from developing collections to providing bibliographic access to all library materials and interpreting these materials to members of the college and university community. Specific services include instruction in the use of print and online library resources and the creation of new tools to enhance access to information available locally, regionally, nationally, or internationally.

Aspects of faculty status covered by the standard include such things as independence of judgment, peer review, faculty governance and participation, compensation, promotion, tenure, leaves, support, and academic freedom.[4]

It is difficult to assess the impact of ACRL's endorsement of faculty status as there have been only sporadic studies conducted; and they have often utilized slightly different methodologies, had a different focus, used different definitions of faculty status,[5] or surveyed a different subset of institutions. In 1981, based on a survey of 836 academic libraries, DePew reported that nearly 79% of academic librarians were covered by some form of faculty status.[6] In 1982, English surveyed members of the Association of Research Libraries (ARL), and found that 61.4% of state institutions and 18.7% of private institutions had granted their librarians faculty status.[7] A 1989 study by Park and Riggs found that librarians at 41% of institutions surveyed enjoyed faculty status,[8] while, nine years later, Lowery determined that an aggregate of 67% of higher education institutions grant their librarians faculty status.[9]

Such inconsistency of data led one author (Lowery) to conclude that: "In general, faculty status for librarians has been vigorously expanded [in the twenty years between 1970 and 1990], though the process has slowed in recent years,"[10] while another (English) could postulate that the shift from non-faculty to faculty status had "run its course" and that a reversal may have begun.[11] Still another interpretation might be that following a period in which faculty status for academic librarians was adopted by a majority of institutions, a kind of stable state has been reached with few libraries either adopting faculty status anew or discontinuing it.[12]

Regardless of the inconsistency of results, these studies have nevertheless revealed much of interest. They have shown, for instance, that "major private institutions [are] much less likely to grant faculty status to librarians than [are] comparable state institutions"[13] and that comprehensive universities are more likely to grant such status to librarians than are institutions in all the other Carnegie classifications;[14] further, not all those that offer faculty status offer the possibility of gaining tenure.[15] Among those that do, there are often significant differences from institution to institution as regards titles and ranks, review processes, facets of work evaluated and their relative weights, and expectations for tenure or promotion.[16] Indeed, Chait's observation regarding teaching faculty, that " . . . identical or similar policies yield considerably different norms and interpretations when actually implemented. In other words, to understand how tenure works on one campus is to understand how tenure works on one campus"[17] appears to be at least equally true for library faculty, if not more so. Such widespread differences make generalization difficult. Those seeking to understand either general or particular situations, therefore, or to find solutions to existing problems must look for commonalities and have a certain tolerance for dissimilarities.

THE MINORITY CULTURE

Notwithstanding the consistency of ACRL's stand, the validity and desirability of faculty status for academic librarians will probably always remain a matter of debate. Points raised in opposition are varied, but most have at their core the reality that the faculty status and tenure system was originally devised to be used by a different profession.[18] The language, values, and mechanisms reflect what is effective and relevant for those whose primary practice of profession is teaching. Although it is true that some librarians may teach as a part of their practice of profession and that all academic librarians contribute to the teaching enterprise in some fashion, librarians who may be covered by the same general faculty policies as the teaching faculty nevertheless represent a minority culture on their campuses.

As a minority culture, librarians have limited power to affect the overall faculty and tenure policies of their institutions. Even as they modify general policies to suit the needs of their own unit, librarians may be prohibited from, or reluctant to make, major changes in the language, structure, values, expectations, weights, or mechanisms of evaluation. Instead, faculty librarians use the language and system of the majority culture and interpret it as best they can in ways that are relevant to librarianship.[19] In pursuit of practices that will be understood and honored by the majority, they may even choose to surrender to the power structure and impose some of the requirements of the teaching faculty upon themselves, even if those requirements may not be entirely appropriate.[20]

Most discussions of faculty status and tenure for academic librarians are held from the perspective of a generic Everylibrarian. But just as librarians represent a minority culture on a college or university campus, technical services librarians, most of who are catalogers, represent a minority culture within librarianship. Therefore, while a system originally written for teaching faculty can be a difficult fit for library faculty, a system modified for the majority of library faculty can be a difficult fit for technical services librarians. Considering the numbers of public and technical services librarians in libraries, within any one academic institution there has almost certainly been less experience in tenuring librarians in technical services and an accompanying lesser understanding of challenges that may exist for them. Further, most of those involved in formulation of documents and practices have probably been public services librarians. In some instances, questions may be raised as to whether technical services work is so different that some or all technical services librarians should not have the same faculty status as other librarians;[21] and, among technical services librarians, there is often speculation as to whether it is harder for them to achieve tenure than it is for librarians in other areas.

METHODOLOGY

In order to assess the status and success of technical services librarians with relation to achieving tenure and to gather information about what aspects of their practice of librarianship might contribute to their greater or lesser success, in the fall of 2005, two Web-based surveys were opened on Zoomerang. The surveys were nearly identical, with only such differences as were dictated by how the invitation to participate was formulated.

An invitation to participate in the first survey (called the Closed Survey) was sent to technical services directors or their nearest equivalent in member libraries of the Association of Research Libraries (ARL) where librarians had faculty status with the possibility of achieving tenure.[22] This separate survey was used to assure at least some input from larger libraries, based on the author's supposition that such libraries are likely to have encountered more instances of technical services librarians' being reviewed for tenure and that they might also be more likely to have created special mechanisms for evaluation or review. The author belongs to this target group and also completed the survey. Her answers contribute to the statistics, but her responses to open-ended questions are not quoted. The text of the closed survey may be found in Appendix 1.

An invitation to participate in the second survey (called the Open Survey) was sent to the electronic discussion group AUTOCAT.[23] This message invited individuals who had experience at an academic library where librarians are tenure-stream faculty to visit the Zoomerang site and complete the survey.

Questions 1 through 5 asked about the degree to which technical services librarians are part of the tenure system that exists for other librarians in the same institution. Questions 6 through 8 sought information about whether tenure standards as written or applied make achieving tenure as easy (or hard) for technical services librarians as for others and what kinds of things are most problematic. These first questions set a context for the primary focus of the paper, which was addressed through the comments sections of questions 5, 7, and 8 plus questions 9, 10, and 13. This group of questions elicited open-ended comments about issues that have a special impact on technical services librarians and about evaluation strategies that libraries have implemented to assist technical services librarians to achieve tenure. Numbers used in this paper correspond to the question numbering of the survey.

Both the invitation to participate in the survey and individual survey questions indicated that information was being sought concerning the facet of work termed the Practice of Librarianship. For technical services librarians, this includes such activities as cataloging, workflow management, personnel supervision, etc.; and it is in this facet of their work that technical services librarians differ most from their colleagues. Examination of how technical services librarians fare with regard to scholarly work and service was not undertaken.[24] Because it is, however, impossible to separate issues related to scholarly work and service from librarianship entirely, to the extent they are intertwined, they are included in the discussions that follow.

Invitations to complete the Closed Survey resulted in forty-one visits, six partial responses, and twenty-four completed surveys. The open invitation elicited one hundred and forty visits, twenty-two partial responses, and ninety-five completed surveys. Figures and comments contained in this paper are derived from completed surveys only. Because respondents to the Open Survey were self-selected and no control was exercised against the possibility of more than one response from a given institution, statistics from the two surveys are not combined. Answers to the open-ended questions on both surveys were coded as to content and considered together. When a single comment touched on more than one issue, all were coded.

DISCUSSION OF RESULTS

To what degree are technical services librarians part of the tenure system that exists for other librarians in the same institution? (Questions 1-5)

1. Do librarians at your institution have faculty status, with the possibility of earning tenure?

The purpose of this question was to provide an early exit for those who might have no relevant experience to bring to the survey. One response to the Closed Survey and two responses to the Open Survey were received from individuals at institutions where librarians do not have faculty status with the possibility of earning tenure. Two of these respondents took the early exit and answered no other questions; the third answered the survey based on relevant experience derived from a previous position.

2. Do promotion and tenure recommendations for library faculty receive substantive review by a body or officer outside the library? (Substantive review evaluates the merit of the candidate's record and could conceivably lead to a recommendation at odds with the library's own recommendation.)

If tenure review is conducted by librarians and if recommendations from the library are accepted without question by the parent institution, there may be little need for a library to pay particular attention to the language of tenure justifications or to devise special evaluative mechanisms. When a library's tenure recommendations receive substantive review by faculty and/or university administrators who may know little of libraries or the disciplinary norms of librarianship, the library may need to take considerable care to provide standards, processes, and evaluation that will be understood by these outsiders. Because 82% of respondents to the Closed Survey and 78% of respondents to the Open Survey indicated that tenure recommendations receive substantive review outside the library, findings concerning tenure evaluation for technical services librarians are potentially of interest to a large segment of academic libraries.

3. Do all librarians in your library have equal access to tenure stream positions?

Seventy-eight percent of respondents to the Closed Survey and 80% of respondents to the Open Survey indicated that all librarians at their institutions had equal access to tenure stream positions.

4. If all librarians do not have equal access to tenure stream positions, what types of positions have lesser or no access to tenure stream employment?

Even though discussions of faculty status and tenure for technical services librarians often include debate about the appropriateness of that status for these librarians, occurrences of exclusion appear to be uncommon (represented by two respondents to the Closed Survey and five respondents to the Open Survey). Circulation librarians are just as likely to be denied tenure stream status, and both administrators and systems librarians are at least twice as likely to be denied that status. Most other librarians reported as being hired outside the tenure stream were exceptional hires, such as temporary appointments, visiting faculty, spousal hires, and interns.

5. *What is the rationale for such exceptions? What do you see as the advantages or disadvantages of exceptions being made?*

Rationales for excluding exceptional hires are outside the scope of this paper. Rationales offered for excluding particular types of librarians (catalogers, other technical services librarians, circulation librarians, systems librarians, and some administrators) are very similar and are harbingers of specific issues mentioned in response to later questions. They are typified by the following responses:

- "The new university president has interpreted the [Board of Regents] policies in such a way that may force all faculty ranked librarians to teach semester long courses."
- "The administration decided these librarians did not have an academic function."
- "Technical Services Librarians have fewer opportunities to work with the public and there is a myth that Acquisitions and Cataloging Librarians are reclusive."

Administrators may be excluded for reasons cited above; but they may also be excluded because of a union contract, because of campus-wide practice, or in order not to enable the dean to "return to the faculty" should s/he cease to be dean. Because these results suggest that many different types of librarians may be at some disadvantage in a tenure process and for similar reasons, observations made for technical services librarians may be applicable beyond this one specialty.

Relatively few respondents ventured an opinion as to the advantages or disadvantages of excluding technical services librarians from the tenure process. Two respondents observed that not being on the tenure track made it possible for incumbents to spend more time on "their substantive duties" (e.g., cataloging). Four mentioned greater ease in hiring as an advantage, but for different reasons: a less complicated hiring process; possible greater ease in attracting candidates to a non-tenure stream position; difficulty finding systems librarians with library credentials; and ability to hire graduates of the library program at the same university. Disadvantages cited included the creation of a "class" system among librarians; inability to involve all librarians in faculty governance; an invitation to the university to ask why any librarians should be faculty; and lack of job security for the individual. Another disadvantage, mentioned in a previous AUTOCAT discussion by Evans, is less flexibility to move from one position to another within a library.[25]

Is it harder for technical services librarians to achieve tenure than it is for other types of librarians? (Questions 6-8, plus relevant comments from question 13)

6. In terms of success in achieving tenure as compared to librarians in other positions, are technical services librarians equally/more/less successful than librarians in other positions?

Only four percent of respondents to the Closed Survey and 11% of respondents to the Open Survey indicated that technical services librarians were less successful than their colleagues in achieving tenure. One respondent to the Open Survey reported that technical services librarians were more successful.

7. If technical services librarians are not as successful as other librarians in achieving tenure at your institution, what factors do you believe contribute to this situation?

Of the five responses in the Closed Survey and thirty responses in the Open Survey, two attributed lack of success merely to individual failure of particular candidates to meet standards–the sort of thing that may befall any librarian regardless of specialty. All other responses citing special problems facing technical services librarians fell into the categories of comments given in response to question 8 and many of the responses to question 13. In order not to fragment discussion of these points, all of these answers are considered as a group in the "Comments Combined" section below.

8. Regardless of the actual record of librarians achieving tenure, do you or others perceive that technical services librarians have a more difficult time achieving tenure than their colleagues in other positions? If yes, please explain.

Thirty-five percent of respondents to the Closed Survey and 49% of respondents to the Open Survey believed that despite a near-equal success rate at achieving tenure, technical services librarians have a more difficult time accomplishing it than do many of their colleagues.

Comments combined: Impediments or factors contributing to differential tenure experience for technical services librarians

In this section, comments from questions 7 and 8 and relevant comments from question 13 on both surveys are considered together. Impediments noted fell into relatively few main categories. In the order of frequency mentioned, these include: workload and time management; job content; exposure, involvement and participation; understanding of the work; and majority vs. minority Culture.

Workload and Time Management: Two major workload themes emerged. The first concerned the structure of technical services jobs, especially as contrasted to the structure of public services jobs. The second theme was related to giving appropriate attention to the different facets of work to be done. Representative comments related to job structure include these:

- "Reference librarians have set times when they are 'on' and 'off' the desk. When they are off, they can perform other tasks. Technical services librarians are never officially 'off' their usual duties. They have to fit tenure related tasks around their primary tasks."
- "Generally, public services librarians have more time to work on articles for publication during their regular work week. Technical services librarians have to set aside a specific block of time, and it doesn't always happen."
- "The work load of technical services librarians is constant year round. Our college has not had summer classes, and even during [the] semester there is a certain flu[ct]uation in demand on the reference librarians' time, so the reference work load is more 'seasonal.'"

No doubt reference librarians would point out that their reference work is not limited to the time they spend sitting at the desk; but nevertheless, in the words of another respondent: "The perception is that non-Tech Services librarians have more free time available than those in Tech Services." Regardless of the accuracy of this perception, the comments above highlight two critical kinds of separation often not available to technical services librarians, perhaps especially to catalogers. The first is the ability to separate time into relatively brief periods of being "on call" and longer periods when it may be possible to make personal decisions about how to use available time. The second is the physical and mental demarcation between the public "on call" location and the more private behind-the-scenes location. Comments related to prioritizing among the facets of job content included these:

- "Technical Services librarians are generally in a very production oriented position and, in my exper[ie]nce, often feel they can't–or shouldn't–use 'work' time developing, researching, writing, and publishing."
- "I find it difficult to stop cataloging and spend time on scholarly pursuits, when I know there is so much to be done."
- "Our cataloguers have a quota in terms of the number of titles catalogued per period. It makes it more difficult for them to focus on research activities."

The comments above were selected to illustrate one effect of imperfect communication or understanding of the full scope of a faculty member's job. In an academic library, that job includes day-to-day librarianship responsibilities (such as cataloging or running an acquisitions department); scholarly endeavors; and professional, institutional, or disciplinary service. Consequently, work spent on scholarly pursuits is just as much a part of a cataloger's job as is cataloging. If, however, some faculty are allowed or encouraged to view scholarly work and service as irrelevant add-ons, they may easily see the never-ending flow of information resources to be acquired, cataloged, or preserved as an invitation to shortchange scholarly work or service, which may in turn be an impediment to their ability to achieve tenure. An additional issue highlighted by these comments is the questionable practice of using numeric quotas to evaluate any faculty member, much less to use numbers to evaluate some faculty and not others.

Job Content: The content of the librarianship portion of a technical services faculty member's job can be problematic as it often lacks at least one activity (teaching) that is generally expected in the dossier of a member of the teaching faculty and may often contain activities (management or supervision) that are generally not part of a teacher's dossier. This may be especially serious if standards for performance evaluation for library faculty too closely mirror that of the teaching faculty and have not been appropriately modified or sensitively expressed to reflect the work of librarians. Respondents commented on this general issue as follows:

- "Since the university criteria for tenure include scholarship, service, and teaching, if technical services librarians don't "teach," they have difficulty with that criteri[on]."
- "Many faculty . . . do not think [librarians] should have faculty rank. When faced with the prospect of giving tenure to a librarian, the Technical Services Librarian is the easiest to deny due to lack of teaching responsibility."

Other possible consequences of a too strict requirement for teaching may be imposition of work perceived as extra and of not having the type of teaching and training that technical services librarians do considered teaching for the purpose of evaluation:

- "My perception as a Tech Services librarian is that we have to do extra work, since measurements are based largely on instruction/reference, so the more of such that we do, the better (even though it's on top of our tech services duties)."
- " . . . training staff in ILS and OCLC workflow is not considered teaching on par with that of the teaching faculty."
- "While describing training and presentations as teaching isn't much of a stretch, trying to describe cataloging as teaching is. It supports the instructional program, of course, but it isn't really teaching and trying to describe it as such was quite a stretch."

Meanwhile, the management and supervisory work that is commonly performed by technical services librarians is easily misperceived. For teaching faculty, management is most often seen as something that is performed as a temporary assignment outside normal faculty responsibilities for which additional compensation is granted and which necessitates lesser attention to the scholarly agenda for the duration of the management assignment. One respondent put it succinctly: "[Technical Services] librarians have management responsibilities which [are] not valued by academic departments as important for tenure decisions."

Exposure and Involvement: Tenure and promotion processes frequently rely on assembling a dossier that includes information and evaluation from many sources and also upon the knowledge and judgment of individuals who sit on review committees. Because technical services librarians are not engaged in direct user services, exposure to two important constituencies (non-library faculty and students) from whom to draw evaluators or by which to inform review committee members is usually limited. It is troubling to note that respondents also identified their own library faculty colleagues as a constituency with which they might have too little interaction. Representative comments about exposure to these groups include:

- "[Technical services librarians have no] exposure to academic departmental faculty who often sit on university committees making decisions."
- "... technical services librarians tend not to do the glitzy work that is easily seen by the public and the administration. The public services librarian will often be noticed for creating a nice web page, we never get noticed for creating a great bib record ... so we do not get the written thanks to include in our tenure packet."
- "Technical services librarians do not participate in reference desk service or bibliographic instruction, therefore contact with faculty and students who might provide evaluations, letters of reference, etc., is naturally limited."
- "[Another problem is] their lesser visibility in the library, both physically (we are in the basement), and metaphorically (the effects of good cataloging are not readily visible to all other librarians in the institution)."

Understanding of the work: Teaching faculty may have some intellectual appreciation of the work involved in providing reference service, doing bibliographic instruction, or building collections through resource selection because each of these activities is similar to some aspect of their own job. Understanding the work of technical services, appreciating its professional or intellectual nature, and comprehending its contribution to the teaching enterprise is more difficult. Few teaching faculty may ever make the effort, and few library faculty would expect them to. Even some library faculty may have limited understanding or appreciation of the nature of technical services work. When technical services faculty must rely on effective internal review by their library colleagues and on fair external review by members of the teaching faculty, lack of understanding of the work being evaluated can constitute a serious problem. Many survey respondents identified this as an issue worthy of concern, and their comments illustrate a number of different perspectives from which the work can be misperceived.

- "There is a pronounced tendency among the public services librarians at my institution to view both TS and Systems work as 'non-professional,' clerical, second-class, etc. And since the outside faculty might rely on the librarians on a committee to interpret material in the personnel file, well, it's the blind leading the blind."
- "While all the TS librarians have worked at the Reference Desk, only 1 of the reference librarians had TS experience. This means evaluation of a TS librarian's work is being done by people with no experience in that area."
- "It's much easier for those outside the library to understand what the User Service/Reference/BI librarians do. Much harder to translate cataloging into teaching and not let it seem as if we're mere technicians."
- "The difficulty is in preparing a tenure portfolio which explains the role of a technical services librarian in a manner that [helps] teaching faculty... understand how the T.S. position contributes to academic teaching."

Majority vs. Minority Culture: Finally, a wide variety of comments was received that can best be categorized as illustrating some of the difficulties that arise from being in the minority. These range from having criteria for evaluation and content of dossiers skewed toward the needs of the majority; to limited representation on committees or in development of standards and expectations; to the consequences of being part of a small community. Relevant comments included these:

- "Technical services librarians also typically score lower in internal evaluations than other librarians, probably because the criteria are skewed towards public services duties."
- "Tech. services has traditionally been staffed mostly by para-professionals, so the few professional librarians have little opportunity for professional mentoring or networking within the unit."
- "It can appear that the tenure requirements are geared more toward public services positions and tech. services applicants have the onus of interpreting the requirements and translating them into what is applicable to tech. services librarians that can be understood by public services librarians as well as those outside of the library who will see the documentation."
- "TS librarians are fewer in number, and consequently have less representation on the library tenure evaluation committee . . ."

What strategies might help technical services librarians achieve tenure? (Questions 9-10 and 13)

9. Has your library developed any special procedures for evaluating the practice of librarianship of Technical Services librarians for the purpose of improving their chances of achieving tenure by making their records more understandable to others, by making their dossiers look more like those of other librarians, etc.?

Four percent of respondents to the Closed Survey and 11% of respondents to the Open Survey indicated that their institutions had developed special procedures for evaluation of technical services librarians. None of the institutions where it was reported that technical services librarians were less successful at achieving tenure than their colleagues had developed special procedures. Remembering how many respondents reported a perception that it is more difficult for technical services librarians to gain tenure than it is for other librarians and that respondents identified numerous factors that contributed to this difficulty, it is sobering to note that so few libraries appear to have tried to implement strategies to ease the situation. In some cases, inaction may be a reflection of attitudes expressed through comments such as: "It is up to the untenured to make sure that the system works for them," and "There is no reason that all are not equal unless they are lazy." Other possibilities might include a perception of inability to influence the institution at large, a bias against action, or even a belief that technical services librarians are not part of the teaching enterprise. Alternatively, inaction may spring simply from not yet having recognized or articulated the problem or from not having appropriate models to follow.

10. If your library has developed such procedures, please describe them. (Examples of such mechanisms might be: (1) Training and presentations evaluated as teaching; (2) Interviewing library colleagues about a candidate's work; (3) Soliciting evaluation of librarianship from outside experts, from their personal knowledge, by sending samples of a candidate's work, etc.)

Examination of answers to question 9 suggests that the number of libraries that have developed special evaluative mechanisms is even smaller than survey results indicate as many of the responses concerned not mechanisms of evaluation but strategies for support, and many described practices that are equally valid for librarians in any specialty.

Given the eagerness with which respondents appeared to be trying to identify any practices that benefit technical services librarians, all are considered below in the order of number of comments received.

Mentoring and involvement of senior library faculty: Many different aspects of mentoring were touched upon by survey respondents including: providing a good example to junior faculty; providing encouragement; helping to identify opportunities for service involvement or scholarly work; communicating expectations; clarifying processes; advising as to the content and presentation of tenure documentation; and carrying out a yearly "progress assessment" for all pre-tenured faculty. Mentoring is not specific to technical services librarians; but, given that they tend to be few in number in any given library, it might be argued that they have greater need of purposive mentoring than their public services colleagues. Mentoring is also not an evaluative strategy; but, to the extent that mentoring crosses departmental boundaries, it may result in better-informed evaluation and review by librarians who do not share the same disciplinary specialty.

Effective description of the job and creation of specific performance criteria: It has already been noted in the "Comments combined" section that those who participate in tenure reviews, especially non-library faculty, may have little understanding of the work performed by those in technical services. It should be no surprise, therefore, that a number of respondents identified providing an effective description of the job as being important to a successful tenure review. It was variously noted that such descriptions should "focus on the end product and the impact on library patrons," "emphasize the enduring aspect of what we do (bib records and authority records last a very long time in databases) and also the impact (international database)," and "use language and examples that... would indicate the impact of what we do in a way that was understandable to those who don't understand cataloging."

Even the most thorough description of a job and the most heartrending explanation of its impact on the academic enterprise may not enable reviewers to assess how well a candidate has performed. Several respondents mentioned use of a set of evaluative criteria tailored to job content. Such a document can serve a variety of functions in the tenure process. It can serve as ongoing guidance to the candidate, provide an organizational structure for a candidate's self-statement, provide an organizational structure for evaluative statements supplied by supervisors or other colleagues, and expand on information provided in the general description of the position. It may also give rise to separate evaluation mechanisms and explain the significance of some of the content of the dossier. Care should be taken to assess performance in terms other than numbers produced. Criteria expressed in terms of such attributes as timeliness, effectiveness, thoroughness, independence, creativity, contribution, mastery, flexibility, and service will be much more persuasive.

Composition of Review Committees: When the content and import of work being evaluated for tenure is not well understood by a majority of peers, the composition of review committees can be critical. One respondent who was about to undergo tenure review observed somewhat ruefully that the internal tenure review committee currently had no members who had any technical services experience. Another said: "We just hope that at least 1 person on the P&T Committee is from TS or has worked in a TS operation at another library," while yet another was pleased to note that: "Catalogers are often popular candidates for our internal Library Faculty Review Committee, and that is also helpful." These comments suggest that, in these libraries, a single review committee serves for all candidates being reviewed in a given year and that no special effort is made to assure that committees include at least one person who might be knowledgeable in the work being evaluated.

Special Evaluative Mechanisms; Special Dossier Content: Even though the focus of this question was on evaluative mechanisms specifically designed for technical services librarians that would enhance dossier content, only five answers were received that related directly to this focus; and two of those were reporting the need for such devices rather than their existence. One expressed interest in a mechanism offered as an example in the survey itself (soliciting evaluation of librarianship from outside experts, from their personal knowledge, by sending samples of a candidate's work, etc.). Another observed that "one of our issues for the Technical Services librarians is finding or generating an assessment instrument comparable to the evaluations submitted when librarians teach BI/Information Literacy sessions."

Of the three remaining responses, one reported utilizing all three methods used as examples in the question. A second reported using outside experts who evaluated from personal knowledge and noted that: "If and when no TS librarians are part of the tenured library faculty, several outside experts are asked to review the dossier and write a letter of review." The final response reported, "I did have samples of cataloging, along with explanations of the problems that the samples illustrate, in my portfolio . . . "

RECOMMENDATIONS AND SUGGESTIONS

None of the impediments that were identified as posing differential difficulties for technical services librarians seeking tenure appears to be intrinsically insurmountable, and many potential solutions can be identified. Solutions outlined below arise from comments supplied in response to survey questions, from the author's own experience, and from two discussions initiated by the author on AUTOCAT. The first was initiated in 2003 under the thread title "Evaluating cataloging for tenure."[26] The second, initiated in July 2005, under the title "Tenure for TS librarians," was a pre-cursor to the Zoomerang surveys.[27]

Each library has its own set of political realities. Some measures that may be critical at one library may be unnecessary at another. Some that may be feasible at one library may be impossible at another. But no library in which librarians may be seeking tenure can afford to dismiss the possibility that the evaluative mechanisms and tenure review processes may be inequitable.

Provide All Librarians Equal Access to Tenure Stream Positions

Excluding particular classes of librarians from tenure stream positions by virtue of their professional subdiscipline fails to recognize the intensely interdependent nature of librarianship and the importance of each librarian to the success of the overall organization. It creates two classes of librarians and diminishes critical facets of the profession. It imposes barriers to cooperation and narrows the perspective of the library faculty in addressing issues of concern to the whole library. It offers university administrations an opening to ask why any librarians at all should be faculty.

Assure That the Library's Tenure Standards and Evaluative Practices Encompass All Types of Librarians Equitably

Do not rely on a single set of processes to provide effective and informative evaluation of librarians in all subdisciplines. Make sure that more than the majority culture is reflected in standards and processes by involving librarians from all subdisciplines in the process of examining, modifying, and creating standards and practices.

Address Issues of Workload–Both Real and Imagined

Redefine the issue as one of time management. Assure that workload and time expectations are equitable for librarians working in all sub-disciplines. Consider such strategies as:

- Communicate effectively to all librarians that the job of a faculty member consists of different facets and that the practice of librarianship *per se* is only one of them and that work on scholarly endeavors and service activities is also part of the "real job."
- Communicate to all technical services librarians that they are afforded an amount of time equal to that afforded librarians in other specialties to engage in scholarly and service pursuits. Make librarians responsible for taking advantage of that time, and make managers responsible for enabling it.
- Establish reasonable production expectations that take into account the time that must be spent on scholarly and service pursuits. Such expectations should not be phrased as numeric quotas. Some redistribution of work, alteration of priorities, addition of staff, etc., may be necessary.
- Seek means for technical services librarians to be obviously "off the desk." This might include moving them out of shared open space and into offices specifically designed to allow separation of day-to-day activities from scholarly or service endeavors.

Confront the Issue of "Teaching"

Recognize the power of word choice and rephrase the discourse. Using terms such as "Practice of Profession" or "Practice of Librarianship." Remember that the terminology and reasoning put forth in the ACRL and AAUP statements is that librarians should be faculty not because they teach but because they make "unique contributions to the academic community and to higher education itself." Consider strategies such as:

- Incorporate statements in the institution's policy manuals such as: "... In recognition of the unique role the librarians play in advancing the University's educational mission, the teaching criteria for librarians will include activities in teaching and/or librarianship."[28]

- Evaluate teaching for librarians who have those responsibilities, but make it clear that teaching is only one of the tenure-worthy activities that they and other librarians perform.
- Evaluate training, workshops, and instructional presentations as teaching by using the same forms or practices used for others.

It may be tempting to surrender to expectations established for the majority (the teaching faculty) and to require all librarians to engage in classroom teaching, but technical services librarians already have difficulty making time for scholarly and service activities. Adding another type of work to be performed will increase this difficulty and impose a special hardship on these librarians.

Confront the Issue of Management

Acknowledge and describe library management as a disciplinary specialty. Recognize that non-library faculty may regard management as temporary, often trivial, service outside their practice of profession. Recognize that teaching faculty may not understand that normal library activities such as workflow management, innovation, policy formulation, process documentation, interdepartmental cooperation, training, and supervision are a part of the practice of librarianship.

Create Evaluative Mechanisms That Mirror or Replace Standard Teaching Evaluation Mechanisms

Teaching faculty are used to seeing in dossiers such things as student course questionnaires, reports from classroom observers, or reports from student interviews. They are not used to seeing letters from supervisors, and even the concept of having a faculty member supervised may be foreign to them. Possible strategies to create familiar-looking dossier content might include:

- Solicit letters from senior colleagues within the library. Be explicit that this letter is to be based on observation of the candidate's work and is therefore, in effect, a classroom observer report.[29]
- Solicit letters from supervisors, and encourage them to use language that makes it clear that they are reporting from the vantagepoint of the equivalent of a constant classroom observer.

- Conduct a focused group interview of persons who are in a position to comment on the candidate's mastery and performance or her/his job, and then summarize the interview for the dossier.
- Solicit letters from other colleagues in the library who are in a position to comment on some aspect of the candidate's work.

Decrease the Differential Effect of Letters in the Dossier from Non-Library Faculty and Students

A dossier that lacks letters of support from non-library faculty and students may appear to be thin and may seem to external reviewers to contain implied comment as to the importance or quality of a candidate's work. Consider alternative dossier content for those whose jobs do not bring them into contact with non-library faculty and students. Some alternatives might be:

- Include substantive electronic discussion-group contributions and solicit letters from other discussion-group participants that address the candidate's librarianship as demonstrated by those contributions.
- Solicit letters from reviewers engaged in cooperative programs (e.g., NACO, CONSER, etc.) that address the candidate's librarianship as demonstrated by contributions to the projects.
- Request external review of librarianship by submitting bibliographic records, documentation for standards and processes, projects overseen, etc.

If it is the institution's practice to solicit external comment on a candidate's scholarly and service contributions, make a clear distinction between those standard external review letters and letters such as are described above that are solicited specifically to comment on the practice of librarianship. To underline this distinction, consider providing a form rather than asking for a free-form letter.

Increase Exposure of Technical Services Faculty to Library Faculty, Non-Library Faculty, and Students

Make a concerted effort to involve technical services faculty in projects and committees that cross-departmental boundaries and include non-technical services faculty on committees and working groups addressing technical services issues. Include technical services faculty on campus committees and working groups. Some libraries increase exposure of technical services librarians by requiring all librarians to serve as a liaison to a teaching department and/or to engage in collection development activities or to serve on the reference desk. While this will certainly give librarians increased exposure, it has the same basic disadvantage as requiring teaching of all librarians–it is an additional activity that must be added to the existing work assignment and can interfere with the ability of the librarian to pursue scholarly or service activities.

Develop an Understanding of a Teaching Portfolio and Create Analogs for Technical Services Librarians

A teaching portfolio may include such items as class syllabi, course plans, sample tests given, proposals for new courses or programs, and evidence of innovation in the classroom. Analogous inclusions for technical services librarians might be:

- Copies of bibliographic or authority records accompanied by the candidate's explanation of special issues illustrated.
- Copies of bibliographic or authority records from a particular project accompanied by the candidate's explanation of the significance of the project; or, in Stuhlman's words: "To show off in a dossier you could mention special cataloging projects such as the cataloging and integration of a valuable gift or the preparation of a display that highlights the librarians' special abilities. Numbers of books cataloged do not count; importance to the collection counts for this show."[30]
- NACO, SACO, etc., headings submitted.
- Project proposals or position papers proposing processing innovations.
- Documentation developed for projects, including implementation of new automation systems, rules, or practices.
- Plans and instructional materials for training or workshops delivered, tutorials developed.
- Web pages created, maintained, edited, etc.

Increase Involvement of Technical Services Librarians in Matters Pertaining to the Tenure Process

Consciously seek input from librarians in all specialties when developing tenure and evaluation standards and processes. Form evaluation committees suited to individual candidates rather than having one committee handle all evaluations in a given year.[31] Do not rely on election to assure a sufficiently diverse committee.

Develop a Mentoring Program or Culture

A small academic library or even a large one with a great many librarians not yet tenured may be unable to support a formal mentoring program, but mentoring can take place in the absence of such a program. Encourage pre-tenured faculty to seek advice from tenured colleagues, regardless of their disciplinary specialty. Encourage all tenured faculty to be open to providing advice and guidance to all those still working toward tenure. Active mentoring has the ancillary benefit of expanding the community of colleagues who have an interest in and some knowledge of technical services librarians and the work they do.

Explain the Work

Develop descriptions of the content of jobs in technical services. Such descriptions should be as free of library jargon as possible and should be couched in terms that relate the work to such things as its impact on library users, learning, access to information, educational outcomes, and the overall mission of the institution. Other persuasive aspects might include the centrality of the organization of information to librarianship as well as the national and international cooperative aspects of the work. As possible and appropriate, speak of the catalog as a reference tool or a bibliography; describe subject analysis as taxonomy; refer to the work as user service. Actively collect, save, and share particularly effective descriptions that can be incorporated into a self-statement or filed elsewhere in the dossier.

CONCLUSION

The work of technical services librarians is different from the work of those in public services and less widely understood, but it is no less critical to the success of the library or to the needs of the academic community. Tenure standards and practices for librarians have been created to reflect the needs of those librarians who are in the majority (reference, bibliographic instruction, collection building). They may not satisfactorily portray or evaluate the Performance of Librarianship facet of the record for librarians who are present in smaller numbers (technical services, circulation, systems, administration). A number of problematic practices and issues that affect technical services librarians' pursuit of tenure can be readily identified, and the perception that navigating the tenure process is more difficult for them than for others is common. All issues can be addressed, but few libraries have made an attempt to do so.

Libraries as organizations depend on intense cooperation and interaction among all of their librarians, and the success of the whole depends on the ability of individuals to be successful within it. Thus, it is undesirable for one group within the organization to be subject to special difficulties. Tenure-granting academic libraries should examine their tenure-related practices and develop or modify them as necessary to ensure that a technical services librarian's pursuit of tenure is no more difficult than that of a librarian working in public services. Libraries should take note of possible differential experiences for other types of non-public-services librarians and address these as well. All development of new or modified practices or standards should be informed by an understanding of the underlying purposes and rationales for a tenure system and how those are reflected in the practices that apply to the majority. Although the primary work toward change must be accomplished in individual libraries, the Association of College and Research Libraries is also in a position to provide guidance. But just as individual libraries need to recognize that tenure standards and practices must suit more than the majority, ACRL must also recognize that it represents all types of librarians who work in academic institutions and actively seek participation from representatives of minority subdisciplines.

REFERENCES

1. Faculty Status Movement–Chronology." Accessed: http://ublib.buffalo.edu/libraries/faculty/fec/libfac/chron.html. (Dec. 10, 2003).
2. Robert G. Sewell. "Faculty Status and Librarians: The Rationale and Case of Illinois," *College & Research Libraries*, 44, no. 3 (May, 1983): 212-222.
3. E-mail correspondence from Mary Ellen Davis, Executive Director, Association of College and Research Libraries. October 25, 2005.

4. ACRL Committee on the Status of Academic Librarians. "Standards for Faculty Status for College and University Librarians." Accessed: http://www.ala.org/ala/acrl/acrlstandards/standardsfaculty.htm. (Dec. 20, 2005).

5. Betsy Park and Robert Riggs, "Tenure and Promotion: A Study of Practices by Institutional Type," *Journal of Academic Librarianship*. 19, no. 2. (May, 1993): 73. In this study, the term faculty status was "reserved for librarians who are eligible for both tenure and promotion, and who are accorded the same titles as other faculty (i.e., instructor, assistant professor, associate professor, professor. Librarians at all other institutions were designated as having "professional status."

6. John N. DePew, "The ACRL Standards for Faculty Status: Panacea or Placebo," *College & Research Libraries*. 44, no. 6. (November, 1983): 407.

7. Thomas G. English, "Librarian Status in the Eighty-Nine U.S. Academic Institutions of the Association of Research Libraries: 1982," *College & Research Libraries*. 44, no. 3. (May, 1983): 199.

8. Betsy Park and Robert Riggs, "Status of the Profession: A 1989 National Survey of tenure and Promotion Policies for Academic Librarians," *College & Research Libraries*, 52, no. 3. (May, 1991): 279.

9. Charles B. Lowery, "The Status of Faculty Status for Academic Librarians: A Twenty-Year Perspective," *College & Research Libraries*. 54, no. 2. (March, 1993): 163.

10. Lowery, "The Status of Faculty Status," p. 163.

11. English, "Librarian Status," pp. 199, 200-202, 207.

12. This is the author's own interpretation, based upon monitoring the literature and upon personal observation.

13. English, "Librarian Status," p. 200.

14. Lowery, "The Status of Faculty Status," p. 165.

15. Lowery, "The Status of Faculty Status," p. 168.

16. Many such variations are noted in Park and Riggs and are also touched on by Lowery, and by English. Examination of tenure standards contributed by respondents to the author's survey revealed many of these same differences.

17. Richard P. Chait. "Gleanings," *The Questions of Tenure*, Richard P. Chait, ed., (Cambridge, MA: Harvard University Press, 2002), p. 310.

18. Danielle Borero Hoggan. "Faculty Status for Librarians in Higher Education," *Portal: Libraries and the Academy*. 3, no. 3 (2003): 431-445. Accessed: http://muse.jhu.edu/journals/portal_libraries_and_the_academy/v003/3.3hoggan.html. (Jan. 6, 2006). This balanced paper touches on nearly every reason ever argued for and against tenure for academic librarians.

19. Janet Swan Hill. "Wearing Our Own Clothes: Librarians as Faculty," *Journal of Academic Librarianship*, 20, no. 2. (May, 1994): 71-76. The section of this paper that begins on p.72 contains the interpretation of librarianship that the author created for the purpose of explaining librarians' dossiers to a campus-wide review committee. The statement may also be found on the Web in the University of Colorado Libraries at Boulder's faculty handbook. Accessed: http://ucblibraries.colorado.edu/internal/fac/V.B.1_sumfield.pdf. (Jan. 6, 2006).

20. Such adoptions might include requiring all librarians regardless of specialty to teach classes or requiring additional advanced degrees for hiring, promotion, or tenure. Survey responses indicated that one or the other had been implemented in at least some libraries.

21. Responses to the survey included these observations: "We explored excluding TS librarians but didn't. It was the quality of the TS librarians then not their jobs," and "I've found that some (not all) non-TS librarians also question the work we do as meeting tenure criteria."

22. Libraries were identified through spreadsheets supplied via e-mail by Lee Ann George of ARL. Spreadsheets were part of raw data collected for *The M.L.S. Hiring Requirement*, compiled by Julia C. Blixrud; series editor, Lee Ann George, (Washington, DC: Association of Research Libraries, 2000), (SPEC Kit 257).

23. AUTOCAT is an international electronic discussion list for issues related to cataloging. The topic of faculty status and tenure for catalogers has been discussed there on numerous occasions including the two discussions cited in notes 25 and 26.

24. These aspects were not included because the author believes that a fair assessment of the quality and extent of a librarian's scholarly or service record does not depend on the particular sub-discipline being pursued, and that all tenure-stream librarians in a given academic institution are treated equitably with regard to importance ascribed to, and support provided for scholarly and service activities. In order to provide a total picture of the tenure situation for technical services librarians, other investigators may wish to explore the validity of these two assumptions.

25. Anaclare F. Evans, "Evaluating cataloging for tenure," message posted to AUTOCAT, July 29, 2003.

26. The original message was posted on July 25, 2003 under the thread title "Evaluating cataloging for tenure." Discussion of the thread continued until July 30.

27. The original message was posted on July 25, 2005 under the title "Tenure for TS librarians." Most responses were received privately.

28. University of Colorado. "Implementation of Tenure Policies for Librarians," Administrative Policy Statement, dated 2/8/83. Accessed: http://www.cusys.edu/policies/Personnel/tenurelibr.html. (Jan. 5, 2006). Excerpts from the statement may also be found in the *University of Colorado Faculty Handbook*. Boulder, 1988. III-16.

29. An individual institution may distinguish between "solicited letters" (those solicited for the dossier by the review committee), and "unsolicited letters" (those that are either genuinely unsolicited, or which have been solicited by the candidate her/himself). The author makes no distinction between the two types of solicitation in this paper.

30. Daniel Stuhlman, "Evaluating cataloging for tenure," message posted to AUTOCAT July 25, 2003.

31. At the author's institution, all tenured faculty are eligible for service on review committees in any given year. Individual review committees are formed for each candidate, taking care to include on each review committee at least one person who has knowledge of the candidate's specialty or a specialty sufficiently similar to enable informed evaluation.

doi:10.1300/J104v44n03_01

APPENDIX 1. Faculty Status and Tenure for Technical Services Librarians

This questionnaire is part of a research project examining issues that have an impact on the success of technical services librarians achieving tenure, with particular emphasis on how the practice of librarianship is evaluated for the tenure decision. Questions below address:

- The degree to which all or some technical services librarians are part of the tenure system that exists for other librarians in the same institution.
- Whether tenure standards as written or applied make achieving tenure as easy (or hard) for technical services librarians as for others, and what kinds of things are most problematic.
- What special mechanisms for evaluating technical services librarians for tenure might be used to ensure fair consideration.

The term **librarian** is used here to indicate an individual with a professional library, archives, or information science degree who occupies a professional position relevant to her/his degree. Questions concern practices that pertain to librarians who are hired into full-time, permanent positions under **current** employment practices.

1. Do librarians at your institution have faculty status, with the possibility of earning tenure? If the answer is no, please go to the end of the questionnaire and SUBMIT it. Thank you for your attention.

2. Do promotion and tenure recommendations for library faculty receive substantive review by a body or officer outside the library? (Substantive review evaluates the merit of the candidate's record, and could conceivably lead to a recommendation at odds with the library's own recommendation.)

3. Do all librarians in your library have equal access to tenure stream positions regardless of type of work they do, or the department in which they are employed?

4. If all librarians do not have equal access to tenure stream positions, what types of positions have lesser or no access to tenure stream employment? (check all that apply)

    Catalogers
    Other Technical Services Librarians
    Administrators
    Systems Librarians
    Other (please specify)

APPENDIX 1 (continued)

5. What is the rationale for such exceptions, and what do you see as the advantages or disadvantages of exceptions being made?

6. In terms of success in achieving tenure as compared to librarians in other positions, are technical services librarians: Equally successful at achieving tenure? More Successful than librarians in other positions? Less Successful than librarians in other positions?

7. If technical services librarians are not as successful as other librarians in achieving tenure at your institution, what factors that you believe contribute to this situation?

8. Regardless of the actual record of librarians achieving tenure, do you or others perceive that technical services librarians have a more difficult time achieving tenure than their colleagues in other positions? If Yes, please explain.

9. Has your library developed or considered any special procedures for evaluating the practice of librarianship of Technical Services librarians for the purpose of improving their chances of achieving tenure by making their records more understandable to others, by making their dossiers look more like those of other librarians, etc.?

10. If your library has developed such special procedures, please describe them. (Examples of such mechanisms might be: (1) Training and presentations evaluated as teaching; (2) Interviewing library colleagues about a candidate's work; (3) Soliciting evaluation of librarianship from outside experts, either from their personal knowledge, by sending samples of the candidate's work, etc.)

11. If your library's tenure standards are available on the Web, please supply the url.

If your library's tenure standards are not available on the Web, but you are willing to share them, please send a copy via U.S. mail, e-mail, or fax to:

>Janet Swan Hill
>Professor, Associate Director for Technical Services
>University of Colorado Libraries
>CB 184, Boulder, Colorado, 80309
>Janet.hill@colorado.edu
>Fax: (303) 492-0494

12. If you are willing to be contacted in case I need to seek clarification concerning your answers, please supply your e-mail address.

13. Please feel free to add any additional comments or observations.

The "Works" Phenomenon and Best Selling Books

Richard P. Smiraglia

SUMMARY. Studying works allows us to see empirically the problem of instantiation of works, both at large and in the catalog. The linkage of relationships among works is a critical goal for information retrieval because the ability to comprehend and select a specific instantiation of a work is crucial for the advancement of scholarship. Hence, the present study examines the instantiation of works among a set of entities known to be popular–best selling books of the 20th century. A sample of best selling works (fiction and non-fiction) from 1900-1999 was constructed. For each work in the sample, all bibliographic records were identified in both OCLC and RLIN as well as instantiations on the World Wide Web. All but one work in the sample exists in multiple instantiations; many have large networks; and complex networks of instantiations have begun to appear in full text on the Web. The results

---

Richard P. Smiraglia is Professor, Palmer School of Library and Information Science, Long Island University, Brookville, NY 11548 (E-mail: Richard.Smiraglia@liu.edu).

A preliminary report of this research appeared in "Crossing Cultural Boundaries: Perspectives on the Popularity of Works." In *Challenges in Knowledge Representation and Organization for the 21st century, Integration of Knowledge across Boundaries, Proceedings of the 7th International ISKO Conference, 10-13 July 2002, Granada, Spain*, ed. Maria J. Lopez-Huertas. Wurzburg: Ergon, 2002, pp. 530-9.

[Haworth co-indexing entry note]: "The 'Works' Phenomenon and Best Selling Books." Smiraglia, Richard P. Co-published simultaneously in *Cataloging & Classification Quarterly* (The Haworth Information Press, an imprint of The Haworth Press, Inc.) Vol. 44, No. 3/4, 2007, pp. 179-195; and: *Cataloger, Editor, and Scholar: Essays in Honor of Ruth C. Carter* (ed: Robert P. Holley) The Haworth Information Press, an imprint of The Haworth Press, Inc., 2007, pp. 179-195. Single or multiple copies of this article are available for a fee from The Haworth Document Delivery Service [1-800-HAWORTH, 9:00 a.m. - 5:00 p.m. (EST). E-mail address: docdelivery@haworthpress.com].

Available online at http://ccq.haworthpress.com
© 2007 by The Haworth Press, Inc. All rights reserved.
doi:10.1300/J104v44n03_02

of this study demonstrate the importance of continuing to gather statistical data about works. Solutions devised for the catalog will need to be modified for use in the chaotic environment of the World Wide Web and its successors. doi:10.1300/J104v44n03_02 *[Article copies available for a fee from The Haworth Document Delivery Service: 1-800-HAWORTH. E-mail address: <docdelivery@haworthpress.com> Website: <http://www.HaworthPress.com> © 2007 by The Haworth Press, Inc. All rights reserved.]*

KEYWORDS. Works, instantiation, best sellers, popular culture, canonicity, FRBR

1. INTRODUCTION: WORKS AS ENTITIES OF RECORDED KNOWLEDGE

The "works phenomenon" has been of much interest lately. Sorting a large set of collocated editions of a work and keeping them in order adjacent to commentaries, translations, and other versions has always presented problems in the catalog. Studying the works phenomenon has allowed us to see empirically the actual dimensions of this issue. Whether we describe this colloquially as the problem of works and their editions or scientifically as the concatenation of evolving intellectual entities that constitute instantiations of a work (an instantiation is an occurrence of a work–an edition, for instance), the analysis of their evolution has been the focus of much study. Early research into what was then called "derivative bibliographic relationships" has given way to more sophisticated analysis of works and their instantiations. The implementation of the "work" entity in the FRBR model (i.e., *Functional Requirements for Bibliographic Records* (IFLA 1998)) has consumed much effort in the cataloging community. Several studies about works were reported collectively in Smiraglia (2001).

Works are deliberate creations that stand as the formal records of knowledge. Other terms that describe the same phenomenon are opera, oeuvres, Werke, etc. We now understand that works constitute key entities in the universe of recorded knowledge. Core bodies of works–canons–function to preserve and disseminate the parameters of the culture from which they spring. Why study works? We study works because, in the catalog, entries for works must be clustered in a variety of ways. Techniques used in the past (e.g., uniform titles) have yielded alphabetico-classified arrays. Yet this clustering has not been effective at providing users with clear choices among alternative instantiations of works. For example, the headings:

Kroetsch, Robert

[Studhorse man]

and

Kroetsch, Robert

[Studhorse man. French]

serve to distinguish in the catalog between the English-language original edition of this 1969 novel. But the second heading makes no differentiation between the 1985 and 1990 French translations of it nor between the different editions of the two translations that exist (see Smiraglia 2001, 103-105). Consequently, empirical observation is required to more fully understand the work phenomenon in order to better make explicit links and differentiations in the catalog. Explicit linkage of relationships among works is a critical goal for information retrieval because the ability to comprehend and select a specific instantiation of a work is crucial for the advancement of scholarship.

Works, defined as entities for information retrieval then, are seen to constitute sets of varying instantiations of abstract creations. Smiraglia (2001) includes a report of several studies that quantify the extent of instantiations of works by demonstrating patterns of mutation and derivation. Works consist of both semantic and ideational content. Progenitor works are those that are followed by the appearance of new instantiations over time. When there is little or no change in ideational content, a new instantiation is said to be a derivation, even if the semantic content is entirely changed (as in the case of a translation or transposition). When the ideational content also experiences change, the new instantiation is said to be a mutation. The progenitor work together with its related instantiations is said to constitute an instantiation network (sometimes this is called a "bibliographic family"). There is some evidence that popularity of works is a contributing factor to the phenomena of mutation and derivation. For instance, in the early studies of works, novels seemed to demonstrate a high incidence of both derivation and mutation. Commercial interests combined with cultural forces propel the evolution of popular novels (translation, serialization, screenplays, comics, etc., not to mention sequels) as interest in them spreads across language and geographic boundaries.

Semiotic analysis has also been used to demonstrate the cultural role of works (cf. Smiraglia 2002). Some works assume cultural roles–consider for example the *Mona Lisa*, the *Bible*, the *Moonlight Sonata*, or even the *Rocky Horror Picture Show*. This acculturation seems to lead to further instantiation of the work, and particularly to its mutation, as cultural needs shape the market demand for the work. When this happens over time, the work itself (the progenitor) comes to coexist with a number of mutated instantiations, all of which are identified by the commonly accepted historically constructed citation for the original work. Works in a cultural canon are therefore seen as signifying, mutable, and dependent on reception for their interpretation.

The concept of instantiation itself was analyzed (Smiraglia 2005) and demonstrated to exist among all kinds of information objects. Instantiation simply means realization in time. It seems that networks of instantiation arise whenever information objects assume canonical qualities associated with cultural inculcation. Variant instantiations and the networks among them must be explicitly identified in future systems for documentary information retrieval. An expanded perception of works helps us understand the variety of ways in which mechanisms for their control and retrieval might be shaped in the future.

Earlier studies also support a concept of the work as a collaborative entity that is changed over time by those who embrace it. One way to think of this phenomenon is this: the more popular the work, the more likely we will observe change over time. The more we can observe cultural embrace of a work, the more likely we can also observe change in the texts and instantiations of the work over time. Qualitative analysis by Leazer and Smiraglia (1999) suggested the same effect could be observed among sets of instantiations of works that are truly "popular" in the colloquial sense. Hence the present study, which was undertaken in 2002 to examine the instantiation of works among a set of entities known to be popular–best selling books of the 20th century. One measure of cultural embrace, or "popularity," might reasonably be considered to be the judgment of the marketplace by which works wind up on best seller lists. Analysis of best sellers could potentially yield useful data for comprehension of the content and extent of the "canon" (as it were) of popular works. Evidence of the derivation and mutation of best sellers can also augment our understanding of the social role of works as cultural signs. Thus, the over-riding research question for the study reported here was:

> Will best selling books demonstrate patterns of derivation and mutation similar to those observed among works in other literary or academic "canons"?

2. METHODOLOGY

A sample of best selling works (fiction and non-fiction) from 1900-1999 was constructed. Specifically, a frame of 1,836 best selling works was assembled by downloading titles for the ten best selling books each year from 1900-1995. These lists were assembled from *Publisher's Weekly*'s list of best selling hardcover books for the entire century (http://www.caderbooks.com/bestintro.html). The frame itself is self-stratified into fiction (992 works) and non-fiction (844 works). One limitation of this frame is its United States orientation–the data must be understood to be descriptive of the American market only (even though some of the works represented are of Canadian origin).

Since there were no data from the earlier studies on best selling books, it was decided to use an approximation to calculate sample size. One useful approximation is the reported size of instantiation networks in earlier studies. In Smiraglia (1992), the mean was 4.7; sample-size calculation using this estimate suggested a sample of 30 cases in each stratum would be sufficient to yield results with 95% confidence. *SPSS* was used to generate a random sample. To eliminate potential bias that might be introduced by works that were listed more than once in the sampling frame, each work in the initial draw was searched against the frame to remove cases that represented other than the first occurrence of a work on the best seller list. Eventually a sample of 84 cases was drawn at random from the entire list of best sellers–45 fiction and 39 nonfiction. The entire list of works in the sample appears in Appendix 1.

For each work in the sample, all bibliographic records were identified in both OCLC and RLIN. An attempt was also made to locate instantiations on the World Wide Web. The collected bibliographic records were then examined and codified (as in the earlier studies) into derivative relationship-types. (See Appendix 3 in Smiraglia 2001 for details about this methodology.) *SPSS* was used to provide statistical data for quantitative analysis. The bibliographic data reported here were current in July of 2002.

3. CHARACTERISTICS OF BEST SELLING BOOKS 1900-1995

A simple read through the lists of best selling books from the twentieth century provides a qualitative summary of social and cultural trends throughout the century. The lists begin with romantic and cowboy fiction and proceed through tales of rural and urban life and love. Table 1 includes a few examples from the fiction sample. Such analyses are perhaps better left to social historians or experts in comparative literatures, but it is easy to observe the shape of the century's cultural evolution in the works on this list. The century opens looking back at the glorification of the American West, then depicts the harsh reality of war and depression in the first half of the century, and follows with the social upheaval of the post-World War II era. The century ends with a fascination with science fiction and the imagined horrors of the impending future.

Similarly and perhaps more directly, the nonfiction list mirrors the cultural evolution of the century (see Table 2). The nonfiction list moves from themes of women's suffrage through the whimsy of the late 1920s and early 1930s but also includes such icons of culture as General Marshall's report on post-World War II Europe, the Kinsey report on sexual function, Woodward and Bernstein's accounts of the Watergate affair, the sexual liberation of women, and the economic uncertainty of the millennial era (not to mention quite a few cookbooks–see Appendix 1 for examples).

The sampling frame itself contained 1836 works (992 fiction and 844 nonfiction). Some authors repeated (Winston Churchill, Danielle Steele, James Michener, Shirley McLaine, and Rush Limbaugh, for example), but not many. One-hundred and seventy-eight authors of fiction and 176 of nonfiction appeared on the list more than once. Only a small number of works remained best sellers over time. Many works can be identified as having spawned sequels that also appeared on the list while others originally appeared in serialized form. Other cultural influences had impact on the list as well; for instance, during World War I separate lists of "war books" were ranked alongside the regular best sellers.

4. RESULTS

All but one work in the entire sample generated an instantiation network. Thus the rate of derivation was .98 for all best sellers, 1.0 for works of fiction, and .97 for works of nonfiction (in earlier studies, this

TABLE 1. Some Best Selling Fiction of the 20th Century

Year:Rank	Author	Title
1902:1	Owen Wister	The Virginian
1917:5	Zane Grey	Wildfire
1936:10	Aldous Huxley	Eyeless in Gaza
1939:1	John Steinbeck	The Grapes of Wrath
1969:2	Mario Puzo	The Godfather
1978:1	James Michener	Chesapeake
1979:5	Kurt Vonnegut	Jailbird
1994:2	Tom Clancy	Debt of Honor
1996:3	Stephen King	Desperation
1996:4	Michael Chrichton	Airframe

TABLE 2. Some Best Selling Non-Fiction of the 20th Century

Year:Rank	Author	Title
1912:9	Olive Schreiner	Woman and Labor
1921:4	Margot Asquith	Autobiography
1924:8	Bernard Shaw	Saint Joan
1935:3	Clarence Day	Life with Father
1945:7	U.S. War Dept.	General Marshall's Report
1947:9	Margaret Boni et al	Fireside Book of Folksongs
1948:4	Kinsey	Sexual Behavior in the Human Male
1958:9	Van Buren	Dear Abby
1971:5	David Reuben	Any Woman Can
1991:7	Charles J. Givens	More Wealth Without Risk

rate varied from .302 in OCLC's WorldCat to .499 in Georgetown University's catalog) (Smiraglia 2001, 87). Curiously, the one work that failed to generate more than an original edition was Clare Barnes Jr.'s *Campus Zoo*, which was ranked ninth in 1950. One other work, the *Better Homes & Gardens Dessert Book*, which ranked fifth in 1960, had only one subsequent edition.

Other generally indicative figures are those regarding the size of instantiation networks. For the sample as a whole, the mean was 28.17 members (earlier studies ranged from 3.54 to 8.44). For fiction the mean was 33.37, and for nonfiction the mean was 22.3. Clearly, best selling works generate larger instantiation networks overall than their less popular counterparts.

In all studies of works, a statistically significant barometer has been the age of the progenitor work; and the results were confirmed again in this study. The mean age of progenitor work was 52 years–for fiction it was 57.64 and for nonfiction 45.48. The mean age of progenitor approaches 50, which is understandable in a study in which all the subjects are works generated within the recent century. But, the relationship between an older progenitor work and an accompanying large instantiation network, which is seen in this study, has been uncovered in prior research as well. In this case, the regression coefficient was .002; and the constant was .039 (see Figure 1).

4.1 Relationship Types–The Makeup of Instantiation Networks

Instantiation networks have been described by assigning instantiations to taxonomical categories that are descriptive of the evolution of the

FIGURE 1. Regression Plot of Age of Progenitor with Size of Instantiation Network

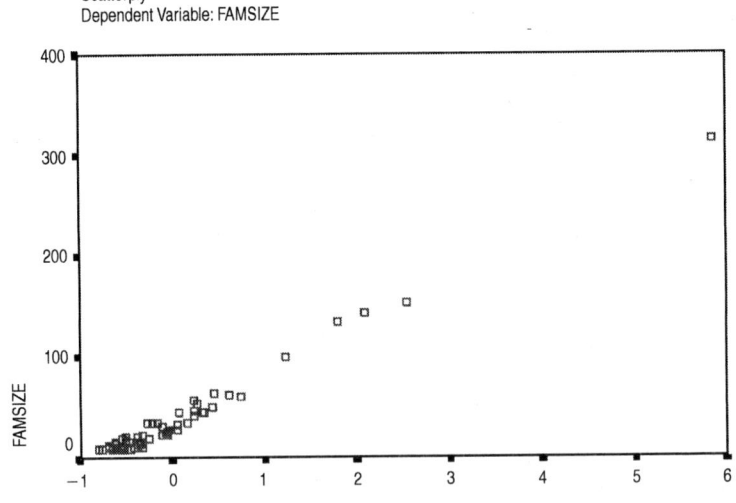

work over time. The original taxonomy (Smiraglia 1992, 28) included seven categories:

1. Simultaneous derivations–works that are published in two editions simultaneously in different places.
2. Successive derivations–new editions.
3. Translations.
4. Amplifications–illustrated texts; musical settings; and criticisms, concordances, and commentaries that include the original text.
5. Extractions including abridgments, condensations, and excerpts.
6. Adaptations including simplifications, screenplays, librettos, arrangements of musical works, and other modifications; and,
7. Performances including sound or visual (i.e., film or video) recordings.

Two additional categories were added to the tabulation for this study, both originally generated for the Leazer and Smiraglia (1999) study. These were "predecessor" and "accompanying material" relations. A predecessor is tabulated in the face of evidence that a "progenitor" in the current sample is derived somehow from an earlier work (e.g., when a monograph originates as a newspaper serial). Accompanying material is tabulated when derived intellectual material physically accompanies the work in question (a map or sound recording in a pocket at back are both common in mid-twentieth century publications).

Tables 3.1 through 3.3 include data about the instantiation networks analyzed in this study. As noted above, the mean instantiation network for works of fiction had 33 members while nonfiction had 22. The mean age of the progenitor was 58 for works of fiction, and 45 for nonfiction. Nonfiction works, in general, then, had younger and smaller instantiation networks.

The average instantiation network overall had 2 simultaneous, 10 successive, 8 translation, 1 adaptation, 4 performances, and negligible instances of the other relationship types. The shape of instantiation networks for fiction versus nonfiction followed the overall mean closely except that works of fiction had more translations (the mean was 11). The largest instantiation networks were for works of fiction and included 12 simultaneous, 101 successive, 109 translations, 22 amplifications, 5 extractions, 20 adaptations, and 47 performances, for a total of 315 members (Steinbeck's *The Grapes of Wrath*). This was by far the largest network–the next largest were *The Godfather* with 152, *Saint Joan* with 147, and *The Virginian* with 134.

TABLE 3.1 Instantiation Networks at Large

	#	Network Size	Age of Work	Simultaneous	Successive	Predecessor	Translation	Amplification	Extraction	Adaptation	Performance	Accompanying
All	84	28.23	52	2.18	10.43	.24	8.21	.67	.3	1.11	4.33	.12
Fiction	45	33.37	57.64	2.78	11.67	.02	11.29	.76	.33	1.4	4.69	.04
Non-Fiction	39	22.3	45.48	1.49	9	.49	4.67	.56	.26	.77	3.92	.21

TABLE 3.2 Instantiation Networks: The Difference of Persistence

	#	Network Size	Age of Work	Simultaneous	Successive	Predecessor	Translation	Amplification	Extraction	Adaptation	Performance	Accompanying
All	84	28.23	52	2.18	10.43	.24	8.21	.67	.3	1.11	4.33	.12
≤7	21	4.66	63.9	1.24	1.95		.24	.76	.33	.1	.14	
>7	63	36	48	2.49	13.25	.32	10.87	.89	.4	1.4	5.73	.16

TABLE 3.3 Instantiation Networks: The Difference Between Fiction and Non-Fiction

	#	Network Size	Age of Work	Simultaneous	Successive	Predecessor	Translation	Amplification	Extraction	Adaptation	Performance	Accompanying
All	84	28.23	52	2.18	10.43	.24	8.21	.67	.3	1.11	4.33	.12
F	45	33.37	57.64	2.78	11.67	.02	11.29	.76	.33	1.4	4.69	.04
>7 F	34	42.44	47.82	3.09	14.71	.03	14.91	1	.44	1.79	6.21	.06
NF	39	22.3	45.48	1.49	9	.49	4.67	.56	.26	.77	3.92	.21
>7 NF	29	28.6	48.2	1.79	11.55	.66	6.14	.76	.34	1.03	5.17	.7

Simultaneous editions were ubiquitous in this study. Clearly, one part of the publication strategy for a work expected by its publisher to become a best seller is to publish the work in more than one place. In the early part of the twentieth century, this meant that books in the sample appeared in two North American cities, such as New York and Toronto, or New York and Indianapolis, or sometimes all three. Toward the end of the century, the phenomenon was international with simultaneous publication in New York and London seemingly the norm. Also, Braille editions are frequently produced simultaneously with the printed progenitor.

4.1.1 Canonicity–Persistent Works

Every work but one in the sample demonstrated over time mutation and derivation from instantiations. That is, only one work existed in only its initial edition. Best selling works, therefore, demonstrate wider cultural impact through the promulgation of editions and translations over time than is true of the works observed in earlier studies of academic canons. However, many best selling works in the sample exist in a small set of instantiations: the progenitor, one or two simultaneous editions, and one or two successive editions. Twenty-one (or 25%) fell into this category. If we look at instantiation networks for works that do persist over time (in this study, 63 such works with instantiation networks greater than 7), we see a slightly different set of descriptors. Comparing the works in these two groups was revealing. In fact, it turns out that even best selling works demonstrate a concept of "canonicity"; only some works are culturally embraced sufficiently to generate large instantiation networks. A correlate of this observation is that "popularity" cannot be directly associated with "canonicity." Some catalyst apart from mere popularity is a determinant in the persistence of best selling works.

For the purposes of this analysis, we have denoted the works with instantiation networks greater than 7 in number as "works that persist" to contrast them with those that did not. The mean instantiation network for works that did not persist had approximately 5 members, of which 1 was simultaneous, up to 2 were successive, and only on rare occasions were translations or other mutations present. These works had an older mean age (64 years). In fact, three quarters of these works were more than forty years old. These works were evenly divided among fiction (88 years, 2 simultaneous, and 2 successive) and nonfiction (37 years, 1 simultaneous, and 2 successive). This might reflect greater skill either in market projection or market performance among publishers of best sellers as the years passed. The shape of instantiation networks for works that persisted was approximately the same as for the overall mean. Or, we have to admit the possibility that this difference is an artifact of retrospective conversion; it will require another study to rule this out.

Among the works that persisted, the instantiation networks for fiction were larger but not older than non-fiction with translations accounting for the majority of the difference. Removing the non-persistent works leaves larger but not older instantiation networks but does not change the basic shape of differentiation between fiction and non-fiction.

4.1.2 Other Notes on Instantiation Networks

A few other observations arise from analysis of these instantiation networks. The relationship types are all populated throughout the sample, demonstrating the efficacy of the expanded taxonomy. However, the majority of relationships are derivative (simultaneous and successive editions). The majority of mutations are translations and performances. All other relationship categories are sparsely populated. Best sellers have many editions and are likely to be turned into performance works, but few other mutations are present. For more recent works, those with progenitors after 1980, it was observed that performances develop prior to successive editions or translations, reversing a trend earlier in the century. Works with translations fit one of two patterns–in the early part of the century translations appeared first in French and German; by the end of the century (after 1980), the first translations to appear are in Spanish, Japanese, Korean, and Persian.

4.2 Films

The cultural appetite for entertainment is easily observed by looking at works that originate in writing but get appropriated for production as film or television programs. While the continued publication of reprintings or new editions (e.g., paperback editions or condensed editions) stretches the marketplace to new readers, the mutation of the text into a screenplay that is then filmed creates an entirely new market for the work. And following production of the film, new mutations, such as recordings of sound-tracks, novelizations, and even the production of related paraphernalia such as lunchboxes, all provide illustration of the cultural inculcation of a work.

In this study, 19 bestsellers, or 22.6%, were made into films or had film instantiations, e.g., *Alistair Cooke's America*. The mean instantiation network surrounding works made into films was 71.8. Works from both strata fell into this category. Eight works of fiction (e.g., *Grapes of Wrath*) and 11 works of nonfiction (e.g., *All the President's Men*, *Elements of Style*) were made into films. One interesting case was Scott Turow's 1987 *Presumed Innocent*. A movie was made within a year of publication, and a novelization of the movie makes up a substantial proportion of the successive editions in the instantiation network.

George Bernard Shaw's *Saint Joan* was a best selling book in 1924. It spawned a very large and complex network including 147 instantiations tallied in this study. The performance history alone (see Table 4 for a summary). demonstrates the social and cultural influence of the marketplace that can propel a work across time into the consciousness of millions.

The list includes a television play based on an excerpt distributed on video; differing dramatic performances captured on audio media; a motion picture; its sound track separately released; and its subsequent colorization released on video–the list ends with a musical composition created as a compilation of music associated with the work over time. In the cultural imagination, a plethora of images of the valiant Joan of Arc take root; in the library catalog, a plethora of different bibliographic entities, all associated with Shaw's *Saint Joan*, introduce potential chaos for the searcher.

4.3 Electronic Resources

Web-searching was employed for the first time in the present study to begin to understand how the multiple instantiation of works might or might not present challenges in the digital environment. Preliminary data were inconclusive; at the time of data gathering in 2002, few works in the sample were represented in full in the digital environment. Twenty-four bestsellers or 28.5% had electronic resources, which were roughly evenly divided between fiction (13 or 28.8%) and nonfiction (11 or 28.2%).

The entire sample was searched again in 2006 for this report. Each author-title combination was searched in Google™ and also in Google™ Book Search Beta. As could be expected, results were dramatically different. The proportion now available online is 42% and is rapidly approaching half the works (20 or 44% of fiction, 15 or 38% of

TABLE 4. Some Performances of Shaw's *Saint Joan*

- 1955, Omnibus television, Excerpt of Trial scene, videocassette
- 1957, Capitol sound disc, Music from the sound track of the Preminger movie, mono analog LP disc
- 1998, Audio book, Narration of book, 3 analog cassettes
- 1982, Argo sound cassette, Recording of play starring Barbara Jefford, 2 cassette re-release of 1966 recording
- 1973, Caedmon cassette, Recording of play starring Siobhan McKenna, mono 2-track cassettes of 1966 LP
- 1969, CMS sound disc, Reading of Shaw's preface, mono analog LP disc
- 1966, Argo sound disc, Recording of play starring Siobhan McKenna, 3 stereo LP discs
- 1966, Argo sound disc, Recording of play starring Siobhan McKenna, 3 mono LP discs
- 1988, Video Treasures, Colorization of Preminger 1957 movie starring Jean Seberg, 1 VHS cassette
- 1987, Video Treasures, Colorization of Preminger 1957 movie starring Jean Seberg, 1 VHS cassette
- 1925, Piano transcription, Foulds' Suite from incidental music, piano music

nonfiction). E-resources are predominantly full text (fiction) and excerpts (non-fiction). New media are appearing tentatively in the cyber realm. There is one audio file; one e-sequel that does not otherwise appear in print; one official website that contains a link to the full-text of a novel; and two electronic exhibitions of manuscripts that are essential predecessors. Copyright is clearly an influence as fiction before 1925 is all represented online but only sparsely after that date. Nonfiction is completely represented to 1928 and then only very selectively after. Fascinating to see was the smattering of e-books, all indistinguishable from each other except for varying dates of origin and varying page lengths. In some cases, electronic versions of the progenitor appear side by side with sequels and motion pictures. The largest electronic instantiation network was Harold McGrath's 1907 novel *Half a Rope*; the most complex was Judy Mazel's 1981 *Beverly Hills Diet*. Clearly, there will soon be a need for sorting devices to organize these displays to facilitate retrieval.

5. IMPLICATIONS

Owen Wister's *The Virginian* was published as a novel in 1902 in New York. Over time, this work has been observed in at least 134 instantiations, including 89 successive editions, 14 translations, at least 20 performances, and a variety of adaptations, including the generation of a comic-book version based on a set of excerpts. Many of these instantiations demonstrate more than one type of derivation. For instance, the successive editions often are issued simultaneously (new editions might be issued in three cities at once each year). These patterns demonstrate both the working of the marketplace and the cultural embrace of the work. The present research seems to promise to add to the growing body of empirical evidence about the derivation and mutation of works in instantiations over time. Repeated observation of quantitatively demonstrable phenomena supports the notion that a theory of the instantiation of works over time can be developed. Such a theory would have predictive power critical for the design of sophisticated work-retrieval engines.

The results of this study demonstrate both the fascinating evolution of instantiation networks across time and the importance of continuing to gather statistical data about them. We can observe the confirmation of what has been learned in earlier studies. Mean sizes of instantiation networks in the present study have 95% confidence intervals of ±9, meaning the true mean size among all 1,836 best sellers could range between 19 and 37. Despite that wide variability, it is still much larger than the means of 3.5 (in the catalog at Georgetown University) and 8.4 (in the OCLC WorldCat) observed in earlier studies (Smiraglia 2001). Instantiation networks for best selling works are, then, more than twice as large as for other works. Works that achieve the cultural status of membership in a canon are likely to evolve over time. At the very least, they will appear in many subsequent editions and translations. If they have older progenitors, these works will have larger instantiation networks. All nine categories of instantiation occur among the descendants of these progenitors, indicating the richness and utility of the taxonomy.

Extending the concept of canonicity, we discovered the tendency of some best sellers to persist over time. Apparently, although all best selling books start out with a large market niche, not all remain in the public consciousness. However, interestingly enough, all of these best sellers in the public domain have begun to appear in full-text online, sometimes complete with electronic instantiation networks. Solutions devised for the catalog, whether it be more complex uniform titles or more sophisticated linkages in *FRBR*-based systems, will need to be modified for use in the otherwise chaotic environment of the World Wide Web and its successors.

REFERENCES

International Federation of Libray Associations. 1998. *Functional Requirements for Bibliographic Records.* Munich: K.G. Saur, 1998. Available http://www.ifla.org/VII/s13/frbr/frbr.htm or http://www.ifla.org/VII/s13/frbr/frbr.pdf.

Leazer, Gregory H., Richard P. Smiraglia. 1999. Bibliographic families in the library catalog: A qualitative analysis and grounded theory. *Library resources & technical services* 43: 191-212.

Smiraglia, Richard P. 2001. *The nature of "a work:" Implications for the organization of knowledge*. Lanham, Md.: Scarecrow Press.

Smiraglia, Richard P. 2002. "Works as signs, symbols and canons: The epistemology of the work *Knowledge organization* 28 (2002): 192-202.

Smiraglia, Richard P. 2005. "Instantiation: Toward a theory." In Vaughan, Liwen, ed. *Data, information, and knowledge in a networked world: Proceedings of the Canadian Association for Information Science annual conference June 2-4 2005*. http://www.cais-acsi.ca/2005proceedings.htm.

doi:10.1300/J104v44n03_02

APPENDIX 1. Sample of Best Selling Works

		FICTION				NON-FICTION	
Year	Rank	Title	Author	Year	Rank	Title	Author
1901	3	The Helmet of Navarre	Bertha Runkle	1912	9	Woman and Labor.	Olive Schreiner
1902	1	The Virginian	Owen Wister	1920	5	White Shadows in the South Seas.	Frederick O'Brien
1907	3	The Por of Missing Men	Meredith Nicholson	1921	4	The Autobiography of Margot Asquith.	Margot Asquith
1907	10	Half a Rogue	Harold MacGrath	1923	7	Self-Mastery Through Conscious Auto-Suggestion.	Emile Coué
1912	7	The Just and the Unjust	Vaughan Kester	1924	8	Saint Joan.	Bernard Shaw
1913	9	The Valiants of Virginia,	Hallie Erminie Rives	1928	10	The Intelligent Woman's Guide to Socialism and Capitalism.	George Bernard Shaw
1914	7	Penrod	Booth Tarkington	1931	7	Fatal Interview.	Edna St. Vincent Millay
1917	2	The Light in the Clearing	Irving Bacheller	1932	3	A Fortune to Share.	Vash Young
1917	4	The Road to Understanding	Eleanor HPorter	1935	3	Life with Father.	Clarence Day
1917	5	Wildfire	Zane Grey	1935	6	Francis the First.	Francis Hackett
1917	6	Christine	Alice Cholmondeley	1936	1	Man the Unknown.	Alexis Carrel
1917	9	The Definite Object	Jeffrey Farnol	1940	7	New England: Indian Summer.	Van Wyck Brooks
1918	1	The UPTrail	Zane Grey	1941	2	The White Cliffs.	Alice Duer Miller
1918	2	The Tree of Heaven	May Sinclair	1944	10	Ten Years in Japan.	Joseph C. Grew
1920	10	Harriet and the Piper	Kathleen Norris	1945	7	General Marshall's Report.	U.S. War Dept General Staff
1923	1	Black Oxen	Gertrude Atherton	1947	9	The Fireside Book of Folk Songs.	Margaret B. Boni, editor
1925	1	Soundings	A. Hamilton Gibbs	1948	4	Sexual Behavior in the Human Male	A.C. Kinsey et al.

		FICTION				NON-FICTION	
1927	5	Jalna	Mazo de la Roche	1950	3	Look Younger, Live Longer.	Gayelord Hauser
1928	7	Old Pybus	Warwick Deeping	1950	9	Campus Zoo.	Clare Barnes Jr.
1933	3	Ann Vickers,	Sinclair Lewis	1955	5	How to Live 365 Days a Year.	John A. Schindler
1933	6	Forgive Us Our Trespasses,	Lloyd C. Douglas	1958	9	Dear Abby.	Abigail Van Buren
1933	7	The Master of Jalna,	Mazo de la Roche	1959	7	The Elements of Style.	William Strunk Jr., E. B. White
1936	10	Eyeless in Gaza,	Aldous Huxley	1960	5.	Better Homes and Gardens Dessert Book	
1939	1	The Grapes of Wrath,	John Steinbeck	1964	7	The Kennedy Wit.	compiled by Bill Adler
1941	4	The Sun Is My Undoing,	Marguerite Steen	1969	10	Twelve Years of Christmas.	Rod McKuen
1942	5	Drivin' Woman,	Elizabeth Pickett	1971	5	Any Woman Can!.	David Reuben, M.D.
1946	10	The Snake Pit,	Mary Jane Ward	1973	9	Alistair Cooke's America.	Alistair Cooke
1949	9	Pride's Castle,	Frank Yerby	1974	2	All the President's Men.	Carl Bernstein and Bob Woodward
1958	10	Victorine,	Frances Parkinson Keyes	1976	1	The Final Days.	Bob Woodward and Carl Bernstein
1960	6	The Constant Image	Marcia Davenport	1979	7	Lauren Bacall By Myself.	Lauren Bacall
1965	6	Those Who Love,	Irving Stone	1981	1	The Beverly Hills Diet.	Judy Mazel
1966	10	All in the Family,	Edwin O'Connor	1983	4	The One Minute Manager.	Kenneth Blanchard and Spencer Johnson
1969	2	The Godfather,	Mario Puzo	1985	2	Yeager: An Autobiography.	Gen. Chuck Yeager and Leo Janos
1970	9	Travels with My Aunt,	Graham Greene	1991	7	More Wealth Without Risk.	Charles J. Givens
1978	1	Chesapeake,	James A. Michener	1994	1	In the Kitchen with Rosie.	Rosie Daley
1979	5	Jailbird,	Kurt Vonnegut	1995	2	My American Journey.	Colin Powell
1981	5	Gorky Park,	Martin Cruz Smith	1995	7	Mars and Venus in the Bedroom.	John Gray
1985	8	Lucky,	Jackie Collins	1995	10	The Moral Compass.	William J. Bennett
1986	1	It,	Stephen King	1997	1	Angela's Ashes.	Frank McCourt
1987	7	Presumed Innocent,	Scott Turow				
1988	8	To Be the Best,	Barbara Taylor Bradford				
1989	4	Star,	Danielle Steel				
1994	2	Debt of Honor,	Tom Clancy				
1996	3	Desperation,	Stephen King				
1996	4	Airframe,	Michael Crichton				

Measuring Typographical Errors' Impact on Retrieval in Bibliographic Databases

Jeffrey Beall
Karen Kafadar

SUMMARY. Typographical errors can block access to records in on-line catalogs; but, when a word contains a typo and is also spelled correctly elsewhere in the same record, access may not be blocked. To quantify the effect of typographical errors in records on information retrieval, we conducted a study to measure the proportion of records that contain a typographical error but that do not also contain a correct spelling of the same word. This article presents the experimental design, results of the study, and a statistical analysis of the results. We find that the average proportion of records that are blocked by the presence of a typo (that is, records in which a correct spelling of the word does not also occur) ranges from 35% to 99%, depending upon the frequency of the word being searched and the likelihood of the word being misspelled. doi:10.1300/J104v44n03_03 *[Article copies available for a fee from The Haworth Document Delivery Service: 1-800-HAWORTH. E-mail address: <docdelivery@haworthpress.com> Website: <http://www.HaworthPress.com> © 2007 by The Haworth Press, Inc. All rights reserved.]*

Jeffrey Beall is Catalog Librarian, Auraria Library, University of Colorado at Denver and Health Sciences Center, 1100 Lawrence Street, Denver, CO 80204 (E-mail: jeffrey.beall@cudenver.edu). Karen Kafadar is Professor, Department of Mathematical Sciences, University of Colorado at Denver and Health Sciences Center, P.O. Box 173364, Denver, CO 80217 (E-mail: kk@math.cudenver.edu).

[Haworth co-indexing entry note]: "Measuring Typographical Errors' Impact on Retrieval in Bibliographic Databases." Beall, Jeffrey, and Karen Kafadar. Co-published simultaneously in *Cataloging & Classification Quarterly* (The Haworth Information Press, an imprint of The Haworth Press, Inc.) Vol. 44, No. 3/4, 2007, pp. 197-211; and: *Cataloger, Editor, and Scholar: Essays in Honor of Ruth C. Carter* (ed: Robert P. Holley) The Haworth Information Press, an imprint of The Haworth Press, Inc., 2007, pp. 197-211. Single or multiple copies of this article are available for a fee from The Haworth Document Delivery Service [1-800-HAWORTH, 9:00 a.m. - 5:00 p.m. (EST). E-mail address: docdelivery@haworthpress.com].

Available online at http://ccq.haworthpress.com
© 2007 by The Haworth Press, Inc. All rights reserved.
doi:10.1300/J104v44n03_03

KEYWORDS. Errata, cataloging errors, online library catalogs

1. INTRODUCTION AND PREVIOUS STUDIES

Typographical errors limit retrieval of bibliographic records in online catalogs. If a given word is spelled both correctly *and* incorrectly in the same record, retrieval is often (but not always) not blocked because the correctly spelled word matches the search argument and hence the record is successfully retrieved in the search results.

Using keyword searches of typographical errors to study database quality originated with "The Dirty Database Test" proposed by Beall and described in a sidebar in *American Libraries* in 1991.[1] The test involves searching a set of ten misspelled words and then adding the total number of hits to use as a rough measure of data quality in a bibliographic database. Numerous studies have followed this methodology,[2] but most of these studies attempt to measure overall database quality.

Only a single previous study has attempted to measure the impact of correctly spelled words that complement a typographical error in the same bibliographic record, thereby ameliorating retrieval. That study, "Spelling Errors in the Database: Shadow or Substance?" by Barbara Nichols Randall,[3] found that spelling errors are "shadow." The author concluded: "Most spelling errors are redundant errors and thus do not prevent users from finding the needed record."[4] However, the study included only a small number of test words, did not indicate whether the test words were selected randomly, and did not include calculations of statistical confidence for the conclusions.

We decided to investigate this phenomenon with a statistically designed experiment. If a misspelled word appears in a record, what proportion of the records with the misspelled word fail to contain the word again, correctly spelled? If this proportion is low, then Randall's assertion can be confirmed quantitatively. But if it is high, then a large number of records will be missed.

This article describes the investigation and results. Section 2 describes the methodology and experimental design. Section 3 presents the results. Conclusions are given in Section 4. Further details on the statistical analysis appear in the Appendix.

2. METHODOLOGY

2.1 Selecting the Words

We randomly selected 135 words from the Web site "Typographical errors in library databases"[5] based on two criteria. First, because the frequency with which the word might be misspelled might have an effect on the results, we selected words based on "typo frequency." The site that lists the typographical errors is divided into five sections, based on a measure of how often a given typo is likely to occur in bibliographic databases. These categories are Very High, High, Moderate, Low, and Very Low. We combined the top two and bottom two categories to make three groups of typo frequency, which we called Frequent (F), Semi-Frequent (S), and Infrequent (I).

Second, it seemed plausible that more-common words might have different outcomes than less-common words. That is, more-common words are more likely to appear again elsewhere in the record; the target proportion of records that would be missed when the search word is a common one would be lower than if it were an uncommon word. Therefore, we also considered word frequency itself to see if it had any impact on our results. We sought word frequency data that would enable us to search words based on their frequency of occurrence in bibliographic records. We assumed that a general English language word frequency list would not be appropriate because the word frequency from bibliographic records would likely differ from a general word frequency list because bibliographic records are a specialized set of language data. No word frequency list of words in bibliographic records existed, so we generated one using a set of records taken from the online library catalog at the Downtown Denver Campus of the University of Colorado at Denver and Health Sciences Center. This generation involved selecting at random one thousand records from the catalog. We then tabulated the frequency of all words in these 1,000 records. Because numbers, such as specific years like 1990, were so common in the sample data, we eliminated them from the sample. After generating the sample, we took the most common 684 words from the sample and divided them into two equal sections of 342 words. The top 342 words formed our "High Word Frequency" category, and the next 342 words formed our "Moderate Word Frequency" category. All the other words fell into the "Low Word Frequency" category.[6]

Next we designed a grid that contained nine sections. The horizontal axis of this grid corresponded to the three levels of word frequency; the vertical axis was for the three levels of typo frequency. We used numbers from a random number table to select 15 words for each of the 9 boxes in the grid. The table below shows all 9 categories with one of the 15 words in each category. The complete table of all $9 \times 15 = 135$ words appears in the Appendix.

Table 1 shows the grid we created to guide us in the selection of misspelled words from all three categories of word and typo frequency. This grid and our random number tables led to the 15 words in each of the 9 word frequency/typo frequency categories shown in Table 2. Because we eliminated dates from our word frequency sample, we did not use dates when the randomization process led us to select a typo that was a date. In the Web site *Typographical Errors in Library Databases*, some of the typos occur in dates, such as using the letter "l" instead of the initial "1" in *1990*. In this case, we skipped the word and selected another one from the next random number. Had we included dates, we expect that our estimated proportion of missed records would be much higher.

2.2. Gathering the Data

We selected the WorldCat database as our test database, and we searched using the FirstSearch search interface. The searching was done in August 2005. For each typo, we performed two keyword searches. The searches were not qualified in any way (by date or by language, for example). We searched:

Search	Example
Typographical error	congess*
Incorrect not correct	congess* not congress*

One valuable feature of the FirstSearch interface is that it informs the searcher about the exact number of hits retrieved for each search. Our raw data consisted of the number of hits for each of the two searches listed above for each of the 135 words. In a few cases, the system returned errors stating it was unable to complete the search because it exceeded its capacity. In this case, we selected new words by using the randomization process to replace these words that the system could not search.

The list of typos contains many truncated words, which is a method of listing several variant forms of a word together. The asterisk is used

TABLE 1

		Typo Frequency Category		
		B1 Frequent	B2: Semi-frequent	B3: Infrequent
Word Frequency Category	A1: High	A1 B1 congess*	A1 B2 ternational*	A1 B3 prress
	A2: Moderate	A2 B1 Philadelh*	A2 B2 contemporay*	A2 B3 Japnes*
	A3: Low	A3 B1 aquir*	A3 B2 manufactuer*	A3 B3 Nashvile*

The grid we used to guide our selection of words from all possible combinations of word and typo frequency. Each of the nine cells in the table lists one the 15 words in the complete study. The complete table is given in Table 2.

to represent truncation. For example, the typo *congess** represents *congess, congesses, congessional*, etc. We maintained this truncation in our searching. By doing this, we hoped to test simultaneously several forms of a given misspelling. Most searches done on a public interface such as FirstSearch are probably unqualified keyword searches–the type of search performed in this study. It is acknowledged that, if a user were performing a subject search, if the subject contained a misspelled word, and if a correct spelling of that word occurred elsewhere in the record, the record would not be retrieved because the search was limited to the subject headings. Therefore, this study tests search failure only for unqualified keyword searches that are not limited to a specific search type such as author, title, subject, etc. The data were collected and recorded using Microsoft Excel, and the statistical analysis was performed using R (http://www.r-project.org).

3. STATISTICAL ANALYSIS

The results of the investigation are shown in Table 2 grouped by A-category (word frequency: high, moderate, low) and B-category (typo frequency: frequent, semi-frequent, infrequent). Within each group are listed the misspelled word, the number of records in which it was misspelled, the number of records in which the word did not appear correctly spelled, and the proportion (i.e., the ratio of those two numbers). For example, the first word in the "high-frequency, frequently mistyped" category that was searched was "congess*," which appeared in 282 records. Among them, "congress*" appeared (correctly) in only 32 of these 282 records; i.e., in 246 records, the correctly spelled "con-

TABLE 2

B: Frequency of Typos

		B1: Frequent				B2: Semi-Frequent				B3: Infrequent		
		N	X	P		N	X	P		N	X	P
A1	congess*	282	246	0.872	ternational*	9	5	0.555	prress	4	4	1.000
	unied*	84	29	0.345	instituio*	148	89	0.601	bioraph*	50	37	0.740
	seriv*	477	203	0.425	statess*	115	0	0.000	ccounc*	6	2	0.333
	nationa	204	103	0.504	engish*	74	47	0.635	systms	14	6	0.429
	assocaition*	74	35	0.472	boook	13	2	0.154	libbrar*	2	2	1.000
	United_State	1398	487	0.348	biogaph*	29	22	0.759	incld*	333	323	0.970
	sevice*	330	147	0.445	intellign*	64	37	0.578	ciivi*	3	0	0.000
	langauge*	407	155	0.380	reprot	39	22	0.564	governent	26	19	0.731
	musuem*	297	99	0.333	cutlur*	55	26	0.473	conservation	3	1	0.333
	Yrok*	23	8	0.347	teachng*	73	33	0.452	desingn*	11	5	0.455
	manange*	204	76	0.372	finace*	114	63	0.553	sschool*	17	7	0.412
	conditon*	142	86	0.605	survy*	104	43	0.413	technoloy	20	6	0.300
	Goerge	362	271	0.748	edcuat*	268	63	0.235	vidorecording*	3	2	0.667
	Afica*'t	107	28	0.261	educaion	156	45	0.288	cenral	60	21	0.350
	civl*	269	114	0.423	librara*	101	84	0.832	conferrence*	31	11	0.355
A2	Philadelh*	33	14	0.424	contemporay*	62	48	0.774	Japnes*	66	28	0.424
	foreward*	7550	7410	0.981	resorce*	82	33	0.402	perspetive	13	10	0.769
	distrubut*	55	46	0.836	estem	178	158	0.888	gropu*	40	29	0.725
	colection*	273	193	0.706	criminial*	49	16	0.327	beteween*	7	6	0.857
	compositon*	177	126	0.711	vocatin*	25	6	0.240	desision*	45	26	0.578
	mathmati*	356	132	0.370	Columib*	103	44	0.427	childhod	9	5	0.556
	litle*	688	472	0.686	persepect*	54	37	0.685	gelogy	18	4	0.222
	resouc*	286	113	0.395	military*	154	83	0.539	sympsoium	61	18	0.295
	chilrl*	342	306	0.894	dicton*	475	378	0.796	childerns	13	7	0.538
	decison*	127	71	0.559	veiw*	88	61	0.693	studetn*	45	26	0.578

	athelete*	89	57	0.640	elecronic*	31	13	0.419	fulfillem*	9	9	1.000
	enviroment*	443	195	0.440	cooperti*	239	132	132	expereinc*	39	26	0.667
A2	communite*	338	293	0.866	Spainish	79	53	0.671	natrual*	35	21	0.600
	electoni*	125	49	0.392	apprao*	129	98	0.760	Alask	8	1	0.125
	genral*	478	285	0.596	japanse*	370	171	0.462	nighi	1	0	0.000
	aquir*	339	318	0.938	manufactuer*	79	52	0.658	Nashvile*	19	13	0.684
	temperment*lt	172	148	0.860	scandel	39	32	0.821	jugdment*	26	2	0.077
	anced*	43	32	0.744	severly	54	48	0.889	editd	94	89	0.947
	avaiab*	77	63	0.818	microfom	2	2	1.000	apprp*	30	16	0.533
	Cincinati*	96	51	0.531	Brazillian	90	77	0.856	variou	941	939	0.998
	Carribbean	257	146	0.568	commetar*	146	87	0.596	beuty*	10	8	0.800
	adultr*	125	97	0.776	biliotheque	68	43	0.632	sypplement	5	4	0.800
A3	jospeh*	1006	281	0.279	encyclopoedi*	55	39	0.709	singng	3	1	0.333
	Chrisit*	293	113	0.385	citzenship	22	9	0.409	wthin	18	16	0.889
	Buddis*	320	139	0.434	quarangle	9	5	0.556	Louisis*	25	10	0.400
	manucript*	74	36	0.486	tradegy	69	56	0.812	bucaneers	15	13	0.867
	Pennyslvania*	207	82	0.396	huamn*	16	11	0.688	tourch*	21	21	1.000
	Austrailia*	142	69	0.485	atmopsh*	28	10	0.357	questionnia*	19	10	0.526
	disabilit*	18	5	0.277	allumin*	106	63	0.594	scieniti*	10	5	0.500
	fascim*	766	653	0.852	comissione*	213	141	0.662	inpeach*	1	0	0.000

gress*" did not appear. Thus, a search for the word beginning with "congress" would fail to return 246 of the 282 records, or 87.2% of them. We will denote the number of hits in the first search (e.g., 282) by "N" and the proportion of missed records (e.g., 0.872) as "P." Figure 1 displays the variability in these proportions via boxplots,[7] grouped by word and typo frequency.

Each boxplot displays the median, quartiles, and extremes among the 15 transformed proportions in each word/typo group. (In some cases, the minimum or maximum of the 15 numbers was quite different from the other 14 numbers so it is designated separately; e.g., see boxes labeled 12, 13, 23, 33, whose minimum is 0 but the next closest value is 0.3 or higher.) The label for each box designates the A/B category; e.g., "12" indicates A1/B2 group, or high frequency word, semi-frequently mistyped. Panel A (left) of Figure 1 groups together the three A1 categories, followed by the three A2 categories, and finally the three A3 categories; in general, the level of the first three boxes (A1, high frequency words) tends to be lower than that of the next three boxes (A2, moderately frequent words), which in turn have lower proportions than the last three boxes (A3, low frequency words). That is, the proportions tend to increase with decreasing word frequency. This is sensible: the higher the word frequency, the more likely it is to appear again in the record; and hence the more opportunities for it to be correctly spelled elsewhere in the record. Panel B (right) groups the boxes together by the three B1 categories, then the three B2 categories, and lastly the three B3 categories. The trends in the proportions by typo frequency is less clear, indicating that word frequency has a greater influence on the proportions than does typo frequency.

Part of the complication in interpreting the raw proportions is due to the fact that the uncertainty in the proportions (P) is a function of both P and N, roughly $\sqrt{P(1-P)/N}$.[9] Thus, the closer P is to 0.5 and the smaller the N, the larger the uncertainty. We can minimize the dependence of this uncertainty on P by transforming P to $Y = (\arcsin \sqrt{P})$: the uncertainty in Y is $1/\sqrt{N}$. Figure 2 shows another boxplot display using the same structure as in Figure 1 but displaying the transformed proportions instead. When we examine the three left-most boxes in Figure 2A, we see that the proportions tend to increase with decreasing typo frequency (B1,B2,B3) among the High frequency words (A1); this appears to be true also for the Low frequency words (A3). Among the moderately frequent (A2) words (i.e., the three middle boxes in Figure 2A), the proportions seem to slightly decrease or to stay about the same.

FIGURE 1

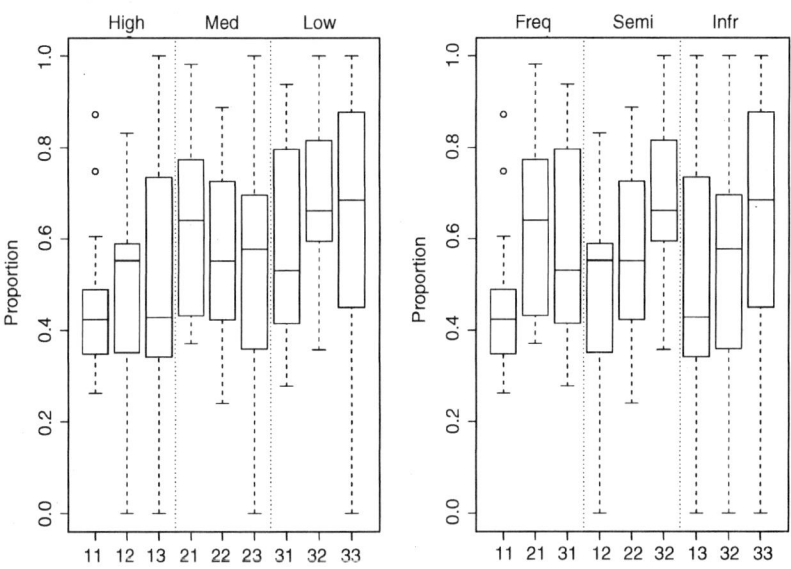

A: Word frequency = 1 (high) 2 (medium) 3 (low)
B: Typo frequency = 1 (frequent) 2 (semi-frequent) 3 (infrequent)

Thus, the trend in the proportions as a function of typo frequency seems to depend mostly on the frequency of the word. The boxes in Figures 1 and 2 as well as Table 2 show substantial variability in the proportions (P) as well as in the numbers of occurrences (N).

We summarize the proportions by A- and B-categories by averaging the transformed (arcsine-square root) proportions, weighted by the inverse of their variances (i.e., by N). We calculate the standard errors of the weighted averages and then calculate approximate upper and lower 95% confidence limits on the transformed scale using allowances of plus or minus two standard errors around each weighted average. (The standard error of the weighted average is approximated using a propagation of error formula–see Ku[8]–and is usually smaller than the standard error of the unweighted average, so we will use the more conservative (larger) standard error for this interval.) Finally, we transform both the weighted average and the limits back to the original P scale by squaring the sine of the values. The results are shown in Table 3. For comparison, we also show the unweighted mean and standard error (i.e., the mean of the 15 proportions and their standard deviation divided by $\sqrt{15}$).

FIGURE 2

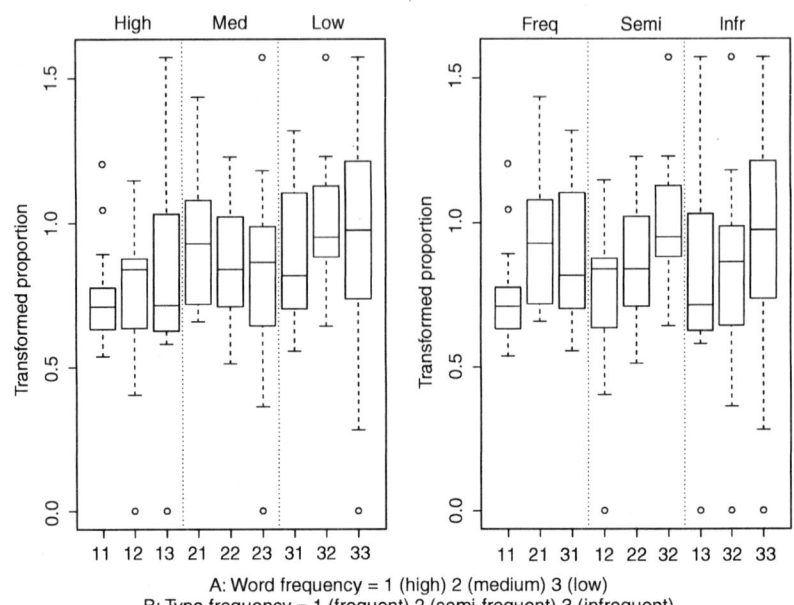

A: Word frequency = 1 (high) 2 (medium) 3 (low)
B: Typo frequency = 1 (frequent) 2 (semi-frequent) 3 (infrequent)

The most obvious feature in Tables 2 and 3 is the magnitude of the proportions: all exceed 40%; and the highest proportions occur in the A3/B3 category (low frequency words, infrequently mistyped). The weighted and unweighted average proportions are similar (within ± 0.05) except in categories 2 (A2/B1), 7 (A1/B3), and 9 (A3/B3). The cause of these large differences is the appearance of one word with an extremely high number of occurrences (N). For example, N ranges from 33 to 688 for the words in category 2, except "foreward*" (7550). Likewise, the counts in category 7 range from 2 to 60 except "incld*" which occurred in 333 records; and the counts in category 9 range from 1 to 30 except for "editd" (94 times) and "various" (941 times). In all 4 cases, the observed proportions were 0.95 or higher. (No relationship between N and either P or arcsin ($\sqrt{P}$) appears in general; see Figure 3.) Due to the high weight attributed to these high proportions in the weighted average, the difference between it and the unweighted average for these three categories was quite high (0.26). However, because the proportions based on large N are more reliable (uncertainties are inversely proportional to $\sqrt{N}$), the weighted average is more reliable.

TABLE 3. Average of the Proportions (Weighted and Unweighted Averages) with Intervals of Plus or Minus Two Standard Errors, by A-Category and by B-Category

		$Y = \arcsin(\sqrt{P})$				$P = \text{proportion} = (\sin(Y))^2$			
A	B	weighted avg (Y)	unweighted mean	standard error	lower limit	upper limit	weighted avg (P)	unweighted mean	lower limit	upper limit
1	1	0.7356	0.7471	0.0459	0.6438	0.8274	0.4503	0.4617	0.3603	0.5420
2	1	1.2598	0.9404	0.0612	1.1374	1.3821	0.9063	0.6525	0.8237	0.9648
3	1	0.8695	0.8886	0.0636	0.7423	0.9967	0.5837	0.6024	0.4569	0.7051
1	2	0.6893	0.7406	0.0714	0.5465	0.8322	0.4045	0.4553	0.2701	0.5467
2	2	0.9246	0.8678	0.0531	0.8184	1.0309	0.6374	0.5821	0.5329	0.7358
3	2	0.9746	0.9959	0.0576	0.8593	1.0899	0.6847	0.7044	0.5736	0.7860
1	3	1.1331	0.8503	0.1052	0.9227	1.3435	0.8203	0.5648	0.6356	0.9492
2	3	0.8182	0.8141	0.0923	0.6336	1.0029	0.5328	0.5287	0.3505	0.7107
3	3	1.4084	0.9365	0.1102	1.1879	1.6288	0.9738	0.6488	0.8604	0.9966

The Appendix contains two additional tables. Table 4 lists the averages by A-factors, B-factors, and jointly (A- and B-factors), when calculated in the (T) transformed scale (transformed back to original scale) and (O) original, untransformed scale, along with 95% intervals of uncertainty. For comparison, unweighted averages are listed also. Table 5 contains a formal analysis of variance on the transformed proportions, weighted inversely proportional to their variances; it confirms the significance of factor A, word frequency, as the primary effect on the results and also, to a lesser extent, of factor B, typo frequency.

4. CONCLUSION

This study quantified the effect of typographical errors in bibliographic databases by sampling records in the WorldCat database. If a user searches for all records in which a (correctly spelled) word is sought, a rather high proportion of records that contain the incorrectly spelled word will be missed because the word does not appear again, correctly spelled, in the record. The proportion of missed records ranges from 40% (95% confidence interval: 27% to 55%) to 97% (95% confidence interval: 86% to 99%) and depends on word frequency (lower proportions of missed records for more-frequent words, higher proportions for less-frequent words) and, to a lesser extent, on typo frequency.

FIGURE 3. Weighted Averages with Limits of One Standard Error, First as a Function of A-category (Figure 3A, left panel) and Then as a Function of B-category (Figure 3B, right panel)

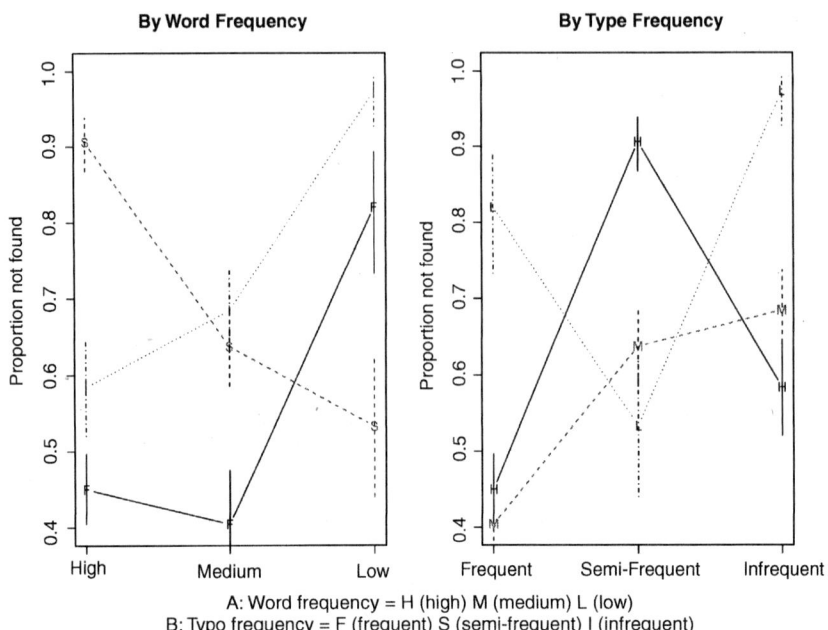

A: Word frequency = H (high) M (medium) L (low)
B: Typo frequency = F (frequent) S (semi-frequent) I (infrequent)

Due to the enormous variability in the numbers of records in which randomly selected words appeared, it would be important to confirm these results with a larger study. Also, if the retrieval limits on FirstSearch are increased, the study should be repeated using the words that maxed out the system and therefore could not be included in this study. It would also be useful to confirm these findings on other databases. These studies are underway and will be reported in a future article.

REFERENCES

1. Jeffrey Beall, "Ideas: the Dirty Database Test," *American Libraries* 22:3 (1991): 197.
2. For an excellent summary see: D.W. Bade, *Theory and Practice of Bibliographic Failure, or, Misinformation in the Information Society* (Ulaanbaatar: Chuluunbat, 2004).
3. Barbara Nichols Randall, "Spelling Errors in the Database: Shadow or Substance?" *Library Resources & Technical Services* 43:3 (1999):161-169.

4. Randall, p. 168.
5. Terry Ballard, "Typographical Errors in Library Databases," http://faculty.quinnipiac.edu/libraries/tballard/typoscomplete.html.
6. The ten most common words found (in order) are: And, The, Of, Includes, Bibliographical, References, States, United, New, A.
7. John W. Tukey, *Exploratory Data Analysis* (Reading, Mass.: Addison-Wesley, 1977).
8. Harry Ku, "Notes on the Use of Propagation of Error Formulas," in *Statistical Concepts and Procedures*, ed. Harry Ku (Washington: U.S. Govt. Print. Off., 1969), 331-341.
9. George W. Snedecor and William G. Cochran, *Statistical Methods*, 8th ed. (Ames, Iowa: Blackwell, 1989).

doi:10.1300/J104v44n03_03

APPENDIX

Table 5 provides the analysis of variance for the transformed proportions, arcsin ($\sqrt{P}$), in terms of the two factors A and B and their interaction, A × B. This table confirms our visual assessment that both factors influence the response with the larger effect coming from factor A. Because factors A and B have three levels, Table 4 lists each factor with 2 degrees of freedom, each of which can be decomposed into two 1-degree of freedom contrasts and their interaction has 2 × 2 = 4 degrees of freedom. The sum of squares for A can be decomposed into two separate one-degree-of-freedom contrasts, one that represents the linear effect of A, say A_L, and one that represents its quadratic effect, say A_Q, and likewise for B (B_L and B_Q). Table 4 shows that these two factors, A and B, account for 48% of the variation in the response, arcsin ($\sqrt{P}$) and that the largest contributor is factor A (27.7%), specifically its quadratic component A_Q (21.6%). The interaction $A_Q \times B_L$ accounts for 10.7%, followed by B_Q (7.8%) and A_L (6.2%). The contributions from the other 4 degrees of freedom amount to only 1.6%.

The linear and quadratic effects of A (A_L, A_Q) confirms the conclusion seen in Figures 1 and 2 and Table 3: as word frequency decreases, the proportion of missed records increases (less frequent words are less likely to appear again in the record and hence be spelled correctly elsewhere), but the increase is not perfectly linear (.49 to .59 and .59 to .65). The effect may be linear if the categories were defined differently. The p-values confirm significant trends for A_L (p-value 0.0002) A_Q (p-value 4.3 x 10^{-11}) and the quadratic effect for B, B_Q (p-value 0.0003).

TABLE 4. Weighted and Unweighted Averages, by Factors A (Word Frequency) and B (Typo Frequency)

		Transformed & Weighted Average					
		(transformed back to original scale) Typo Frequency			weighted average Typo Frequency		
		B1	B2	B3	B1	B2	B3
		Frequent	Semi-freq	Infrequent	Frequent	Semi-freq	Infrequent
A1	High	0.4503	0.4045	0.8203	0.4479	0.4266	0.7650
A2	Med	0.9063	0.6374	0.5328	0.8593	0.6284	0.5281
A3	Low	0.5837	0.6847	0.9738	0.5675	0.6777	0.9272

A-averages

	A1	A2	A3
Trans +wtd	0.5584 (0.4220, 0.6793)	0.6922 (0.5690, 0.8038)	0.7474 (0.6303, 0.8292)
wtd	0.5465	0.6720	0.7241
unwtd	0.4939 (0.3482, 0.6375)	0.5877 (0.4518, 0.7182)	0.6518 (0.5005, 0.7879)

B-averages

	B1	B2	B3
Trans +wtd	0.6468 (0.5469, 0.7373)	0.5756 (0.4589, 0.6895)	0.7757 (0.6155, 0.8855)
wtd	0.6249	0.5776	0.7401
unwtd	0.5722 (0.4600, 0.6797)	0.5806 (0.4625, 0.6950)	0.5807 (0.3780, 0.7690)

TABLE 5. Analysis of Variance for Arcsin ($\sqrt{P}$), Weighted Inversely Proportional to its Variance ($1/N$)

Response: asin(sqrt(P))

	Df	Sum	Sq Mean	Sq F-value	Pr(> F)		%Variance
Factor A	2	864.69	432.34	33.52	2.128e-12	***	
AL (linear)	1	192.14	192.14	14.90	0.0001805	***	6.17
AQ (quadratic)	1	672.54	672.54	52.14	4.316e-11	***	21.58
Factor B	2	265.27	132.63	10.28	7.300e-05	***	
BL (linear)	1	21.14	21.14	1.64	0.2028186		0.68
BQ (quadratic)	1	244.13	244.13	18.93	2.778e-05	***	7.84
Interaction:							
AXB	4	360.66	90.16	6.99	4.087e-05	***	
AL:BL	1	23.07	23.07	1.79	0.1835457		0.74
AL:BQ	1	0.14	0.14	0.01	0.9169674		0.00
AQ:BL	1	332.61	332.61	25.79	1.338e-06	***	10.67
AQ:BQ	1	4.84	4.84	0.38	0.5410820		0.16
Residuals	126	1625.23	12.90				52.16
Total	134	3115.84					

*** = highly significant—less than 0.001 chance that the effect showed significance but is not real

Error Rates in Monograph Copy Cataloging Bibliographic Records Before and After Outsourcing at the University of Saskatchewan Library

Vinh-The Lam

SUMMARY. This comparative study was conducted to compare error rates encountered in monograph copy cataloging bibliographic records before and after a cataloging outsourcing program was implemented at the University of Saskatchewan Library. The findings of the study were twofold: (1) The error rates were low and acceptable; (2) There was no significant difference between error rates before and after outsourcing. doi:10.1300/J104v44n03_04 *[Article copies available for a fee from The Haworth Document Delivery Service: 1-800-HAWORTH. E-mail address: <docdelivery@haworthpress.com> Website: <http://www.HaworthPress.com> © 2007 by The Haworth Press, Inc. All rights reserved.]*

KEYWORDS. Academic libraries, cataloging, outsourcing, monograph cataloging, copy cataloging, error rates, Saskatchewan

---

Vinh-The Lam is Original Cataloguer, Technical Services Division, University of Saskatchewan Library, 3 Campus Drive, Saskatoon, Saskatchewan, S7N 5A4, Canada (E-mail: vinhthe.lam@usask.ca).

[Haworth co-indexing entry note]: "Error Rates in Monograph Copy Cataloging Bibliographic Records Before and After Outsourcing at the University of Saskatchewan Library." Vinh-The Lam. Co-published simultaneously in *Cataloging & Classification Quarterly* (The Haworth Information Press, an imprint of The Haworth Press, Inc.) Vol. 44, No. 3/4, 2007, pp. 213-220; and: *Cataloger, Editor, and Scholar: Essays in Honor of Ruth C. Carter* (ed: Robert P. Holley) The Haworth Information Press, an imprint of The Haworth Press, Inc., 2007, pp. 213-220. Single or multiple copies of this article are available for a fee from The Haworth Document Delivery Service [1-800-HAWORTH, 9:00 a.m. - 5:00 p.m. (EST). E-mail address: docdelivery@haworthpress.com].

Available online at http://ccq.haworthpress.com
© 2007 by The Haworth Press, Inc. All rights reserved.
doi:10.1300/J104v44n03_04

BACKGROUND

During my sabbatical leave from the University of Saskatchewan Library (July 2003-June 2004), I conducted a research project to investigate various issues of quality control in cataloging outsourcing programs carried out at U.S. and Canadian academic libraries.[1] The quality of cataloging was defined as a combination of the following components: accuracy, consistency, adequacy of access points, and timeliness. One of the major findings of the research was that, for a large majority of outsourcing libraries (62.79%), the quality of cataloging after outsourcing remained the same. Only about a quarter of these libraries (25.58%) reported that the quality of their cataloging increased, and less than one-eighth of them (11.63%) reported that the quality of their cataloging decreased. For both groups, reported data were obtained not from an in-house survey but mostly from personal observations/opinions or discussions with colleagues within the cataloging department or from public services. During my sabbatical leave, the University of Saskatchewan Library began its outsourcing program for monograph copy cataloging. After my sabbatical leave, I was made responsible for the quality control of outsourced materials. As part of my new responsibilities, I conducted an in-house survey of the error rates encountered in copy cataloging bibliographic records for monographs before and after we implemented our outsourcing program.

METHODS

This comparative study was conducted to answer the following questions: (1) What were the error rates of monograph copy cataloging bibliographic records? (2) Were the error rates affected by the outsourcing program?

Two samples of bibliographic records were taken for this comparative study. The first one was a systematic sample of 5% of a list of 6,569 OCLC/LTS records of the first year of the outsourcing program (2003-2004). This was done by taking every 20th record from the list (n1 = 329). The second one was taken from a list of 22,385 in-house records created the year before the outsourcing program started (2002-2003). Excluded from this list were records for the following types of materials: audiovisual materials, maps, music, government documents, and serials. Also excluded from the list were original cataloging records and records bought from e-book vendors. Based on the population size of

22,385 and the desired confidence level of 95% with a 5% significance level, the desired sample size was calculated to be 378 (n2 = 378). The records were randomly selected using a random function in Excel.

Based on the technical specifications in the contract that the University of Saskatchewan Library had signed with the outsourcing vendor, the review of records was performed only for the following key fields in the records in both samples:

Non-access points:

- 008
- 040
- 250 $a
- 260 $b, and $c
- 300 $a
- 590 (for our Local Series only)

Access Points:

- 020
- 090
- 1XX
- 245 $a
- 4XX
- 6XX (for LCSH only)
- 7XX
- 8XX

The error rate was calculated as the number of errors per total number of key fields in the samples.

FINDINGS

Some Statistics About the Materials Cataloged

Distribution by Locations:

Location	Outsourced Sample	In-House Sample
Main Library	235 (71.4%)	281 (74.3%)
Education Library	31 (9.4%)	30 (7.9%)
Engineering Library	16 (4.8%)	11 (2.9%)

Location	Outsourced Sample	In-House Sample
Health Sciences Library	26 (7.9%)	14 (3.7%)
Law Library	5 (1.5%)	16 (4.2%)
Natural Sciences Library	13 (3.9%)	24 (6.3%)
Veterinary Medicine Library	3 (0.9%)	2 (0.5%)
Total	329 (100%)	378 (100%)

Distribution by Subjects:

LC Class	Outsourced Sample	In-House Sample
Non-LC (Dewey, Fic.)	7 (2.1%)	17 (4.4%)
Class B	20 (6.0%)	43 (11.3%)
Class C	0 (0.0%)	3 (0.7%)
Class D	12 (3.6%)	36 (9.5%)
Class E	4 (1.2%)	4 (1.0%)
Class F	6 (1.8%)	11 (2.9%)
Class G	9 (2.7%)	19 (5.0%)
Class H	38 (11.5%)	42 (11.1%)
Class J	5 (1.5%)	16 (4.2%)
Class K	4 (1.2%)	16 (4.2%)
Class L	19 (5.7%)	12 (3.1%)
Class M	5 (1.5%)	2 (0.5%)
Class N	7 (2.1%)	13 (3.4%)
Class P	75 (22.7%)	53 (14.0%)
Class Q	41 (12.4%)	37 (9.7%)
Class R	33 (10.0%)	19 (5.0%)
Class S	17 (5.1%)	4 (1.0%)
Class T	23 (6.9%)	19 (5.0%)
Class U	1 (0.3%)	6 (1.5%)
Class V	0 (0.0%)	3 (0.7%)
Class Z	3 (0.9%)	3 (0.7%)
Total	329 (100%)	378 (100%)

Types of Records

There was a fairly large majority of LC records in the outsourced sample as demonstrated in the following table:

Sample of Outsourced Records: (n1 = 329)

Types of Records	Total Records
LC Records	245 (74.47%)
Non-LC Records	84 (25.53%)
Total	329 (100%)

By contrast, there was almost an even split between LC and non-LC records in the in-house sample as we can see from the following table:

Sample of In-House Records: (n2 = 378)

Types of Records	Total Records
LC Records	195 (51.58%)
Non-LC Records	183 (48.42%)
Total	378 (100%)

A closer look at the two samples revealed that the in-house sample included almost twice (31) the number of National Library of Canada (NLC) records than the outsourced sample (16). This factor was an important contribution to the quality of records in the in-house sample.

Types of Errors

Following is the distribution in the key fields of the types of errors encountered in records with errors (45 records from outsourced cataloging and 56 records from in-house cataloging) from the two samples:

MARC Tags with Errors	Outsourced Records	In-House Records
008	17 (31.3%)	20 (27.7%)
040	0 (0.0%)	13 (18.0%)
020	0 (0.0%)	2 (2.7%)
090	1 (1.7%)	3 (4.1%)
1XX	0 (0.0%)	3 (4.1%)
245 $a	1 (1.7%)	4 (5.5%)
250 $a	1 (1.7%)	2 (2.7%)
260 (Missing whole Tag)	0 (0.0%)	1 (1.3%)
260 $b	0 (0.0%)	0 (0.0%)
260 $c	10 (17.8%)	0 (0.0%)
300 (Missing whole Tag)	0 (0.0%)	1 (1.3%)
300 $a	1 (1.7%)	4 (5.5%)

MARC Tags with Errors	Outsourced Records		In-House Records	
4XX	2	(3.5%)	2	(2.7%)
590 (Local series)	0	(0.0%)	0	(0.0%)
6XX	20	(35.7%)	4	(5.5%)
7XX	3	(5.3%)	13	(18.0%)
8XX	0	(0.0%)	0	(0.0%)
Total Errors	56	(100%)	72	(100%)

General Error Rate

The total number of key fields was calculated for both samples. The general error rate from both samples was almost the same as we can see from the following table:

Sample	Total Errors	Total Fields	Error Rate
Outsourced	56	4023	56/4023 = 0.0139%
In-House	72	4560	72/4560 = 0.0157%

Major Errors

A major error was defined as an error that would result in loss of access to the item cataloged. Included in this category were errors in all the key fields for access points: 020, 090, 1XX, 245, 4XX, 6XX, 7XX, and 8XX. The following table shows the distribution of major errors in both samples:

MARC Tags with Errors	Outsourced Records		In-House Records	
020	0	(0.0%)	2	(6.4%)
090	1	(3.7%)	3	(9.6%)
1XX	0	(0.0%)	3	(9.6%)
245 $a	1	(3.7%)	4	(12.9%)
4XX	2	(7.4%)	2	(6.4%)
6XX	20	(74.0%)	4	(12.9%)
7XX	3	(11.1%)	13	(41.9%)
8XX	0	(0.0%)	0	(0.0%)
Total	27	(100%)	31	(100%)

Major Error Rates

The total numbers of key fields for access points were calculated for both samples. Again, the major error rate from both samples was almost the same as can be seen in the following table:

Sample	Total Errors	Total Fields	Major Error Rate
Outsourced	27	2639	27/2639 = 0.0102%
In-House	31	2877	29/2877 = 0.0107%

DISCUSSION

The characteristics of the two samples were very similar. In terms of locations of cataloged materials, almost three quarters of them (71% for the outsourced sample and 74% for the in-house sample) were for Main Library. In terms of subject content of the cataloged materials, both samples included large numbers of records for the same LC classes, namely classes B, D, H, L, P, Q, R, and T. This similarity made the comparison of the two samples statistically meaningful.

In general, the error rates for both samples were quite low and more than acceptable. In both samples, there were also more errors in the non-access point key fields than in access point key fields. The ratio for non-access-point errors vs. access-point errors was 29/27 (or 1.07) for the outsourced sample, and 41/31 (or 1.32) for the in-house sample. It was also interesting to note that both samples included a fairly large number of errors in Field 008 and that the number was quite equal for both samples: 17 in OCLC/LTS records and 20 in in-house records. The distribution of these errors in both samples is presented in the following table:

Codes Used For	Outsourced Sample		In-House Sample	
Contents (bibliography)	4	(23.5%)	4	(20.0%)
Country	3	(17.6%)	4	(20.0%)
Date	0	(0.0%)	1	(5.0%)
Government documents	1	(5.8%)	0	(0.0%)
Illustrations	5	(29.4%)	8	(40.0%)
Index	4	(23.5%)	3	(15.0%)
Total	17	(100%)	20	(100%)

In the access point key fields, the groupings of errors in the two samples were different. There were 20 errors in the 6XX for the outsourced sample and 13 in the 7XX for the in-house sample. The following table shows the distribution of all the 20 errors in 6XX of the outsourced records:

Types of Errors	Number of Occurrence	
Wrong Topical Subject Headings (650) Used	1	(5.0%)
Wrong Type of Subject Headings Used (650 was used instead of 651)	1	(5.0%)
Additional Topical Subject Headings (650) Needed	5	(25.0%)
Subdivisions Changed	2	(10.0%)
Subdivisions Added	10	(50%)
Dates Removed from Name Subject Headings (600)	1	(5.0%)
Total	20	(100%)

The following table shows the distribution of errors in 7XX of the in-house records:

Types of Errors	Number of Occurrence	
Personal Name Heading Changed (Typo in author's last name)	1	(7.7%)
Additional Personal Name Headings Needed	3	(23.1)
Personal Name Headings Deleted	3	(23.1)
Additional Corporate Name Headings Needed	6	(46.1%)
Total	13	(100%)

CONCLUSION

The answers to the two research questions of this comparative study were: (1) The error rate was quite low and very acceptable; (2) The error rate remained the same after outsourcing. The findings of this survey, however, apply only to monograph copy cataloging. Further research is needed to investigate the impact of outsourcing upon other aspects of cataloging such as original cataloging of monographs and on original cataloging and copy cataloging of other types of materials.

NOTE

1. Vinh-The Lam. Quality Control Issues in Outsourcing Cataloging in U.S. and Canadian Academic Libraries, *Cataloging & Classification Quarterly*, v. 40, no. 1 (2005), p. 101-122.

doi:10.1300/J104v44n03_04

Meeting the Needs of Special Format Catalogers: Ideas for Professional Organizations, Library Schools, and Professional Catalogers

Robert L. Bothmann

SUMMARY. Catalogers are essential for cataloging and classification of resources in library catalogs to create a resource discovery tool to aid users in their research and public service librarians to assist users. The number of catalogers in libraries has declined in past decades; and many more are on the cusp of retirement, resulting in an impending loss of collective history. Previous literature addressed catalogers in general, the training and recruitment of catalogers, and the expected retirements of librarians in general. The purpose of this study is to assess the specific needs of nonprint or special format catalogers in relation to education, training, and mentorship. A voluntary online survey conducted in 2004 asked questions about special format catalogers' current work, involvement in professional organizations, source of their training, their opin-

---

Robert L. Bothmann is Electronic Access/Catalog Librarian, Assistant Professor, Library Services, Minnesota State University, Mankato, P.O. Box 8419, ML3097, Mankato, MN 56001 (E-mail: robert.bothmann@mnsu.edu).

[Haworth co-indexing entry note]: "Meeting the Needs of Special Format Catalogers: Ideas for Professional Organizations, Library Schools, and Professional Catalogers." Bothmann, Robert L. Co-published simultaneously in *Cataloging & Classification Quarterly* (The Haworth Information Press, an imprint of The Haworth Press, Inc.) Vol. 44, No. 3/4, 2007, pp. 221-232; and: *Cataloger, Editor, and Scholar: Essays in Honor of Ruth C. Carter* (ed: Robert P. Holley) The Haworth Information Press, an imprint of The Haworth Press, Inc., 2007, pp. 221-232. Single or multiple copies of this article are available for a fee from The Haworth Document Delivery Service [1-800-HAWORTH, 9:00 a.m. - 5:00 p.m. (EST). E-mail address: docdelivery@haworthpress.com].

Available online at http://ccq.haworthpress.com
© 2007 by The Haworth Press, Inc. All rights reserved.
doi:10.1300/J104v44n03_05

ions of library school education, and demographic questions. The survey results indicate nearly half of all special format catalogers will retire within fifteen years, and the majority have had special format cataloging added to their workflow over time. Memberships in professional organizations are low, but one-third hold some sort of office in an organization. Special format catalogers are interested in more training and felt that library schools do not offer enough training. Ideas dealing with cooperative professional development among special format catalogers, professional organizations, and library schools are proposed based on the survey results. doi:10.1300/J104v44n03_05 *[Article copies available for a fee from The Haworth Document Delivery Service: 1-800-HAWORTH. E-mail address: <docdelivery@haworthpress.com> Website: <http://www.HaworthPress.com> © 2007 by The Haworth Press, Inc. All rights reserved.]*

KEYWORDS. Special format catalogers, professional development, cataloging training and education, mentorship, library education, professional organizations

I. INTRODUCTION

In the discipline of librarianship, cataloging and classification are arguably the most complex, essential, and theory-driven fields among the various types of professional librarians. Without catalogers to analyze resources and create surrogate records, there would be no catalog of any meaningful or useful kind; and it is the catalog that all other types of librarians use for instructing and locating resources in a library for users. Without proper cataloging and classification, collection development librarians would not be able to ascertain strengths or weakness within a collection; serials librarians would be unable to locate preceding or succeeding or ceased journals; instruction librarians would be unable to teach users how to access materials; and reference librarians would be unable to locate resources that could aide a patron. Without a proper catalog, a library is nothing more than a building full of books with no map to guide the user to the resources. Thus, catalogers are essential to the function and use of a library so that the education and training of catalogers is essential to the continued viability and health of the library catalog.

It is therefore alarming that the essential nature of the cataloger's role in the healthy functioning of a library has been demoted in many libraries. The ratio of catalogers to resources acquired appears to have declined over the past two decades,[1] with many libraries employing fewer catalogers. Many library schools have dropped the teaching of cataloging and classification from the core courses, some even from the curriculum altogether.[2] Those who wish to be educated in the field of cataloging and classification, either in graduate school or post-graduation, find themselves with a very limited options. Without a large selection of library schools that provide courses geared for those who wish to be professional catalogers, new professionals must content themselves with on-the-job training and any cataloging-related workshops that may be available.

To compound the problem, the current population of experienced professional librarians is expected to decrease drastically due to retirement over the next decade. Not only is the profession on the verge of losing a wealth of collective history and knowledge, it is also losing those professionals who would be the best candidates as mentors and recruiters of the next generation of catalogers. With the move of many libraries toward outsourced cataloging, more catalogers find themselves cataloging nonprint or special format materials that have a complexity that does not lend itself to outsourced cataloging. The purpose of this article is to examine the current state of those catalogers who identify themselves as non-print or special format catalogers, to assess their needs with respect to training, education, and mentoring, and to discuss how professional organizations and library schools can contribute to the continued professional development of the special formats cataloger.

II. LITERATURE REVIEW

There are a number of articles relating to the various issues concerning catalogers that are covered in this article, including surveys of catalogers, reports on mentoring, and many articles related to the education and training of catalogers. Leysen and Boydston[3] surveyed one hundred heads of cataloging at Association for Research Libraries (ARL) libraries in 2003. Their survey, which focused on catalogers' responsibilities and future demand for their roles in academic libraries, found that the number of catalogers in half of the responding libraries has decreased since 1998, generally due to retirements and the reallocation of those positions to other areas. Other findings indicated that one-third of ARL catalogers could retire in the next decade and that ARL libraries see future professional catalogers providing more training and focusing on administrative tasks. In an earlier survey, Buttlar and Garcha[4] surveyed academic catalogers to see how their jobs had changed from 1987 to 1997. Their findings show that catalogers' responsibilities for special format and electronic resource cataloging has increased, and that catalogers do their work with a smaller professional and support staff.

With the numbers of professional librarians, including catalogers, expected to retire in the next decade, recruitment and mentoring have become two important topics of discussion for the American Library Association (ALA) and some of its divisions. ALA commissioned an analysis of the professional workforce in 2001 and reported the results in the March 2002 issue of *American Libraries*.[5] The analysis indicated that more than 18,000 professional librarians will reach the age of sixty-five between 2010 and 2014. An update on this study based on 2000 census data reported that retirements for the 45% of professionals reaching the age of 65 between 2010 and 2014 will likely occur between 2015 and 2019 and that the number of working professionals increased by 22% between 1990 and 2000.[6] In light of these expectations, ALA and the Association for College and Research Libraries (ACRL) have listed recruitment as a top priority.[7]

Fennewald and Stachacz describe the ACRL Delaware Valley Chapter's mentoring program which recruited students at nearby library schools as mentees for the project. The program has been successful with matching students to mentors and benefits both the students and the mentors. With specific regard to the mentoring of catalogers, Aulik et al. reported a generally good experience in which Dominican University library school students learning electronic resource cataloging in an online course were partnered with a professional mentor for a two-week period.[8] Harcourt and Neumeister also reported a good experience as mentors for the Dominican course. In particular, they noted that mentoring helped to improve their own skills by requiring them to check rules and to comment on the students' work.

Views and discussion on the education and training of catalogers is very well represented in the literature. Two different theme issues of *Cataloging & Classification Quarterly* (*CCQ*) (1987 and 2002) have been devoted to this very topic as well as two monographs from the March 1989 Simmons College Symposium on Recruiting, Educating, and Training Cataloging Librarians: Solving the Problems.[9] The articles in the publications from the Simmons College Symposium focus on the changes in the nature of cataloging as a result of automation during the 1970s and 1980s, the decline in cataloging and classification course work in library schools, and the poor image of catalog librarians in the profession as it affects the recruitment of new catalogers. The 1987 *CCQ* theme issue also addresses the education of catalogers in changing times and focuses on the theoretical education and practical training of catalogers. Interestingly, the 2002 *CCQ* theme issue revisits many of the same questions, problems, and discussions of the previous decade but differs in noting the need for the continuing education of catalogers on account of the rapid changes in technology and the increase in the number of nonprint and special formats catalogers work with today. Connaway supports this notion and concludes that library school education should include theory *and* practice in its curriculum.[10]

III. METHOD

To understand the current state of special format catalogers, a survey instrument consisting of fifty-six questions divided into four sections was developed.[11] Section one asked questions about current and past cataloging work, types of formats cataloged, and changes in workflow. Section two asked questions about professional organizations in which special format catalogers have membership, hold offices or elected positions, and participate in conferences as well as which organizations special format catalogers perceive to best support and least support special format cataloging. Section three asked how special format catalogers obtained their training, if they felt library schools offered acceptable training, and about mentorship. Section four consisted of demographic questions, including gender, age range, salary, institution type, range of patron population, geographic location, length of time in the profession, and if retirement was anticipated in the next five to fifteen years.

In an effort to reach the largest possible number of catalogers who identify as a special format cataloger, the survey was sent to four different electronic discussion lists: AUTOCAT, OCLC-CAT, OLAC-List, and Serialist.[12] AUTOCAT and OCLC-CAT were chosen to access the largest number of catalogers of all types of formats. Serialist was chosen to invite those serials catalogers who work with electronic and microform cataloging. OLAC-List, the electronic list for the OnLine Audiovisual Catalogers, Inc. (OLAC), devoted to the discussion of special format cataloging, was chosen to survey special format catalogers. The survey was open for nine days from 29 April through 7 May, 2004.

IV. FINDINGS

The survey results represent the answers from 354 librarians who identify as professional or paraprofessional special format catalogers who subscribe to one or more of the electronic discussion lists at the time the survey invitation was sent. In May 2004, the electronic lists had the following number of subscribers: AUTOCAT, 4,145; OCLC-CAT, 2,672; OLAC-List, 931; and Serialist 3,106. Many respondents indicated receiving the survey invitation on more than one of these lists. Of the total number of respondents completing the survey, 259 were professionals and 95 were paraprofessionals.

Since the survey was not sent to a specific number of pre-selected individuals, there is no method to provide a response rate of special format catalogers to this survey. However, of the total number of respondents, 99 indicated they were members of OLAC, which had a membership of 379 personal members in May 2004.[13] Assuming that OLAC personal members are representative of the special formats cataloger community, there was a 26% response rate from special format catalogers in general from all of the lists. This indicates that the survey was delivered and answered by a fairly representative number of special format catalogers in the cataloging community.

The demographic section of the survey indicates a predominately female, mid-career composition of special format catalogers. Women make up 82% of respondents, and half the survey population are between the ages of 45 and 59. Half the respondents indicated they earn between $30,000 and $44,000 per year; 64% are employed by an academic library; and 93% of respondents are from the United States. Professional librarians comprise 78% of the population of which half have faculty or faculty-like status. Finally, half of all respondents anticipate retirement within the next fifteen years; 12% indicated they will retire within five years; 19% within ten years; and 21% in fifteen years.

The majority of respondents reported that the nature of their current special format cataloging work consisted of cataloging electronic resources, sound recordings (both audio and music), and video resources. The cataloging of other types of special format materials came in at a distant second as is shown in Table 1. Three-quarters of the survey respondents had not actively sought a position specifically for cataloging of special formats, and 74% of respondents have had special format responsibilities assigned over time. Half of all respondents indicated their cataloging department consists of one to three catalogers with only 19% indicating their department has more than ten catalogers.

TABLE 1. Percentage of Formats Cataloged

Formats Cataloged	Response Rate
Videocassettes, DVDs, Film, etc.	76%
Electronic Resources	68%
Sound Recordings (Audio & Music)	67%
Microforms	39%
Kits	36%
Music (Scores, etc.)	31%
Cartographic Resources	27%
Realia & Three-Dimensional Artefacts	21%
Graphic Materials	19%

To get a sense of special format catalogers' involvement in professional organizations, the survey listed twelve professional organizations that address or support the needs of catalogers as indicated in Table 2. Almost half (48%) indicated they are members of ALA, while only 27% were members of the Association for Library Collections and Technical Services (ALCTS), the division of ALA that addresses cataloging and classification. As for other professional organizations, only 31% were members of OLAC, which specifically addresses special format cataloging issues. One third (34%) were members of their state library association, and 41% belong to some other group not listed in the survey.

Although membership in professional organizations on the whole is relatively low, nearly one third (30%) of respondents indicated that they hold an elected or appointed office in an organization, primarily in a state library association, ALA, ALCTS, and the Music Library Association (MLA). The majority of respondents indicated that ALA, their state library association, OLAC, and ALCTS workshops are their most commonly attended conferences (Table 2).

When asked which organizations best support special format cataloging, the majority indicated OLAC, ALCTS, MLA, and ALA; they cited the state library associations as overlooking special format cataloging needs. Not surprisingly, more than half of the respondents said OLAC provides the best support for special format cataloging. One-third perceived that training opportunities in the U.S. are adequate, and half felt opportunities are less than adequate.

The survey provided five areas for respondents to indicate where they would like to have more training and gave the option to indicate

TABLE 2. Memberships in Professional Organizations

Professional Organizations	Hold Membership	Attend Conferences
American Library Association (ALA)	48%	34%
Other	41%	45%
State Library Association	34%	37%
OnLine Audiovisual Catalogers (OLAC)	31%	19%
Assoc. for Library Collections & Technical Services (ALCTS)	27%	14%
Music Library Association (MLA)	11%	10%
Music OCLC Users Group (MOUG)	11%	6%
Medical Library Association	3%	2%
Society of American Archivists	3%	2%
American Association of Law Libraries	2%	3%
Canadian Library Association	2%	3%
American Association of School Librarians	1%	0%
Public Library Association	1%	2%

other areas. The topics provided were access points, authority control, classification, description, and subject analysis. When asked about continuing education, the response for all five areas was strong, as can be seen in Table 3. Other topics that special format catalogers added for this question include training for continuing resources and for metadata schemes such as MARC21 and the Dublin Core.

Finally, respondents were asked abut their perceptions of their training in library school (Table 4) and their experience with mentorship (Table 5). Most respondents indicate that they had little or no training for cataloging special formats and feel even more strongly that library schools offer little to no training for special format cataloging. Only 40% indicate they have had a professional mentor; 29% are currently mentors; and 55% would consider being a mentor. However, only 15% said that their institution has a formal mentoring program, a fact that indicates that mentoring is very informal.

V. DISCUSSION

With regard to education and training specifically for special format catalogers, the survey data indicate a number of different possibilities and partnerships among catalogers, professional organizations, and li-

TABLE 3. Training Needs

Desired Areas of Training	Response Rate
Description	63%
Authority Control	58%
Subject Analysis	48%
Access Points	44%
Classification	31%
Other	11%

TABLE 4. Perception of Cataloging Training

Training Perception	Did you have sufficient training when you began cataloging special formats?	Do library schools offer adequate training for special formats cataloging?
No Training	23%	41%
Some Training	47%	55%
Adequate Training for most formats	28%	5%
Excellent Training on all special formats	2%	0%

TABLE 5. Mentoring

Mentoring Questions	Yes	No
Did/do you have a mentor?	40%	60%
Are you a mentor now?	29%	71%
Have you been a mentor in the past?	31%	69%
Would you consider being a mentor?	55%	45%
Does your institution have a formal mentoring program?	15%	85%

brary schools to meet the needs of special format catalogers. These include targeted training opportunities, coordinated mentoring programs, and involvement in professional organizations.

Foremost among these possibilities is a need to address the education of cataloging and classification provided by library schools in general. Cataloging literature over the past two decades has critically indicated that library schools are not providing adequate education in cataloging and classification. Assuming that bibliographic control of resources is a primary and necessary tenet of the provision of access to information, it logically follows that library schools ought to provide sufficient theoretical and practical course work in cataloging. It is therefore incumbent upon library schools to reexamine their curricula to provide the education and training future catalogers require. Furthermore, the ALA should re-examine the accreditation requirements related to cataloging and classification education in library schools to ensure curricular support.

As a mechanism for providing adequate training, professional organizations and library schools could benefit from creating and administering a formal mentorship program for library school students as well as for practicing librarians. While some schools and institutions do offer this opportunity, a coordinated effort would benefit both the schools and the catalogers, and promote recruitment efforts. With less than one third of special format catalogers currently acting as mentors and half of survey respondents indicating a willingness to be a mentor, there is sufficient interest and talent available to institute such a program. With the impending retirement of almost half of the special format catalogers who replied to this survey, it is extremely important for the profession to act on a mentoring program as soon as possible, before our most experienced special format catalogers retire.

Another partnership for professional special format catalogers to explore is their involvement with professional organizations. Organizations are only as strong as their memberships make them. In light of the numbers in Table 2, it would be prudent for special format catalogers to join and become more active in the professional organizations that best support special formats cataloging and training such as OLAC and ALCTS. It is equally important that these professional organizations target and sponsor training opportunities regionally and hold them more frequently. In particular, respondents noted that their state library associations, in which many hold memberships and offices and whose conferences they attend, are the very associations that do not support special format catalogers. Therefore, those special format catalogers holding offices or membership in the state associations could use their leadership roles to advocate for more training opportunities to be sponsored by the larger professional organizations at the state conferences since this would thus provide better access to training for a broader audience of catalogers.

VI. CONCLUSION

The results of this survey show that the characteristics of special format catalogers are remarkably similar to demographic data drawn from surveys of catalogers and librarians in general. The results also support the notion held by many professional catalogers that library schools do not provide enough training for new professionals to begin special format cataloging. However, the data also show a relative weakness on the part of the special format cataloger to be a member of professional organizations and to attend conferences. The fact that so many special format catalogers would consider mentoring suggests that special format catalogers are an untapped force for leadership and change in the profession. The obvious next step is to lobby the larger professional organizations to bring these pieces together to promote the change and the support required for a strong and healthy pool of special format catalogers.

NOTES

1. Stanley J. Wilder, "Demographic Trends Affecting Professional Technical Services Staffing in ARL Libraries," *Cataloging & Classification Quarterly* 34, no. 1/2 (2002): 53-7. Wilder provides statistical data demonstrating a decline in the number of technical services librarians, primarily catalogers. Joan M. Leyson and Jeanne M. K. Boydston, "Supply and Demand for Catalogers: Present and Future," *Library Resources & Technical Services* 49, no. 4 (Oct. 2005): 250-65. Leyson and Boydston's findings confirm a general loss in the number of catalogers since 1998 (p.254). Sheila S. Intner, "Scholars and Media: An Unmixable Mess of Oil and Water or a Perfect Meld of Oil and Vinegar?" *Cataloging & Classification Quarterly* 31, no. 3/4 (2001): 297-312. Intner reports that statistics of nonprint media have not been taken in recent years. Her research demonstrates a general increase in the acquisition of nonprint media, particularly electronic media. Martha Kyrillidou and Mark Young, "ARLStatistics 2003-04," http://www.arl.org/stats/arlstat/04pub/04intro.html, accessed 15 January 2006. The Association for Research Libraries does not address nonprint or special format resources in its statistics. However, their statistics indicate a general increase in the expenditure of ARL libraries for one-time purchases of electronic resources.

2. Jerry D. Saye, "Where Are We and How Did We Get Here? Or, The Changing Place of Cataloging in the Library and Information Science Curriculum: Causes and Consequences," *Cataloging & Classification Quarterly* 34, no. 1/2 (2002): 121-43.

3. Leyson and Boydston, "Supply and Demand for Catalogers."

4. Lois Buttlar and Rajinder Garcher, "Catalogers in Academic Libraries: Their Evolving and Expanding Roles," *College & Research Libraries* 59, no. 4 (July 1998): 311-21.

5. Mary Jo Lynch, "Reaching 65: Lots of Librarians Will Be There Soon," *American Libraries* 33, no. 3 (March 2002): 55-6.

6. Mary Jo Lynch, "Retirement and Recruitment: A Deeper Look," *American Libraries* 36, no. 1 (Jan. 2005): 28.

7. W. Lee Hisle, "Top Issues Facing Academic Libraries," *C&RL News* 63, no. 10 (2002): 714; John W. Berry, "Addressing the Recruitment and Diversity Crisis," *American Libraries* 33, no. 2 (Feb. 2002): 7.

8. Judith L Aulik, Holly Ann Burt, Michael Geeraedts, Elizabeth Gruby, Bongjoo Moon Lee, Anita Morgan, and Corey O'Halloran, "Online Mentoring: A Student Experience at Dominican University," *Cataloging & ClassificationQuarterly* 34, no. 3 (2002): 289-92.

9. Ruth C. Carter, ed., *Education and Training for Catalogers and Classifiers* in *Cataloging & Classification Quarterly* 7, no. 4 (1987); Janet Swan Hill, ed., *Education for Cataloging and the Organization of Information: Pitfalls and the Pendulum*, Parts I and II, in *Cataloging & Classification Quarterly* 34, no. 1/2-3 (2002); Sheila S. Intner and Janet Swan Hill, editors, *Recruiting, Educating, and Training Cataloging Librarians: Solving the Problems,* New Directions in Information Management, no. 19, New York: Greenwood Press, 1989; Sheila S. Intner and Janet Swan Hill, editors, *Cataloging: The Professional Development Cycle*, New Directions in Information Management, no. 26, New York: Greenwood Press, 1991.

10. Lynn Silipigni Connaway, "Educating Catalogers to Meet the Needs of Diverse Users in a New Technological Environment," *Colorado Libraries* 25, no. 3 (fall 1999): 48-50.

11. The survey questions are available on the author's Web site at http://mavweb.mnsu.edu/bothmr/2004/sfc-survey.html.

12. AUTOCAT (http://ublib.buffalo.edu/libraries/units/cts/autocat/) is an independent electronic discussion list for cataloging and authority control topics. OCLC-CAT is a discussion list for library staff using OCLC products and the discussion of cataloging in OCLC's World Cat. OLAC-List (http://www.olacinc.org/olaclist/) is the electronic discussion list of the OnLine Audiovisual Catalogers, Inc. (OLAC), which is devoted to the discussion of cataloging nonprint or special format media. Serialist (http://www.uvm.edu/~bmaclenn/serialst.html) is devoted to the discussion of issues related to serials processing, including serials cataloging. This particular list was chosen to reach out to catalogers who deal with electronic and microform serials.

13. OnLine Audiovisual Catalogers, Inc., *OLAC Newsletter* 24, no. 2 (2004): 5. The OLAC-L list is not closed, thus list members need not be OLAC members.

doi:10.1300/J104v44n03_05

Copy Cataloging for Print and Video Monographs in Two Academic Libraries: A Case Study of Editing Required for Accuracy and Completeness

Carolynne Myall
Sydney Chambers

SUMMARY. This article presents the results of a case study of editing required on OCLC bibliographic records for print monographs and video/DVD monographs during a three-month test at two mid-sized academic libraries. First, the authors reviewed the literature of cataloging/catalog quality and consider the problems this literature presents in terms of creating meaningful and measurable standards of "quality." Next, they define "quality" for the purposes of the case study and describe case-study procedures for determining and comparing extent of editing required for records to meet comparable standards. They then present results indicating that records for print monographs acquired at

---

Carolynne Myall, MS, CAS, is Head of Collection Services, John F. Kennedy Library, Eastern Washington University, Cheney, WA 99004 (E-mail: cmyall@mail.ewu.edu). Sydney Chambers, MLS, is Catalog Librarian, Foley Center, Gonzaga University, Spokane, WA 99258 (E-mail: chambers@gonzaga.edu).

[Haworth co-indexing entry note]: "Copy Cataloging for Print and Video Monographs in Two Academic Libraries: A Case Study of Editing Required for Accuracy and Completeness." Myall, Carolynne, and Sydney Chambers. Co-published simultaneously in *Cataloging & Classification Quarterly* (The Haworth Information Press, an imprint of The Haworth Press, Inc.) Vol. 44, No. 3/4, 2007, pp. 233-257; and: *Cataloger, Editor, and Scholar: Essays in Honor of Ruth C. Carter* (ed: Robert P. Holley) The Haworth Information Press, an imprint of The Haworth Press, Inc., 2007, pp. 233-257. Single or multiple copies of this article are available for a fee from The Haworth Document Delivery Service [1-800-HAWORTH, 9:00 a.m. - 5:00 p.m. (EST). E-mail address: docdelivery@haworthpress.com].

Available online at http://ccq.haworthpress.com
© 2007 by The Haworth Press, Inc. All rights reserved.
doi:10.1300/J104v44n03_06

the two institutions usually required little or no editing (many of these records were U.S. national-level records), while records for video/DVD monographs required considerably more editing (U.S. national-level records for this category of acquisition were not available). Finally, the article proposes establishment of a cooperative program to create U.S. national-level bibliographic records for videorecordings/DVDs as a means of reducing redundant institution-level editing and ensuring availability of comparable records across formats. doi:10.1300/J104v44n03_06 *[Article copies available for a fee from The Haworth Document Delivery Service: 1-800-HAWORTH. E-mail address: <docdelivery@haworthpress.com> Website: <http://www.HaworthPress.com> © 2007 by The Haworth Press, Inc. All rights reserved.]*

KEYWORDS. Video cataloging, DVD cataloging, book cataloging, local cataloging practice, cataloging standards

In conditions of tight budgets, reduced staff, and high expectations for timely access to new library resources, cataloging operations in mid-sized academic libraries are under pressure to process materials promptly and to complete as many records while using as little staff time per record as possible. How have they attempted to accomplish this?

A common strategy is to accept cataloging records as acquired, whether from a bibliographic utility or a vendor, particularly if they are created by the Library of Congress or if they appear to match standards of full-level cataloging as defined by utilities such as OCLC. Cataloging literature of the last two decades includes many statements of practice along these lines:

- "The point of copy cataloging is to process materials expeditiously; therefore, NLM attempts to keep editing of copy records to a minimum" (Boehr and Horan, p. 347).
- "We usually accept an LC record as it stands, and changes will not be made unless serious mistakes are identified" (Tsao, p. 62).
- "Never alter Library of Congress cataloging, except where that cataloging is clearly in error or reflects obsolete cataloging codes or practices" (Bland, p. 51).
- Or, conversely, described as a practice to avoid: ". . . too often we have looked on [records] as lumps of clay to be molded into some-

thing usable" rather than accepting them as presented (Bolin, p. 358).

Thus, in the hope of making cataloging "ends" meet, many libraries accept this admonition and adopt minimal editing of copy cataloging records as policy.

Does this strategy work equally well for all types of library materials? Or is it more workable for some formats and less so for others? Can a consistent level of accuracy and completeness of information be maintained with minimal editing of records across formats, or do records for materials in some formats typically require more editing for consistency with other records in the catalog and for conformity with national standards?

While textual materials, whether in traditional print or digital format, remain the bulk of academic library collections, non-textual materials are also present in most academic libraries and are entered into most public catalogs. A 1997 study of U.S. and Chinese libraries with large collections reported that about 60% of the U.S. libraries owned videorecordings and an average of 90% of those did full-level cataloging for nonprint holdings (Ma, Miller, and Liu, p. 48). A survey of nonprint materials in Canadian academic libraries published in 1995 reported that "the highest percentage of inclusion in library collections was videorecordings"–78.2%, or 262 of 335 responding libraries (Weihs and Howard, p. 186). No doubt, the number of libraries holding nonprint materials, and specifically videorecordings, has grown since these surveys.

Audiovisual cataloging is, however, widely viewed as "Different, Difficult, and Diverting (or resource-intensive)" (Howarth, p. 3); and cataloging for videorecordings presents some specific complexities. One notable example is transcription of title. AACR prescribes the chief source as the title frame, but title-frame title often differs from container information clients encounter in shelf browsing. Repackaging of titles originally broadcast in television series and the inclusion of "special features" in DVDs also creates situations requiring attention (Weitz). Under these conditions, of what does minimal editing to meet full-level cataloging standards–a common cataloging policy–consist? Is minimal editing for video records comparable to minimal editing for print monograph records?

This paper reports on a project comparing number and kinds of editing changes made to copy cataloging records by two mid-sized academic libraries–at Eastern Washington University and Gonzaga

University-for two formats of material: print monographs and video (VHS and DVD) monographs. In both these libraries, the policy is to edit copy cataloging only to the extent necessary to maintain consistent record quality as defined by OCLC I-Level in order to provide predictable access to all kinds of resources. The purpose of the project was to determine whether applying the same basic policy resulted in different numbers of editing changes for the two types of records and, if so, what the differences were.

QUALITY IN CATALOGING: THE LITERATURE

In her detailed study of cataloging records for Korean materials in OCLC, Shin states: "Quality is well defined in the literature, as several authors have proposed evaluative criteria and methodology" (p. 56). One of the papers she cites, however, asserts that quality in cataloging is "difficult to define, and though it is often assumed and praised in the literature of bibliographic control, it doesn't seem to be well delineated" (Graham, p. 214). This sort of contradiction runs through the literature of cataloging quality. Further, Chapman and Massey believe that there "is a profusion of literature on what makes good catalogues, or at least good catalogue records, but fewer studies have attempted to measure quality" (p. 315). And while most papers about cataloging quality declare the importance of focusing on user needs, such statements are usually accompanied by a disclaimer about the difficulty of actually doing so, considering the variety of users.

Adding to the difficulty of using the literature to define cataloging quality and to show how it might be measured is the fact that authors discuss a number of related and overlapping but not identical topics without necessarily distinguishing among them. Cataloging quality may refer to:

- Quality of individual cataloging records in terms of the data enabling functional objectives and/or matching input standards.
- Quality of the overall structure and presentation of the catalog.
- Quality of cataloging service as part of total library service, particularly including timeliness of record entry.

Most numerous are studies of individual record quality; among them are Chapman, Intner, Shin, Shoenung, Simpson, Tsao, and Zeng (and to some extent Lam). These studies typically identify standards for accuracy and completeness of information required in a cataloging record, define a set of "reportable" errors of omission or commission that do not match these standards, select a sample or group of records, locate all reportable errors in these records, and compile totals. These studies, particularly Chapman, provided models that were adaptable for the purposes of this case study.

Some authors distinguish between record quality from a functional point of view–that is, the record meets objectives of providing clients access to collections–and record quality from the point of view of compliance with existing standards (see, for example, Bland, p. 48). Cataloging rules and practices have historically been intended to meet Cutter's 1904 objects of the catalog (Cutter, p. 67). Currently, however, cataloging principles and rules are under review to meet the user tasks defined by Functional Requirements for Bibliographic Records: find, identify, select, and obtain (IFLA Study Group . . . p. 8-9). FRBR's user tasks are not, in our opinion, very different from Cutter's objects. Based on the fact that cataloging practices are generally devised to comply with Cutter (and now FRBR), a failure to conform to current rules and standards does appear to us to represent a quality problem, with some exceptions. One exception, in our view, is errors in punctuation or spacing specified by ISBD that have little or no impact on retrieval either by keyword or controlled-vocabulary searching.

The literature indicates that individual cataloging records created by the Library of Congress remain the national standard for U.S. libraries. (See Bland, p. 56, and Svenonius and McGarry, p. 27 among others.) Many libraries, however, including the two in this study, now regard LC-authenticated records and records created or authenticated through the Program for Cooperative Cataloging (PCC) as representing reliable levels of accuracy and correctness roughly equaling those of LC copy.

Quality of the overall catalog appears to be less frequently the subject of study, notwithstanding Chapman and Massey's comment (quoted above) and notwithstanding the fact that both Cutter's objects and much of FRBR's approach are focused on the catalog as a whole rather than on individual records. Presumably, the limited extent of study at this level is due to the complexity and multi-faceted nature of the task, which now must include not only content and structure of the database, but also completeness and presentation of the data on various screens, search engine execution, presence of context-sensitive help, and other elements in an environment in which users are familiar with many other Web-based information tools. We found that this (so far limited) literature was not explicitly pertinent to our project though it is already having an impact on cataloging theory.

Discussions of quality of cataloging service as part of library service attempt to balance the benefits of two service components: providing more extensive and consistent catalog data about items in the collections versus making the items physically available and providing some catalog access with records available in the catalog quickly. As Thomas remarks, the last twenty years have seen "an increasing awareness of costs in libraries and a shift from quality of records as an absolute toward a redefinition of quality service rather than strictly quality cataloging . . . " (Thomas, S., p. 497). Tillett's well-known statement derived from responses submitted to a LC Cataloging Forum attempts to achieve this balance: cataloging quality is defined as:

- *accurate bibliographic information that
- *meets the users' needs and provides
- *appropriate access in a
- *timely fashion (Tillett, p. 28).

The variability of user needs and the subjectivity of the term "appropriate" make uniform application of this definition problematic. While we wished to identify differences in the amount of editing required for available records for two formats, we decided not to measure the difference explicitly in terms of time expended. The implications in terms of staff time as well as skill required should, however, be evident and are considered in the discussion of results.

USING THE OPAC: SOME PERTINENT RECENT STUDIES

Only a few published studies specifically address client use of the OPAC to find, identify, select, and obtain videorecordings. The few that exist, however, along with some other recent studies of user OPAC behavior, are helpful in identifying important data elements for clients.

Ho reports in her study of faculty and graduate students in departments' making heavy use of a closed-stack video collection that title searching was most common and resulted in greatest satisfaction (pp. 76, 79). This result points to a need for inclusion of variant-title information. Second in frequency of use by Ho's clients was subject though its lower satisfaction rating indicated problems in obtaining desired results. Interestingly, the "greatest proportion of users (86%) perceived the original author of the work a video is based on as useful ..." (p. 79); and cast was rated the next most useful information. Again, these results suggest the importance of including this data, beyond the minimal-cataloging level, in order to match user searches. Hume's study of faculty and student media users in three academic departments indicates that clients want extensive information for these materials: in the words of one, "The user approaches a record with a problem he is trying to solve. The more access the better'" (p. 9)–including title, director, cast, contents, summary, etc. A recent study of OPAC use not specifically focused on nonprint materials found that the field users rated most highly in terms of usefulness was MARC 520, summary note–required for videorecordings but not required or typically input for print monographs (Thomas, D., p. 37).

OPAC user studies indicate that clients typically do not employ the full range of searching options available. Allison and Childers, for example, found that "user search strategies were basic and did not take advantage of available advanced features" (p. 152). Chisman, Diller, and Walbridge also found that clients do not use advanced features, including the limit feature for type of material, which presumably would be helpful in finding videos (p. 557). These results suggest to us that inputting data that might match the initial search string–for example, names of director and cast members–is a critical cataloging task since clients typically do not use system features to improve results.

Recent studies have begun to consider the impact of user experience with Internet search engines and specific Web sites. "Web searching is shaping user expectations of what an information retrieval system looks like, how it behaves, and how to interact with it," note Campbell and Fast in a recent study of university student library users (p. 27). Novotny echoes this assessment, and reports that users "focused their attention on the fields in the catalog that were hyperlinked" (p. 532). Novotny's finding suggests that clients may benefit from hyperlinked entries for directors, etc., if these are present in records for videos, as well as from subject fields.

DEFINING QUALITY FOR PURPOSES OF THIS STUDY

Following this review of the literature, we defined the level of quality that would require no editing of the record. As we have indicated, we accept that most current cataloging practice, with some exceptions, is intended to meet a user task so that our definition is standards-based:

- Accurate, without errors in transcription, MARC tagging, etc.
- Access points match LC authority records and follow AACR practice.
- Full level in extent of information: complying with standards for completeness as defined for OCLC Encoding level blank or I.
- Includes LCC classification.

Is "completeness of information" in records, as shown by the information actually used by library clients, the same for all formats; or should the concept of completeness be adjusted based on format of material? Based on the few studies of OPAC use to find videos and considering the popularity of IMDb with its searching and linking capabilities, we believe that input standards requiring performer/cast information, for example, are responding to a real client need. Our standards for completeness of content for video records therefore matched OCLC input standards requiring 508, 511, 520, etc. This results in a longer record with, of course, more opportunity for errors and omissions.

THE TWO LIBRARIES IN THE PROJECT

Eastern Washington University in Cheney and Spokane, Washington is a public comprehensive university with approximately 10,000 students and offers many undergraduate and masters programs and one doctoral degree. Its libraries have an annual acquisition budget of approximately $1.2 million. Gonzaga University in Spokane, Washington, is a private Jesuit institution with approximately 6,200 students in undergraduate and masters programs, the JD, and one PhD program. Although the law school has a fully autonomous library, the Foley Center Library serves the entire campus. Foley Center Library has an acquisitions budget of approximately $850,000. While there is overlap between the two collections, EWU has more money to spend on electronic resources, print subscriptions, and approval plans for print monographs. Gonzaga, on the other hand, has deeper collections in some areas such as philosophy and religion and adds a higher percentage of non-English language monographs. Both libraries have growing, active collections of videos, both videocassettes and DVDs, arranged by LC call number on open shelves. Both libraries are OCLC members. Neither is a research library.

METHODOLOGY OF THIS PROJECT

We assume, as Chapman states, that editing records–particularly when library policy is generally to avoid editing–indicates "dissatisfaction with the quality of the record in some respect" (p. 203). We therefore established a plan to identify editing changes made to records by comparing a printout of the record on OCLC at the time the material was cataloged with a printout of the record as entered in the local system of the library.

Our procedures were as follows.

1. Identified errors and changes to be tracked.

Cataloging literature has emphasized the importance of errors in access points and particularly in controlled fields; but, as Chapman and Massey note, clients' use of "keyword searching require[s] accuracy throughout all fields . . . " (p. 315). We therefore treated uniformly all bibliographic corrections and additions required to meet input standards with the following exceptions:

- Matters of judgment were not counted as corrections or additions.
- Corrections due to changes in MARC format definitions were not counted.
- Changes in punctuation and spacing, including ISBD-required formatting, were not counted if keyword or controlled-vocabulary access was not affected.
- Changes in formatting and wording of notes were not counted.
- Editing for any local practice or purpose was not counted since there are options in some cases and since these changes typically did not affect either access point or keyword access.
- Editing that was done in error or that was not necessary to meet full level member contributed (OCLC-defined I level) standards (e.g., adding more subject headings) was not counted.

2. Developed an error table/spreadsheet with categories/encoding-levels of records on the horizontal axis and record fields on the vertical axis.

We began by identifying different levels of records based on a combination of Encoding Level values and information about record contributors and authenticators in the 040 and 042 fields. Initially, we identified all the encoding level/contributor categories we expected to encounter; but we then cut back to the following eleven categories, which covered all the records identified for review:

- Blank, Library of Congress (i.e., Enc Lvl value was blank and only LC appeared in the 040 string).
- Blank, not only Library of Congress (i.e., Enc Lvl value was blank and other institutions, usually in addition to LC, appeared in the 040 and/or 042 string). These are called "full national" in the tables that summarize results.
- 4, Library of Congress (i.e., Enc Lvl value was blank and only LC appeared in the 040 string).
- 4, not only Library of Congress (i.e., Enc Lvl value was blank and other institutions, usually in addition to LC, appeared in the 040 and/or 042 string). These are called "core national" in the tables that summarize results.
- I, member-contributed (by library/institution member with possible additions by other libraries or vendors).
- I, vendor-contributed (with possible additions by other libraries or vendors).
- K, member-contributed (by library/institution member with possible additions by other libraries or vendors).
- K, vendor-contributed (with possible additions by other libraries or vendors).
- M, member-contributed (by library/institution member with possible additions by other libraries or vendors).
- L, vendor-contributed (with possible additions by other libraries or vendors).
- 4, member-contributed (by library/institution member with possible additions by other libraries or vendors).

We considered the first two categories to be U.S. national-level, full-level records though creators/contributors of the records may or may not include LC. "Vendors" in this usage typically refer to vendors of library resources.

In general, we divided categories finely so that types of problems could be separately identified. We then combined results in various ways. This meant tracking most fixed-field elements and variable fields separately rather than initially grouping them into categories such as 5XX notes. We did not track errors by subfields except in a few cases.

- 007 was parsed finely by subfield because of the role of these subfields in the sort/limit function of some library systems.
- 245 a through c subfields were tracked separately. Information in the 245 a/b/c in records for videos is often complex and extensive, is often misunderstood, and therefore must often be edited.
- 260 a through c subfields were also separately tracked, following the same reasoning as for 245 a/b/c.
- 300 subfields were tracked, based on experience of these bits of information as likely to be edited in video records.
- Some specific types of 500 fields, such as source of title and "based on" notes, were separately tracked. On the other hand, we tracked 700-710 editing together rather than separating the fields. For videos, adding name access points on video records, whether for persons or companies, typically is the same cataloging function.

We separately compiled two categories of editing changes: information that needs to be inserted into the record to meet standards of completeness, called *additions*, and errors to be corrected, called *corrections*. In addition to tracking print monographs and video monographs separately, we tracked Gonzaga and EWU records separately.

This slicing up of data resulted in long, complicated worksheets, particularly since some fields ended up having no corrections made in the 302 bibliographic records reviewed. Appendix I shows a sample worksheet.

3. Identified records for review.

Chapman and Massey state that "[r]andom sample may be impractical, necessitating a convenience sample..." (p. 317). We found this observation to be true for this operational research project. In order to minimize disruption of EWU's Cataloging & Acquisitions Unit and not require that a printout be made of all records in process pre- and post-editing, we attached the study to the unit's regular tracking of selected print monographs. On a day that "moves" through the month, up to fifty print monographs received in the unit get tracking slips. These items are monitored through unpacking, receipt and payment, cataloging, shelving, etc., to see if standards for timeliness are met. While tracking-day items are not a random sample, tracking is a long-established practice at EWU that has yielded useful information with no indication that tracked items are not representative. Using tracking-day procedures, 97 records for print monographs were identified during September, October, and November 2005 (three months that do not have heavy receipts). Videos are expedited and not part of the tracking process. To get a comparable set of records, we identified 97 videos being cataloged during the same three months; this represented most of the videos cataloged during that time. Gonzaga records included every videocassette and DVD cataloged during the three months of record collection and resulted in a group of 54 records. Then a set of 54 print monograph records was selected by choosing every tenth record of all those print monographs cataloged during the same time period. Thus, there were 151 print monograph records and 151 video monographs records selected for review in the project.

4. Collected printouts of the OCLC record at the time of cataloging and the record as entered in the local catalog.

Staff printed the OCLC record of each selected print or video monograph just before they reviewed and edited the record as necessary. They made a second printout of the record when work on it was completed so that changes could be compared.

5. Checked access points in the OCLC authority file.

One of the two institutions does not do authority work on copy cataloging records prior to loading the records into the local system (this library mostly uses a combination of system-generated headings reports and vendor-supplied updating for authority maintenance). For consistency in this project, all headings were checked at the point of record editing.

6. Reviewed each pair of printouts and tallied editing changes as corrections and additions.

We scrutinized printouts, categorized the editing changes as corrections or additions, entered them into the spreadsheet by field or subfield, and totaled corrections and additions for each encoding level of record for print monographs and video monographs at the two institutions.

RESULTS OF RECORD REVIEWS

Our results can be briefly summarized:

- U.S. national-level, full-level records, defined by us as Enc Lvl blank and LC and/or other institutions in the 040/042, require little editing to meet standards of accuracy and completeness. On average, these records for print monographs in the study required .47 additions per record and .13 corrections per record for a total of .59 edits per record (rounded up).
- There were no U.S. national-level, full-level records for videorecordings.
- Full-level member- or vendor-input records for print monographs in this study required 1.45 additions and .55 corrections, on average, for a total of 2 edits per record.
- Full-level member- or vendor-input records for videorecordings required 4.47 additions and 1.91 corrections per record, on average, for a total of 6.39 edits per record.
- Core-level records for print monographs required .27 additions and .23 corrections per record for a total of .5 edits per record.
- There were no core-level records for videorecordings.
- Minimal-level records for print monographs required .8 additions and .6 corrections, on average, for a total of 1.4 edits per record.
- Minimal-level records for videorecordings required 5.63 additions and 1.63 corrections per record for a total of 7.26 edits per record.
- The most commonly required additions for print monograph records were 246, 020, and 6xx (descending order).
- The most commonly required additions for videorecordings were 700-730, 538, and LC class/call number.
- The most commonly required corrections for print monograph records were 6xx, 260 a, and 505 (descending order).
- The most commonly required corrections for videorecordings were 700-730, 546, and 500 (special features) (descending order).
- There was little difference in number of corrections made to records at the two different institutions in either format. However, Gonzaga, though having an editing policy similar to EWU's policy, made almost twice as many additions per record for both print monographs and video monographs. Further study would be necessary to explain this difference in practice under comparable policies. We speculate that the reason may be that different levels of

staffing are assigned to some tasks at the two institutions (e.g., a professional catalog librarian completes all copy cataloging of videos at one institution while high-level support staff does so at the other).

One unexpected finding not specifically related to the project's objectives was the discovery that there were very few recent records for print monographs having only the Library of Congress in the 040/042 fields: most Encoding Level blank records have multiple contributors, often vendors. (It would be interesting, though beyond the scope of this project, to track the changes made over the life of these records and by whom.)

There were few records for non-English language materials, which made it difficult to determine what effect, if any, language of cataloged material might have on editing.

Table 1, "Total Number of Edits by Encoding Level/Cataloging Source," shows a summary of additions and corrections made for categories of print monographs versus video monographs. Since there were no U.S. national-level, full-level video records, no comparable comparison of editing requirements for print and video records with Encoding Level value of blank can be made. Overall, records for video monographs clearly required more editing, particularly in terms of additions. Table 1A, "Total Number of Edits by Summary Encoding Level," groups together additions and corrections made for records with comparable Encoding Level regardless of cataloging source.

Table 2, "Number of Edits Per Record by Encoding Level/Cataloging Source," shows the average number of additions, corrections, and total edits for each type of record. Some categories of records for both print and video monographs clearly required more editing. Again, though, the video format lacked the highest level of Encoding Level. Table 2A, "Edits Per Record by Summary Encoding Level," groups together record categories with a similar Encoding Level and shows the number of edits per record by Encoding Level.

Table 3, "Most Common Edits for Print and Video Monographs," shows the five most common additions and corrections made to the records in the review group.

Table 4, "Edits Per Record by Institution," compares the two institutions in terms of number of edits per record for print and video records. Interestingly, the number of corrections was very close; but the number of additions varied.

TABLE 1. Total Number of Edits by Encoding Level/Cataloging Source

	Print monographs				Video monographs			
	Additions	Corrections	Total edits	n =	Additions	Corrections	Total edits	n =
Blank DLC	5	0	5	4	0	0	0	0
Blank full national	25	8	33	60	0	0	0	0
4 DLC	0	0	0	0	0	0	0	0
4 full national	12	12	24	57	0	0	0	0
I member contributed	32	12	44	22	437	178	615	95
I vendor contributed	0	0	0	0	65	38	103	20
K member contributed	3	2	5	4	59	14	73	10
K vendor contributed	0	0	0	0	114	36	150	21
M member contributed	1	1	2	1	24	7	31	4
L vendor contributed	0	0	0	0	17	6	23	1
4 member contributed	4	2	6	3	0	0	0	0
Overall	82	37	119	151	716	279	995	151

TABLE 1A. Number of Edits by Summary Encoding Level

	Print monographs				Video monographs			
	Additions	Corrections	Total edits	n =	Additions	Corrections	Total edits	n =
Full national	30	8	38	64	0	0	0	0
Full contributed	32	12	44	22	519	222	741	116
Less than full contributed	4	3	7	5	197	57	254	35
Core national and contributed	16	14	30	60	0	0	0	0

Full national = Blank DLC and Blank full national; full contributed = I-level member- and I- and L-level vendor-contributed records; less than full contributed = K- and M-level member- and vendor-contributed; core national and contributed = 4 DLC, full national and member-contributed.

TABLE 2. Number of Edits Per Record by Encoding Level/Cataloging Source

	Print monographs				Video monographs			
	Additions	Corrections	Total edits	n =	Additions	Corrections	Total edits	n =
Blank DLC	1.25	0.00	1.25	4	0.00	0.00	0.00	0
Blank full national	0.42	0.13	0.55	60	0.00	0.00	0.00	0
4 DLC	0.00	0.00	0.00	0	0.00	0.00	0.00	0
4 full national	0.21	0.21	0.42	57	0.00	0.00	0.00	0
I member contributed	1.45	0.55	2.00	22	4.60	1.87	6.47	95
I vendor contributed	0.00	0.00	0.00	0	3.25	1.90	5.15	20
K member contributed	0.75	0.50	1.25	4	5.90	1.40	7.30	10
K vendor contributed	0.00	0.00	0.00	0	5.43	1.71	7.14	21
M member contributed	1.00	1.00	2.00	1	6.00	1.75	7.75	4
L vendor contributed	0.00	0.00	0.00	0	17.00	6.00	23.00	1
4 member contributed	1.33	0.67	2.00	3	0.00	0.00	0.00	0
Overall	0.54	0.25	0.79	151	4.74	1.85	6.59	151

TABLE 2A. Edits Per Record by Summary Encoding Level

	Print monographs				Video monographs			
	Additions	Corrections	Total edits	n =	Additions	Corrections	Total edits	n =
Full national	0.47	0.13	0.59	64	0.00	0.00	0.00	0
Full contributed	1.45	0.55	2.00	22	4.47	1.91	6.39	116
Less than full contributed	0.80	0.60	1.40	5	5.63	1.63	7.26	35
Core national and contributed	0.27	0.23	0.50	60	0.00	0.00	0.00	0

Full national = Blank DLC and Blank full national; full contributed = I-level member- and I- and L-level vendor-contributed records; less than full contributed = K- and M-level member- and vendor-contributed; core national and contributed = 4 DLC, full national and member-contributed.

TABLE 3. Most Common Edits for Print and Video Monographs

	Print	Videos	Overall
Additions	246 (n = 14)	700-730 (n = 190)	700/730 (n = 196)
	020 (n = 11)	538 (n = 64)	538 (n = 68)
	6XX-0 (n = 7)	090/050 (n = 56)	090/050 (n = 60)
	Illus (n = 5)	245 c (n = 52)	245 c (n = 54)
	300 a (n = 5)	Date1/2 (n = 33)	246 (n = 40)
Corrections	6XX-0 (n = 8)	700-730 (n = 77)	700-730 (n = 77)
	260 a (n = 3)	546 (n = 20)	6XX-0 (n = 24)
	505 (n = 3)	SpecFeat (n = 14)	546 (n = 20)
	Cont (n = 2)	TitleSrce (n = 13)	TitleSrce (n = 15)
	Illus (n = 2)	Ctry (n = 11)	SpecFeat (n = 14)
	LitF (n = 2)	007 l (n = 11)	
	090/050 (n = 2)		
	245 a (n = 2)		
	245 c (n = 2)		
	504 (n = 2)		
Combined edits	6XX-0 (n = 15)	700-730 (n = 267)	700-730 (n = 273)
	246 (n = 14)	538 (n = 65)	538 (n = 69)
	020 (n = 12)	245 c (n = 59)	245 c (n = 65)
	300 a (n = 6)	090/050 (n = 56)	090/050 (n = 64)
	504 (n = 6)	SpecFeat (n = 41)	6XX-0 (n = 61)
		546 (n = 41)	

TABLE 4. Edits Per Record by Institution

	Print monographs			Video monographs		
	Additions	Corrections	Total edits	Additions	Corrections	Total edits
EWU (print n = 97, video n = 97)	0.072165	0.216495	0.28866	3.845361	1.814433	5.659794
GU (print n = 54, video n = 54)	1.388889	0.296296	1.685185	6.351852	1.907407	8.259259

DISCUSSION OF SOME IMPLICATIONS OF THESE RESULTS

Expected Extent of Editing for Print Monographs and Video Monographs

Records for video monographs in this case study typically required more total editing than records at comparable Encoding Levels for print monographs. This result suggests that, in general, libraries should expect video monograph cataloging to be more staff intensive than comparable print monograph cataloging.

But the database of print monograph records and the database of video monograph records available in OCLC WorldCat are *not* comparable in terms of national-level authentication. For print monographs, there is a database of national-level, full-level records that may be expected to require very little editing per record. For libraries attempting to maintain consistent standards across formats, these results suggest, however, that there are likely to be few records for videos that do not require editing. The most reliable category of Encoding Level is entirely absent for videos, and it is reasonable to believe that the total difference in editing required for print and video records in this case study is partly attributable to that absence.

For the time being, it appears that a library may choose among limited options:

1. Do not attempt or expect to bring copy cataloging records for video monographs up to the same standard as records for print monographs since this will generally require editing, sometimes a lot of editing. Accept that cataloging for video monographs will generally not be as accurate or complete as cataloging for print monographs.
2. Attempt to bring copy-cataloging records for video monographs up to the same standard as records for print monographs. Accept that cataloging for videos will require more editing and be more time-intensive so that productivity in terms of numbers of records completed will be lower. Accept that higher-level cataloging skills will be required for these resources.

Much cataloging quality literature asserts that completeness of cataloging and rapid local cataloging cannot be achieved simultaneously.

Again, if reliably high quality copy cataloging records are available, this assertion does not seem to be true for all materials; but such records are not routinely available for videos. Productivity in terms of numbers of records for videos therefore seems likely to be lower than productivity for print monographs if the library follows a policy of consistent records across formats.

Benemann, though, suggests that quality and productivity may reinforce rather than compete with one another: Increasing the complexity of the task, rather than simplifying it, along with communicating the long-term value of the product, may actually increase productivity. Under present circumstances, Benemann's attitude may be the only optimistic one to adopt with regard to video cataloging if the library opts for accurate, complete, and functional catalog records for visual materials. At the least, given the absence of nationally authenticated records for video monographs, the library should expect that the extent of editing will be greater for copy cataloging of videos and that, as a corollary, higher-level cataloging skills are likely to be required.

IMPORTANCE OF CATALOGER SKILLS IN VIDEO CATALOGING

Porter and Bredderman reported on nonprint catalogers in ARL libraries almost a decade ago. They concluded that catalogers of nonprint materials received most of their education in nonprint cataloging from on-the-job training and that, the more cataloging of nonprint materials they did, the more confident catalogers became in their skills (Porter, p. 146). Given the prevalence of on-the-job training (often self-training), perhaps staff are expected to perform video cataloging before having acquired knowledge of special-format cataloging issues. If this is so, it could explain much of the inconsistency in the way comparable information was presented in the records reviewed in this project.

Many libraries sort print materials based on an Encoding level/Cataloging source triage and direct the national-level cataloging requiring little review to a lower staff level than minimal-level cataloging needing more revision to bring it up to the library's standards. Such a triage is difficult or impossible to perform with video records. Through experience, a library can develop a "white list" of preferred record sources on an institution-by-institution basis. However, a white list of this sort should be based on constant observation and evaluation of bibliographic records–in itself requiring a high level of discerning judgment and knowledge of current cataloging, then constant maintenance as the cataloging policies and practices of institutions both on and off the approved list change over time.

Without record triage based on assumptions about record quality, libraries have few choices if they want to provide fully functional cataloging records for video materials. They must invest in a deeper skill set involving both knowledge of cataloging generally and of video issues specifically; they must develop or acquire expertise and judgment beyond the range expected for many support staff cataloger positions. Ideally, this would mean hiring or assigning experts in video cataloging at a staffing level high enough to develop specialized skills and to exercise judgment.

Interestingly, most advertisements for professional cataloger positions do not mention expertise or experience with specific formats; instead they lump everything together with phrases such as "variety of formats," "all formats," or even "print and non-print," unless the position is specifically devoted to a cataloging specialty. During the same time period that we were collecting cataloging records to review for this case study, we also collected employment advertisements for catalogers. We inspected job ads published in *American Libraries*, *College & Research Libraries News*, *Library Journal*, and *The Chronicle of Higher Education* or posted on their online counterparts, *ALA's Hot Jobs Online*, *Library Journal and School Library Journal Job Board*, and *Chronicle Careers*. We observed how positions were framed with regard to the expectations for specific knowledge of special areas of cataloging.

Out of 63 positions described, 40 were for general cataloging duties; and 23 were for specialized cataloging duties. Most of the specialized cataloging jobs were for language-related specialties, such as Korean or Slavic languages, and listed language knowledge as a required skill. A few were for special collections duties, requiring skills with rare books and archival materials, or music cataloging, requiring music degrees or experience with scores and sound recordings. The nine positions specializing in nonprint materials mostly focused on electronic resources, requiring knowledge of metadata standards and skills with metadata formats. Of the positions, both general and specialized, that mentioned nonprint materials other than electronic resources in the scope of duties, only two listed experience with cataloging nonprint formats in MARC as a requirement. The problems of video cataloging that this case study encountered do not seem to be recognized by libraries in cataloger job advertisements. Special skills in the area of video cataloging are not specified.

A THIRD APPROACH?

Must libraries that are committed to consistent treatment of resources expect to devote significant amounts of high-level time to video cataloging? Or, lacking that commitment, must they accept that records for an important category of materials will be inferior?

We believe that there is a third possibility. If a national cooperative program for video cataloging were established, similar to or part of PCC for example, with many libraries bearing part of the responsibility for creating a database of national-level, full-level records, these circumstances could change. In this case study, the low number of additions and corrections made by staff in two academic libraries to national-level records for print monographs suggests that a policy of limited editing can be workable under the right circumstances, without compromise in quality, when there is a database of nationally authenticated records. Such a database of nationally authenticated records could be created for videos.

The establishment of a national cooperative program to provide authoritative cataloging records for videos could also develop a larger, more widely distributed, and more knowledgeable cohort of audiovisual catalogers as well as improve the accuracy, completeness, and consistent treatment of bibliographic records for these materials. The cooperative program would provide an established path for developing this expertise and for contributing to the national database of authenticated records if the library wished to make this contribution. But every library desiring to provide quality, consistent records across formats to its clients would not have to have a specialist to do so.

A cooperative solution would, indeed, cost some libraries staff time and development. But if these libraries are currently attempting to provide consistent, fully functional records across formats, they may already be devoting time to local editing of video records as the two libraries in this case study are. Why not invest the same resources in a cooperative program to save library time nationally while improving the functionality of catalog records for an important category of materials? The results of this case study suggest that libraries may already be spending time on video records and that, in the long run, the more visionary approach may be a practical one as well.

REFERENCES

Allison, Dee Ann and Scott Childers. "Index Relativity and Patron Search Strategy." *portal: Libraries and the Academy* 2 (1) (2002): 145-153.

Benemann, William E. "The Cathedral Factor: Excellence and the Motivation of Cataloging Staff." *Technical Services Quarterly*, 10 (3) (1993): 17-25.

Bland, Robert. "Quality Control in a Shared Online Catalog Database: The LAMBDA Experience." *Technical Services Quarterly* 4 (2) (Winter 1986): 43-58.

Boehr, Diane L. and Meredith L. Horan. "Non-Print Media at the National Library of Medicine." *Cataloging & Classification Quarterly* 31 (3/4) (2001): 341-354.

Bolin, Mary K. "Make a Quick Decision in (Almost) All Cases: Our Perennial Crisis in Cataloging." *Journal of Academic Librarianship* 16 (1991): 357-361.

Campbell, D. Grant and Karl V. Fast. "Panizzi, Lubetzky, and Google: How the Modern Web Environment is Reinventing the Theory of Cataloguing." *Canadian Journal of Information and Library Science* 28 (3) (Sept. 2004): 25-38.

Chapman, Ann. "Up to Standard? A Study of the Quality of Records in a Shared Cataloguing Database." *Journal of Librarianship and Information Science* 26 (4) (Dec. 1994): 201-210.

Chapman, Ann and Owen Massey. "A Catalogue Quality Audit Tool." *Library Management* 23 (2002): 314-324.

Chisman, Janet, Karen Diller, and Sharon Walbridge. "Usability Testing: A Case Study." *College & Research Libraries* 60 (Nov. 1999): 552-569.

Chung, Heeja Hahn. "User-Friendly Audiovisual Material Cataloging at Westchester County Public Library System." *Cataloging & Classification Quarterly* 31 (3/4) (2001): 313-325.

Cutter, Charles A. "Rules for a Dictionary Catalog: Selections." In: *Foundations of Cataloging: A Sourcebook*, edited by Michael Carpenter and Elaine Svenonius. Littleton, Colo.: Libraries Unlimited, 1985, pp. 62-71.

Graham, Peter S. "Quality in Cataloging: Making Distinctions." *Journal of Academic Librarianship* 16 (Sept. 1990): 213-218.

Hafter, Ruth. *Academic Librarians and Cataloging Networks: Visibility, Quality Control, and Professional Status*. New York: Greenwood Press, c1986.

Harmon, Joseph C. "The Death of Quality Cataloging: Does it Make a Difference for Library Users?" *Journal of Academic Librarianship* 22 (July 1996): 306-307.

Ho, Jeannette. "Faculty and Graduate Student Search Patterns and Perceptions of Videos in the Online Catalog." *Cataloging & Classification Quarterly* 33 (2) (2001): 69-89.

Howarth, Lynne. "AudioVisual Cataloging: From Orphan Child to Cinderella." *Technicalities* 19 (2) (Feb. 1999): 1, 3-5.

Hume, Margaret. "Searching for Media in the Online Catalog: A Qualitative Study of Media Users." *MC Journal: The Journal of Academic Media Librarianship* 3 (1) (Spring 1995): 1-28.

IFLA Study Group on the Functional Requirements for Bibliographic Records. *Functional Requirements for Bibliographic Records: Final Report*. München:| K.G. Saur, 1998. Viewed online 12/8/2005 at: www.ifla.org/VII/s13/frbr/frbr.pdf.

Intner, Shelia S. "Much Ado About Nothing: OCLC and RLIN Cataloging Quality." *Library Journal* 114 (Feb. 1, 1989): 38-40.

Lam, Vinh-The. "Quality Control Issues in Outsourcing Cataloging in United States and Canadian Academic Libraries." *Cataloging & Classification Quarterly* 40 (1) (2005): 101-122.

Ma, Yan, Steven J. Miller, and Yan Quan Liu. "Cataloging Nonprint Resources in the United States and China: A Comparative Study of Organization and Access for Selected Electronic and Audiovisual Resources." *International Cataloguing and Bibliographic Control* 26 (2) (Apr./June 1997): 46-49.

MacEwan, Andrew and Thurstan Young. "Quality vs. Quantity: Developing a Systematic Approach to a Perennial Problem." *Catalogue & Index* 152 (Summer 2004): 1-7.

Mann, Thomas. *Cataloging and Classification Quality at the Library of Congress.* Washington, DC: Cataloging Forum, Library of Congress, 1994.

Naun, Chew Chiat and K.C. Elhard. "Cataloguing, Lies, and Videotape: Comparing the IMDb and the Library Catalogue." *Cataloging & Classification Quarterly* 41 (1) (2005): 23-43.

Novotny, Eric. "I Don't Think I Click: A Protocol Analysis Study of Use of a Library Online Cataloging in the Internet Age." *College & Research Libraries* 65 (Nov. 2004): 525-537.

Porter, Galey and Paul Bredderman. "Nonprint Formats: A Survey of the Work and Its Challenges for the Cataloger in ARL Academic Libraries." *Cataloging & Classification Quarterly* 24 (3/4) (1997): 125-148.

Schoenung, James Gerald. *Quality of the Member Input Monograph Records in the Oclc On-Line Union Catalog.* Ph.D. dissertation, Drexel University, 1981.

Shin, Hee-sook. "Quality of Korean Cataloging Records in Shared Databases." *Cataloging & Classification Quarterly* 36 (1) (2003): 55-90.

Simpson, Fung-Yin K. "Quality Control of Chinese Monographic Records: A Case Study." *Journal of East Asian Libraries* 116 (Oct. 1998): 31-40.

Svenonius, Elaine and Dorothy McGarry. "Objectivity in Evaluating Subject Heading Assignment." *Cataloging & Classification Quarterly* 16 (2) (1993): 5-40.

Thomas, David H. "The Effect of Interface Design on Item Selection in An Online Catalog." *Library Resources & Technical Services* 45 (Jan 2001): 20-46.

Thomas, Sarah E. "Quality in Bibliographic Control." *Library Trends* 44 (Winter 1996): 491-505.

Tillett, Barbara. "Postscript: "'Cataloging Quality Is . . . ': A Summary of Responses to the October 1994 Cataloging Forum." In: *Cataloging Quality: A Library of Congress Symposium.* Washington, DC: Cataloging Forum, Library of Congress, 1994, pp. 28-29.

Tsao, Jai-hsya. "The Quality and Timeliness of Chinese and Japanese Monographic Records in the RLIN Database." *Library Resources and Technical Services* 38 (1994): 61-63.

Waysylenko, Lydia W.:Building Quality That Counts Into Your Cataloging Operation." *Library Collections, Acquisitions & Technical Services* 23 (1) (Spring 1999): 101-104.

Weihs, Jean. "A Somewhat Personal History of Nonbook Cataloguing." *Cataloging & Classification Quarterly* 31 (3/4) (2001): 159-188.

Weihs, Jean and Lynne C. Howarth. "Nonbook Materials: Their Occurrence and Bibliographic Description in Canadian Libraries." *Library Resources & Technical Services* 39 (April 1995): 184-197.

Weitz, Jay. "Videorecording Cataloging: Problems and Pointers." *Cataloging & Classification Quarterly* 31 (2) (2001): 53-83.

Zeng, Lei. *An Evaluation of the Quality of Chinese-Language Records in the OCLC OLUC Databases and a Study of a Rule-Based Data Validation System Online Chinese Cataloging.* Ph.D. Dissertation. University of Pittsburgh, 1992.

doi:10.1300/J104v44n03_06

APPENDIX I. Example of Worksheet for Additions and Corrections to Bibliographic Records

	Added data to record		Other full national level records		Contributed records				Vendor contributed records		
	Library of Congress records										
	Added LC blank	Added LC 4	Added full nat blank	Added full nat 4	Added Contrib I	Added Contrib K	Added Contrib M	Added Contrib 4	Added Vendor I	Added Vendor K	Added Vendor L
Audn	0	0	0	0	0	0	0	0	0	0	0
Cont	0	0	1	0	2	0	0	0	0	0	0
Ctry	0	0	0	1	2	0	0	0	0	0	0
Date1/2	0	0	0	1	1	0	0	0	0	0	0
DtSt	0	0	0	1	1	0	0	0	0	0	0
Elvl	0	0	0	0	0	0	0	0	0	0	0
Form	0	0	0	0	1	0	0	0	0	0	0
Gpub	0	0	0	1	0	0	0	0	0	0	0
Illus	0	0	2	0	2	0	0	0	0	0	0
Indx	0	0	0	0	2	0	0	0	0	0	0
Lang	0	0	0	0	0	0	0	0	0	0	0
LitF	0	0	0	0	0	0	0	0	0	0	0
Tech	0	0	0	0	0	0	0	0	0	0	0
Time	0	0	0	0	0	0	0	0	0	0	0
Tmat	0	0	0	0	0	0	0	0	0	0	0
006	0	0	0	1	0	1	0	0	0	0	0
007	0	0	0	0	0	0	0	0	0	0	0
007d	0	0	0	1	0	0	0	0	0	0	0
007e	0	0	0	0	0	0	0	0	0	0	0
007f	0	0	0	0	0	0	0	0	0	0	0
007g	0	0	0	0	0	0	0	0	0	0	0
007h	0	0	0	0	0	0	0	0	0	0	0
007i	0	0	7	0	1	1	0	0	0	0	0
010	0	0	0	1	0	0	0	0	0	0	0
020	2	0	0	0	0	0	0	0	0	0	0
024 ISBN13	0	0	0	0	0	0	0	0	0	0	0
028	0	0	0	0	0	0	0	0	0	0	0
041	0	0	0	0	0	0	0	0	0	0	0
043	0	0	0	0	0	0	0	0	0	0	0
090/050	0	0	0	0	2	0	0	0	0	0	0
1xx	0	0	0	0	2	0	0	0	0	0	0
700-730	0	0	1	0	2	0	0	0	0	0	0
240	0	0	0	0	1	0	1	0	0	0	0

APPENDIX I (continued)

Field											
245 a	0	0	0	0	1	0	0	0	0	0	0
245 b	0	0	0	0	0	0	0	0	0	0	0
245 c	0	0	0	0	0	0	0	0	0	0	0
246	1	0	6	1	4	1	0	0	0	0	0
740	2	0	0	0	0	0	0	1	0	0	0
250	0	0	0	0	0	0	0	0	0	0	0
260 a	0	0	0	0	1	0	0	0	0	0	0
260 b	0	0	0	1	0	0	0	0	0	0	0
260 c	0	0	0	0	1	0	0	0	0	0	0
300 a	0	0	2	2	1	0	0	0	0	0	0
300 b	0	0	1	0	1	0	0	0	0	0	0
300 c	0	0	0	0	1	0	0	0	0	0	0
4xx/8xx	0	0	0	0	2	0	0	0	0	0	0
500	0	0	0	0	2	0	0	0	0	0	0
SpecFeat	0	0	0	1	0	0	0	0	0	0	0
TitleSource	0	0	0	0	0	0	0	0	0	0	0
OrigProd	0	0	0	0	0	0	0	0	0	0	0
Based on	0	0	0	0	0	0	0	0	0	0	0
Includes	0	0	0	0	0	0	0	0	0	0	0
502	0	0	0	0	0	0	0	0	0	0	0
504	0	0	0	0	2	1	0	0	0	0	0
505	0	0	1	1	1	0	0	0	0	0	0
506	0	0	0	0	0	0	0	0	0	0	0
508	0	0	0	0	0	0	0	0	0	0	0
511	0	0	0	0	0	0	0	0	0	0	0
518	0	0	0	0	0	0	0	0	0	0	0
520	0	0	1	1	1	1	0	1	0	0	0
521	0	0	0	0	0	0	0	0	0	0	0
533/590	0	0	0	0	0	0	0	0	0	0	0
538	0	0	0	0	0	0	0	0	0	0	0
546	0	0	0	0	0	0	0	0	0	0	0
550	0	0	0	0	0	0	0	0	0	0	0
590	0	0	0	0	0	0	0	0	0	0	0
6xx-0	0	0	4	1	1	0	0	2	0	0	0
655-0	0	0	0	0	0	0	0	0	0	0	0
69x	0	0	0	0	0	0	0	0	0	0	0
76x-78x	0	0	0	0	0	0	0	0	0	0	0
856	0	0	0	0	0	0	0	0	0	0	0
Total	5	0	25	12	32	3	1	4	0	0	0

257

Are Technical Services Topics Underrepresented in the Contributed Papers at the ACRL National Conferences?

Robert P. Holley

SUMMARY. This study tests the hypothesis that the contributed papers at the 12 ACRL national conferences do not cover topics of interest to technical services librarians in proportion to their membership in ACRL. The analysis showed that 14.66% of contributed papers dealt with subjects that were part of the charge of ALCTS, the technical services division in ALA, and its five sections. This percentage dropped to 7.52% with the removal of collection development papers that are also of high interest to many public services librarians. Current overlap statistics indicate that 18.83% of ACRL members also belong to ALCTS–an indication of potential ACRL member interest in technical services topics. An unexpected discovery was that the contributed papers became much more holistic with the arrival of the Internet and electronic resources in academic libraries and, starting with the 1999 Detroit national conference, were much more difficult to categorize into specialized niches. The author speculates that the attendance at the national conferences by a high proportion of librarians from small to mid-size academic libraries discourages papers on

---

Robert P. Holley is Professor, Library and Information Science Program, Wayne State University, Detroit, MI 48201 (E-mail: aa3805@wayne.edu).

[Haworth co-indexing entry note]: "Are Technical Services Topics Underrepresented in the Contributed Papers at the ACRL National Conferences?" Holley, Robert P. Co-published simultaneously in *Cataloging & Classification Quarterly* (The Haworth Information Press, an imprint of The Haworth Press, Inc.) Vol. 44, No. 3/4, 2007, pp. 259-269; and: *Cataloger, Editor, and Scholar: Essays in Honor of Ruth C. Carter* (ed: Robert P. Holley) The Haworth Information Press, an imprint of The Haworth Press, Inc., 2007, pp. 259-269. Single or multiple copies of this article are available for a fee from The Haworth Document Delivery Service [1-800-HAWORTH, 9:00 a.m. - 5:00 p.m. (EST). E-mail address: docdelivery@haworthpress.com].

Available online at http://ccq.haworthpress.com
© 2007 by The Haworth Press, Inc. All rights reserved.
doi:10.1300/J104v44n03_07

technical services topics since technical services librarians are more likely to work in large ARL libraries. doi:10.1300/J104v44n03_07 *[Article copies available for a fee from The Haworth Document Delivery Service: 1-800-HAWORTH. E-mail address: <docdelivery@haworthpress.com> Website: <http://www.HaworthPress.com> © 2007 by The Haworth Press, Inc. All rights reserved.]*

KEYWORDS. ACRL national conferences, publications in technical services, holistic librarianship

The following paper initially set out to test the hypothesis that the contributed papers presented at the 12 national conferences of the Association of College and Research Libraries (ACRL) did not adequately cover topics of interest to technical services librarians and especially to catalogers, who most frequently work in large academic libraries. My concern was that they were an underrepresented constituency and were forgotten in ACRL in contrast with their public service counterparts.

While I will show that the subjects of the papers selected for presentation generally support this hypothesis, the review of the papers also uncovered an unexpected discovery that the arrival of the Internet, the growth of the World Wide Web, and the resulting increased use of online resources has led to a more holistic view of academic librarianship that has made it more difficult to place the contributed papers into well-defined interest niches. This change became evident starting with the Detroit national conference in 1999. Even before that time, I found some difficulty in neatly determining the audience for several papers because the themes of many papers would appeal to multiple academic constituencies; but the number of such papers has increased in recent years.

METHODOLOGY

I examined all contributed papers from the 12 national ACRL conferences from Boston in 1979 to Minneapolis in 2005. I excluded invited papers, panels, and any other type of presentation that did not fall into the reviewing process for contributed papers. Each conference has published proceedings except for the 8th conference in Nashville (1997) whose contributed papers are available on the ACRL Web site. (See Appendix I for a bibliography of the conference proceedings.)

I read the abstract for each paper and then the paper itself for those that fell into my sample as being of potential interest to technical services librarians. While many of the conference proceedings organized the papers by broad headings, I did my best not to let this pre-analysis influence my decision and read all abstracts no matter where they appeared in the volume. This was a wise decision because occasionally technical services papers appeared in other areas such as special collections when the subject matter was the acquisitions, cataloging, or preservation of special materials.

To structure my analysis, I used the organizational units of the ALA division, the Association for Library Collections and Technical Services (ALCTS), that has responsibility for technical services concerns. The subject interest coding that I used was therefore:

TS	Technical services in general
ACQ	Acquisitions
CAT	Cataloging
COL	Collection development
SER	Serials
PRE	Preservation and reformatting

I put one article on indexing in Cataloging (CAT) and several articles on intellectual freedom in Collection Development (CD). If an article treated three specific areas, I counted it as a general article on Technical Services (TS). In a small number of cases, an article seemed so evenly split between two areas that I assigned two codes where each is given a .5 weighting in my analysis. In three cases, the second area was outside of technical services so that the final count includes a fraction.

RESULTS

As can be seen from Table 1, the total number of technical services papers represents only 14.66% of the 638 contributed papers at the 12 national conferences. These figures undoubtedly overstate the number of papers that were intended for a technical services audience. The largest number of contributed papers in the chart above, 45.5 or 48.6% percent of technical services presentations, treat collection development issues. While collection development is represented in the ALCTS

TABLE 1. Total Number of Papers for All Conferences

	Number	% Total	% TS
General Technical Services	8	1.25%	8.56%
Acquisitions	10	1.57%	10.70%
Cataloging	19.5	3.06%	20.86%
Collection Development	45.5	7.13%	48.66%
Preservation	8.5	1.33%	9.09%
Serials	2	0.31%	2.14%
Total Number of TS Papers	93.5		
Total Number of Papers	638		
Percentage TS Papers	14.66%		
Percentage TS Papers without Collection Development	7.52%		

structure by the Collection Management and Development Section (CMDS), the Reference and User Services Association (RUSA) also has a collection development unit, Collection Development and Evaluation Section (CODES), a fact that indicates that collection development is of interest to both technical services and public services librarians. In many organizations, collection development responsibilities reside primarily, if not completely, in public services. Without the collection development papers, the percentage of papers firmly focused on technical services drops to 7.52%. While less important in numbers, several of the papers put into the acquisitions category (ACQ) discuss the acquisitions budget, a subject that would be of interest to administrators and collection development specialists outside of technical services.

While cataloging has a respectable number of articles, 19.5 or 20.86% of technical services presentations, this number is most likely not in keeping with their percentage among technical services staff with degrees in library science. On the other hand, preservationists, a group known for their dedication to their area of expertise, may have more articles than their numbers in the profession would warrant.

I understand, of course, that many librarians have diverse responsibilities and may do a little bit of everything. While statistical evidence from the ACRL registration records would be necessary to support this claim, it is my impression from attending all the ACRL national conferences that the number of attendees from small to mid-size academic libraries is a larger percentage wise than this same group's attendance at the national ALA conference where librarians from ARL libraries are much more common.

Table 2 and Chart 1 indicate the percentage of technical services presentations at each individual conference. The most striking feature is the steep decline in the mid-1990s to a low of 1.9% for the 1999 Detroit national conference. From having looked at all the articles, I would attribute this decline to the increasing importance of the Internet, the World Wide Web, and electronic resources. I could have perhaps categorized a few of the papers on the electronic resources as collection development, but most seem to be more focused on the content of these resources and their uses in libraries rather than the collection development aspects of how to choose them. While the percentage of technical services papers has increased since then for the three subsequent conferences (6.8%, 7.1%, and 8.7%), this figure is still well below the percentages for the earlier ACRL national conferences.

DISCUSSION

ALA and Its Divisional Structure

An issue for ALA members is the fact that they can choose divisions according to their type of work (technical services, systems, reference) or their type of library (public, academic, school). I believe that a case

TABLE 2. Percentage of Technical Services Papers by Conference

Year	Place	Percent
1978	Boston	15.2%
1981	Minneapolis	23.2%
1984	Seattle	27.7%
1986	Baltimore	23.3%
1989	Cincinnati	22.1%
1992	Salt Lake	15.4%
1995	Pittsburgh	11.1%
1997	Nashville	7.5%
1999	Denver	1.9%
2001	Detroit	6.8%
2003	Charlotte	7.1%
2005	Minneapolis	8.7%

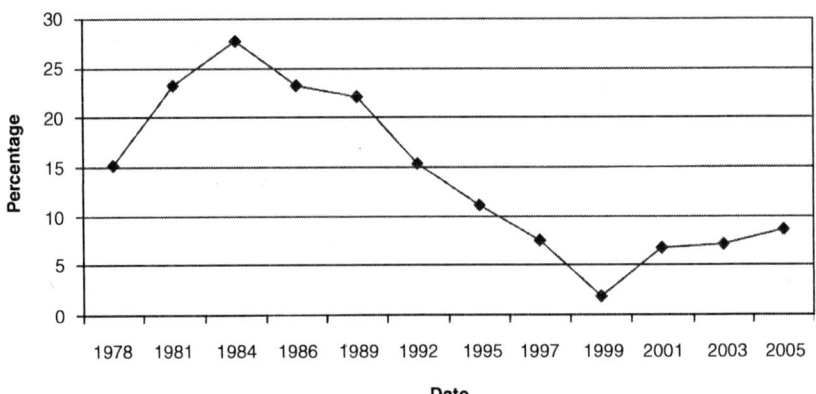

CHART 1. Percentage of TS Presentations

can be made that technical services librarians have generally made the choice to focus their professional participation in ALCTS rather than ACRL, perhaps in part because ALCTS is mostly a division of academic librarians and larger academic libraries are most likely to have a significant mass of technical services librarians. I am aware from my long participation in ALCTS that the number of public librarians who actively participate in the division is relatively small.

For whatever reason, ACRL members seem to have felt the need to create "type of work" sections (Distance Learning Section, Instruction Section, Rare Books and Manuscripts Section) and "subject sections" (Arts Section, Law and Political Science Section among many others) in addition to the sections that focus on subgroups of academic libraries (College Libraries Section, Community and Junior College Libraries Section, and Universities Libraries Section). The "type of work" and "subject sections" have a strong focus on public services activities and provide few opportunities for relevant committee appointments for technical services librarians.

Another interesting statistic for this article is the strong member overlap between ACRL and ALCTS as can been seen in a report prepared for the 2006 Midwinter Meeting in San Antonio.[1] On the ALCTS side, 2,301 members also belong to ACRL for a 50% overlap. Thus, half the ALCTS membership also belongs to ACRL, which is a strong indication of technical services librarians' interest in academic libraries. The issue is less clear on the ACRL side with its higher membership, but the same 2,301 overlap members make up 18.83% of ACRL's total membership. The issue could be how many of these dual members actively participate in none, one, or both of the divisions. Some may join for the publications since both divisions publish high quality journals. Some may join either division, but more likely ALCTS, from having past ties with the division even when job duties or type of library has changed. Nonetheless, it is clear that many ACRL members, 18.83% percent, indicate some interest in technical services through their membership in ALCTS.

REASONS FOR THE LACK OF PAPERS ON TECHNICAL SERVICES TOPICS, NOTABLY CATALOGING

There are two main possible reasons for the lack of papers, especially those on cataloging, though a detailed analysis of historical records, if they even exist, would be needed to "prove" the relative merits of the two choices. The two reasons are not mutually exclusive.

1. *Technical service librarians have not submitted papers for the ACRL national conferences.* To test the validity of this reason would require looking at all the submissions and analyzing their subject content. If many were submitted, the next issue would be the quality of the papers as discussed below. If few papers were submitted, the next step would be to try to understand why. Did potential writers not want to attend the ACRL conference? Did potential writers not consider the ACRL conference as a good outlet for their publications in comparison with other publication opportunities? Did the lack of technical services publications at the early conferences, especially on cataloging topics, discourage potential writers from considering the ACRL national conferences?
2. *The review panels rejected a higher proportion of technical services publications.* This hypothesis is also difficult to prove or disprove because it would require access to the deliberations of the review panels, which are by their very nature secret, and also an indication of the subject matter of rejected papers. I did consider looking at the make up of these panels, but ALA records give only the names of the panel members and peer reviewers.[2] The difficulty in discovering position titles over the past 25 years for so many librarians would be a more formidable task than warranted

by the importance of this topic. Rejection can also occur for a combination of two reasons. The first would be the poor quality of the submitted paper. The second would be the perception that the paper, though of high quality, would have limited appeal to the attendees of the conference. Thus, a decent paper on information literacy, a topic of high interest within ACRL, might have a better chance of being accepted than an excellent paper on a narrow "niche" topic in technical services. A final consideration might be the level of prior knowledge required to understand the presentation. For papers on technical services subjects, the audience might be required to have more specialized knowledge while more general papers would be accessible to a higher proportion of conference goers.

This process could become a vicious cycle as few technical services librarians submit papers because they get rejected and the review panels select fewer papers because technical services librarians do not attend the conference.

CONCLUDING REMARKS

If the goal of each national conference is to encourage member participation and involvement with ACRL, perhaps the topic of this paper is irrelevant in any case because the ACRL national conferences have been wildly successful whether or not there are contributed papers that appeal to technical services librarians. Attendance set a record at the 2005 Minneapolis conference. "Close to 4,000 attendees from every state and 15 countries joined the Association of College & Research Libraries (ACRL) at its 12th National Conference in Minneapolis, April 7 to 10. About 3,490 people attended the 2003 ACRL conference in Charlotte."[3] I find it hard to argue against such success. If my perception that a high percentage of the attendees come from smaller libraries is correct, this audience may be less interested in technical services because acquisitions and cataloging are normally less complicated in smaller libraries and are more often handled by library support staff who are probably less likely to attend an ACRL conference.

On the other hand, the lack of technical services papers may reinforce the perception that ACRL is a division for public services academic librarians with much less appeal for academic librarians who work behind the scenes in cataloging, acquisitions, and systems. From my dealings with students, I can confirm that the stereotypes about catalogers being "different" still persist and that they perceive a "gulf" between public and technical services. I would hope that ACRL, as the division for academic librarians, would do all that it can to minimize this "gulf" and speak for all academic librarians. At the very least, ACRL should assure that the selection panels and peer reviewers for contributed papers include a fair proportion of technical services librarians if this is currently not the case.

NOTES

1. "Division and Round Table Overlap Prepared for Midwinter 2006 San Antonio." http://www.ala.org/ala/pla/plaorg/reportstopla/2006.23.1.xls (accessed August 2006).
2. "On the lists of contributed papers readers, there are no affiliations given, so you'd have to know the players." Email from Karen Muller, ALA Librarian, September 20, 2005.
3. Association of College & Research Libraries conference draws record-breaking attendance in Minneapolis. (2005, April 11). *Press release*.

doi:10.1300/J104v44n03_07

APPENDIX I. Bibliography of ACRL National Conferences

1st National Conference, Boston, MA, 1978

"New Horizons for Academic Libraries: Papers Presented at the First National Conference of the Association of College and Research Libraries, Boston, Massachusetts, November 8-11, 1978." Eds. Robert D. Stueart and Richard David Johnson. New York: K.G. Saur Pub., 1979. (Print version)

1st National Conference, Boston, MA, 1978

"New Horizons for Academic Libraries: ACRL 1978 National Conference: Contributed Papers" Eds. Martha J. Bailey. [Chicago]: American Library Association, 1978?. (Microfiche Version)

2nd National Conference, Minneapolis, MN, 1981

"Options for the 80s: Proceedings of the Second National Conference of the Association of College and Research Libraries." Eds. Michael D. Kathman and Virgil F. Massman (Foundations in Library and Information Science; v. 17). Greenwich, CT: JAI Press, 1982.

APPENDIX I (continued)

3rd National Conference, Seattle, WA, 1984

"Academic Libraries: Myths and Realities: Proceedings of the Third National Conference of the Association of College and Research Libraries." Eds. Suzanne C. Dodson and Gary L. Menges. Chicago: Association of College and Research Libraries, 1984.

4th National Conference, Baltimore, MD, 1986

"Energies for Transition: Proceedings of the Fourth National Conference of the Association of College and Research Libraries, Baltimore, Maryland, April 9-12, 1986." Ed. Danuta A. Nitecki. Chicago: Association of College and Research Libraries, 1986.

5th National Conference, Cincinnati, OH, 1989

"Building on the First Century: Proceedings of the Fifth National Conference of the Association of College and Research Libraries, Cincinnati, Ohio, April 5-8, 1989." Ed. Janice C. Fennell. Chicago: Association of College and Research Libraries, 1989.

6th National Conference, Salt Lake City, UT, 1992

"Academic Libraries: Achieving Excellence in Higher Education: Proceedings of the Sixth National Conference of the Association of College and Research Libraries, Salt Lake City, Utah April 12-14, 1992." Ed. Thomas Kirk. Chicago: Association of College and Research Libraries, 1992.

7th National Conference, Pittsburg, PA, 1995

"Continuity & Transformation: The Promise of Confluence: Proceedings of the Seventh National Conference of the Association of College and Research Libraries, Pittsburgh, Pennsylvania, March 29-April 1, 1995." Ed. Richard AmRhein. Chicago: Association of College and Research Libraries, 1995.

8th National Conference, Nashville, TN, 1997.

"Choosing Our Futures: Nashville, Tennessee April 11-14, 1997." http://www.ala.org/ala/acrl/acrlevents/nationalconference/conference8.htm

9th National Conference, Detroit, MI, 1999

"Racing toward Tomorrow: Proceedings of the Ninth National Conference of the Association of College and Research Libraries, April 8-11, 1999." Ed. Hugh A. Thompson. Chicago: Association of College and Research Libraries, 1999.

10th National Conference, Denver, CO, 2001

"Crossing the Divide: Proceedings of the Tenth National Conference of the Association of College and Research Libraries, March 15-18, 2001." Ed. Hugh A. Thompson. Chicago: Association of College and Research Libraries, 2001.

11th National Conference, Charlotte, NC, 2003

"Learning to Make a Difference: Proceedings of the Eleventh National Conference of the Association of College and Research Libraries, April 10-13, 2003, Charlotte, North Carolina." Ed. Hugh A. Thompson. Chicago: Association of College and Research Libraries, 2003.

12th National Conference, Minneapolis, MN, 2005

"Currents and Convergence: Navigating the Rivers of Change: Proceedings of the Twelfth National Conference of the Association of College and Research Libraries, April 7-10, 2005, Minneapolis, Minnesota." Ed. Hugh A. Thompson. Chicago: Association of College and Research Libraries, 2005.

PART IV: POSITION PAPERS

Quo Vadis, Cataloging?

Elizabeth N. Steinhagen
Mary Ellen Hanson
Sharon A. Moynahan

SUMMARY. Under the leadership of Ruth Carter's generation, cooperative, shared cataloging grew and flourished among academic and research libraries. The authors provide an overview of trends and challenges from a golden age of expanding budgets and international cooperation during the 1970s and 1980s and later responses to the economic retrenchment and demographic changes of the 1990s and early 2000s. Responses to current challenges, including the impact of outsourced cataloging, increasing complexity of cataloging rules, and emerging technological options, are discussed. doi:10.1300/J104v44n03_08 *[Article copies available for a fee from The Haworth Document Delivery Service: 1-800-HAWORTH. E-mail address: <docdelivery@haworthpress.com> Website: <http://www.HaworthPress.com> © 2007 by The Haworth Press, Inc. All rights reserved.]*

Elizabeth N. Steinhagen, MA, MLS, is Coordinator of Resource Management, Bibliographic Access (RMBA) group, University of New Mexico University Libraries, Albuquerque, NM 87131 (E-mail: ens1@unm.edu). Mary Ellen Hanson, MA, MA, PhD (E-mail: mehanson@unm.edu), and Sharon A. Moynahan, MA, MSLS (E-mail: smoynaha@unm.edu), are both Catalogers in RMBA.

[Haworth co-indexing entry note]: "Quo Vadis, Cataloging?" Steinhagen, Elizabeth N., Mary Ellen Hanson, and Sharon A. Moynahan. Co-published simultaneously in *Cataloging & Classification Quarterly* (The Haworth Information Press, an imprint of The Haworth Press, Inc.) Vol. 44, No. 3/4, 2007, pp. 271-280; and: *Cataloger, Editor, and Scholar: Essays in Honor of Ruth C. Carter* (ed: Robert P. Holley) The Haworth Information Press, an imprint of The Haworth Press, Inc., 2007, pp. 271-280. Single or multiple copies of this article are available for a fee from The Haworth Document Delivery Service [1-800-HAWORTH, 9:00 a.m. - 5:00 p.m. (EST). E-mail address: docdelivery@haworthpress.com].

Available online at http://ccq.haworthpress.com
© 2007 by The Haworth Press, Inc. All rights reserved.
doi:10.1300/J104v44n03_08

KEYWORDS. Cataloging, outsourcing, cooperative cataloging, catalog rules, catalog standards, keyword searching

INTRODUCTION

Dr. Ruth Carter, in one of her last *Cataloging & Classification Quarterly* editorials, stated: "transitions are a norm in bibliographic control, albeit often slowly. They are also a fact of life in general." In the same piece, she pointed out that "it is always good when a transition is positive."[1] On her retirement from professional life, Dr. Carter, one of the icons of cataloging in the late twentieth century who has personified the golden age of the profession, felt positive about moving on to other activities. However, one wonders if her departure, and that of other leading figures in academic library cataloging, might be the harbinger of a long transition leading cataloging and its practitioners to profound changes in the new millennium.

THE GOLDEN ERA

Over the past century our role as catalog librarians "has evolved from traditional cataloging and classification."[2] We have been the content providers for databases and have created an enormous structure of bibliographic data that is the backbone of most catalogs, in card format or online, that are in use in libraries around the world. Of course, the demise of technical services in general, and of cataloging in particular, has often been predicted over the past one hundred years. In fact, Charles A. Cutter, in 1904, observed that the implementation by the Library of Congress of its card services for libraries would bring about the end of the then golden age of cataloging. However, throughout the twentieth century, catalog librarians flourished as their activities included receiving items, creating bibliographic records either by typing cards or later by entering records in online utilities, doing authority work, and processing materials. This was, and continues to be, a massive and labor-intensive operation that has proven expensive for most libraries. Even the advent of technology–especially after the introduction of the MARC record and OCLC in the early 1970s–did not reduce many personnel expenses as had been somewhat naively anticipated. Yes, we were able to eliminate boring and repetitive tasks such as typing, correcting, filing, and pulling cards; but we had to acquire new skills that included the manipulation of online bibliographic and authority records. Suddenly, the product of our work was exposed for the library world to see, to evaluate, and to use. Shared cooperative cataloging "was really a giant step toward modernization of cataloging, [and] quantity and quality of cataloging have been improved enormously."[3]

Catalogers have had to sharpen their skills, embrace new technologies, and take on diverse additional responsibilities. In the 1960s and '70s enrollments at universities and colleges skyrocketed; library budgets grew; and publishers rushed to supply the ever-increasing number of titles demanded by academic libraries competing to reach the top echelons of the Association of Research Libraries (ARL). These developments ensured that catalog librarians were kept busy managing burgeoning workloads in large departments, contributing original cataloging records to national databases, and trying to stay on top of changing cataloging codes, rule interpretations, and new computer systems. Academic libraries benefitted from cooperative activities in this electronic environment that allowed many to reduce costly duplication of effort, create high quality bibliographic and authority records for international use, and bring equally high quality records contributed by other libraries into their own online catalogs.

TROUBLE IN PARADISE

After the economic expansion of the 1970s, libraries faced leaner times with flat or decreasing budgets and increasing inflationary costs. These new challenges affected both the performance of cataloging and the perception of its value. Huge backlogs of materials acquired during earlier flush times were often left uncataloged, and some backlogs reached the tens of thousands. The RLIN and OCLC cataloging utilities were good, but not fast enough. Catalogers were also slowed down by multiple rule changes and constant technological upgrades. Cards were still being produced and filed. As libraries converted to online catalogs, thousands of older titles required retrospective conversion in competition with new titles to be cataloged. The advent of OCLC did not reduce the need for professional catalogers, at least not in academic catalog departments that did the lion's share of original cataloging. Many public libraries simply abandoned customization and purchased cards from vendors; but this option was less applicable to academic libraries with diverse, unique research collections. As the complexity and new formats of published materials increased, the Library of Congress issued hundreds of pages of rule interpretations used by research libraries to keep their catalog records in line with LC's quality standards. Library budgets supported annual subscription costs for cataloging utilities in addition to the cost for in-house cataloging staff. These developments forced budget-challenged administrators to look for economies in technical services. Cooperative acquisitions and cataloging agreements, such as those developed by the Seminar on the Acquisition of Latin American Library Materials (SALALM), were seen as a means to address soaring costs by sharing expertise and reducing duplication of collections and cataloging effort.

COOPERATION, COMPETITION, AND STRUCTURAL CHALLENGES

In the new millennium, demographics have begun to affect the state of cataloging. As catalogers in the boomer generation retire, many are not being replaced; and fewer new catalog professionals are being trained. Library administrators eager to staff new initiatives view attrition in cataloging as a source for budget reallocation. Those MLS catalogers who remain are often occupied with competing duties in supervision, reference, instruction, and selection. These duties lessen their ability to keep up with changes in cataloging practice and reduce the time available to contribute catalog records to shared databases. In addition, as their numbers decrease, professional catalogers have less influence on library policy and staffing priorities.

By the year 2000, online AACR2R, automated classification schedules, and improved cataloging modules had greatly speeded up the cataloging process. Library catalogs were online; no cards had to be filed; and administrators felt it was not necessary to replace cataloging personnel. University budgets were, at best, flat and, in many cases, shrinking. Staffing costs had become burdensome; the costs of paper and electronic resources skyrocketed. Other developments caused library administrators to question the need for full cataloging. New technologies promised partial alternatives to the in-house library collection and its well-crafted catalog. Vendors offered serials, reference, and book packages that changed monthly, making cataloging of those materials impractical. Decisions to provide access to information rather than ownership reduced the need to acquire and catalog in-house collections as did reliance on inter-library loan for materials that previously would have been purchased.

Library administrations now look to outsourcing of cataloging as a way to reduce personnel costs. Like public libraries in the 1970s, administrators are willing to give up customization for monetary savings. Even the Library of Congress (LC) began "outsourcing" LC-quality original cataloging through programs such as BIBCO, NACO, and CONSER. No longer able afford its de facto role as a national cataloging agency, LC has shifted some of the burden for quality records to a wide range of catalogers in public, academic, and research libraries. These efforts in shared cataloging provide real benefits for many libraries but at increased expense to contributing libraries that receive less than $5.00 credit from a utility for a record that might cost up to $30-50 to create in-house. In effect, shared cataloging has become the gift of these libraries not only to the library community but also to vendors, who advertise the cost savings of purchasing this "shared" cataloging via outsourcing. Library directors relying on outsourcing may forget that *someone* had to create those records originally and that additional IT staff time is required to manage the loading of outsourced bibliographic and authority records after purchase and to continue their maintenance.

The rise of electronic searching tools, notably Google, has also contributed to the assumption that formal cataloging is no longer necessary for access. Librarians themselves have contributed to this perception as they laud Google's coverage and ease of use in reference and information queries. Since Google can now access library catalog records, who needs the OPAC? But those catalog records must be electronically present somewhere for Google to access. Google Print proposes to digitize the contents of many of the world's books so that anyone can find, for example, information on the Battle of Algiers.[4] This is truly a great leap forward. However, users freed from the need to navigate controlled vocabulary must now be able to input the name of the battle in French or Arabic. Thomas Mann makes a strong case for focused browsing in library bookstacks as a way to find information for which exact key words are not known. He suggests that reliance on keyword searching and the prospect of finding "something" quickly really sacrifices true scholarship.[5] Librarians especially need to distinguish between the mechanisms needed for an information search and those needed for detailed, scholarly research. Libraries need to support both levels of research via electronic search engines and electronic catalogs. In a society obsessed with instant gratification, the Google search is ideal and encourages the casual searcher's acceptance of "good enough." In the academic context, shared bibliographic records are necessary for access to unique, off-Web resources. Administrators must balance budgets with increasing demands from students and researchers for more online information as well as more of everything else.

While cataloging faces the challenge of external factors such as shrinking budgets and the impending retirement of a generation of skilled practitioners, it also faces challenges from within the profession that sets its standards and establishes its rules of practice. National and international cataloging codes provide a complex framework for detailed, standardized bibliographic access; but this complexity is perceived by library administrators as an expensive process that is rendered unnecessary by the online keyword search.

Agents of our profession establish the cataloging rules and formats and continually revise and elaborate upon them. The rules change and proliferate with careful deliberations at an abstract level, but with little apparent regard for the cataloger's reality–increased workload due to staff reductions, additional assigned duties outside of cataloging, and reduced travel funds for training workshops. These factors mean less time and opportunity for catalogers to keep current with changing practice. The sheer magnitude of text encompassed by codes, rule interpretations, and technical bulletins (not including classification schedules and subject heading lists which also grow and change) can be daunting to those who use them daily.

Cataloging standards are necessary to provide access and to enable cooperative sharing of records. Too much complication that requires the cataloger to synthesize rules, rule interpretations, and precedents, coupled with required redundancies within each MARC format, frustrates efforts to describe materials efficiently. Those who formulate the rules and interpretations strive for a perfect, all-encompassing system. Catalogers must deal with the reality of balancing quality, as defined by the profession, with quantity, as demanded by their employers. If the complexity of standards means that libraries contribute fewer records, then local use as well as national and international cooperation via cataloging utilities is compromised. The result is fewer records for libraries–or outsourcing vendors–to use.

GOING FORWARD

What Can the Cataloging Profession Do?

It is essential to groom a new generation of catalogers to advance international, national, and local access to public knowledge. Library schools should continue to offer formal coursework in cataloging theory and practice as a fundamental access service and promote cataloging as a fundamental component in the organization of information. Professional library associations should continue to provide regional workshops in the current theory, practice, and new developments of cataloging.

Perhaps we should acknowledge that increasingly complex rules and interpretations, the coming of Functional Requirements for Bibliographic Records (FRBR), and other changes geared to the long-standing dream of universal bibliographic control are intended for a few large and well-funded academic and research libraries. At this level, simplification is not a priority; but many other libraries would benefit from less complex cataloging options. Perhaps we ought to lobby for simplified cataloging protocols and introduce different levels of description for different materials. Even the "core" level of bibliographic description may not be simple enough for many understaffed libraries. It may be necessary to recognize that the golden age of cataloging as our generation knew it cannot be sustained given current budget and staffing constraints.

It is necessary for national and international cataloging rule makers to realize that the level of complexity in current practice is not realistic under the working conditions most libraries face. Similarly, we catalogers must be more pragmatic in striking a balance between adequate records for our local users and the prestige and visibility resulting from international cataloging contribution. Perhaps cataloging will become a divided profession consisting of two tiers of staff: those who check-in shelf-ready materials and bibliographic records and a well-trained few who create full records for unique research materials.

What Can Cataloging Utilities and Vendors Do?

Although our library administrators have enjoyed the benefits and national prestige resulting from participation in programs such as PCC, BIBCO and NACO, these mandates are largely unfunded and might be considered unnecessary luxuries when budgets are tight. While member libraries receive small rebates for each original record contributed to catalog utilities, the utilities and outsourcing vendors sell these full-level records many times over. It is worth asking vendors to compensate libraries that produce high-quality records at a level which realistically reflects their ongoing commercial value.

What Can Library Administrators Do?

Library administrators have a difficult role to play as they attempt to strike a balance between the bottom line and the needs of their patrons. Academic libraries, especially, have to continue serving their research faculty as well as their undergraduates and must acknowledge the need for in-house cataloging expertise in order to provide access to research and special materials. Library administrators should cultivate local cataloging expertise through on-the-job training and professional workshops for catalogers. In the longer run, administrators must recognize that outsourcing cataloging to vendors and/or utilities has its limitations, if fewer original catalogers are left to populate and refine the databases. As one of the strongest advocates of cataloging, Michael Gorman, has said: "Technical services areas can be cut, and the disservice to future users of the library and to reference librarians could take years to become a crisis." And, "Also, OCLC and the others" [i.e., RLIN or the former WLN] "are cooperative enterprises depending on their members to contribute as well as take records."[6] Thus, cooperative cataloging activities should continue so that all can benefit from the growth of international databases that will bring us closer to the dream of universal bibliographic control. Last, but definitely not least, administrators and catalogers will have to lobby agencies at the national and international levels that are engaged in establishing and revising the cataloging codes so that these can be simplified, rather than made more complex. During this anticipated long transition to a more "mechanized" inputting of data, utilities should also be required to provide input screens and online work forms that do not require catalogers to bother with punctuation, subfield delimiters, and other data that are still geared to card production or electronic displays which mimic the appearance and content of a catalog card.

CONCLUSIONS

In 1998, E. Steinhagen and S. Moynahan proposed a set of changes aimed at helping catalogers caught between a rock and a hard place.[7] Today, caught between diminished staffing and increasing complexity in cataloging and technological advances, catalog librarians struggle to meet their objectives for rapid, functional records in record time. Some of their needs for better cataloging technology are being met. Outsourcing cataloging for unique as well as trade publications has been generally accepted by the profession and is especially welcome when certain language skills are not available locally. However, catalogers have not succeeded in simplifying complex processes, and administrators have not succeeded in getting fair compensation for original cataloging records.

As we ponder the developments of recent years, we realize that most of our professional activity has become technology-driven. This trend will continue to affect cataloging practice profoundly. Major innovations in computer technology will likely come from outside the profession; and, after a significant transition period, we see the day when catalogers no longer have to worry about the details of descriptive elements in bibliographic records, MARC tags, and punctuation. We anticipate that title pages will be scanned, perhaps even by the publishers; and tables of contents, abstracts, or other information (and not copyrighted!) will be linked to these records. Librarians' skills will then be needed to provide access to the intellectual content of the work through controlled subject vocabularies and authoritative headings for names. In libraries with open stacks, it may still be necessary for professionals to provide access to related items through classification schedules that group items by subject. With increased reliance on keyword searching and sophisticated information retrieval systems, complete bibliographic description of an item might become less important as information seekers gain online access to title pages and related data. The concept known as FRBR poses a "model to facilitate the collocation of related entities in the vast bibliographic universe."[8] Although concerned with the need for international cataloging rules to help reduce the global costs for bibliographic control, FRBR "still puts the user first" according to Barbara Tillett and "should influence the design of future systems, cataloging codes and cataloging practices."[9]

The profession and indeed the process of cataloging as we know it today will change dramatically; but, in the words of Google's Vice President in charge of Google Print Library Project, Susan Wojcicki: "The stores of knowledge inside libraries, combined with research skills offered by librarians, are an irreplaceable asset."[10] Ruth Carter's generation has successfully led catalogers through profound changes. Her work with *Cataloging & Classification Quarterly* has given catalogers a venue for sharing ideas and solutions. By following her example of flexibility, perseverance, innovation, and cooperation, catalogers will be able to contribute significantly to the world of information access in the 21st Century.

As for the process of cataloging, we can safely assume it will continue to evolve, driven by a technology that controls the creation of catalog records and by the appearance of new media in need of access. By making use of new electronic tools and new concepts such as FRBR, we should finally be able to get away from replicating the old paper catalog card in electronic form and focus cataloging on the intellectual process of access for research.

NOTES

1. Carter, Ruth C., Editorial. *Cataloging & Classification Quarterly*, v. 40, no. 2 (2005), p. 2.

2. Hall-Ellis, Sylvia D. "Descriptive Impressions of Entry-Level Cataloger Positions as Reflected in *American Libraries,* Auto-CAT, and the *Colorado State Library Jobline,* 2002-2003. *Cataloging & Classification Quarterly*, v. 40(2), (2005), p. 36

3. Tan, Wendy. "The Status of Catalogers in Academic Libraries and Implications for Chinese American Librarians." Available online at: http://www.white-clouds.com/iclc/cliej/clltan.htm.

4. Schmidt, Eric. "Books of Revelation." *Wall Street Journal,* (October 18, 2005), p. A18.

5. Mann, Thomas. "Google Print vs. Onsite Collections." *American Libraries,* v. 36 no. 7 (August 2005), p. 46.

6. Gorman, Michael. "The Corruption of Cataloging." Available online at: http://www.lib.csufresno.edu/libraryinformation/publications.

7. Steinhagen, Elizabeth N. and Sharon A. Moynahan. "Catalogers Must Change! Surviving Between the Rock and the Hard Place." *Cataloging & Classification Quarterly*, v. 26, no. 3 (1998), p. 3-20.

8. Tillett, Barbara B. "FRBR and Cataloging for the Future." *Cataloging & Classification Quarterly*, v. 39, no. ¾ (2005), p. 200.

9. Ibid, p. 197.

10. Interview: Straight Answers from Susan Wojcicki." *American Libraries*, v. 36, no. 10 (November 2005), p. 31.

doi:10.1300/J104v44n03_08

Principia Bibliographica? Balancing Principles, Practice, and Pragmatics in a Changing Digital Environment

Dick R. Miller

SUMMARY. This article explores the emphasis on control in cataloging versus the chaos found on the Web. It delves into adversarial relationships between catalogers and technologists. It seeks commonalities and suggests that new alternatives addressing both perspectives might offer superior and more satisfying results. A series of examples juxtapose current practices, enrichment possibilities, and flaws in current digital solutions to suggest potential opportunities where catalogers might excel. Speculation on ways to promote cataloging principles and values

---

Dick R. Miller, MLS, is Associate Director for Resource Management, Lane Medical Library and Knowledge Management Center, Information Resources and Technology, Stanford University Medical Center, Stanford, CA 94305 (E-mail: dick@stanford.edu).

The author is indebted to Ruth Carter for always being open to publishing new ideas, even controversial ones, and to his many supportive colleagues at home and abroad. Lane Medical Library, celebrating its centennial in 2006, continues to provide an environment for exploring new ideas and pursuing excellence.

[Haworth co-indexing entry note]: "Principia Bibliographica? Balancing Principles, Practice, and Pragmatics in a Changing Digital Environment." Miller, Dick R. Co-published simultaneously in *Cataloging & Classification Quarterly* (The Haworth Information Press, an imprint of The Haworth Press, Inc.) Vol. 44, No. 3/4, 2007, pp. 281-305; and: *Cataloger, Editor, and Scholar: Essays in Honor of Ruth C. Carter* (ed: Robert P. Holley) The Haworth Information Press, an imprint of The Haworth Press, Inc., 2007, pp. 281-305. Single or multiple copies of this article are available for a fee from The Haworth Document Delivery Service [1-800-HAWORTH, 9:00 a.m. - 5:00 p.m. (EST). E-mail address: docdelivery@haworthpress.com].

Available online at http://ccq.haworthpress.com
© 2007 by The Haworth Press, Inc. All rights reserved.
doi:10.1300/J104v44n03_09

via more direct participation in the unruly digital environment hints at a more promising future for our profession. doi:10.1300/J104v44n03_09 *[Article copies available for a fee from The Haworth Document Delivery Service: 1-800-HAWORTH. E-mail address: <docdelivery@haworthpress.com> Website: <http://www.HaworthPress.com> © 2007 by The Haworth Press, Inc. All rights reserved.]*

KEYWORDS. Cataloging, relationships, principles, transparency, balance, cooperation, control, time, Open Access, tradition, innovation, MeSH, XML

From the principle of vanity that holds a prominent place in every man's heart, there is too great a tendency to dwarf the past of our science, to exaggerate its present, and to greatly magnify its future.

–Levi Cooper Lane,
surgeon and namesake of Lane Medical Library[1]

Periods of rapid change make it challenging to maintain information management models that may have served well for many years. The nature of change itself invites controversy, and even confrontation, as interested parties seek to adjust past practices or to establish new models better suited to the changing conditions. Rather than lamenting loss or dismissively forging ahead, it is useful to explore the balance between the two perspectives, old and new. Inevitably, there will be lessons to be learned from traditions, which underwent their own controversial developments, and from the bold promise of emerging paradigms that may falter from lack of universal adoption and the validation of long practice.

The beginning of the twenty-first century finds libraries, and cataloging in particular, embroiled in such conundrums. Forging the future through the lens of the past may well augur greater success and stability for libraries than emulating the wasteful competition found in the business world. Open and cooperative endeavors, designed to enable and foster catalogers' traditional talents, could flourish in Web environments–too often viewed by this constituency as threatening.

BALANCING THE BOOKS?

At the 2005 LITA National Forum, Michael Gorman observed that today's plethora of metadata schemes parallel the early history of cataloging when libraries had their own cataloging rules, classification schemes, etc., and operated largely independently of one another. However, instead of the apparent lone option to continue establishmentarian practice as is, catalogers need to seek ways to demonstrate the value of cataloging principles in an open Web environment. Are the nouveau information organizers reinventing the wheel under our noses? What could they learn from cataloging, and what could catalogers learn that might foster greater respect all around and provide improved library services?

Catalogers know the value of clearly identifying works to distinguish between them and recognize the growing importance of this in anchoring relationships. They appreciate the value of authority control and controlled vocabularies, the value of details that may not interest one user but are crucial to another or to enable automated retrieval, the value of reliable and persistent information, the complexity of representing the actual facts, the importance of context in interpreting bibliographic data, and the fundamental value of doing a social good. Wouldn't we and our users be better off if the world were more aware of these qualities and the difference they can make in information retrieval? As metadata troves grow, the value of cataloging skills will become more apparent. We should be stretching our thinking to be ready for the inevitable opportunities that will arise and that would recognize and take advantage of our unique skills.

To explore areas that may offer possibilities for "building a better catalog" and beyond, the following broad strokes and selected details present some problems and possibilities to ponder in thinking about the role of catalogers in the development of more robust and flexible information systems. The reality is a very competitive Web environment with commercial and specialist interests often ignoring the library, other than perhaps LC, OCLC, and RLIN. In this ramble through the information landscape, consider the potential for libraries' less restrained participation in an open environment–without compromising our values.

A SEMI-OPEN UNION CATALOG?

Is the big picture in focus? Could a Web-based Metalog, an ersatz combination of OpenWorldCat and Wikipedia elements, provide a more robust shared authority file and union catalog? It is not so radical to consider combining libraries' dispersed and diluted efforts to provide a semi-open, yet structured, framework for organizing information. Rather than being a source for copy cataloging, local systems could link to it for transient bibliographic needs and use Google subsets of it to identify local holdings. "Accredited" catalogers could create and edit records freely by fixing errors or adding information on the spot. (OpenWorldCat isn't really open; it only permits appending notes.) By using an "OpenID" structure, terminology could change; record enhancement, without breaking external links, could flourish. Although reminiscent of the CataWiki prototyped at Access 2005 in Edmonton to permit group editing of MARC records and to "break the cataloguing cartel," this is not the intention. There is need for responsibility, detail, thoroughness, erudition, etc., and catalogers do have a certain "je ne sais quoi" in these regards.

Some of our redundant cataloging effort could be pooled as an experiment in demonstration projects to show how groups of libraries could cooperatively create and maintain a Web-based and Web-embedded catalog and authority files far more valuable than the many separate silos. Supervised volunteers and specialists could be enlisted to extend the possibilities. Quick responses to a suggestion/contribution box would encourage the unaccredited to flag errors and submit records. Library programmers could be enlisted to make batch changes. Also, by encouraging other websites to link in at the appropriate level, a looser array of resources could cluster around the more formal managed core. The open, cooperative environment should appeal to grant agencies, which might fund projects to map records and holdings, enrich the data with FRBR relationships, encourage international cooperation, and other similar projects. Protocols for ironing out data conflicts and other policies could develop gradually without discouraging participation, i.e., accepting that it is OK to make mistakes.

Google Book Search and others are making complete books available on the Web with little or limited metadata, but libraries are largely keeping their cataloging efforts isolated and straight-jacketed. This disconnect is not to our advantage. Libraries' interests would be better served by a convergence of interests and efforts.

Criticisms of cataloging vis-à-vis new technologies have called for the "death of MARC" and used strident phrases such as "rearranging the deck chairs on the Titanic" and "putting lipstick on a pig." While inflammatory, they often contain kernels of truth. Efforts by the concerned parties would be more productively spent together in exploring both XML's benefits and pitfalls and cataloging's values and reticence in an open and constructive manner. The issues are fundamental and not restricted to a particular purview. Focusing the ardor on effective communication and joint involvement would likely promote more innovative solutions to the shared problems.

VALUE-ADDED METALOGING?

In addition to reviewing the big picture, detail needs scrutiny as well. Should catalogers be scribes or illuminators? Cataloging in a full text environment calls for a greater emphasis on judgment and evaluation to create the best metadata. Identifying key concepts and translating them to a controlled vocabulary enhances findability, and constructing relationships provides valuable context. These professional skills will likely retain or increase our value whereas transcription is likely to become a mostly automated extraction taken for granted. Likewise, enrichment of authorities by supplying alternative terms and by determining and normalizing relationships will help users navigate masses of information more effectively. The value of such information need not be limited to the catalog but could support interfaces to other databases and Web resources and act as a device to automatically provide synonymy and offer alternatives before sending an enriched search request to chosen targets.

Words

Fill-in-the-box keyword searching is popular. The "Did you mean" option in Google is a useful feature; a search for "psuedo" yields a respectable 880,000 hits; however, this represents only 3% as the suggestion of "pseudo" produces over 30 million, no doubt enhanced by Google's stemming algorithm. Misspelling is an interesting phenomenon because word processing software can automatically correct this error, and yet savvy EBay shoppers actually seek sleepy listings containing misspellings in search of bargains overlooked by compliant spellers. But, maybe you meant "fake" (43 million), "false" (132 million), "faux" (16 million), or "counterfeit" (6.5 million)? The "pseudo" retrieval is only 14% of these near synonyms; and then there's "artificial," "bogus," "not genuine," "simulated," etc.

Roget's has been around since 1852, but thesaural relationships have not been incorporated effectively into search retrieval software. Because word searching is so popular, help in selecting semantically related words could distinguish catalogs. Do searchers always think of dirigibles or Zeppelins when seeking blimps? Browsable keyword indexes could identify variants and related terms, e.g.:

house, abode, domicile, dwelling, habitation, residence [near synonymy]
apartment, castle, condominium/condo, digs, home, mansion, etc. [related]
casa, Haus/Häuser, maison, [other languages]
House of . . . [more sophisticated options for royalty, government bodies, etc.]

Entries

Deliberate catalog entries are often touted as superior to free text. However, without building richer references, the same problems in finding the right word are likely to occur as in locating the right entry. The still brewing *Resource Description and Access* (RDA) code emphasizes relationships,[2] but the new title signals the traditional mantra while downplaying its Anglo-American slant. Hopefully, the new standard will balance a combination of the identification/characterization of resources and the articulation of relationships among them to improve access–not only to the resources, but to the underlying and underutilized authority structures. Whether the code is truly "designed for use in a digital environment" may lie in its answer to questions such as: Will users be able to generate standard citations from bibliographic records?

Even when structures are available, will reluctance to go beyond the traditional persist? Might catalogers adopt a more value-added orientation? The following example may stretch cataloging attitudes more than it does MARC coding. Consider a literary movement, La Pléiade. In December 2005, the LC catalog had 46 records with the heading "Pléiade" and 581 records containing the keyword, many from series. In contrast, an exact phrase search produced 188,000 results in Google, 3,560 in Google Scholar, and 2,040 in Google Books. This is the related LC authority:

150 __ |a Pléiade

550 __ |w g |a French literature |y 16th century

550 __ |w g |a French poetry |y 16th century

670 __ |a Levi, A. Guide to French literature : beginnings to 1789, 1994: |b p. 610 (hdg.: Pléiade, La; list of 7 French poets active mostly in the third quarter of the 16th cent., drawn up by Ronsard)

670 __ |a New Oxford companion to lit. in French, 1995: |b p. 627 (hdg.: Pléiade, La; constellation of 7 poets active from 1549 to 1589, under leadership of Ronsard)

From the cross references, we learn that this heading is related to sixteenth century French literature and poetry. The non-public notes justifying the entry add scant additional scope.

Contrast this with the first paragraph of the Wikipedia entry in English in December 2005:[3]

> The Pléiade is the name given to a group of 16th-century French Renaissance poets whose principal members were Pierre de Ronsard, Joachim du Bellay and Jean-Antoine de Baïf. The name was a reference to another literary group, the original Alexandrian Pleiad of seven Alexandrian poets and tragedians (3rd century B.C.), corresponding to the seven stars of the Pleiades star cluster. The name "Pléiade" was also adopted in 1323 by a group of fourteen poets (seven men and seven women) in Toulouse.

The Wikipedia entry is much richer in both informational content and links. The entry covers two French entities of the same name in some detail, identifies the star cluster namesake, and provides links to selected individual poets and to an ancient Alexandrian Pleiad. The French Wikipedia includes an entry, Pléiade (XVIe siècle), which provides even more specifics. Oddly, there is another archived French version, Pléiade, which contains additional useful information not included in the current entry.

In considering context and relationships, it is not difficult to tease out information from these hyperlinked descriptions and, with additional effort, to unearth salient details from Google's 2.24 million entries on the stemmed word, including full text of the *Dictionary of Phrase and Fable* (1894). This exploration anticipates the need for disambiguation and variant access–perhaps as follows:

```
150 __  |a Pléiade (France : 16th cent.)
450 __  |a French Pleiade, First
450 __  |a Groupe Pléiade
450 __  |a Pléiade française
450 __  |a French Renaissance Pléiade
450 __  |a Pleiad (France : 16th cent.)
450 __  |a Brigade |f 1553-1556
```

Who "belonged" to this movement? There were initially seven poets, but actually more due to replacements. Potential personal name relationships with their duration lead to those involved. While sometimes the names encountered did not match entries established in LC authorities, it was not difficult to locate all of them as well as a couple of other related names:

    500 1_ |e Leader |a Ronsard, Pierre de, |d 1524-1585.
    500 1_ |e Member |a Du Bellay, Joachim, |d 1525 (ca.)-1560.
    500 1_ |e Member |a Baïf, Jean-Antoine de, |d 1532-1589.
    500 1_ |e Member |a Jodelle, Étienne, |d 1532-1573.
    500 1_ |e Member |a Tyard, Pontus de, |d 1521-1605.
    500 1_ |e Member |9 1553-1582 |a Peletier, Jacques, |d 1517-1582.
    500 1_ |e Member |9 1582- |a Dorat, Jean, |d 1508-1588.
    500 1_ |e Member |9 1553-1554 |a La Péruse, Jean de, |d 1529-1554.
    500 1_ |e Member |9 1554- |a Belleau, Remy, |d 1527?-1577.
    500 1_ |e Associated |a Des Autels, Guillaume, |d 1529-ca. 1581.
    500 0_ |e Inspiration |a Francis |b I, |c King of France, |d 1494-1547.

Related headings, perhaps coded to indicate their "semi-established" status, would provide awareness of the six other septets known by the same name, benefiting both catalogers and users:

    550 __ |a Pléiade (Alexandria, Egypt : Tragic)
    550 __ |a Pléiade (Alexandria, Egypt : Poetic)
    550 __ |a Pléiade (Carolingian)
    550 __ |a Pléiade (France : 17th cent.)
    550 __ |a Pléiade (Toulouse, France : 14th cent. : Men)
    550 __ |a Pléiade (Toulouse, France : 14th cent. : Women)

Additional relationships and a public scope note would also help:

    550 __ |a Renaissance
    551 __ |e Locale |e France
    551 __ |e Namesake |a Pleiades
    678 __ |a This constellation of roughly seven French poets promoted French as a language of literary expression. The name, derived from the seven visible stars of the Pleiades, references the group of ancient Alexandrian tragic poets.

Catalogers with a knowledge of French literature would be better suited to provide such enhancements and the above "straw" record may contain inaccuracies in addition to the nouveau MARC subfields. This type of effort is a bargain when considering that subsequent explorers can avoid sifting through the haystack repeatedly. The level of effort need not be applied consistently, but perhaps proportionately to the prominence or confusedness of the topic. One can argue what to include, but balanced/neutral assertions can help avoid errors of omission and allow the searcher to decide which relationships to pursue.

Other than tedium and frustration, the difficulty in providing this enrichment was in the delineation/disambiguation of the groups and in identifying/finding the authorized forms of the related names. Both are professional activities, and even drudgery can result in the delight of identifying a missing link. Standards to address form of entry create stability and address weaknesses in open systems. The Wikipedia is not without problems; recently it had to bar unregistered users from creating new pages due to controversial content. Despite disclaimers of validity, it is interesting that citations to it occur in authority records:

970 __ |a Wikipedia home page, via WWW, July 11, 2003 |b (Friedrich II., German king, emperor of the Holy Roman Empire; b. Dec. 26, 1194, d. Dec. 13, 1250)

The Wikipedia is a work in progress. While more than one Pléiade is distinguished in its entry, this is not reflected in its page devoted to disambiguation of Pleiades; nor does it reference the separate, relevant "Alexandrian Pleiad" page.

Pleiades (disambiguation)

Pleiades can refer to:

* Pleiades (star cluster)–an open cluster of stars in the constellation Taurus;

* Pleiades (mythology)–the seven sisters of Greek mythology;

* Pleiades (volcano group)–a group of volcanoes in Antarctica;

* La Pléiade–a group of 16th-century French poets.

The Wikipedia's limitations can be subtle. In reading one of its biographical sketches of a noted scientist, it was poignant to learn that the luckless researcher had not received any of the leading awards in his field, despite his fundamental contributions that were so obvious to the writer. Only from unrelated references in the text was it possible to discern that the page had been based on content written in the 1970s and that the subject had been fully honored in the 1980s. Although the entry was a recent creation, it relied on an earlier document that the author had failed to verify as to currency. In this case, the reader fixed the error but forgot the scientist's name and cannot cite it. The importance of such time factors is treated further below.

While the Wikipedia's limited controls leave it susceptible to controversies, its model could be adapted so that catalogers could share efforts in building a more effective authority file focused on anticipating users' needs rather than so strictly relying on literary warrant of collections. In reality, libraries rely heavily on books to establish the need for entries. Books are typically several years in the making; and thus terminology lags rather than being ready when books arrive.

STRUCTURE AND FUNCTION IN INFORMATION SYSTEMS

Bibliographic data elements, their attributes, and their relationships to other records determine to a large extent how flexibly this information can be processed for varied tasks, whether to support discovery, circulation, bibliometrics, or Web displays. While MARC has stretched about as far as possible to accommodate all manner of data, many recognize that it is hampering the fullest utilization of bibliographic data in Web environments. XML has shown much greater flexibility in deploying cataloging information, but schema development has been hampered by blind fidelity to MARC. Exceptionally, Martha Yee has responded formally to questions raised about MARC.[4] Unfortunately, her response preceded the detailed presentation of deficiencies in AACR and MARC included in *Putting XML to Work in the Library*.[5] These issues are beyond the current scope of this article; but, regardless of one's stance in this protracted controversy, more open dialogue is needed.

Browse Entry (Sequential Access) vs. Keyword Search (Random Access)?

Web search engines focus on keywords/phrases with relevance ranking. Their proprietary algorithms and policies largely shroud the systems' internal workings from scrutiny although much can be ferreted out by the persistent.[6] Powerful keyword access relies on *random access* to uncontrolled data. Library catalogs usually provide this but also emphasize browsing or *sequential access* to controlled data elements in discrete indexes. Library portals fall back on keyword access even when database driven from cataloging data.

Is it easier to find "library resources" on the Web than in the catalog? Every day, more full text and more metadata appear directly on the Web. Sometimes this sketchy metadata is directly associated with available full text–sometimes searchable with only a peek permitted and sometimes entirely separate. The following three examples illustrate the blurring of catalogs and Web searches; the disregard, de-emphasis, or disappearance of controlled vocabulary; and the meager bibliographic information even when full text originates from libraries.

1. Amazon.com's limited metadata is offset by additional features such as sales ranking (popularity); searches of full text (when available and after the book is found) via its "Search inside! the book" feature; CAPs (CApitalized Phrases, e.g., proper nouns, occurring in the full text); SIPs (Statistically Improbable Phrases to identify unique content); and access to teaser full text samples.

   French Intellectuals And History. The

   Nouvelle Revue Francaise under Jean

   Paulhan, 1925-1940. (Faux Titre 93)

   (Paperback)

   by Martyn Cornick

   Product Details

   Paperback: 224 pages

   Publisher: Rodopi Bv Editions (January, 1995)

   Language: English

   ISBN: 9051837976

2. Google Book Search allows searching full text of books, which are also searchable in regular Google, but reduces bibliographic information drastically. The inclusion of "Publication Date" is significant in view of disregard for dating Web content, and "Related information" recognizes bibliographic relationships.

Related information

- Web search for reviews of Cambridge History of Classical Literature
- Other web pages related to Cambridge History of Classical Literature

Bibliographic information

Title	Cambridge History of Classical Literature
Author(s)	E.J. Kenney
Publisher	Cambridge University Press
Publication Date	Apr 1, 1982
Format	Hardcover
Dimensions	6.25 × 9.50 × 2.25 in
ISBN	0521210437

Scanned library books have the same links for related information but even less metadata although pagination is sometimes given:

Bibliographic information

Title	The History of Civilization
Author(s)	Amos Dean
Publisher	J. Munsell
Publication Date	1868

Bibliographic information

Title	Michigan law review
Publisher	Michigan Law Review Association, etc.

To date, it is apparent that Google does not encourage direct linking to full text books since the lack of a control number or Digital Object Identifier does not make this simple and persistent.

3. OCLC's "Find in a Library" maps selected cataloging data, including contents notes, and is searchable in Google or separately. Some codes are burst to text values. The overall emphasis is on links to library holdings and provision of options for users to add contents and notes.

> La Pléiade
>
> by Yvonne Bellenger
>
> Type: French: Book: Non-fiction
>
> Publisher: Paris: Presses universitaires de France, 1978.
>
> ISBN: 2130357733
>
> Subjects: French poetry--History and criticism--16th century | Pléiade. | Pléiade.

The segregation of controlled bibliographic data elements in catalogs limits their usefulness. There should be ways of creating more peaceful coexistence between controlled and uncontrolled access on the Web. It should not be an either/or choice.

Undated Documents? Timeless

Many digital resources parallel published documents and include proper attribution and date of issuance. Too many other digital resources lack normative data elements, thus preventing retrieval by the date of content. Unfortunately, digital documents produced by libraries are not immune. An appeal to a search engine company suggested defining content dates for Web pages and using its clout to promote them. A representative from the company answered that it would not work as creators would falsify values to make content appear newer. Bracketed dates provided in cataloging records may become the only indication of the date of some Web content, especially in cases where pages are moved and copied without content change since each time they receive new date/time stamps. This is another case of the digital environment reflecting too well the manual one of handwritten manuscripts.

While seemingly a small point, it is just one facet of what eventually leads to historical revisionism. Those concerned primarily with publicity and marketing tend to ignore facts by taking liberties that run the gamut from vague or inaccurate literature citations to what amounts to misrepresentation or falsification of the scholarly record. Some of the most egregious examples of this occur when back files of periodicals are mounted online retrospectively. This example lumps three titles under the current title:

> Journal of Cancer Research and Clinical Oncology (Historical Archive)
>
> Publisher: Springer-Verlag GmbH
>
> ISSN: 0171-5216 (Paper) 1432-1335 (Online)
>
> [covers 1904 to 1996; 1997- listed separately with same ISSNs]

The following earlier titles, each having separate ISSNs, are not mentioned.

> 1971-1978: Zeitschrift für Krebsforschung und klinische Onkologie 0084-5353
>
> 1903-1971: Zeitschrift für Krebsforschung 0301-1585

For a century, articles in these German titles have been cited by the title *as published*, indexed *as published*, and searched *as published*. This practice creates problems for link resolvers; and, when users reach the "right" place, they are confused in not seeing the title sought. The separation of a current file from the archive hampers navigation by introducing an unnecessary boundary.

Citation practice is hampered further when online versions of publications drop pagination, withdraw superseded editions of books, etc. Similarly, organizations claim accomplishments under current names; and sometimes appear to try to eradicate their earlier names. Libraries have shown that information retrieval nightmares due to such practices are avoidable by respecting bibliographic history and the scholarly record as does Project Muse. NLM practice regarding retracted publications accurately reflects changes without compromising the original. Inclusion of the Publication Type, "Retracted Publication," and displaying this relationship prominently at the beginning of the record corrects errors without altering the facts:

> Retraction in: Clin Infect Dis. 2004 Jul 1;39(1):152.

Accurate reflection of bibliographic history, including the date of content, will benefit catalogers in the long run. As the Web grows and ages, time's critical role in delineating information currency and historicity will become more evident to users.

Proliferation or Prevention of Errors?

Once created, deliberate or inadvertent misinformation can proliferate. This is particularly true of often-copied Wikipedia content but also occurs in copy cataloging. The Wikipedia entry for the MacArthur Foundation lists "John Cairns (biologist)" under 1981 fellowships, which used to link in error to a preacher who had died in 1892, until corrected on August 29, 2005. However, as of December 22, 2005, a Google search for "'john cairns' macarthur wikipedia" yielded 14 websites on the first two screens of a total 246 results. The results may be classed as correct (3), failed (5), and incorrect (6) as shown in the following sequence retrieved. Of the two screens of highly ranked pages in Google, only two had picked up the Wikipedia correction after several months.

Site	Result
1. en.wikipedia.org	Correct (John Cairns (biologist) with no link)
2. answers.com	Incorrect (link to biography of 19th century preacher)
3. reference.com	Incorrect
4. searchspaniel.com	Failed ("Not Found" message)
5. biocrawler.org	Incorrect
6. factbug.com	Failed (redirect to search form)
7. thefreedictionary.com	Correct
8. lowide.com	Incorrect
9. oldion.com	Correct
10. peopledump.com	Failed (redirect to pornography)
11. mygoinfo.com	Failed ("Not Found" message)
12. carluvers.com	Incorrect
13. bharathnet.com	Failed (peculiar link to generic Wikipedia news)
14. netipedia.com	Incorrect

The LC Authority files include 10 different John Cairns, including "Cairns, John, 1922-," the one who received the MacArthur Fellowship in

1981 although this information is not provided. Another one born in 1923 is also a biologist. The *Biographical and Genealogical Master Index* lists 20 entries with some duplication, but none born in 1922. The MacArthur site lists him as "H. John Cairns," but this search in Google only yields the same site. The *Boston Globe* announces his award under "Hugh John Cairns."

Unfortunately, listings of major award winners do not lead directly into the bibliographic apparatus. Conversely, authority files do not identify instances of topical headings. The LC catalog does list works by this author, but nothing about him. A potential relationship:

100 1_ |a Cairns, John, |d 1922-
550 __ |e Awardee |9 1981 |a MacArthur Fellowship

Better integration of library catalogs, authority files, and reference tools are long overdue. If authority information were more apparent on the Web, those creating resources might avail themselves of using preferred forms and become more aware of the value of context and disambiguation. Currently, they are more likely to consult the Wikipedia, which does have disambiguation pages, but not in this case as there is only a biography of the 19th century preacher.

Sometimes there is a lot of noise and not much information. Elements that could lead to clarity regarding people, organizations, and events are sadly dispersed across incompatible systems, unarticulated with their counterparts. Disclaimers about the veracity of information likely go unread. Perhaps herein lies opportunity for the cataloger. Authorities for selected cyclical data, such as new Nobel laureates, could contain triggers to prompt creation of new instances as they are announced.

Extensible Relationships?

The importance of relationships in the bibliographic apparatus continues to gain currency. This could be due to the ease of "hotlinking" in online catalogs, the influence of hyperlinking in web documents, buzz in publications advocating this, or other factors. The influence of FRBR on the RDA hopefully bodes well in addressing this strategic aspect of bibliographic information. As rule simplification is a goal, a generic linking mechanism is easily imaginable. Currently, linking entry fields, along with some of their 2nd indicators, provide approximately 30 specific relationships, mostly relating to seriality. Consider the following examples that omit related control numbers, etc.:

780 00 |t Journal of the American Medical Association
760 0_ |t American journal of hygiene
767 0_ |t Finance & development. Spanish. Finanzas y desarrollo
785 07 |t Quarterly review of pediatrics
785 07 |t Clinical pediatrics
785 00 |t New England journal of medicine

In other cases, a linking entry complexity note (580) describes a "non-specific" relationship:

580 __ |a "Companion to Rohen/Yokochi Color atlas of anatomy."
787 1_ |a Rohen, Johannes W. |q (Johannes Wilhelm). |t Color atlas of anatomy.

Linking entry fields could be reduced to one field (possibly 788) by defining a relator subfield (possibly |e) to explicitly name the relationships. Recommended display constants could serve as an initial set of values and be expanded to cover cases unnecessarily relegated to notes. Consider these entries paralleling the foregoing examples:

788 __ |e Continues |t Journal of the American Medical Association
788 __ |e Subseries of |t American journal of hygiene
788 __ |e Translated as |t Finanzas y desarrollo
788 __ |e Merged with |t Quarterly review of pediatrics
788 __ |e Continued by |t Clinical pediatrics
788 __ |e Continued by |t New England journal of medicine
788 __ |e Companion to |t Color atlas of anatomy (2003)

Other data specific to relationship would be better covered as part of the relationship field. Generally, serials have notes in a separate area, despite MARC linking entry fields including a notes subfield (|n). The following section contains an example of a note embedded in a relationship.

Whatever the reason that series are treated as a distinct ISBD area, they inherently express a relationship to an implied parent work, either via a numbered sequence of another title (indistinguishable from a serial) or via sharing a collective title alone. The simplifying mechanism could be extended by inclusion of a subfield for sequence note.

788 |e Series |t Advances in cardiology |v v. 10

Such practice would simplify a confusing array of fielding and support series display in numeric or alphabetic sequence in particular. Moreover, this would help in interfiling links for analytics and component parts.

> ▼Advances in cardiology [serial]
>
> v. 10 Body surface mapping of cardiac field [analytic]

Instead of:

> Advances in cardiology [serial]
>
> Advances in cardiology; v. 10. [analytic]

Simplicity in structuring bibliographic linking would support more intuitive and advanced approaches to information management and use, e.g., links from maps to geographic entries; from a periodic table of chemical elements to entries for elements and isotopes; graphical displays of time lines including works created, active creators at the time, extant organizations, events of the time, works about the time period, places existing at the time, etc. Further refinements could permit literary maps of periods, chronologies of concepts in a field, and visual displays of relationships as seen in products from Antarctica Systems, KartOO, etc.

RELATIONSHIPS IN CONTROLLED VOCABULARIES

Development and use of controlled vocabularies are often associated with libraries and indexing agencies. These tend to focus on a topic or field of study with the aim of providing consistent terminology, cross-references from variant terms and related terms, and sometimes hierarchical relationships and other features–all focused on facilitating users' access to information. Vibrant schemes continue evolving to keep current with advances relevant to their scope and to associated reinterpretations of terminology. Due to such change, it is inevitable that previously valid terms persist in some databases, despite significant effort to maintain currency. Without constant vigilance and ongoing maintenance, obsolescence can seriously hinder the realization of the benefits of a controlled vocabulary. For example, how many libraries using *Medical*

Subject Headings would claim their catalogs' full compliance with 2006 MeSH?

Insubordinate Subheadings?

While the National Library of Medicine's use of MeSH is exemplary, limitations other than obsolescence are more challenging, even for national libraries. A long-standing feature of both MeSH and LCSH (*Library of Congress Subject Headings*) is the use of subheadings. How many integrated library systems effectively use subheadings to eliminate clutter in alphabetical subject indexes (displaying the substructure on demand) or to break a large topic into organized subsections? Would it really be so difficult to display subject indexes to reflect the careful coding that went into them?

A subject browse in Lane's Voyager catalog recently retrieved 208 topics beginning with the word "heart." The following subheadings are widely dispersed amongst intervening terms, many of which also have subheadings, e.g., "Heart Valve Diseases" with 10 subheadings. One may argue that a combined alphabetical list is useful, but what about the 50 entries beginning with "cardiac"? Is this vocabulary out of control?

Subheading	Position in Retrieval
abnormalities	2nd (xref to precombined term)
anatomy & histology	3rd
blood supply	37th
drug effects	95th
embryology	96th
growth & development	117rd
injuries	(xref suppressed; matches Heart Injuries)
innervation	124th
metabolism	131st
physiology	139th
pathophysiology	140th
radiography	141st
radionuclide imaging	142nd
surgery	162nd (xref to precombined terms)
transplantation	(xref suppressed; matches Heart Transplantation)
ultrasonography	171st

Hierarchical Relationships

Hierarchical structures can effectively reveal relationships as seen in the MeSH Browser[7] and in PubMed.[8] However, some of the content is not displayed there, and a great deal of it disappears in the context of the catalog. In 2005, MeSH was restructured via an XML schema into three levels: Descriptor, Concept, and Term.[9] The influence of NLM's Unified Medical Language System (UMLS) is evident in provision for a richer array of relationships.

In trying to grasp this major reorganization, mapping the XML structure to the relatively flat MARC structure proves an interesting exercise. The quasi-MARC below distinguishes the typical inclusion of synonyms under a preferred term from the subsumption of terms with narrower meanings. Both are most often intermixed but distinguished in XML MeSH data.

```
035 __ |a (DNLM)D002397
150 __ |a Catfishes |3 M0003649 |4 T006951 |9 1989-11-17
450 __ |1 -- |a Catfish |3 M0003649 |4 T006952 |9 1999-01-01
450 __ |1 -- |a Siluriformes |3 M0003649 |4 T421188 |9 2000-08-09
450 __ |1 -- |a Cat Fish |h [local] |3 M0003649 |9 2006-01-02

450 __ |e Includes |a Arius |2 Genus of the family Ariidae (sea catfishes).
        |3 M0367470 |4 T421189 |9 2000-08-09
450 __ |e Includes |a Eremophilus mutisii |2 A fish species of the order
        SILURIFORMES, family Trichomycteridae. |3 M0438709 |4 T519813
        |9 2002-09-18
450 __ |1 -- |e Eponym |a Colombian Catfish |3 M0438709 |4 T519814 |9 2002-09-18
450 __ |e Includes |a Heteropneustes |3 M0003651 |4 T006958 |9 1986-04-15
450 __ |e Includes |a Plotosus |3 M0003652 |4 T006959 |9 1986-04-15

550 __ |e Broader |a Fishes |w (DNLM)D005399
550 __ |e Narrower |a Ictaluridae |w (DNLM)D007059
680 __ |i Common name of the order Siluriformes. This order contains many families
        and over 2,000 species, including venomous species. Heteropneustes and
        Plotosus genera have dangerous stings and are aggressive. Most species are
        passive stingers.
```

This coding of a MeSH record for Catfishes has a unique Descriptor ID in field 035. The first group of fields includes the base Concept in field 150 and three variants in field 450. One of these, Cat Fish, illustrates with "|h [local]" one way of distinguishing this local enhancement from NLM's data. Note that each synonym shares the same Concept ID, given in |3. Other subfields are explained in the next group.

In the second group, four Concepts each have a relator "|e Includes" to indicate more clearly their subsumption under Catfishes. Note that each of these subsumed Concepts has a separate Concept ID, again in |3, implying that they could be established separately. Like the base Concept, synonyms of a particular subsumed Concept share its Concept ID. Each synonym for the base Concept or for a subsumed Concept is "indented" by use of a pair of hyphens in |1 to enforce the hierarchy. Similarly, "|e Eponym" uses a relator for type of subsumed Concept. Each term, regardless of type, has a unique Term ID appearing in |4. Notes specific to a subsumed Concept appear with the Concept in |2, and the date a specific Term was added appears in |9.

The third group includes references to related Descriptors and a public note. The mapping is fabricated but fairly literal. Additional fields not of interest were omitted, and the example of a local enhancement added.

The following group of fields could be included to subsume a new local Concept in the MeSH data. The only difference is an arbitrary local Concept ID to group the terms within this record.

    450 __ |a Includes |a Malapteruridae |h [local] |3 L1 |9 2004-12-18
    450 __ |1 -- |a Electric Catfishes |h [local] |3 L1 |9 2004-12-18
    450 __ |1 -- |a Catfishes, Electric |h [local] |3 L1 |9 2004-12-18

Potentially, the data thus far could be displayed more transparently. Base concepts are in bold and subsumed concepts in italics:

Topic: **Catfishes**

Scope: Common name of the order Siluriformes. This order contains many families and over 2,000 species, including venomous species. Heteropneustes and Plotosus genera have dangerous stings and are aggressive. Most species are passive stingers.

Varia: -- Catfish

-- Siluriformes

-- Cat Fish [local]

Includes:

Arius Genus of the family Ariidae (sea catfishes).

Eremophilus mutisii A fish species of the order SILURIFORMES, family Trichomycteridae.

-- Eponym: Colombian Catfish

Heteropneustes

Plotosus

Malapteruridae [local]

-- Electric Catfishes [local]

-- Catfishes, Electric [local]

Related: Broader:

Fishes

Narrower:

Ictaluridae

To further stretch the example, consider adding more local subsumption:

450 __ |a Includes: |a Ariidae |h [local] |3 L2 |9 2005-12-18
450 __ |1 -- |a Sea Catfishes |h [local] |3 L2 |9 2005-12-18
450 __ |1 -- |a Catfishes, Sea |h [local] |3 L2 |9 2005-12-18
450 __ |1 -- |e Includes: |a Arius |2 Genus of the family Ariidae (sea catfishes). |3 L3 |3 M0367470 |4 T421189 |9 2000-08-09
450 __ |1 -- -- |a Arius seemani |h [local] |3 L4 |9 2005-12-29

It is possible to introduce a local intermediate level subsumed Concept, Ariidae, in this record. The existing MeSH subsumed Concept, Arius, is logically subordinate to the new local one. Making the Concept ID subfield |3 repeatable could introduce processing problems. Adding another subordinate term, Arius seemani, implies the need for an awkward second level of indention.

The example in this rather tortured mapping exercise illustrates the limitations of the flat MARC structure. Elsewhere, the XML MeSH data exhibits two other types of relationship coding that this author has dubbed as 'suprasumption' (subordinate inclusion of a broader term) and 'circumsumption' (subordinate inclusion of a related term). These examples are not just curiosities, but illustrate the broader structural issues of maintaining clarity of relationships of an evolving topic. A preferred term becomes a sort of holding pen under which to lump other terms while maintaining the actual relationships among the subsumed terms until such time that these might merit separate headings.

This example further illustrates the challenges of localization when using a centralized data source. Another example is editing of bibliographic records, where local changes are not always reconciled when the host record changes. This blurred shift of locus of control to the local catalog may be offset by coding conventions to keep track of local practice. At a broader level, MARC's |5 (Institution to which field applies) and RLIN's clustering partially support these distinctions.

This lumping phenomenon is fairly common. Similar bibliographic challenges are found in latest entry serial cataloging, the single-record approach to print/digital versions with multiple holdings records, structured contents notes, etc. Currently, NLM's MeSH in MARC format avoids problems by omitting the troublesome data and its substructure. Oddly, the MeSH Browser and PubMed also do not display the added information found in the XML data. The advantages of cooperation are diminished by informal solutions. Libraries need more robust shared mechanisms to encourage inclusion and maintenance of complementary local data.

MY SILO IS BETTER THAN YOUR SILO vs. DISTRIBUTED COOPERATION?

There are many interesting and successful examples of library-created websites, portals, repositories, etc. However, these do not seem much different than the plethora of competing commercial products in their striving to be *the* information destination for a target audience. Efforts to federate resources recognize the value of integration but do not fair particularly well when disparate data structures are involved. Better solutions, such as NLM's products and Elsevier's Scopus, have melded content and context by creative treatment of relationships and categorizations. However, these work well precisely because they largely *control* the creation and deployment of the data involved.

Silos or silo-complexes, including catalogs, remain islands of organization in a generally chaotic Web environment. The boundaries have blurred further, e.g., Google's crawling the controlled content of PubMed. Thus, PubMed gems sometimes pop up in Google searches. However, such controlled metadata often occupies the bottom of the Google heap since few Web pages link directly to them. These hits also represent an ill-defined, unevenly-updated, partial subset of the host data. The lack of transparency in Google's coverage is unfortunate. The tendency of search engines to obscure their workings and make retrieval appear to be magic is questionable.

Is control or chaos the only choice? Could we compete to find better ways to cooperate? Could we create generalized ways to add specialized metadata? Developing robust mechanisms aimed at coordinated retrieval in a distributed digital environment could take advantage of both useful controls and widespread Web technologies. Libraries have a history of cooperation, but are union silos enough? Structured metadata intended for retrieval on the Web could add coherence without being prescriptive. Emphasis on structured relationships could facilitate retrieval in search engines if citations of a work represented by its metadata could be made equivalent in relevance to Web page links.

Taken together, libraries' scarce catalogers could accomplish more by coordinating efforts and upholding higher standards in the open Web environment rather than by duplicating efforts. By seeking ways to address both local and shared needs concomitantly, cataloging could be recast and potentially enjoy a renaissance. The distributed creation and maintenance of quality metadata in a virtual structure directly on the Web could consolidate our singular diluted efforts and garner recognition of our unique contributions. Instead of increased polarization, we need to learn from cooperative efforts such as the Wikipedia and seek to balance control and chaos. Even Google recently has recognized that they and librarians share the same mission.[10] Considering what has happened since Dr. Lane's observation, we can expect great things in the future; but the wisdom of balancing past lessons, present exigencies, and future prospects remains as true today as in 1886.

NOTES

1. Levi Cooper Lane, "Things old and new, with a chapter from Caelius Aurelianus," *Pacific Medical and Surgical Journal and Western Lancet* v. 29, no. 6 (July 1886):398-9.

2. Joint Steering Committee for Revision of Anglo-American Cataloging Rules, *RDA: Resource Description and Access*, (Dec. 20, 2005), http://www.collectionscanada.ca/jsc/rda.html.

3. La Pléiade (Jan. 6, 2006). In: Wikipedia, http://en.wikipedia.org/wiki/Pleiade.

4. Martha M. Yee, "New Perspectives on the Shared Cataloging Environment and a MARC21 Shopping List," *Library Resources & Technical Services* v. 48, no. 3 (2004):165-78.

5. Dick R. Miller and Kevin S. Clarke. *Putting XML to Work in the Library* (Chicago: American Library Association, 2004), p. 101-136.

6. Nancy Blachman, *Google Guide*, http://www.googleguide.com/. Although Google cooperated in this endeavor, they advocate that the system should be intuitive and not need extensive documentation.

7. National Library of Medicine (U.S.), *MeSH Browser*, http://www.nlm.nih.gov/mesh/MBrowser.html.

8. National Library of Medicine (U.S.), *PubMed*, http://www.ncbi.nlm.nih.gov/entrez/query.fcgi. Select MeSH on pulldown menu.

9. National Library of Medicine (U.S.), *Introduction to MeSH in XML Format*, (Oct. 4, 2004), http://www.nlm.nih.gov/mesh/xmlmesh.html.

10. Google's Newsletter for Librarians, (Dec. 2005), http://www.google.com/newsletter/librarian/librarian_2005_12/newsletter.html. This is also called Google Librarian Newsletter, 1st ed.

doi:10.1300/J104v44n03_09

Cataloging Compared to Descriptive Bibliography, Abstracting and Indexing Services, and Metadata

Martha M. Yee

SUMMARY. Cataloging is compared to descriptive bibliography, to enumerative bibliography and abstracting and indexing services, as well as to metadata created by Web search engines or nonprofessionals at sites such as Amazon.com. These four types of metadata are compared with regard to object of the description, functions, scope, number of copies examined, collective vs. individual creation, standardization, authority control, evidence, amount of descriptive detail, degression, time span the data is intended to last, and degree of evaluation. doi:10.1300/J104v44n03_10 *[Article copies available for a fee from The Haworth Document Delivery Service: 1-800-HAWORTH. E-mail address: <docdelivery@haworthpress.com> Website: <http://www.HaworthPress.com> © 2007 by The Haworth Press, Inc. All rights reserved.]*

KEYWORDS. Cataloging, metadata, descriptive bibliography, enumerative bibliography, abstracting and indexing services, Web search engines, Google, Amazon.com, authority control, standardization, degression

---

Martha M. Yee, MLS, PhD, is Cataloging Supervisor, UCLA Film and Television Archive (E-mail: myee@ucla.edu).

[Haworth co-indexing entry note]: "Cataloging Compared to Descriptive Bibliography, Abstracting and Indexing Services, and Metadata." Yee, Martha M. Co-published simultaneously in *Cataloging & Classification Quarterly* (The Haworth Information Press, an imprint of The Haworth Press, Inc.) Vol. 44, No. 3/4, 2007, pp. 307-327; and: *Cataloger, Editor, and Scholar: Essays in Honor of Ruth C. Carter* (ed: Robert P. Holley) The Haworth Information Press, an imprint of The Haworth Press, Inc., 2007, pp. 307-327. Single or multiple copies of this article are available for a fee from The Haworth Document Delivery Service [1-800-HAWORTH, 9:00 a.m. - 5:00 p.m. (EST). E-mail address: docdelivery@haworthpress.com].

Available online at http://ccq.haworthpress.com
© 2007 by The Haworth Press, Inc. All rights reserved.
doi:10.1300/J104v44n03_10

INTRODUCTION

Powerful library administrators have been making negative comparisons between library catalogs and bookseller catalogs, such as Amazon.com, and between library catalogs and Web search engines, such as Google (Marcum, 2005; Flecker, 2005). Commercial abstracting and indexing tools are also sometimes used as examples of access tools that are created more quickly and therefore provide more timely access to current literature than do library catalogs. Such comparisons are like comparing apples and oranges. These are all very different tools with very different goals and objectives. One purpose of this article is to point out these very different goals and objectives to try to provide a little more clarity to these discussions.

The term metadata is now being used in a very loose fashion by both librarians and computer scientists. While some argue that cataloging is a kind of metadata, it is clear from actual metadata projects that much metadata is very far from being cataloging. An important distinction between cataloging and other kinds of metadata is in danger of being lost. Another purpose of this article is to make some needed distinctions in this area.

The final purpose of this article is related to the fact that new cataloging rules are on the way; it is planned for *Resource description and access* to replace the *Anglo-American cataloguing rules*, 2nd ed. rev. (RDA). The designers of these new cataloging rules seem to have a desire to create rules that can be used by a much wider community than that of libraries that create item-level cataloging records. It appears that an attempt will be made to design rules that can be used to create metadata for electronic documents, descriptions of rare books and museum objects, and collection-level records for unpublished materials in collections based on provenance. *Functional requirements for bibliographic records* (FRBR), a model that underpins the new cataloging rules, is aiming at an even wider audience, including scholars of folklore, descriptive bibliographers, and computer scientist designers of projects that analyze raw data using computers with no human intervention whatsoever. The assumption seems to be that all these diverse areas have more in common than they have differences. There is a danger that some important distinctions will be lost in the rush to be so all-inclusive. For all these reasons, this paper was written to try to make these distinctions and raise some questions about where we are headed.

For the purposes of this paper, "cataloging" is defined as "the creation of catalogs"; and a "catalog" is defined as: a guide to a particular collection or aggregate of collections created using standards that govern both the choice and the labeling of data in such a way as to result in the choice of preferred names for authors, works, subjects, and disciplines, with provision for access under variant forms, such that a user who searches under any variant is led to everything of interest (all works on the subject sought, or all works by the author sought, or all editions or expressions of the work sought). In any given catalog record, sufficient data is recorded to allow a user to identify and distinguish one edition or expression from another and to select a desired work or expression of a work.

I. CATALOGING COMPARED TO DESCRIPTIVE BIBLIOGRAPHY

Object of the Description

Tanselle argues that the essential difference is that descriptive bibliography describes the ideal copy, while cataloging describes a particular copy (Tanselle, 1977, p. 4). This is not completely accurate; the ordinary cataloger, in describing a particular copy, aims at describing both the edition or expression to which it belongs, as issued, and the work of which it is an edition or expression; a conscious effort is made not to include copy-specific details in the bibliographic record or at least to differentiate clearly which details are copy-specific. Tanselle himself recognizes this when he characterizes AACR collation as aiming at "extent of work" (Tanselle, 1977, p. 52), although "extent of expression" would be more accurate within the FRBR model.

Functions

Lubetzky quotes Pierce Butler–"A catalog is a bibliography of the books in a particular collection"–and goes on to elaborate the function of the catalog as being that of serving as a guide to a particular collection, indicating relationships between items in the collection (Lubetzky, p. 269). Note that modern cataloging is also called on to serve the functions of a national bibliography, and this can create tensions between local and national/international needs, and make the demonstration of relationships quite a complex task. The function of descriptive bibliography is essentially to record physical evidence that bears on printing history of particular texts and on printing and publishing history in general.

Scope

Most writers, including Lubetzky and Tanselle, emphasize that the scope of a catalog is a particular collection (Lubetzky, p. 269; Tanselle, 1977, p. 10). This is an important distinction in that it points up the fact that, in contrast to catalogers, bibliographers are free to define their scope as necessary to serve their particular purposes and the fact that catalogers can usually examine only those copies that are in their particular collections. However, in the last hundred years, it has become increasingly the case that catalogers catalog not just for their local catalog, but also to contribute to the national bibliography.

Number of Copies Examined

Tanselle rejects this criterion in favor of the object of description as the essential difference. This seems to be a very important difference, however. It is only after examining *all* copies of a text that one can be sure of what the discriminatory details are in any particular case, i.e., the details that discriminate between particular states, issues, impressions, and editions of a text. Since this extent of research cannot be performed by catalogers, it is impossible for them not just to describe an ideal copy (in Tanselle's sense) but even to be sure that they are including in their descriptions the pieces of evidence that a bibliographer would need to tell exactly what is held in that particular collection. The cataloger can examine copies outside his or her collection only in surrogate form (i.e., in the form of cataloging records created by other catalogers in other collections) and only if surrogates for them are readily available. These surrogates will have been created under the same handicap; that is, their creators will not have been able to examine all extant copies in order to identify variations and determine the important discriminatory detail to describe them.

Collective vs. Individual Creation

It is extremely rare for even a single local catalog to be the product of the work of a single person. A descriptive bibliography is usually the product of a single person, who plans the scope, looks at all of the items described, decides on what kinds of evidence are relevant, and records the relevant evidence according to his or her own rules that are devised to fit the circumstances of that particular project. Surely, a descriptive bibliography is likely to be carried out in a more uniform and predictable fashion than can a catalog, which is gradually built up over many years, due to the efforts of countless catalogers. It should be noted, of course, that non-institutional catalogs, such as bookseller's or collector's catalogs, may be the work of a single person. Union catalogs, such as OCLC or the ESTC, are bound to have even more inconsistencies due to differences in cataloging policy from one institution to another.

Standardization

Because catalogs are created collectively, rules and other standards are written to try to attain some measure of uniformity from one cataloger to another and from one institution to another (to allow construction of union catalogs or national bibliographies). Because the data in a catalog is gathered in a predictable fashion and presented in a predictable fashion, it is possible to design complex indexes and displays of records from many different institutions; for example, it is possible to display all the editions of a particular work, along with all of the works related to it and all of the works about it in response to a user's search that uses a variant of the author's name and a variant of the title of the work.

A descriptive bibliographer is much freer than a cataloger is to tailor-make descriptive rules and formats to fit the materials being described although the necessity to communicate findings does impose some requirements for use of standard terminology, standard collation formulae (or at least comprehensible ones), etc.

Authority Control

Authority control of names, work identifiers, and subjects is a special kind of standardization that is much more likely to be necessary in large cataloging and union cataloging projects than in descriptive bibliography projects. When authority control is applied effectively, users are enabled to find the works they seek under any variant of author name (Mark Twain vs. Samuel Clemens), variant of title (Tom Sawyer vs. Adventures of Tom Sawyer), or subject synonym they might use in their search (e.g., hypnosis vs. hypnotism). In addition, homonyms are differentiated (e.g., cold the disease vs. cold the temperature), people with the same name are differentiated (e.g., George Bush) and works with the same title are differentiated (e.g., 5th symphony). And finally, a structure is created that allows a user to broaden and narrow a search as desired.

Evidence

In ordinary cataloging, the title page and preliminaries are the primary evidence; and they are taken at face value, unless there is clear evidence of falsehood or error. The title page is only roughly transcribed. The descriptive bibliographer may use a much vaster array of evidence: signatures, running titles, paper (format, watermarks, chain lines, etc.), typography (quasi-facsimile transcription, identification of type faces, etc.), binding, ownership, textual variation (catchwords, fingerprints), etc. Tanselle is right to reject this as an essential criterion in differentiating between cataloging and descriptive bibliography (Tanselle, 1977, p. 5) since rare book catalogers, to one degree or another, often record much of the same evidence that descriptive bibliographers do. However, in this criterion lies much of the distinction between ordinary cataloging and descriptive bibliography. Although edition is defined in AACR2 as all copies produced from substantially the same type image, the evidence employed to determine whether two items are the same edition are in practice essentially the title page transcription and the paging (at least in ordinary cataloging).

Amount of Descriptive Detail

Tanselle is right to reject this as a criterion as well (Tanselle, 1977, p. 5) as there is wide variation among catalogs and bibliographies alike. It is interesting, though, to contrast Bowers' assertion that a more fully detailed description should be given if fewer copies have been examined (Bowers, 1953, p. 5) with Schneider's assertion that entries in catalogs must be brief while entries in bibliographies must be full (Schneider, p. 51). Schneider is talking primarily about enumerative bibliographies; the implication is that a fuller description may be needed to aid users in finding listed works, whereas less detail may be needed in a catalog that can lead the user directly to the work itself (or at least an edition of it). Bowers seems to mean that the more investigation a bibliographer has done, the more assurance with which he or she can eliminate particular details as non-discriminatory. However, the messages from these two bibliographers about the amount of detail appropriate to a catalog is contradictory!

Degression

Degression, in the modern sense (the use of only discriminatory detail for editions after the first), is used only in some book catalogs and descriptive bibliographies. Card and online catalogs historically have used unit records. One suspects that in the case of the card catalog this was due to a reluctance to modify a card once filed. In the online environment, it surely is connected with a shared cataloging environment in which records are copied into thousands of different catalogs.

Degression in Madan's sense (Madan) sounds like the modern cataloging concept of levels of description. For economic reasons, many catalogs contain minimal records for classes of materials identified by librarians as less important. The differences between rare book cataloging and ordinary cataloging might be considered to be due to degressive practice in Madan's sense of the term as well. Libraries identify particular materials as being rare or special, and these may be given descriptions using many of the techniques developed by descriptive bibliography, e.g., transcription of capitalization, punctuation, and/or line endings, transcription of full imprints without transposition, collation by signatures, notes on binding, typography, paper, etc.

It would seem that a certain amount of degression in this sense might be a wise thing. Elizabeth Tate has shown that the common 80:20 ratio operates on the number of works which ever appear in more than one edition (Tate). Even though bibliographers protest that any book is interesting as a physical object regardless of its content, in fact there has been a marked tendency in the past to invest bibliographical effort in investigating classic and influential literary texts that have gone into many editions and for which scholars and students require authoritative texts. Greg actually defined bibliography as "the science of the material transmission of literary texts" (Greg, 1914, p. 83).

Time Span

Descriptive bibliographies, like catalogs, are meant to be used in perpetuity by future generations and are not considered by their makers to be of transient or ephemeral interest. A catalog or a descriptive bibliography is designed to be part of the permanent documentation of humanity's cultural record.

Evaluation

It could be argued that works described using the techniques of descriptive bibliography are inherently valuable to scholarship, or the considerable investment in time and travel involved in creating the descriptive bibliography would not have been made by members of the scholarly community.

Not all works collected by libraries are valued that highly by the scholarly community, but works collected by a library still represent a considerable investment in processing time and in storage costs and have not been acquired lightly. There is a selection process involved, first in the publishing process (reputable publishers make value judgments in deciding which works to publish), and secondly in the library selection process. No library has an unlimited budget, and works are acquired only when they are considered useful to the community served by the library. Thus, only the more reliable and reputable works on a subject even appear in the library catalog. In addition, a library catalog allows a user to determine which writers have published the most works on a subject of interest, a fact that should also bear some weight in the process of evaluating the best works on a subject. However, once works are included in a library (and its catalog), librarians are careful not to include evaluative comments in their actual descriptions. When librarians compose summary notes, they are scrupulously careful to avoid reviewing or critiquing works; instead the aim is to provide an objective description of the subject matter of the work.

Section Summary

The essential criterion would seem to be that of function since from it all else follows. The function of a library catalog is to serve as the guide to a particular collection. The function of a descriptive bibliography is to record the findings of an investigation into printing and publishing history of a particular work or works. The latter is *not* a function of a library catalog. Aside from whether or not it should be the function of a library catalog, no particular collection is likely to have enough of the evidence to make such an investigation feasible. While other kinds of catalogs have different functions, e.g., the bookseller's catalog is designed to sell books, the private collector's catalog is designed to reflect glory on the collector, in listing the contents of particular collections, these catalogs are as limited as library catalogs in how much evidence they can contain to support studies of printing and publishing history. All these catalogs can draw on the findings of descriptive bibliographers to identify and describe precisely the publications that they list, but the catalogers who construct them cannot carry out the investigations themselves.

Tanselle's criterion of ideal copy seems unsatisfactory for the following reason. One could argue that a library cataloger aims at describing the ideal copy as well in that he or she aims at excluding from the description (or at least clearly indicating) details which are specific to the copy cataloged and including those details which apply to the entire edition as issued. The cataloger differs from the descriptive bibliographer only in the methods of investigation and kinds of evidence that he or she brings to bear in this process.

The function of the library catalog is to serve as the guide to a particular collection. As such, it must be able to tell the users which subjects and which authors are represented in the collection, which works of those authors, and which editions of those works. It is in the last object that the work of the descriptive bibliographer can be tapped to allow us to more clearly identify and describe, e.g., identical editions hiding under differing title pages or different editions hiding under identical title pages.

Those users of the library who are not bibliographers are assumed to be more interested in the content of the works or editions they seek than in physical variation that does not affect content. The bibliographers themselves are interested in physical variation that does not affect content essentially because it is evidence that ultimately supports either the establishment of authoritative texts or the description of printing and publishing practice that can later support the establishment of authoritative texts. Thus, the bibliographer's work will ultimately serve the library's users; and librarians and bibliographers must cooperate to that end.

Unfortunately, before the bibliographer has done his or her work, the cataloger cannot be sure of what details are discriminatory in any particular case. In ordinary cataloging, we rely on rough title page transcription and overall paging as the primary evidence for variation in edition. When this is not enough, we must wait until the bibliographer has done his or her work before we can do ours.

II. CATALOGING COMPARED TO ENUMERATIVE BIBLIOGRAPHY AND ABSTRACTING AND INDEXING SERVICES

Object of the Description

The object of a description is a published item as in cataloging. Frequently, however, more analysis will be practiced. In other words, articles in journals, papers, short stories, poems, and the like in compilations, pamphlets, and other materials not generally cataloged in libraries will be included in an enumerative bibliography; abstracting and indexing services specialize in the journal articles that are not cataloged by libraries.

Functions

Instead of a guide to a particular collection, an enumerative bibliography (sometimes called systematic or reference bibliography) or an abstracting and indexing service serves to aid the user interested in a particular subject to discover the existence of works on that subject; but generally no help is provided in locating an actual copy of a given publication. In fact, the American Film Institute catalogs (actually enumerative filmographies) are an example of an enumerative bibliography that lists titles that probably no longer exist; it is known that many films listed in the AFI catalogs no longer exist from having been lost to nitrate film deterioration (*American Film Institute Catalog*).

Some attempts have been made to provide more linking from abstracting and indexing services to available electronic copies in the on-line environment; but, so far, the mechanisms do not work very well. First, the mechanisms are very dependent on numerical identifiers such as ISSNs, which may be erroneous, treacherous, or non-existent. Second, these mechanisms must navigate an impenetrable tangle of rights management algorithms.

Scope

Scope is usually defined as limited to a particular subject or academic discipline, as opposed to a catalog, the scope of which is defined by the collection to which it is a guide.

Number of Copies Examined

The creator of an abstract or an indexing entry or an entry in an enumerative bibliography is probably seeing only the copy in front of them and is unaware of other copies or versions although, depending on the subject area, some will list the various extant editions of a particular work of interest.

Collective vs. Individual Creation

An enumerative bibliography is likely to be created by a single person who will have defined a consistent scope and style. Abstracting and indexing services typically employ staffs of abstracters and indexers, who will presumably be following some sort of in-house guidelines.

Standardization

Standardization will be employed within the enumerative bibliography project or in-house at the abstracting and indexing service, but it is rare for outside standards to be followed. Abstracting and indexing services generally see their function as being that of providing speedy access to current materials that will be of interest for only a short time. Their tools are generally not designed to be used in perpetuity by future generations and are considered by their makers to be of transient or ephemeral interest. Thus, for example, it is not uncommon for older records to be formatted or indexed differently than newer records with no attempt being made to bring the records into sync. Because of the lack of standardization over time, it can be difficult to design anything other than very simple indexes and displays, especially if the index or display must cover records from more than one time period. Interoperable displays of records from more than one institution or indexing service would probably necessarily have to resemble a primitive Google-like display.

Authority Control

As with standardization in general, there are few incentives for abstracting and indexing services to provide elaborate authority control. Speed of publication is valued over quality of output. They see their role as that of helping someone find out what a particular author wrote in this past year, not helping someone find out what he or she has written over his or her entire career. Frequently, authors' forenames will be represented by initials with no attempt to distinguish one AB Smith from a different AB Smith. Users who search under variant author names or variant titles will be out of luck. There are the exceptional abstracting and indexing services that use, for example, Library of Congress subject headings (LCSH); however, they are unlikely to invest any resources in changing older records to match newer forms of heading when LCSH headings change over time. Often abstracting and indexing services do use a thesaurus since the emphasis is usually on subject access rather than on access to authors and works. However, the thesaurus usually bears no relationship to any other thesaurus or subject heading list; and, even internally, no effort will be made over time to keep older records in sync with newer ones when the thesaurus changes.

Evidence

Enumerative bibliographers are likely to use title pages and preliminaries in much the same way that ordinary library catalogers do. Often particular style manuals, such as the *Chicago Manual of Style*, will be followed. Abstracting and indexing services usually derive titles from the actual publications being indexed although liberties may be taken with authors' names as noted above.

Amount of Descriptive Detail

Probably only enough detail will be provided to allow the user to find the work described in a bookstore or a library; usually, little attention will be paid to discriminatory details pertaining to expression or edition beyond explicit title page edition statements and publication dates.

Degression

Since there is usually little interest in providing a record of the various extant editions or versions of a listed work, degression is not a factor in either enumerative bibliography or abstracting or indexing services.

Time Span

Tools are generally not designed to be used in perpetuity by future generations and are considered by their makers to be of transient or ephemeral interest.

Evaluation

See above for a disquisition on the degree to which library catalogs evaluate the works they contain. Enumerative bibliography exists primarily for the purpose of evaluation. An enumerative bibliography is usually a list of the best books on a subject created by a scholar or expert in the given subject. Abstracting and indexing services exercise evaluation at the point of determining which journals will be indexed. There is generally some effort to include only reputable journals and to exclude those that do not follow acceptable scholarly practices.

Section Summary

The function of a catalog is to provide a permanent record of the works held in a particular collection with the underlying assumption that they will be held in perpetuity as part of the cultural record of humanity. Even if a title is withdrawn or discarded in a particular collection, this is done only when it is known to survive in another. The function of enumerative bibliography and of abstracting and indexing services is quite different; it is to provide temporary and timely access to citations to works on a subject without guaranteeing that the user will actually be able to obtain those works. The user must take a second step of visiting a library and searching the catalog (or, nowadays, searching the catalog over the Internet and authenticating themselves as users who are entitled to access electronic documents that are licensed by a library) in order to obtain the works themselves. Abstracting and indexing services especially are in the business of analyzing what is held by libraries; they do not collect the resources themselves.

III. CATALOGING COMPARED TO METADATA

Many consider cataloging to be a type of metadata. In fact, by that broad definition of metadata (data about data), descriptive bibliography is metadata; abstracts and indexes are metadata; and, for that matter, encyclopedias, dictionaries and telephone books are metadata. Here, I would like to use a somewhat narrower definition of metadata, that of metadata that is neither cataloging, nor descriptive or enumerative bibliography, nor abstracts and indexes. I would like to consider here both metadata that is automatically generated by Web search engines and other computer software for which the data is the metadata (e.g., Google), and metadata that is created by humans who are not trained and educated in cataloging and authority control or any other kinds of standards (e.g., Amazon.com or the metadata created by an aerospace engineer and attached to his paper on the Internet). Here I am using a definition of metadata similar to Campbell's: "Metadata is not designed or created by a specially-trained cohort of professionals who have a specific skill set and a common slate of objectives" (Campbell, p. 59). In other words, we define metadata in this paper in such a way as to exclude cataloging.

Object of the Description

There can be quite a bit of fluidity in determination of the object of a description. One metadata creator will create a separate metadata record for each chapter of a given work or each page of a web site, and another will create a metadata record only for the work as a whole. Since many electronic documents are diverse conglomerations of image, text, and audio, different metadata creators will make different decisions about levels of analysis. When the computer is left to make the decision about the object of a description on its own, as in web search engines, the results can be inexplicable and bewildering. As Bernhard Eversberg points out, "Search engine operators cannot afford to disclose their methods of searching and indexing" (p. 11).

Functions

One of the main functions is often that of capturing the attention of potential users, much like the function of advertising. It has been said that the economy of the Internet is an economy of attention. Instead of vying for capital, competitors are vying for the scarce moments of attention that each Internet user has available on a given day.

Scope

For Amazon.com, the scope is current trade publications plus out-of-print titles available for purchase. It could be argued that the scope for metadata as narrowly defined above is the entire Internet. One could also argue that one of the reasons that the Internet is so appealing to people who have never been taught research skills is that it allows people to search for facts (Eversberg, p. 11) within disembodied texts, thereby losing all context. One of the main ways in which the metadata on the Internet differs from cataloging, descriptive bibliography or abstracting and indexing service data is precisely this loss of context. Because of the loss of context, it provides information of often dubious authenticity and reliability and cannot provide the discourse that can lead to knowledge and finally wisdom in minds that are trained in research and critical thinking.

Number of Copies Examined

Only the copy in front of the metadata creator will be examined.

Collective vs. Individual Creation

This is the ultimate in collective creation.

Standardization

Little standardization is possible when metadata creators are not trained or educated in the principles of bibliographic organization, and none is possible when only computer manipulation of data is available as in the case of Google. As Bernhard Eversberg points out: "The database consists of nothing but large inverted files, derived directly from the documents" (Eversburg, p. 12). Thus, complex indexes and displays become impossible as the data is completely unpredictable.

Remember that here we define metadata more narrowly than does, for example, Lynne Howarth, who vividly describes the cacophany that results when many different cataloging standards are followed in creating metadata, in her case broadly defined to include cataloging (Howarth, p. 48-49). We have excluded metadata created according to standard rules from our definition of metadata in this paper.

Authority Control

As with any kind of standardization, authority control is probably impossible. Users interested in precision and recall will succeed only if they have all synonyms or variant names and titles available for searching and if they are patient in wading through an ocean of homonyms. Since there are few such users in the world, precision and recall will be possible only for searches for authors, subjects or works with unique and unchanging names. Thomas Mann writes vividly about how much users lose in the transition from library catalog to Web search engine.

Thus, in Amazon.com, a person who looks up Thomas Mann's work *Library Research Models* will be told that users who bought this work also bought *Death in Venice* and *The Magic Mountain*. A person interested in reading the great Chinese novel by Cao Xueqin will find some English language translations under *Dream of the Red Chamber*, some under *Dream of Red Mansions*, some under *The Story of the Stone*, and some under *Hung Lou Meng*, with nothing to guide the user back and forth among them.

Evidence

Since data is unlikely to be marked up in any standard way, it is hard for computer programs to find automatically the title or creator of a particular assemblage of bytes. Human mark-up may improve computer performance a bit in this regard; but, if, as humans often seem to do, they display one title prominently on their electronic document and then put a different title into their metadata, they are not doing much better.

Amount of Descriptive Detail

Most extant metadata systems seem to be trying to reduce the amount of descriptive detail collected compared to the amount collected in ordinary cataloging in libraries.

Degression

The problem of describing the differences among multiple editions or expressions of the same work has not been tackled yet in the metadata world although the librarian interested in science fiction might contemplate a future in which all documents have been digitized and are therefore available for electronic comparison. Such comparison might be able to signal to a descriptive bibliographer controlling the comparison process where there are significant variations in text, sound, or image sequencing. Only a human, however, would be able to identify which electronic documents represent the same work and should be compared in this fashion. With current Web search engines, it would be impossible to assemble all of the expressions and manifestations of a given work in the first place in order to conduct a subsequent comparison.

Time Span

Currently, the major interest in Internet access seems to be focused on the extremely current and ephemeral. So far, because of its lack of organization and its bewildering magnitude, the Internet does not seem to be a good place to keep the permanent cultural record although bits of it are starting to show up there in the form of electronic texts.

Evaluation

Web search engines often provide what is called relevance ranking. This can mislead users into thinking that the most valuable and useful indexed Web sites are at the top of the tens of thousands of hits that result from just about any search done using a Web search engine. In fact, all that any relevance ranking algorithm can do is to weight certain words (e.g., those that occur least frequently) more heavily, add up the results, and put the sites with the highest score at the top. Because this process has nothing to do with the actual meaning of the terms being weighted and because language is one of the most complex of human capacities and one which is not available to computers, this can frequently lead to ludicrous results.

Google, perhaps the most popular of all search engines, is so successful because, instead of using the standard relevance ranking algorithms, it ranks sites based on their popularity. Google is capitalizing on an insight that lies behind citation indexing tools long familiar in the library world: one way to evaluate the quality of a document is to ask how many other people have cited it in their writings. Google ranks sites based on how many other sites link to them. This can often give valuable results, but it is a method that should be used with caution. Popularity does not always equal excellence!

Section Summary

These various kinds of metadata have an even more ephemeral function than does enumerative bibliography or an abstracting and indexing service; and, consequently, even less control is exerted to facilitate ready access. Users are left on their own with no human intervention to organize data for access. These systems profit from the ignorance of users who do not know about what they do not find, and are so bedazzled by computers that they place extra value on whatever they did find because they did not have to travel anywhere to get it and did not have to humiliate themselves by asking for help from someone else to get it.

CONCLUSION

If librarianship is to continue to be a profession, it is going to have to find a way to provide the majority of our users with what they need (rather than what they think they want) and be content, for awhile perhaps, with pleasing only an educated minority that realizes what it needs. Otherwise, humanity is in danger of losing access to its cultural record.

There is a folk tale about a man who captures a leprechaun and is therefore entitled to the gold belonging to the leprechaun. Unfortunately for him, however, the gold is buried in the ground under a particular tree; and he has not brought a shovel with him. He does have a red ribbon with him, however; and he ties it around the tree and makes the leprechaun promise not to remove it. When he returns with his shovel, of course, every tree in the forest has a red ribbon tied around it. Lest humanity is left to search through such a forest for its cultural treasure, we need to use our ingenuity to figure out how to defend the value of the type of human intervention for information organization that we carry out as a profession from the many advocates of the cheap fix that leaves human intervention out of the solution.

REFERENCES

Alden, John E. "Cataloging and Classification." In: *Rare Book Collections*. Ed. Richard Archer. ACRL Monograph no. 27. (Chicago: ALA, 1965), p. 65-73.

Alston, Robin and M.J. Jannetta. *Bibliography, Machine Readable Cataloging and the ESTC*. (London: British Library, 1978)

Alston, Robin. "Computers and Bibliography: the New Approach in ESTC." *Papers of the Bibliographical Society of America* 75:4 (1981), p. 371-389.

Alston, Robin. "The History and Description of Books." In: *Searching the Eighteenth Century*. (London: British Library, 1983), p. 15-27.

Alston, Robin and Richard Christophers. "Machine-readable Cataloguing and Early Printed Books." *International Cataloguing* 8:1 (Jan./Mar. 1979), p. 9-12; 8:2 (Apr./June 1979), p. 16-18.

American Film Institute Catalog of Motion Pictures Produced in the United States. (Berkeley, Calif.: University of California Press, 1971-1999).

Anglo American Cataloguing Rules. 2nd ed., 2002 rev. (Chicago: American Library Association, 2002).

Bowers, Fredson. "Bibliography, Pure Bibliography and Literary Studies." *Papers of the Bibliographical Society of America* 46 (1952), p. 186-208.

Bowers, Fredson. "The Function of Bibliography." *Library Trends* 7:4 (April 1959), p. 497-510.

Bowers, Fredson. "McKerrow, Greg and 'Substantive Edition.'" *The Library* 5th ser. 33:2 (June 1978), p. 83-107.

Bowers, Fredson. *Principles of Bibliographic Description.* (New York: Russell & Russell, 1949).

Bowers, Fredson. "Purposes of Descriptive Bibliography with Some Remarks on Methods." *The Library* 5th ser. 8:1 (March 1953), p. 1-22.

Butler, Pierce. "The Bibliographical Function of the Library." *Journal of Cataloging and Classification* 9:1 (March 1953), p. 3-11.

Campbell, D. Grant. "Metadata, Metaphor, and Metonymy." *Cataloging & Classification Quarterly* 40:3/4 (2005), p. 57-73.

"Critical Bibliography." *Encyclopedia of Library and Information Science.* (New York: Marcel Dekker, 1971), v. 6, p. 276-286.

Crump, Michael. "Introduction." In: *Searching the Eighteenth Century.* (London: British Library, 1983), p. 3-12.

Crump, Michael. "Stranger than Fiction: the Eighteenth Century True Story." In: *Searching the Eighteenth Century.* (London: British Library, 1983), p. 59-73.

Currier, Thomas Franklin. "What the Bibliographer Says to the Cataloger." *Catalogers' and Classifiers' Yearbook* 9 (1941), p. 21-37.

Davis, Stephen Paul. "Computer Technology as Applied to Rare Book Cataloging." *IFLA Journal* 10:2 (1984), p. 158-169.

Davis, Stephen Paul. "Night Thoughts on Automation and Rare Books." Typescript of lecture delivered July 30, 1984, Columbia School of Library Service Rare Book School.

"Descriptive Bibliography." *Encyclopedia of Library and Information Science.* (New York: Marcel Dekker, 1972), v. 7, p. 1-17.

Dunkin, Paul S. *Bibliography: Tiger or Fat Cat?* (Hamden, CT: Archon books, 1975).

Dunkin, Paul S. "On the Catalog Card for a Rare Book." *Library Quarterly* 16:1 (Jan. 1946), p. 50-56.

Eversberg, Bernhard. *On the Theory of Library Catalogs and Search Engines.* Supplement to a talk on Principles and Goals of Cataloging, given at the German Librarians' Annual Conference, Augsburg, 2002. Available on the Internet at: http://www.allegro_c.de/formate/tlcse.htm.

"The First Phase: an Introduction to the Catalogue of the British Library Collections for ESTC." *Factotum* 4 (1983).

Flecker, Dale. *OPACs and Our Changing Environment.* (Washington, D.C.: Program for Cooperative Cataloging, January, 2005). Available on the Internet at: http://www.loc.gov/catdir/pcc/archive/opacfuture-flecker.ppt.

Foxon, David F. *Thoughts on the History and Future of Bibliographical Description.* (University of California, 1970).

Functional Requirements for Bibliographic Records. (Munich: K.G. Saur, 1998).

Functional Requirements for Bibliographic Records: Hype or Cure-all? Ed. by Patrick le Boeuf. (New York: The Haworth Information Press, 2005).

Greg, W. W. "Bibliography–an Apologia." (1932) In: *Collected Papers.* Ed. by J.C. Maxwell. (Oxford: Clarendon Press, 1966), p. 239-266.

Greg, W. W. "The Present Position of Bibliography." (1930) In: *Collected Papers.* Ed. by J.C. Maxwell. (Oxford: Clarendon Press, 1966), p. 207-225.

Greg, W. W. "What is Bibliography?" (1914) In: *Collected Papers.* Ed. by J.C. Maxwell. (Oxford: Clarendon Press, 1966), p. 75-88.

Hibberd, Lloyd. "Physical and Reference Bibliography." *Library* 5th ser. 20 (1965), p. 124-134.

Howarth, Lynne. "Metadata and Bibliographic Control: Soul-Mates or Two Solitudes?" *Cataloging & Classification Quarterly* 40:3/4 (2005), p. 37-56.

Laurence, Dan H. *A Portrait of the Author as a Bibliography.* (Washington, D.C.: Library of Congress, 1983).

Library of Congress. Processing Dept. *Studies of Descriptive Cataloging: a Report to the Librarian of Congress by the Director of the Processing Dept.* (Washington, D.C.P: Library of Congress, 1946).

Lubetzky, Seymour. *Writings on the Classical Art of Cataloging.* (Englewood, Colo.: Libraries Unlimited, 2001).

McKenzie, D. F. "Printers of the Mind: Some Notes on Bibliographical Theories and Printing-House Practices." *Studies in Bibliography* 22 (1969), p. 1-75.

Madan, Falconer. "Degressive Bibliography." *Transactions of the Bibliographical Society* 9 (1906-8), p. 53-65.

Mann, Thomas. *Survey of Library User Studies.* (Washington, D.C.: AFSCME 2910, July, 2005). Available on the Internet at: http://www.guild2910.org/google.htm.

Mann, Thomas. *Will Google's Keyword Searching Eliminate the Need for LC Cataloging and Classification?* (Washington, D.C.: AFSCME 2910, 2005). Available on the Internet at: http://www.guild2910.org/searching.htm.

Marcum, Deanna B. *The Future of Cataloging.* Address to Ebsco Leadership Seminar, Boston, Mass. (Washington, D.C.: Library of Congress, January 16, 2005). Available on the Internet at: http://www.loc.gov/library/reports/CatalogingSpeech.pdf

Mitchell, Jim. "Investigating False Imprints." In: *Searching the Eighteenth Century.* (London: British Library, 1983), p. 43-58.

Osborn, Andrew D. "The Crisis in Cataloging." In: *Readings in Library Cataloguing.* Ed. and introd. by R.K. Olding (London: Crosby Lockwood & Son, 1966), p. 225-41.

Osborn, Andrew D. "Relation Between Cataloguing Principles and Principles Applicable to Other Forms of Bibliographical Work." In: International Conference on Cataloguing Principles (1961: Paris). *Working Papers.* Working Paper no. 1.

Pollard, Alfred W. "Relations of Bibliography and Cataloguing." In: International Library Conference (2nd: 1897: London). *Transactions and Proceedings,* p. 63-66.

Pouncey, Lorene. "The Fallacy of the Ideal Copy." *The Library.* 5th ser. 33:2 (June, 1978), p. 108-118.

RDA: Resource Description and Access: Prospectus. Available on the Internet at: http://www.collectionscanada.ca/jsc/rdaprospectus.html.

Rota, Anthony. *Points at Issue: A Bookseller Looks at Bibliography.* (Washington, D.C.: Library of Congress, 1984).

Schneider, Georg. *Theory and History of Bibliography.* Trans. Ralph R. Shaw. (New York: Columbia University Press, 1934).

Shatford, Sara. "Catalogue Access to Early Children's Books." *AB* (Nov. 12, 1984), p. 3411-3416.

Tanselle, G. Thomas. "Descriptive Bibliography and Library Cataloguing." *Studies in Bibliography* 30 (1977), p. 1-56.

Tanselle, G. Thomas. "The Editorial Problem of Final Authorial Intention." *Studies in Bibliography* 29 (1976), p. 167-211.

Tate, Elizabeth L. "Main Entries and Citations: One Test of the Revised Cataloging Code." *Library Quarterly* 33 (1963), p. 172-191.

Taylor, Archer J. *Book Catalogues: Their Varieties and Uses.* (Chicago: Newberry Library, 1957).

Taylor, Archer J. *Catalogues of Rare Books: a Chapter in Bibliographic History.* (University of Kanasas Publications Library Series no. 5) (University of Kansas Libraries, 1958).

Taylor, Arlene. *The Organization of Information.* 2nd ed. (Westport, Conn.: Libraries Unlimited, 2004), p. 29-48.

Taylor, Earl R. "Cataloguing and Computers: Librarians and Cyberphobia." *Papers of the Bibliographical Society of America* 75:4 (1981), p. 392-400.

Times Literary Supplement.
>July 7, 1966. "Review of William B. Todd's *A Bibliography of Edmund Burke.*"
>Aug. 4, 1966, "Letter from John Carter re: review."
>Sept. 1, 1966, "Letter from William B. Todd."
>Sept. 22, 1966. "Letter from Tanselle."

Todd, William B. "The ESTC as Viewed by Administrators and Scholars." *Papers of the Bibliographical Society of America* 75:4 (1981), p. 389-392.

Tolman, Frank L. "Bibliography and Cataloging: Some Affinities and Contrasts." *Public Libraries* 10:3 (March, 1905), p. 119-122.

Wright, Wyllis E. "Some Fundamental Principles in Cataloging." *Catalogers' and Classifiers' Yearbook* 7 (1938), p. 26-39.

doi:10.1300/J104v44n03_10

Knowledge Structures and the Internet: Progress and Prospects

Nancy J. Williamson

SUMMARY. This paper analyses the development of the knowledge structures–Web directories, thesauri, and gateways/portals–as they are presented on the Internet as aids to information seeking. It identifies problems and suggests improvements. doi:10.1300/J104v44n03_11 *[Article copies available for a fee from The Haworth Document Delivery Service: 1-800-HAWORTH. E-mail address: <docdelivery@haworthpress.com> Website: <http://www.HaworthPress.com> © 2007 by The Haworth Press, Inc. All rights reserved.]*

KEYWORDS. Thesauri, Web subject directories, gateways, portals, subject access

INTRODUCTION

Since its early and somewhat primitive beginnings, the Internet has gone through many changes. It has grown ever larger, and search engines have become increasingly sophisticated. In efforts to improve ac-

---

Nancy J. Williamson is Professor Emeritus, University of Toronto, Faculty of Information Studies, 140 St. George Street, Toronto, Canada, M5S 3G6 (E-mail: nancy.williamson@utoronto.ca).

[Haworth co-indexing entry note]: "Knowledge Structures and the Internet: Progress and Prospects." Williamson, Nancy J. Co-published simultaneously in *Cataloging & Classification Quarterly* (The Haworth Information Press, an imprint of The Haworth Press, Inc.) Vol. 44, No. 3/4, 2007, pp. 329-342; and: *Cataloger, Editor, and Scholar: Essays in Honor of Ruth C. Carter* (ed: Robert P. Holley) The Haworth Information Press, an imprint of The Haworth Press, Inc., 2007, pp. 329-342. Single or multiple copies of this article are available for a fee from The Haworth Document Delivery Service [1-800-HAWORTH, 9:00 a.m. - 5:00 p.m. (EST). E-mail address: docdelivery@haworthpress.com].

Available online at http://ccq.haworthpress.com
© 2007 by The Haworth Press, Inc. All rights reserved.
doi:10.1300/J104v44n03_11

cess and to ease the search for information, old tools have been adapted and reconfigured; and new tools are constantly being developed. The question of how to organize Web sites so users can actually find what they are looking for is a continuing problem. In any event, while information systems may change to achieve greater success, they must continue to meet two fundamental requirements of information seekers: to permit users to locate information on a subject directly and to allow them to browse so as to familiarize themselves with a domain or to refine a request.

In the infancy of the Internet, information providers were working on a trial and error basis. Research findings indicate that the expertise of the providers varied in its sophistication. The medium and its potential were often misunderstood. Information seeking methods were sometimes naïve and the access tools inadequate to the task. These findings were confirmed in the research for two papers previously prepared–"Knowledge Structures and the Internet" (Williamson, 1997) and "Thesauri in the Digital Age" (Williamson, 2000). In 1997, search engines were relatively primitive; and control over the development of the Internet was minimal. Each information provider had his/her own objectives as to how information should be organized to accomplish easy and productive browsing. The literature seldom addressed the intricacies of structuring the data. There existed no standards or generally accepted guidelines for dealing with document content. Moreover, early research and development focused on the societal and technological problems rather on a concern for effective access to data. Indeed, like so many new technological toys, the developers and many users assumed that the entertainment value of 'surfing the net' was its most important function. Research into the possibilities for organization and access had only just begun.

In the 9 years (2006) since that time, much has changed. The Internet is now seen as a serious source of information in the academic, business, and industrial communities as well as in the eyes of the ordinary citizen. In 2006, Web designers and researchers are well into exploiting a full range of knowledge structures and search strategies. Software cannot solve all the problems. There is an urgent need for more user friendly interfaces and greater emphasis on human computer interaction to aid the user in achieving successful searches. From its early beginnings, much effort has been put forward in an effort to "index the Internet." The first approaches were rather simplistic in nature and not always appropriate to the new medium. For example, early use of traditional classification was at a minimal level, usually shallow and sometimes erroneous. Currently, controlled vocabularies of various kinds (e.g., thesauri and taxonomies) as well as other kinds of information structures are deemed to have an important role to play. Most significantly, endeavors to create seamless information systems in many cases have led to the integration of the tools into the databases themselves. At this point, major questions to be addressed are: "How well are these tools performing their task? Is there room for improvement?" Using the aforementioned papers as a starting place, this current research examines the access tools provided for the aid of users. Focus is on those devices that can actually be viewed on the screen by users and can be manipulated to facilitate subject searching. Emphasis is on structure and complexity as embodied in the use of tools that foster browsing subject domains and individual Web sites. Structure has been defined as the bringing together and organization of information in a way that facilitates browsing. Included is classificatory structure as embodied in both traditional and newly developed aids to searching.

METHODOLOGY

As the first step in this investigation, a literature search was conducted to locate relevant research and publications since 1997. There are numerous devices to aid the user such as 'more like this," hyperlinking, site maps, etc. Since the list is long, three major tools were selected for more intense study–Web directories (taxonomies), thesauri, and gateways/ portals. Hyperlinking and mapping are discussed in conjunction with these three. From the results of this search, the investigation was extended further through a critical examination of the design and structure of relevant Web sites in each of the categories. Since much of the literature was published prior to 2003, an accurate picture could be obtained only by viewing current sites themselves.

Some of the sites viewed in 2000 (Williamson) were revisited to see if changes had been made, and new sites were added. The ultimate goal was to find answers to such questions as: Where do things stand in the development of the browsing capabilities of the Internet? What is the nature of the changes that have taken place? Are they changes that truly support users in their searches? Are the new tools being used effectively? Are there obvious improvements that could be made? Where should research and development go from here? Final conclusions have been drawn from the findings from the two areas of investigation.

SEARCH ENGINES

The bottom line on the Internet is the search engine, and the search is constrained and/or supported by what that search engine has to offer. What is the coverage of the data? What parts of the document are searched? What search options are provided? These are things that determine what can be retrieved. The other aspect of the system is its navigation once the search engine has done its job. It is the navigation over which the information seeker has partial control. The nature, strengths, and weaknesses of search engines are not discussed here. The focus is on the tools that aid the user to navigate Web sites through directed searches. The analysis that follows here moves from the simplest to the most complex.

WEB SUBJECT DIRECTORIES

One of the most obvious tools in a directed search of Internet sites is the Web subject directory. Web directories "are, in fact, a form of classification" (Gilchrist, 2003, p. 11) and are described by Gilchrist, along with some other applications, as belonging under the more generic term "taxonomies." These directories fulfill the two basic requirements for searching an information system. They permit searching on specific terms and also allow browsing through the lists of resources. This investigation focused on subject directories of six sites that are reputed to be "good sites"–Yahoo, Open Directory, LookSmart, Librarians' Internet Index (LII), InfoMine, and RDN (Resource Discovery Network) (Notess 2003). In each case, searches were carried out under the terms "health" and "education." The terms in the directories lead through hyperlinking to Web sites which deal with each particular topic.

In each directory, the user is offered a menu of top terms. Selecting one of the terms, the user can move to second and succeeding levels until some information or references are reached; or perhaps the opportunity of using another search engine is offered. Directories are designed by humans for each particular Web site. There are no rules or standards for these directories, but attempts are made to use terminology and structure suitable to the particular site (as opposed to using a standard classification scheme). The number of top terms, the total number of sites involved, and the nature of the domain influence the degree of division, the number of hierarchical levels in a directory, and length of the pathways to particular topics. For example, the Yahoo directory leading to 3,000,000 + locations is much more detailed than RDN's (Resource Discovery Network) leading to 30,000 locations (Notess 2003). Top terms tend to be at the domain level, but popular topics might also be top terms. For example Librarians' Internet Index includes the very broad topics–Arts & Humanities, Science, and Society & Social Science as top terms as well as terms that could be subsumed under these. At the upper levels, terms sometimes included a brief contents note to aid the user in making choices. Web directories are described as being hierarchical, but they are not hierarchical in the classical sense. In some cases, a term may be repeated at different levels. For example in the Yahoo directory, 'cancer' and 'breast cancer' both appear at level 3; but 'breast cancer' appears again at level 4. Also the categories are not "pure." For example, "diseases and conditions" and "news and media" are in the same category in the Yahoo directory. Not every term relative to the various Web sites will appear in a directory. In all the subject directories searched, there was provision for searching on keywords as well as for browsing.

As might be expected, there is wide variation in the structure and usefulness of Web directories. The user controls the search by following a path in the directory. A useful device is a display of the search path at each step of the user's search (Yahoo and Librarians' Internet Index). InfoMine differs from all the other directories. The first page of the site contains the top terms in the directory. A click on the top term leads to a search form designed for selecting search options and for inputting a term that permits a choice of regular display or relevance ranking. As aids in selecting search terms, browsing of LCSH, LCC, keywords, and other indexes is also permitted. Similarly, searching 'biological, agricultural and medical sciences' in RDN permits the use of LCSH, MESH, and LCC.

The large Web directories (Yahoo and Librarians' Internet Index) tend to be the most logically organized and most minutely divided. In the Yahoo example, some paths went down six levels whereas RDN provided division that was only three levels deep in the paths searched. For the user, effective sorting of the material is important. There is need for an increasing number of levels as the size of the database increases. In the Yahoo directory, for example, a search for 'mammography' goes through 5 levels: Health–Diseases and conditions–Cancer–Breast cancer–Mammography. If a directory is to continue to be useful over time, revision and resorting of the directory needs to occur as the number of and types of Web sites grow. There is little indication as to whether this actually happens.

THESAURI

While Web subject directories (taxonomies) provide useful tools to aid in navigating the Internet, thesauri provide much more powerful tools not only by allowing subjects to be arranged hierarchically but also by permitting other kinds of term relationships and linkages. Controlled vocabularies, such as subject headings, go back to the nineteenth century; and the modern thesaurus emerged in the early 1960s. By the late 1990s, it was generally assumed that there was an important role for the thesaurus to play as a tool in online access to information (Milstead 2000). At that time, that role was still being defined. Among other things, it was assumed that thesauri could complement full text access by aiding users in focusing their searches by supplementing the linguistic analysis of the text search engines and even by serving as one of the tools used by the search engine for its analysis. Machine aided indexing could make use of thesauri as a basis for easier term selection by indexers. Also by analogy, the principles of term relationships as applied in thesauri should be applicable in the creation of hyperlinks in large databases and on the Internet.

Over time, a growing number of thesauri have become available through the Internet. There are two basic types of display–static and dynamic. Static thesauri are displayed much as they are in printed form and differ only in that they are available electronically. The contents can be browsed, but there is little or no facility for moving about the list in a dynamic way. For practical purposes, they are clumsy; it would often be easier and more efficient to use a printed volume. This approach was typical of initial attempts to move printed products into digital format and was precipitated by the existing use of electronic sources to create the printed versions. Dynamic thesauri, on the other hand, are presented in such a way that they can be "searched" by inputting thesaurus terms or by browsing a section of the alphabet. Some provide a list of categories as a starting place for beginning a search. Some allow Boolean searching and begin to use hyperlinks that enable users to move from one part of the thesaurus to another; to follow the BT, NT, and RT relationships; and to move from one type of display to another (e.g., from a rotated display to an alphabetical display). Some are derived from a printed product; others are newly created for the Internet and only exist in electronic form. Some (e.g., the *Cook's Thesaurus*) actually led to documents. By 2000, there was considerable improvement in the way thesauri were presented online. At the time, there was evidence of a solid start in the development of online thesauri; but there was still much research to be done on possible ways to enhance the display and the use of thesauri online. There were plenty of examples of what to do and what not to do. Many of the designs were predicated on what the designers knew about databases and not always on what was known about the behavior of users. Some were incomplete and displayed only a portion of the thesaurus as an encouragement to buy the product. However, there were healthy signs of innovation; in particular, many lists now began to lead to actual document citations–confirming the prediction that direct linkage between a thesaurus and documents was on the way.

All thesauri that presently exist were created, more or less, on the basis of the current guidelines for thesaurus construction. These guidelines, while sound in linguistic principles, are technologically somewhat out of date. The ISO 2788 guidelines were published in 1986. The ANSI/NISO Z39.19 guidelines, published somewhat later in 1993, employed the same guiding principles as ISO 2788; but included a section on screen display that recognized that "sophisticated thesaurus display and terminology" (NISO 1993, p. 25) would be appropriate for expert searchers and indexers. Furthermore, it acknowledged the fact that screen viewing is different from print viewing and presents difficulties for the user. In addition, it alludes to the need for standards for human-computer interaction but does not refer directly to the possibility of a dynamic thesaurus. By 1999, at a workshop sponsored by NISO on electronic thesauri, it was recommended that a variety of flexible displays should be provided and that a new standard be established for digital thesauri. Furthermore, it was soon recognized that new guidelines were needed. The work on new standards has now been completed. ANSI/NISO Z39.19-2005 was published in November 2005 and is available on the Web at http://www.niso.org/standards/resources/Z39-19-2005.pdf (accessed 4/3/2006). BS 8723, "*Structured Vocabularies for Information–Guide*," parts 1 and 2, have been published in the UK by the British Standards Institution (BSI). This guide supercedes BS 5723:1987, the *Guide to Establishment and Development of Monolingual Thesauri*, and is described by Leonard Will as being substantially different from BS 5723. "The text has been rewritten in today's idiom and some additional aspects are now covered" (Will, 2006) including facet analysis, presentation via electronic (as well as printed) media, thesaurus functions in electronic systems, and requirements for thesaurus management software" (Will, 2006). Three other parts yet to come will cover "vocabularies other than thesauri, interoperation between multiple vocabularies (with multilingual as a special case), interoperation between vocabularies and other components of information storage and retrieval systems." The hope is that "BS 8723 will pave the way towards a corresponding revision of the international standard ISO 2788." Without having seen the full text of the BSI version, it can be said that both standards support the principles laid out in previous standards and that they are cognizant of the need to provide for electronic manipulation and display of thesauri and for their integration with databases. Problems of interoperability will also be addressed. In NISO Z39.19-2005 (p. 103-104), Section 11.47 sets out requirements for "browsing within hierarchical and alphabetical displays" and the "viewing of a term in the context of its relationships and its complete term record from any display (through hyperlinking)."

These guidelines should lead us into the future. But what is the state of the thesaurus on the Internet today? Much has changed in the way thesauri are handled. Many of the predictions made by Milstead (2000) have come to pass. Clearly, the thesaurus has now assumed its role as a search tool. However, there are some unfortunate links to the past. A revisit to some of online thesauri from the previous research found that some of them are still available on the Internet and have never having updated or improved. However, things have moved on; and the most important developments are the efforts to link thesauri up with the databases and the convergence of a number of databases under on one access point. Online thesauri can be found in one or more of the following forms (Shiri and Revie 2000): (a) simple static text format (e.g., ASFA; NASA Thesaurus); (b) static HTML format; (c) dynamic HTML format with fully navigable hyperlinks (e.g., MeSH; UNESCO Thesaurus; (d) advanced visual and graphic interfaces (Plumb Design Visual Thesaurus); and (e) XML format (Virtual Hyperglossary).

Because of the lack of standards, there are considerable differences in: (a) the way the thesauri are accessed and (b) the provision for their electronic manipulation. Some online versions are incomplete and are online mostly to encourage subscriptions to the full product. Indeed, in many cases, the only sure method of receiving updates is to subscribe. Rarely, except in static format, can a user access the whole thesaurus at once. With the dynamic format, the "black box" effect exists; and access in response to input by the user of a term, partial term, or known descriptor is either a list of descriptors or a group of related thesaurus entries (with BT, NT, RT relationships). Most are forgiving of spelling mistakes and respond to truncation. However, the browsing feature of the printed thesaurus has gone the way of the card catalogue. Perhaps this is not a problem for the searcher, but it may be for the indexer. Users often do not know what the working version looks like without a subscription to the tool. An essential of a good online thesaurus is hyperlinking to permit navigation across the thesaurus, both within a particular display and across displays. The following examples demonstrate some of these features.

The *NASA Thesaurus* is of the static type; and, yes, you can view the whole of the alphabetical display; but it cannot be manipulated online and is not connected to the database. The *CATIE HIV/AIDS Treatment Thesaurus* is a dynamic thesaurus and is accessed through letters and letter combinations (e.g., A–Ana, Anb-Az, B, etc.). Selection of a segment brings up an alphabetical list of terms from which a choice can be made. The chosen term leads to a thesaurus entry with all the necessary relationships, but that list is static and cannot be manipulated further. Having chosen the term, the user must then go to the Web site search page or to the library catalog to get the final information because the thesaurus and the database are not connected.

The *UNESCO Thesaurus* is a multilingual thesaurus containing 7,000 English terms, 8,600 terms in French, and 8,600 terms in Spanish. It is easy to use and has most of the requirements for a good online thesaurus. A search on "UNESCO" brings up the official Web site for UNESCO documents and publications that provides a link to the thesaurus. The thesaurus can be searched both alphabetically and hierarchically. An alphabetical search is initiated by inputting "a few letters" (e.g., "cultur" for culture). The click leads the user to the relevant terms from the permuted list. Each term includes a full thesaurus entry with the number of documents in square brackets. BTs, NTs, and RTs are hyperlinked to their own records so that a user can expand/narrow the search if desired. A click on the number of documents retrieves the records for the documents from unesdoc/bib for that topic. From that point, the full catalogue record can be accessed if there is one; full text can be accessed online if available; and "no full text" is indicated where appropriate. If the hierarchical approach is chosen, the process is slightly different. The user is asked to choose (a) a domain from a list (e.g., Social and human sciences) and (b) a specific subject area (e.g., Social problems). Input again takes the user to full thesaurus entries supported by hyperlinks. There may be more than one record. For example, the request for "social problems" brought up thesaurus records for "crime," "disadvantaged groups," and "social problems." Clicking the number of documents leads to records for the documents. While the user must understand the system, it is simple and effective to use; and the instructions are clear. It gives details of the thesaurus including "how to browse the thesaurus." This format stands alone and is intended for use as a searching thesaurus. Alphabetical access is through an alphabetical list of terms that leads to the thesaurus entries. While this thesaurus would serve the user well, the indexer might have a problem as one cannot browse the whole thesaurus. However, the working format may have some differences. In addition, while the user can move around in the individual format, he/she cannot move directly from the hierarchical format to the alphabetical format without returning to the initial page.

Another format now being introduced is the advanced visual and graphic interface. This approach has great potential, but so far the examples are very simple and applied to a small group of terms. Think Map is one example of this and, at best, might be thought to be "cute." On the Internet, a graphic design is presented that changes when individual terms are clicked on. Another result is a change in the configuration with the adding of new terms and the subtraction of others. Very little information is given, and the user is allowed to play with it for only a few minutes. Access to it is problematic without further information. There may be an alphabetical list linked to the graphics, but only a subscription or questioning the owner would provide answers. One would not want to subscribe without more information. The significance of this format is that this type of graphic design is not new. It was demonstrated by Lauren Doyle (1961) and by Eric Johnson and Pauline Cochrane (1998) in an experiment with the *INSPEC Thesaurus*. This kind of design deserves some further thought.

GATEWAYS AND PORTALS

When an extensive information system becomes extremely large, it is difficult to locate the best materials on a domain or to find all the important databases pertaining to that domain. At that point, there is a need to provide one's clients with improved access through "narrowing the focus to a super discovery tool" (ARL 2005, p. 3). Among the newest tools coming to the aid of information seekers are gateways and portals that provide access to Web resources and/or various databases through one facility. They tend to be either client or subject oriented. Some cover a vast territory, but they may also be developed by individual libraries and special information centers. The particular interest here is subject gateways. More precisely defined:

> Subject gateways are Internet services which support systematic resource discovery, provide links to resources (documents, objects, sites or services), predominantly accessible via the Internet. The service is based on resource description. Browsing access to the resources via a subject structure is an important feature. (Koch 2000, p. 24-25)

These are developed with care to ensure high quality. Quality-controlled subject gateways are created by editors and subject specialists to ensure a high level of quality. Completeness and balance are sought in collection development, and a policy is developed to ensure the contents are up to date. Quality metadata is used that should comply with an acceptable standard. Formalized content description is also recommended. Of particular interest here is the kind of subject access. Koch (2000, p. 25) indicates that there is a need for deeper levels of classification and that subject/browsing structure is important. He also calls for keyword or better controlled vocabularies (e.g., subject headings, thesauri, etc.) for subject indexing as well as advanced search and browse access.

As with thesauri, taxonomies, and ontologies, there is some confusion over the terminology. The terms "gateways" and "portals" appear to be used synonymously (Lancaster, 2003), and some have referred to them as virtual libraries. One example of this is that Lancaster refers to InfoMine and Librarians' Internet Index as portals while they are described elsewhere in the context of Web directories. There are a number of important examples of these structures, and the number is growing rapidly. Founded in 1988, the Ovid gateway provides access to electronic, scientific, and academic research information and provides for multiple ways to carry out searches. The NLM Gateway is a Web-based system that permits users to search simultaneously in multiple retrieval systems at the National Library of Medicine. Users can initiate a search from one Web interface and carry out one-stop searching in all the NLM's databases. One huge gateway is CSA Illumina. CSA describes itself as a world wide information company. It sounds commercial, but it leads to bibliographies and journals in four primary areas–natural sciences, social sciences, arts and humanities, and technology. It provides a single point of access to very large number of electronic resources. One might argue that it is not necessarily a "quality" subject gateway, but it all depends on the resources it leads to. It includes in its long list ERIC and Scholar's Portal. ERIC is having to make some concessions to be included there. The *ERIC Thesaurus* has only recently become accessible again after being reconstructed for inclusion in the CSA Illumina system.

Scholars' Portal is a system developed in 2002 by the ARL Libraries; users of some of those libraries will be familiar with it. There may be different configurations of the portal in different libraries. One example of its application is the one at the University of Toronto Libraries. From the official Web page, four approaches are possible:

1. "Search Illumina" leads to CSA Illumina and a broad list of databases from which user can select (e.g., AGRICOLA, ERIC, LISA) and then be taken to a description of the resource;
2. "Electronic journals" leads to a list of journals that can be browsed and accessed by letter. The journal name is hyperlinked to the actual journal and ultimately to tables of contents that allow particular journals to be searched;
3. "RefWorks" permits the building of a personal bibliography of sources;
4. "RACER" leads to an interlibrary loan function.

However, at the University of Toronto, a user's first encounter with Scholars' Portal may result from a search of such journal indexes as LISA and ISTA where a subject search retrieves a list of references. A particular reference leads to a title and full abstract and a direction to see UTL (University of Toronto Libraries). Response to this command will tell the searcher if and where full text online is available–Scholars' Portal, Haworth Press, HW Wilson, Proquest, etc. A click will bring up the full article. If no full text is available online, the searcher is referred to the library catalogue where it can be determined whether the book or printed journal is available. The bibliographic and interlibrary loan functions are also active here. The system is not finished, and there are improvements to be made. The decision to use Scholars' Portal is University of Toronto's answer to Google.

CONCLUSION

Has control of subject access to the Internet improved since 1997? Definitely yes! There are more and better provisions for access to materials, and serious efforts are being made to single out the best materials. This is happening at four levels–at the gateway/portal level, at the individual database level, at the Web site level, and at the resource level.

Aside from the structures discussed above, lengthy pieces of text are appearing with tables of contents and outlines hypertexted to the appropriate location in the text. There are indexes that look very much like book indexes that bring together related parts internal to a text and other devices. Most importantly, some of this might not have happened without the development of the Web-based OPAC and the emergence of metadata. These two developments have done much to aid the changes that have taken place. However, there is much yet to be done. There could be further improvements in online thesauri to make them more useable for searching and browsing. The gateways and portals will improve as time goes on. Will the Internet ever be a perfect world? No. Things will become more complex; but, in a world where everybody is an information provider, many of them will go their own way. However, it is to be hoped that "quality" information will rise to the top.

REFERENCES

Aitchison, Jean and Clarke, Stella Dexter. (2004). "The thesaurus: a historical viewpoint with a look to the future." *Cataloging & Classification Quarterly* 37 (3): 5-21.

ARL Scholars Portal Working Group. (2002). "Final report" http://www.arl.org/access/scholarsportal/final.html (accessed 12/12/2005).

CSA guide to discovery. http://illumina.scholarsportal.info/ (accessed 2/6/2006).

Doyle, Lauren B. (1961) "Semantic road maps for literature searchers," *Journal of the Association for Computing Machinery* 8 (4): 553-578.

Gilchrist, Alan. (2003). "Thesauri, taxonomies and ontologies–an etymological note." *Journal of Documentation* 39 (1): 7-17.

Garshol, Lars Marius. (2004). "Metadata? Thesauri? Taxonomies? Topic maps! Making sense of it all." *Journal of Information Sciences* 30 (4): 378-391.

Gullikson, Shelley, Blades, Ruth, Bragdon, Marc, McKibbon, Shelley, Sparling, Marnie and Elaine G. Toms. (1999). "The impact of information architecture on the academic Web site usability." *The Electronic Library* 10 (5): 293-304.

International Organization for Standardization. (1986) *Guidelines for the Establishment and Development of Monolingual Thesauri.* ISO2788. 2d .ed. Geneva: ISO.

Johnson, Eric H. And Cochrane, Pauline A. (1998). "Hypertextual interface for a searcher's thesaurus." http://www.csdl.tamu.edu/DL95/papers/johncoch/johncoch.html (accessed 4/3/06).

Koch, Traugott. (2000). "Quality-controlled subject gateways: definitions, typologies, empirical review." *Online Information Review* 24 (1): 24-34.

Lancaster, F.W. (2003). "Portals." In Lancaster, F.W. *Indexing and Abstracting: Theory and Practice.* 3rd ed. Champaign, Il: University of Illinois, School of Library and Information Science. pp. 352-354.

Milstead, Jessica. (2000). "Invisible thesauri: the year 2000." *Online &CDROM Review* 19 (2): 93-94.

Notess, Greg R. (2003). "Internet subject directories." http://www.searchengineshowdown.com/dir/ (accessed 4/3/06).
Renardus. "Gateways defined." http://www.renardus.org/about_us/subject_gateways.html (accessed 10/20/2005).
Shiri, Ali Asghar and Crawford Revie. (2000). "Thesauri on the Web: current developments and trends." *Online Information Review* 24 (4): 273-279.
Will, Leonard. [e-mail received 31/01/06].
Williamson, Nancy J. (1997). "Knowledge structures and the internet." In *Knowledge Organization for Information Retrieval: Proceedings of the Sixth International Study Conference on Classification Research*. Held at University College London, 16-18 June 1997. The Hague, Netherlands: International Federation for Information and Documentation. pp. 23-27.
Williamson, Nancy J. (2000). "Thesauri in the digital age: stability and dynamism in their development and use. In *Dynamism and Stability in Knowledge Organization: Proceedings of the Sixth International ISKO Conference 10-13 July 2000, Toronto, Canada*. Würzburg: ERGON Verlag. pp. 268-274.
Zeng, Marcia Lei and Chan, Lois Mai. (2004). "Trends and issues in establishing interoperability among knowledge organization systems." *Journal of the American Society for Information Science and Technology*, 55 (5): 377-395.

doi:10.1300/J104v44n03_11

Numbers to Identify Entities (ISADNs– International Standard Authority Data Numbers)

Barbara B. Tillett

SUMMARY. The advantages of unique identifiers for the entities described in authority records are outweighed by the costs to manage an international system for assigning and maintaining such unique identifiers. Today's and tomorrow's systems perhaps can do without unique identifiers, but the attraction of unique identifiers still persists. This paper provides a personal recommendation to use the existing machine-generated record control numbers from our authority records as an interim measure until we see what future systems need. doi:10.1300/J104v44n03_12 *[Article copies available for a fee from The Haworth Document Delivery Service: 1-800-HAWORTH. E-mail address: <docdelivery@haworthpress.com> Website: <http://www.HaworthPress.com> © 2007 by The Haworth Press, Inc. All rights reserved.]*

KEYWORDS. Unique identifiers, International Standard Authority Data Number, ISADN, name authority control, subject authority control

---

Barbara B. Tillett is Chief of the Cataloging Policy and Support Office and Acting Chief of the Cataloging Distribution Service, the Library of Congress, 101 Independence Avenue, S.E., Washington, DC 20540-4305 (E-mail: btil@loc.gov).

[Haworth co-indexing entry note]: "Numbers to Identify Entities (ISADNs–International Standard Authority Data Numbers)." Tillett, Barbara B. Co-published simultaneously in *Cataloging & Classification Quarterly* (The Haworth Information Press, an imprint of The Haworth Press, Inc.) Vol. 44, No. 3/4, 2007, pp. 343-361; and: *Cataloger, Editor, and Scholar: Essays in Honor of Ruth C. Carter* (ed: Robert P. Holley) The Haworth Information Press, an imprint of The Haworth Press, Inc., 2007, pp. 343-361. Single or multiple copies of this article are available for a fee from The Haworth Document Delivery Service [1-800-HAWORTH, 9:00 a.m. - 5:00 p.m. (EST). E-mail address: docdelivery@haworthpress.com].

Available online at http://ccq.haworthpress.com
© 2007 by The Haworth Press, Inc. All rights reserved.
doi:10.1300/J104v44n03_12

The idea of a simple unique number that everyone in the world could use to identify the same person, corporate body, work/expression, or subject is very alluring, especially with computer systems on the Web. The idea has been proposed many times over the past 30 years, but is nearly impossible to achieve. Part of the difficulty is that things are viewed differently in different communities and in different parts of the world. Just pinpointing what is to be considered the thing to be numbered varies from one community to another, based on the business need. Things can be given many names, and names often change over time and vary in different languages and scripts.

Yet the idea persists. Numbers are very appealing as an element of naming to uniquely identify an entity. We know that having a unique number helps *avoid duplication*. A number lends itself to international application because, for the most part, it is *language independent*. Using a number can facilitate having systems provide local displays of the locally preferred form of name (language and script). There is the potential for greater international sharing of bibliographic data where the identifying number could be stored in shared bibliographic and authority records, and local systems could display their mapped text name for the entity identified by the number.

Certainly many international standard numbers have appeared over the past decades like a great alphabet soup: ISAN, ISBN, ISSN, ISRN, ISMN, ISIL, ISTC, ISWC, and on and on. Most of these numbers are managed by international organizations that use the numbers for inventory control, tracking, and identification of the entities numbered, such as the International Standard Book Numbers (ISBN) and the International Standard Serials Number (ISSN). We also use standard numbers such as social security numbers to identify people for tax purposes and employment.

Attempts have been made to build systems to create and maintain unique identifying numbers for the entities described in library authority files as well. For example, suggestions were made in the late 1970s within IFLA (International Federation of Library Associations and Institutions) on the system requirements to build an international authority system including a registration system for International Standard Authority Data Numbers (ISADNs). Some have suggested possibilities for building intelligent numbers for ISADN's (e.g., Bourdon). Both centralized and distributed systems have been suggested for registering such numbers. Lots of problems have been identified over the years in regards to the proposals for having such numbers. The proposals break down because there are too many fuzzy areas, too many conflicting perspectives of what such a number would be used for, and too many possibilities for duplication and mis-assignment of numbers when taken to an international level across different communities.

WHAT ENTITY?

Before one even gets to numbering, there are multiple problems with trying to identify across domains those entities that would get numbers. The entities recognized by the library communities do not exactly match those in archives, museums, publishing agencies, rights management agencies, etc. For example, libraries sometimes think of a person as a "bibliographic identity" or "persona"–that is, the entity behind a personal name that we find on a bibliographic resource, such as the author, whether that is a real person or not. For rights management agencies, they need to know the real person to whom they pay the royalties, regardless of how many pseudonyms they may use. So the "person" entity is slightly different, but they can be interconnected by the names used.

WHAT GOVERNANCE?

Then there is the superstructure necessary for administering an international system of numbering. It would likely be prohibitively expensive. The management and governance to assure everyone in the world takes part and follows the agreed conventions is unlikely to happen even within the library world, let alone across communities worldwide.

And is it really even necessary? What tasks are we trying to accomplish by having unique numbers for entities? Could those tasks be accomplished in some other, less resource intensive way? I think so.

TASK OF CONTROLLING NAMES

Having files of authority records has been a big step towards controlling the names given to entities that we identify in our bibliographic files in libraries. Controlled vocabularies as reflected in authority files continue to be important, even essential, to improving the precision and recall of searches. In the past (and even today) in libraries, we provided control by requiring a single authorized form of name to be used for each entity (persons, corporate bodies, works/expressions, subjects), either as an authorized heading, a uniform title, or a subject heading.

When libraries began automating their cataloging operations, some system designers saw the advantage of using a control number in bibliographic records in lieu of the text string name for an entity. The control number would be linked to a corresponding authority record to save on storage, to make global update easier, and in general to provide better control over the displayed forms of names used. Not all systems took this approach, but the elegance of having a number behind the scenes that could be displayed based on the authority record was very attractive, especially for international applications. The script or language in the authority record could be displayed and not need to be stored in the bibliographic records.

One limitation was that the MARC format required the text string for communicating and sharing bibliographic records so that local systems had to supply the text string in lieu of the number when exporting records for data exchange.

With the advent of the Internet and networked systems worldwide, the use of identifiers, again for machine manipulation and navigation, has been successful. The URLs and resolvers to enable connections and links to digital objects are a reality. As Cliff Lynch notes: "The assignment of identifiers to works is a very powerful act; it states that, within a given intellectual framework, two instances of a work that have been assigned the same identifier are the same, while two instances of a work with different identifiers are distinct." This same identification and disambiguation is what authority records also try to accomplish.

Thus, the tasks we hope to perform with unique identifiers for entities represented by authority data include avoiding duplication, providing international sharing, simplifying maintenance of controlled vocabularies, and enabling customization of displayed forms of names/terms.

INTERNATIONAL COOPERATION FOR AUTHORITY CONTROL

There is a wonderful overview of the efforts towards international cooperation in the area of authority data by Françoise Bourdon. She reminds us of the history of these efforts and that the uses for authority files have grown over the years beyond just controlling the forms of names used in an individual library's catalog to becoming more a reference tool available to anyone anywhere (Bourdon, p. 65, 67).

Bourdon proposed an international center to collect all the records and suggested how it might be run. She also described a decentralized international system (Bourdon, p. 84), which she felt would be less effective, as it required strict adherence to the UBC principles about re-using bibliographic and authority data worldwide. There is still a lot to be said for the 1970s and 1980s IFLA push for "Universal Bibliographic Control" (UBC) that among other things encourages national bibliographic agencies to be responsible for providing authority records for its national authors. However, we recognize that not all countries have national bibliographic agencies or national libraries; and some national libraries have a scope that is international rather than national. National bibliographic agencies are not yet truly universal and do not reflect the wider world of archives, museums, rights management, and publishing where authority information is also valued. Bourdon recognized the problem for authors from countries without national bibliographic agencies (NBAs) and concluded that a decentralized model, as she envisioned it, might prove to be more expensive and less effective than a centralized system.

She recommended addressing authority files in cataloguing rules (Bourdon, p. 87), a step which indeed is coming to pass with the IFLA draft *Statement of International Cataloguing Principles* and work towards *RDA: Resource Description and Access*, a new content standard to replace the *Anglo-American Cataloguing Rules*. *RDA* Part III is to cover authority control or access point management. Having instructions for constructing authority records and identifying the elements to be included could lead to more uniformity across the communities using those cataloging instructions.

Two IFLA surveys in 1977/78 and 1989 documented the redundant work going on internationally in establishing authority records for the same entity (Beaudiquez and Bourdon, 1991). It has long been recognized that we could save a lot of that redundant work by sharing authority information. In the 1970s, that would have been through exchanging authority records; but now it can be managed through Internet access to authority data on the Web. And who knows what the future may offer?

We should most certainly continue to work towards an "International Authority System" as those in the 1970s envisioned, at least among libraries. Not only would this help reduce library costs, it may well prove to be one of the building blocks for future international systems such as the Semantic Web. There is also great interest being expressed in the publishing and rights management communities as well as in the archival community about sharing our authority data.

Some recent initiatives over the past couple of decades for linking authority data and building international authority systems include the Project AUTHOR, the LEAF Project among archives and libraries in Europe, efforts within Dublin Core looking at "agents" (including the DELOS/NSF Working Group on "Actors/Roles"), INTERPARTY, the VIAF Proof of Concept Project, and Project MACS (for subjects). Such initiatives help us explore the issues and challenges for shared authority data and help us test the need for international standard authority data numbers.

WHY A NUMBER?

Are we still trying to save storage space? Are we trying to enable international linking or identification of the entity across communities (domains)? Do we need to uniquely identify an entity for any reason or all purposes? Storage space is no longer an issue as the costs keep dropping. The dream of international sharing across domains remains alluring, but do we need a number to enable this dream?

We have several ways we could view providing a unique identifier for an entity through:

> (1) a single "authorized" or default form of name to uniquely identify the entity–i.e., an authorized heading, a unique **text string** (traditional library approach);

or

> (2) a unique number assigned to the entity (function: placeholder in various forms, citations, bibliographic records, authority records, etc; link to variant forms found in a control record for the entity to enable display in the user or system-preferred language/script/format.)–i.e., an **ISADN**;

or

> (3) an **authority data cluster** of variant forms of names, possibly with links to sources locating where the variant name was found, plus other identifying data and links to related entities that together provide a set of information elements to uniquely identify an entity.

There may also be other options in the future. Let's look at each of these three to start.

1. Single "Authorized Heading" (Text String)

The case has been made many times before within IFLA about why it is not practical to have a single "authorized heading" for each entity that everyone in the world would use. People need to have names they can read, in languages and scripts they can read. One form established in China would probably not work in the United States, especially among people who cannot read Chinese characters.

In Dorothy Anderson's 1974 description of the IFLA concept of Universal Bibliographic Control (UBC), national bibliographic agencies were charged with the task of establishing the authoritative form of name for their country's personal and corporate authors. Yet, the single "authorized heading" that everyone in the world would use (a premise of Universal Bibliographic Control) only works when participants share the same standards for cataloging rules, language, and script. It breaks down when moved to the truly international arena and across different communities. For example, Confucius is the English well known name; but it's Kung Fu in China and in Chinese script, and different names in other countries–the same entity, but known by different names and represented in different scripts around the world.

Since 1998 with the publication of the IFLA "MLAR" (Minimal Level Authority Record) report, it has been recognized that:

> requiring everyone to use the same form for headings globally is not practical. There are reasons to use the form of names familiar to our own users, in scripts they can read and in forms they most likely would look for in their library catalogue or national bibliography. Therefore, this Working Group recognizes the important of allowing the preservation of national or rule-based differences in authorized forms for headings to be used in national bibliographies and library catalogues that best meet the language and cultural needs of the particular institution's users. (MLAR, p. 1)

2. ISADN (International Standard Authority Data Number)

Having a unique number assigned to the entity, an ISADN, has the attraction of being:

- language independent–a number could be easily stored in bibliographic records, authority records, or used as an identifying data element in other system applications used worldwide. However, a number needs to be "resolved" to a display name. Having that capability could enable the user to choose a preferred language/script/transliteration scheme, but a system must be able to recognize which text string to display in response to such a request. But is a number really language independent? Since some languages (like Arabic) do not use the "western-style" Arabic numerals, just how international is a "western-style" Arabic number really? We could probably argue that for today's Internet environment, one assumes everyone would use "western-style" Arabic numbers as the de facto universal characters for numbering so that we turn a blind eye to the local variations across the world, which is probably not a politically correct thing to do but may be a practical reality.
- system independent–a number could be used in any system or application without the system having to know any rules or standards. The system would just have to know what to do with a number and how to resolve it to a display that a human could understand (rather than just displaying the numeric code).

However, having a unique number assigned to an entity gets to be a major cost and administrative issue when we look beyond a single institution or a single cooperative program where people share the same standards. On an international level, to assure the uniqueness of such numbers, there would probably need to be a registering system and all the overhead associated with such an operation. Registration of a number also tangentially must relate to a particular application or business need. For some communities beyond libraries, the business need might involve only a subset of the universe of all persons, families, corporate bodies, works/expressions that libraries care about. In other communities, it might be much broader than the "bibliographic identities" needed in libraries.

There is no doubt that having a unique number would be useful. As the IFLA Working Group on Minimal Level Authority Records noted (MLAR report, p. 1): "Within this context, retrieval would be greatly enhanced by the use of some numbering mechanism to link the associated authority records created by the various agencies, either the local system record numbers or an International Standard Authority Data

Number (ISADN) for the entity, as was suggested by IFLA in the 1970s."

However, that group went on to comment on the ISADN (MLAR report, p. 2):

> The Working Group has concerns about the expensive overhead in maintaining such a numbering system. We recommend waiting to see how the emerging international electronic environment and advances in developing technologies impact the linking of records. However, opportunities will be pursued with similar records from the archival community and the realm of publishers and professional associations that maintain databases of members and copyright holders for royalties. We highly recommend a follow-on Working Group be formed in IFLA to pursue these new opportunities and to continue the work to develop a virtual shared resource authority file under the auspices of IFLA.

In 1979, IFLA had a Working Group on an International Authority System, led by Tom Delsey. They proposed (and UNESCO later also recommended) the establishment of an ISADN–International Standard Authority Data Number. As Bourdon notes (Bourdon, p. 79), at that time they felt the ISADN was essential for an International Authority System to work in order to identify entities "unambiguously on an international scale unimpeded by barriers of language." Bourdon recommended: "The ISADN should not just be attributed to the authority form but to the whole of the identification authority record drawn up by the NBA, which is responsible for the author in question" (Bourdon, p. 80). Thus, the ISADN would refer to the authority record as a whole and not just to the authorized form of name so that it can control all forms of names for a given entity. In effect, the number would identify the entity represented by the authority record.

Delsey described this as the view of the IFLA Working Group on an International Authority System:

> The number would serve to identify the object of the authority entry, whether it be a person, a corporate body, a work, or a subject, and would be present in all variant records for that same object as the common element that would link them all regardless of the form of the heading. In an ideal implementation the standard number would be assigned by the national bibliographic agency designated as the agency responsible for establishing the authoritative

heading under UBC. The number would also be recorded in conjunction with the heading in any bibliographic record in which the heading might be used. Once the heading and its corresponding number were registered, any other national bibliographic agency adapting the heading for its own use in its own national authority file would record the standard number with its variant version of the authority. Any subsequent importation either of bibliographic records carrying the heading or of variant authorities emanating from other national bibliographic agencies would trigger an automatic adjustment to conform with the national adaptation, and the records them be cleanly integrated with the national file. (Delsey 1989, p. 24-25)

Even back then, it was recognized that the practical aspects of administrating such a system were "far from simple" (Delsey 1989, p. 25). A basic assumption was the need to reconcile variant authorities and properly register all related variants under the same standard number.

Recent InterParty work also suggests having a standard number and a registration agency and suggests a business model to manage the assignment/registration of such numbers across several communities that would find such information important to their business (MacEwan). Members of that group are pursuing an ISO standard for such an identifying number (i.e., ISPI–International Standard Party Identifier) and continuing their pursuit of a registration agency.

IFLA also continues to hang on to the concept of an ISADN. Within UNIMARC/Authorities, the "0-Identification Block" has the tag 015 reserved for the International Standard Authority Data Number (UNIMARC/Authorities, p. 34-35). It shows up also in IFLA's *Guidelines for Authority and Reference Entries* (GARE) and the later *Guidelines for Authority Records and References* (GARR) as well as in the *Guidelines for Subject Authority and Reference Entries* (GSARE), all of which give instructions on how to present authority numbers in the authority record. However, in GARR there is recognition that an alternative number might be given:

> 1.7.1.3. In the absence of, or in addition to, an ISADN an alternative number assigned by a regional or national agency may be given. This may be generated by the local system of the agency. The alternative number must be preceded by a code identifying the agency that assigned the number. (*GARR*, p. 23) [There is a foot-

note that the codes are in Bell's *An Annotated Guide to Current National Bibliographies.*]

In 2004, Delsey wrote about the ISADN and pointed out how difficult it would be to establish clear territorial boundaries for assigning ISADNs. He noted that even the alternative of "first in" requires a system where everyone can easily check the assignments made in order not to duplicate a number or assign more than one number to an entity–a system to register and search the registration files. He noted that this argues for a centralized registration system; but that also introduces governance and administrative problems, so that he then suggested that perhaps a decentralized system might be better (Delsey 2004, p. 74).

To me, his description of how an ISADN registration system would need to work, demonstrates that we could never have such a system on an international scale. He indicates it:

> will have to support the same basic processes of searching the target file, evaluating the result set to eliminate false hits, and integrating the data retrieved into the host database. In a decentralized system, the processes involved in creating and maintaining a national or regional registration database will be analogous to those involved in contributing authority records to a cooperatively developed national database. Searching across national or regional databases to ensure that an ISADN has not already been assigned for a given entity will parallel the searching of a target database and evaluating search results for purposes of deriving data from an external source. In a centralized system, the processes will parallel those involved in uploading records to a database of linked files from various national sources. (Delsey 2004, p. 74)

He concludes that if an international system such as he describes were feasible, the benefits of the ISADN would be considerable in establishing links between records from multiple international sources.

I personally do not see this happening–the overhead of developing the necessary automated checks and creating a database and registration system do not seem to be in the near future, if at all. So let us look outside this box.

This then brings us back to the question of which entities? What is the scope? For the purposes of IFLA's FRANAR (Functional Requirements and Numbering for Authority Records), we are limiting the discussion to entities that would be represented in authority records: persons, corporate bodies, families, works/expressions, and subjects.

Even if we limit to entities represented in authority records, we still have the problems of which entities, especially when looking internationally where different communities, depending on the cataloguing rules or standards being followed, recognize different entities. Certainly across communities like archives, museums, rights management agencies, publishers, this question becomes even more complex.

What entities do we recognize? When is a change of name for an entity a sign of a new entity or just merely a name change? We have at least the following issues:

- Bibliographic identities or "persona" are recognized as separate entities now in the draft *Statement of International Cataloguing Principles* and *AACR2*, but certainly that view is not yet universal in cataloguing codes worldwide. Rights management agencies would prefer to have all of the names for different "persona" linked to the real person or corporate body to whom they are to pay royalties.
- Name changes over time (persons, corporate bodies, works/expressions) introduce the question of whether we have a new entity or not. Different cataloguing rules tell us to consider some changes as minor and some as major. Major changes require making a new authority record for a new "entity." There is not universal agreement on when this is necessary and in fact some past practices are being challenged (such as (Antelman, p. 245) in exploring "Authority Record Identifiers" as a way to provide a work-level identifier to help cluster the members of a bibliographic family of serial works).
- Fuzzy matches exist. Often there is not enough information to uniquely identify each entity so that our library authority files include records for undifferentiated names. The set of entities represented can change over time as more information is discovered with some entities being added and other being removed as more information is discovered to uniquely identify each persona formerly included. The entities represented by an undifferentiated authority record are not always the same set of entities and may shift over time.
- Is the number for the entity, for the record, or for all the names for the entity? How far do we need to take it? That actually depends on the business need and system design for any particular application.

We need to assume that the number is not for the real person, family, corporate body, or subject (we are not proposing a "Big Brother" approach as in Orwell's *1984*). Most discussions have recognized that the ISADN would be at the record level to provide a number to serve as a surrogate for naming the entity represented by the authority record, but there may be some applications where we would need a number for each name given. For such applications, would they need numbers at the level of all variant names or just for the "authorized forms" in applicable languages and scripts? Again, it would depend on the business need.

Antelman reminds us that the needs of administrative systems that "meet the business needs of their stakeholders" might be different from our needs in library systems (Antelman, p. 245).

There is also an issue of what level of entity and what level of granularity we will we need for unique identifiers. Will we also need to decide whether we need to assign numbers to the different names that could be given to the entity (back to Bourdon's analysis of numbers for the person or the authority record)? Particularly if we need to control display forms, do we also need unique numbers for the names given to entities (persons, families, corporate bodies, works/expressions, subjects)? Some of the issues at this level are well recognized. For example, we can name things in the:

- same language using different words that reflect:
    - cultural differences within same language–as we often find variation among speakers in the United Kingdom, the United States, Canada, or Australia for English and among speakers in France or Canada or other Francophone countries. An example is the need for the French translations of *Library of Congress Subject Headings* (LCSH) to reflect the cultural differences–*RAMEAU* for France and Laval's *Répertoire de vedettes-matière* for French Canadians (see Bélaire, Bourdon, Mingam 2005 and Holley 2002). We also recently saw the differences for Spanish as used in Spain and Latin America/Caribbean when translating the IFLA *Statement of International Cataloguing Principles*.
    - different spellings (e.g., US/UK spellings like labor/labour, cataloging/cataloguing, etc.)

- different languages, which are especially problematic when expressing the:
  - complexity of subject concepts. This was clearly indicated in such projects as MACS and the Unified Medical Language where there are cultural differences in the world view of naming things and especially of naming abstract concepts.
  - word order conventions. Sometimes we use the direct order for transcription as found, inverted order for alphabetical lists/displays and collocation of subject terminology, and some word orders are also culturally significant, such as the order of surnames and forenames in Western versus Asian traditions.

There are thus lots of variations of names. I suggest we *not* consider international standard numbers at the name level. There may be specific applications where it is useful to number names for displays and other purposes, but let us put such ideas aside for now. If we cannot settle on the use of unique identifier numbers and the entities they are to represent, it will be difficult to have a system of numbers.

However, let us assume for now that we solve the issue of which entity we are trying to number and say it is for the entity represented by an authority record. Then what sort of number should we assign to that entity? In 1993, Bourdon felt that the ISADN should be an "intelligent" number; and she went on to propose how it would be constructed automatically by computer within a given national bibliographic agency to include codes for the nationality, the language, and the system's control number of the record (Bourdon, p. 81). Unfortunately this breaks down as not all names have a known "nationality," or they may have multiple nationalities and languages. She proposed the ISADN would be used in authority records and in bibliographic records with or without the authorized heading.

After Bourdon's proposal for an 'intelligent' number was discussed further within IFLA (as during the MLAR discussions), it seemed clear that any identifier number should *not* be intelligent as it would be too difficult to scale up to an international application.

One suggestion has been to just use a system-assigned control number. An example is a proposal to use the number for the "enhanced" authority record being created as part of the Virtual International Authority File proof of concept project with OCLC, the Library of Congress, and Die Deutsche Bibliothek. The problem here is that the number would not necessarily be persistent–as it would be subject to maintenance. If the enhanced authority record was found to be a duplicate (that is, two or more records were found to be for the same entity so that a merge of records would be necessary), a decision would need to be made about what to do with the two or more separate numbers assigned. Likewise, if an enhanced authority record was found to include more than one entity (a split would be needed to recognize separate entities mis-linked by the matching algorithms), another decision would be needed about what to do with the record number for the older undifferentiated record.

If numbers are to be used to clearly identify and distinguish one entity from others, the numbers must be carefully maintained and guarded; and duplicate detection must be in place. Unfortunately, we are not dealing with a perfectly ordered world of entities, as noted above, so that the system is bound to fail and break down but may be doable for a subset that perhaps matters most to the stakeholders that wish to make it work. That is probably as good as we can expect to get, if indeed we want to venture down this path at all.

For library purposes, it may be "good enough" to have the authority record control numbers serve to identify the entities and to have multiple control numbers linked when possible and needed. This might serve the purposes of bibliographic identification and linking. However, it is probably not "good enough" for rights management agencies that will want a different sort of entity (the person to be paid royalties) in any case. Who will identify which of the libraries' entities matches the "real" person to be paid? That also assumes (perhaps mistakenly) that there is a match to a real person from the library authority records. Some fictitious names relate to different individuals or institutions over time.

As Antelman states: "If libraries again adopt an identifier with an administrative data model that is closely bound to the current business needs of publisher and distributors, the inevitable operational pressure will mean that, just as with ISSN, interoperability will be advanced at the expense of basic principles of bibliographic control" (Antelman, p. 248-249). Library needs and publisher needs are not the same.

3. An Authority Data Cluster

Our third option suggests the use of a cluster of authority data that could uniquely identify an entity.

This approach is already taken with the Getty Union List of Artist Names and some search engines that use a clustered approach. For this third option, all of the possible name variations in all languages and scripts could be brought together or linked in various ways (union authority file, linked authority files, etc.).

This begs the question of why would we need a unique identifier. Instead of giving the user the one "right" name, a system could offer the names that potentially match the user's query and suggest pathways to help the user find the name they want. Systems like Endeca, a new breed of search engines offering guided searching, can start with a Google approach of a keyword (or several keywords) and bring back categorized clusters of potential matches that the user can follow depending on the user's needs. Any of the variant forms in bibliographic or authority records are there for retrieval (or data mining); and, with the authority record serving to cluster of variant names for entities, a system can display or utilize each of those forms of names as potential paths for further searching.

This third alternative is probably the most practical approach given today's technology. It avoids the issues of needing an international administrator while taking advantage of what's already being done by libraries worldwide. It does not require exactness or complete matching of all authority records for the same entity but hopefully shows the user the existence of close matches that might meet their needs.

It does require clearly labeling the variant names and related names and specifying the language/script/transliteration scheme so machines can display or link the desired form(s).

The Virtual International Authority File (VIAF) model would be one application of this third alternative. As currently envisioned, the participating institutions in the VIAF system would continue to create and maintain their own authority files as now and would make those records available to an international authority system where the central system "knows" about the various records, makes links among the records when it can, and can display the matches to a search query for the user to select a desired authority record. In the future, the data in such a system could also be used for customized displays of preferred names. Even though the very preliminary research findings of the current VIAF proof of concept model (project with the Library of Congress, Die Deutsche Bibliothek (DDB), and OCLC) show that about 10% of all Library of Congress name authority records would be linked (about 20% of the DDB records), this may be "good enough."

RECOMMENDATION

Since it looks promising that we could take advantage of Internet connections and systems to test VIAF models that would link existing authority records worldwide, across languages and scripts, we may find that for many applications we do not need a unique identifying number.

For those systems that found an ISADN necessary, they might use the automatically generated numbers or system record identifiers for the authority records. However, there would be the understanding that these numbers could change over time (which makes this less attractive). This may be "good enough" for now. Such numbers can be used for displays of "authorized" forms of names, titles, and subject terms.

As for displays to meet user needs for language, script, and transliteration scheme, our current systems need to be improved with more coding at the field level in MARC records and at the data element level for XML schema. The data itself needs better labeling that machines can understand when responding to users' language needs.

Certainly, explorations will continue with the rights management, publishing agencies, and others to see if an international registry can be accomplished. It is still very unclear how such a system would be sustained from a business sense.

I personally still feel that with the use of the newer search engines, like Endeca or similar guided or clustered searching, we can present the user (the cataloger, the reference librarian, the end user, etc.) with the names found in the authority systems, clustered or identified in such a way as to offer clear paths for selecting the name or authority record best suited to the user's needs without requiring unique identifying numbers.

For the cataloger, retrieving a small set of authority records that matched a search query would help in making decisions about using an existing record or in making a new authority record. System capabilities should be able to capture data from the source record found on the VIAF and make it usable in the local system environment–allowing the cataloger to edit it, if needed, and to add information that could be linked as a new local addition to the VIAF. Machines can make matches without ISADNs and can display alternative forms of names without numbers.

I have written for many years on my vision for the future of authority control, and I am still very optimistic that we will find better solutions than the current systems for meeting user needs (Tillett, 2000, 2001, 2004, 2005 as examples of the most recent).

Until there is a compelling business case and cost model for sustained management of an ISADN system, I highly recommend we continue the VIAF efforts and test various models to enable global sharing of authority data.

REFERENCES

Anderson, Dorothy. *Universal Bibliographic Control: a Long-Term Policy, a Plan for Action.*–München: K.G. Saur, 1974.

Antelman, Kristin. "Identifying the Serial Work as a Bibliographic Entity," *Library Resources & Technical Services*, v. 48, no. 4 (Oct. 2004), p. 238-255.

Beaudiquez, Marcelle and Françoise Bourdon. *Management and Use of Name Authority Files: Personal Names, Corporate Bodies and Uniform Titles, Evaluation and Prospects.*–München: K.G. Saur, 1991.

Bélaire, Jo-Anne, Françoise Bourdon & Michel Mingam (2005). "The Répertoire de vedettes-matière and RAMEAU: Two Indexing Languages in French: A Necessary Luxury?" World Library and Information Congress: 71st IFLA General Conference and Council, "Libraries–A voyage of discovery," August 14th-18th 2005, Oslo, Norway. *Conference Programme:* http://www.ifla.org/IV/ifla71/papers/145f-Belair_Bourdon_Mingam.pdf (accessed April 8, 2006).

Bourdon, Françoise. *International Cooperation in the Field of Authority Data: an Analytical Study with Recommendations.* München: K.G. Saur, 1993 (UBCIM Publications, New series, v. 11).

Delsey, Tom (1989). "Authority Control in an International Context" *Cataloging & Classification Quarterly*, v.9, no. 3, p. 13-28.

Delsey, Tom (2004). "Authority Records in a Networked Environment," *International Cataloguing and Bibliographic Control*, v. 33, no. 4 (Oct./Dec. 2004), p. 71-74.

Getty Union List of Artist Names Online. Available online at: http://www.getty.edu/research/conducting_research/vocabularies/ulan/.

Guidelines for Authority Records and References. 2nd ed. München: K.G. Saur, 2001 (UBCIM Publications, New series, v. 23).

Guidelines for Subject Authority and Reference Entries. München: K.G. Saur, 1993 (UBCIM Publications, New series, v. 12).

Holley, Robert P. (2002). "The Répertoire de Vedettes-matière de l'Université Laval Library, 1946-92: Francophone Subject Access in North America and Europe," *Library Resources & Technical Services*, v. 46, no. 4 (Oct. 2002), p. 138-149.

Lynch, Clifford. "Identifiers and Their Role in Networked Information Applications," *Association of Research Libraries Newsletter*, no. 194 (Oct. 12997) available at: www.arl.org/newsltr/194/Identifier.html.

MacEwan, Andrew. "Project InterParty: From Library Authority Files to E-Commerce," *Cataloging & Classification Quarterly*, v. 39, no. 1/2 (2004), p. 429-442.

"MLAR report." *Mandatory Data Elements for Internationally Shared Resource Authority Records*: Report of the IFLA UBCIM Working Group on Minimal Level Authority Records and ISADN, chair Barbara B. Tillett, Françoise Bourdon, Alan Danskin, Andrew MacEwan, Eeva Murtomaa, Mirna Willer. International Federation of Library Associations and Institutions, Universal Bibliographic Control and International MARC Programme, 1998. 95 p. Available online: http://ifla.org/VI/3/p1996-2/mlar.htm.

Tillett, Barbara B. "Authority Control at the International Level," *Library Resources & Technical Services*, v. 44, no. 3 (July 2000), p. 168-172.

Tillett, Barbara B. "Authority Control on the Web," *Proceedings of the Bicentennial Conference on Bibliographic Control for the New Millennium*: Confronting the Challenges of Networked Resources and the Web, Washington, D.C., Nov. 15-17, 2000, sponsored by the Library of Congress Cataloging Directorate, edited by Ann M. Sandberg-Fox. Washington, D.C.: Library of Congress, Cataloging Distribution Service, 2001, p. 207-220. Available online: http://www.lcweb.loc.gov/catdir/bibcontr/tillett.html.

Tillett, Barbara B. "Authority Control: State of the Art and New Perspectives," for the International Conference on Authority Control, Florence, Italy, Feb. 10-12, 2003, *Cataloging & Classification Quarterly*, v. 38, no. 3/4 (winter 2004), p. 23-41 and also issued in: *Authority Control in Organizing and Accessing Information: Definition and International Experience*, edited by Arlene G. Taylor and Barbara B. Tillett. New York: Haworth Press, 2004, p. 23-41.

Tillett, Barbara B. "Virtual International Authority File," *Symposium on 21st Century Cataloging and National Bibliography Policy*, Oct. 18, 2005, held at the National Library of Korea. Seoul, Korea: The National Library of Korea, 2005, p. 61-102. (Also in Korean, p.103-122.)

UNIMARC/Authorities. München: K.G. Saur, 1991 (UBCIM Publications, New series, v. 2).

doi:10.1300/J104v44n03_12

When You Come to a Fork in the Road, Pick It Up: A Case Study in Managing by Self-Responsibility

Lyn Condron

SUMMARY. Focused and limited management theories generally do not cover many important aspects of staff members' and teams' working lives. While most managers implement specific tools that they find helpful from one theory or another, an overriding philosophy that has proven consistently effective for our team is that of self-responsibility by the manager, by the individuals, and by the team as a group. Managers must not only encourage self-responsibility but also set expectations and empower both individuals and teams with the capability to take responsibility for and manage as much of their work life as possible. doi:10.1300/J104v44n03_13 *[Article copies available for a fee from The Haworth Document Delivery Service: 1-800-HAWORTH. E-mail address: <docdelivery@haworthpress.com> Website: <http://www.HaworthPress.com> © 2007 by The Haworth Press, Inc. All rights reserved.]*

KEYWORDS. Management, cataloging, supervision, self-responsibility, teams, staff

---

Lyn Condron, MLS, is Head of Cataloging/Web Manager, Tisch Library, Tufts University, Medford/Somerville, MA (E-mail: lyn.condron@tufts.edu).

[Haworth co-indexing entry note]: "When You Come to a Fork in the Road, Pick It Up: A Case Study in Managing by Self-Responsibility." Condron, Lyn. Co-published simultaneously in *Cataloging & Classification Quarterly* (The Haworth Information Press, an imprint of The Haworth Press, Inc.) Vol. 44, No. 3/4, 2007, pp. 363-375; and: *Cataloger, Editor, and Scholar: Essays in Honor of Ruth C. Carter* (ed: Robert P. Holley) The Haworth Information Press, an imprint of The Haworth Press, Inc., 2007, pp. 363-375. Single or multiple copies of this article are available for a fee from The Haworth Document Delivery Service [1-800-HAWORTH, 9:00 a.m. - 5:00 p.m. (EST). E-mail address: docdelivery@haworthpress.com].

Available online at http://ccq.haworthpress.com
© 2007 by The Haworth Press, Inc. All rights reserved.
doi:10.1300/J104v44n03_13

Theories X, Y, and Z; Total Quality Management; and Management by Walking Around are just a few of the many management models that institutions of all sorts have been implementing for years with the goal of providing the most effective management for their staffs. Much like diets, a "brand new" ism of one fashion or another seems to spawn every few years, assuring us that, if we only adhere to the philosophies and steps outlined in a specific management method, all our supervisory quandaries will be magically solved. But like the diet of the year, we see new management systems come and go, appearing to be great successes for some organizations and woeful failures for others. Consistent throughout the history of management practices seems to be that virtually all theories do have nuggets (often full clusters) of practical, useful, and sustainable philosophies and tools. Again though, as with diets, none have yet completely solved the inevitable issues involved with managing staff. And it seems that none ever will–there are simply far too many variables inherent for any one system to address fully the multitude of facets involved in managing human beings. As with virtually all areas of life, there is no magic pill for managing people. All managers adapt ideas that work best within the dynamics of their personalities and value systems as well as those of each of their staff members and teams as a whole. My experience has consistently shown me that the more responsibility you can give staff for managing as many aspects of their work lives as possible, the better the results–both their actual production and, just as importantly, their attitudes and satisfaction with their work lives.

BASIC MANAGEMENT PHILOSOPHY

From my personal experience and observations throughout my career, I have come to believe strongly that people inherently desire to do well and perform better when taking as much responsibility as possible for those areas of their lives that they can control. Indeed, many areas of our work environment are, for the most part, not within our immediate control. But for those that are, experience and observation have convinced me that staff members function much better if their managers clearly acknowledge that they expect them to take responsibility and, equally importantly, to fit within parameters of the library's, department's, and manager's policies and procedures.

It is important not only to encourage self-responsibility but to set and follow expectations that ensure it. This means developing a great trust–both of the manager for each individual team member and the team as a whole and from each team member and the group for the manager as well as their co-workers. As with all cultural shifts, we cannot expect such a philosophical change from the previous manager to happen overnight (in situations where a self-responsibility theory does present a radical change). This is particularly true when a new manager enters the workplace rather than a new staff member joining the team. Trust of any sort is seldom automatic, and certainly new staff members and managers have to establish this trust over time. The key factor I have found in helping to develop this is to work with staff on their own self-confidence levels.

For example, staff who have routinely informed their supervisors of all personal work schedule fluctuations (medical appointments, etc.), no matter how minute, are often uncomfortable at first with letting go of this type of close supervision experienced with a prior manager. It may at first appear that a supervisor's delegating such a responsibility as managing work schedules to the individual staff members is a relinquishment of sorts by the manager of his or her supervision responsibilities or even a privilege that support staff should not be given. However, this illustration shows the foundation of my philosophy of managing staff of any level: staff should have as much self-responsibility and empowerment to manage their own working lives as possible. Personal responsibility, in my opinion, is what delineates "professional" staff from "non-professional" staff rather than a specific staff level. An abbreviated description of my management philosophy might be to say it fits neatly in with the demarcation of macro-managing over micro-managing. However, I believe it goes much further than that–expecting (not merely espousing) self-responsibility from staff means that managers must invest time working with them in order to empower them to fulfill this goal; it is a resource investment that I have found is well worth it for the results achieved.

I do not purport that my management philosophy is anything new or revelatory at all. In fact, like most managers, I have come to most of my management practices by old-fashioned trial and error, based on my personal value system of self-responsibility as the fundamental building block on which to base work production and work environment policies and practices.

While I concede that the higher the level of staff, the more responsibility should be expected and given to staff for planning and managing their own actual work tasks, much of the responsibility I will be discussing refers to work environment elements that are related to all staff levels–for example, daily work production, schedules, etc.

The remainder of this article will outline some specific tools and actions we implement in the Cataloging Department at Tisch Library, Tufts University, following the philosophy of staff self-responsibility. (Semantics note: While we are officially called a department, I will frequently use the term "team" throughout this article as I prefer the concept and will use "staff" and "team members" interchangeably. "Manager/managing" and "supervisor/supervising" should also be interpreted as synonymous.)

BRIEF BACKGROUND

The cataloging team at Tisch is somewhat unorthodox in that we handle only high-level cataloging and non-book formats. The majority of DLC copy "cataloging" (i.e., essentially verification) is performed by students in the Acquisitions Department. Because we handle only high-level cataloging, all team members in the Cataloging Department are ranked at the highest level of library assistant at Tisch–Library Assistant III. There are only four team members (by design) plus myself.

PERFORMANCE MANAGEMENT

1. Cataloging Production

This article's purpose is not to discuss cataloging philosophies or practices, but I will include a brief word about our current bibliographic access theory. Several years ago, we transitioned from the old-school theory of "cataloging for the cataloger" to "cataloging for the user." That is, with greater advances in online catalogs (and consequent sophistication and expectations of users in their searching capabilities), we began focusing our resources (particularly staff time) on access points and critical information for the user rather than spending time attempting to ensure perfection in every record. For example, reviewing and editing cataloging punctuation such as the proverbial "space-colon-space" does little to actually assist the user (except perhaps in continuity of record format–not to be taken lightly but not critical in rather trivial punctuation points). It is far more important to focus on making bibliographic information accessible to the user, even if knowingly not reviewing and editing every single field to the point of seeming perfection, than to create unnecessary backlogs by spending valuable resources on areas very seldom noticed by the end user. (That being said, we do follow national cataloging standards and practices and perform monthly quality assurance on all aspects of our cataloging. And obviously typos in access points, for example, are critical to indexing and therefore to the user; we do indeed review and edit certain fields and subfields more than others. Additionally, web work [much of which is performed by some of our team] requires a much higher degree of attention to detail than cataloging, in part due to the vastly increased number of potential users as well as the rapid and global sharing of information.)

The Tisch Cataloging Department works very closely with the Acquisitions Department in managing workflow of book cataloging production. Our department catalogs only complex DLC (those having accompanying materials, etc.), member copy, and books for original cataloging; and the two departments have devised a system allowing us to easily maintain a predictable influx of books to be cataloged. Obviously, this number might change enough to affect the team's overall—and therefore, individuals'—production levels if there is a significant change in acquisitions or a special project. Some team member's general work responsibilities require a greater percentage of book cataloging than others but all participate in managing the production. Individuals' and the team's responsibilities exist in a symbiotic relationship and are highly dependent on each other to result in successful outcomes.

The team works together to determine an overall projected production number as far into the future as possible (based on data from Acquisitions). Though monthly consistency in numbers is ideal, it is not always feasible. Taking into account each member's portion of book cataloging, the team determines an average number of books to be cataloged by each member per month. Unless there is some rather drastic unexpected change in the acquisitions or the team dynamics (an unexpected medical leave or a project requiring a large percentage of a team member's time, for example), the group is expected to reach their numerical goals over any given two-to-three-month period. Within those parameters, they balance other work, known absences, etc. Staff consult with me by the beginning of the third month if they realize that something unforeseen will prevent them from reaching their cataloging goals (sooner, of course, if huge reductions are occurring).

Some changes greatly affecting cataloging production are predictable and can be planned for, with me, as the manager, consulting with other departments about temporary changes as necessary. Examples include a known maternity leave or a team member's planned immersion on a systems implementation project. We strive in all cases to maintain full production in current cataloging (i.e., new acquisitions–and have heretofore always reached this goal); and the team generally recommends that specific cataloging projects be relegated to the back burner during the staff reduction (e.g., gift books, older titles, etc.).

As the team's numbers are determined, each member then decides how to balance his or her work to achieve those goals. Some cataloging departments base production goals on an hourly, daily, or weekly basis; but we have found that a monthly goal works well for us. Beyond the other formats they each catalog and other usual work, staff include normal work life realities into their goals: meetings and work for other teams, regular projects, holidays, vacations (averaged for the year), usual sick leave, etc. The team re-evaluates their overall cataloging production goals as necessary and then redistributes their individual work goals.

2. Teams and Meetings

All staff members are responsible for keeping their online calendars up-to-date. This includes any regular work schedules that fall outside the usual 9:00-5:00 hours and any lunch times or breaks they wish to take at specific times (daily or occasionally). If, after accepting a scheduled meeting, a conflict arises, it is their responsibility to contact that meeting's leader. When the conflict involves a one-on-one meeting (e.g., our monthly check-in meetings), they should reschedule the meeting.

Each team member is responsible for being prepared and on time for all meetings, in addition to actively participating in all teams and doing appropriate assignments–without reminders. In our departmental team meetings, they are to know beforehand whose turn it is to take minutes and be prepared to do that. If team members know that they will miss a meeting (intradepartment or otherwise), it is their responsibility to contact the team leader, both before and after the meeting, to ensure that any missed assignments are fulfilled and, depending on the team, to contact another team member to take minutes if necessary.

Team members bring all pertinent project deadlines and discussions of other work to individual monthly check-in meetings. They manage their own internal deadlines; and, except for noting in my calendar when something is due to me, they determine if deadlines become too close together and discuss appropriate dates with me. Deadlines are expected to be met unless something unforeseen arises. When changes are needed, they should contact me well before the date to reschedule. If a deadline falls during a known absence, the work should be completed before that date. For vacations, conferences, etc., that will extend beyond three days, staff are responsible for making arrangements for any upcoming missed work. Cataloging production quantities include vacation time so that individuals' workflow and production include normal work that would be performed during days they will be gone. As necessary, they should contact other staff members (intradepartment and external) to indicate a temporary cessation of pertinent work. For example, a team member who performs regular quality assurance on member copy and original cataloging books will let other catalogers know to send their books on for processing rather than to follow the usual procedure. (Obviously unknown extended illnesses or other emergencies are not subject to this type of self-responsibility actions.)

3. Competency Management

Staff note in their own calendars to prepare documents related to annual goal setting and quarterly goal reviews as well as performance reviews. Their goals and suggestions for areas that need improvement related to performance reviews should include and follow competencies begun by the University for all employees a few years ago, focusing in part on what are commonly known as "soft skills" (communication, leadership, etc.). Regardless of a staff member's level, these competencies link in well with the philosophy of individuals taking responsibility for their own work. Staff members determine which specific competency/ies apply to each of their goals.

We set priorities for their goals together, and usually I prefer to put a stronger emphasis on soft skills goals rather than the more tangible production goals. Soft skills are inherently more difficult to identify, discuss, measure, and improve. Additionally, they are most often the areas of improvement needs that slip through the cracks, in part due to a manager's natural reluctance to deal with challenging situations involving personal behavior. Hence, I believe they generally need a higher priority. Assuming competent skills and knowledge of one's "task work," I usually work with each individual on at least one soft skill area in any given goal setting timeframe (often using Tufts' competencies as a guideline). This is where self-responsibility plays a huge role.

It can indeed be a challenge to set goals related to soft skills that neatly follow the SMART model (specific, measurable, attainable, relevant, timely) that Tufts and many other institutions use, particularly in the area of measuring success. However, I have found ways over the years to work with staff to stress the high degree of importance of specific soft skills; and together we have found creative ways both to improve and to measure success related to such skills. It is not enough just to have staff participate in workshops or read relevant materials, etc. Gaining new knowledge does not automatically turn into implementing new skills; there still must be visible and consistent improvement. An effective tool when setting goals of difficult soft skills is for the staff member and manager to envision what success will look like once this new skill has been mastered, when it has become a true behavioral change. "How will my work performance/environment be different when I have achieved this goal?" A manager must be willing and able to outline and enforce appropriate consequences if repeated attempts and varying methods have not resulted in improvement–certainly this is one of the least favorite aspects of any manager's responsibilities. As with all performance reviews discussing soft skills or work tasks, there should be plenty of ongoing communication throughout the year to prevent any surprises at the actual review time.

As a specific example of the challenge of improving soft skills, I will outline a case with a team member that has had excellent results. This team member has kindly (and bravely) encouraged me to include the illustration here, which is an admirable statement on her commitment to high work standards. (Note: To protect this person's privacy, I will not indicate whether this is a woman or a man or whether this is a current or past staff member. However, for ease of reading, I will resort to the reality that most library staff are women so that I will use the feminine gender and also the present tense in the conclusion of this section.)

This staff member's usual automatic reaction to situations that were uncomfortable for her was to verbally display her response in an often negative way–whether in individual or group meetings. Though further reflection on her part virtually always resulted in her understanding the reasons for her behavior and willingly complying with whatever she had originally found disturbing, the immediate reaction (particularly in group settings) was a continual source of inappropriate behavior (which she definitely understood and accepted). Compounding this was the fact that this truly was the only less-than-stellar work behavior she exhibited. Therefore, it was even more difficult for me to reconcile the necessity–not just desire–of resolving the issue rather than perpetually treating it as a "continue to improve" issue. All the various methods we tried were instilling more understanding of the problem, but not a change in behavior. We both kept falling back on the fact that many soft skills are so ingrained in one's own personality that retraining them can be extremely difficult. That, though, did not solve the problem.

It was not until I acknowledged to myself that I, as a manager, was not fulfilling one of my fundamental responsibilities: enabling staff to succeed. I was unwittingly resorting to the easier method (if still somewhat uncomfortable) of highlighting the issue on improvement needs in goals and performance reviews and of having discussions with her. But this clearly was not working; and we were both frustrated, feeling a bit like the proverbial definition of insanity–doing the same thing over and over again and expecting the outcome to change. I had finally to take ownership for not having taken the necessary, if quite difficult, steps as a manager to facilitate this change; I had to be willing to present and enforce consequences–even involving formal University progressive discipline procedures if necessary. Once I accepted this and we discussed it, I was able to relate to her the need to take whatever responsibility–and actions–necessary to successfully effect this change. It was only then that she was able to fully own the behavior and subsequently find and use resources empowering her to make this important shift in her work performance.

She has very successfully found ways to withhold her initial reactions until she can better review the situation and often uses creative methods to negotiate with others to get her needs met. We have both been extremely pleased with the outcomes; and, in the intervening time span since, there has been virtually no regression to her old, troubling behavior. Just as importantly, she's able to quickly recognize when she does start to slip into past habits (though she rapidly corrects them) and has even come to me with a smile to relate such an incident. Indeed, responsibility as a component of management is critical in both a staff member's and manager's behavior.

4. General Work Environment

As I referred to above, staff are expected to manage their own schedules, including absences. We have policies related to informing the team about planned and unplanned absences, submitting pertinent forms, making up missed time, when appropriate, and work that would have occurred during an absence. Reasonable flex time is encouraged whenever possible in my belief that individuals work better if they can adapt their work schedules to fit their needs. (Obviously the fact that we do not work directly with library users allows us more freedom in the area of scheduling.)

In addition to self-responsibility, I personally feel that individuals are entitled to privacy if they so choose. For example, it is not required that individuals discuss with me why they'll be at a medical appointment or even that the absence is medical in nature–just that they will be out and to follow the team's relevant procedures for absences. (Indeed many individuals do feel comfortable and desire the comradeship of discussing personal situations with their managers or co-workers.)

All staff are expected to be able to perform specific basic computer and Word tasks (documented in our policies) as well as to check e-mail regularly for important information. An issue often overlooked is that of the proverbial e-mail message lost in cyberspace (or otherwise not responded to). We have internal policies about timeframes before resending or seeing the recipient. I encourage and expect staff to determine solutions that are within their areas of responsibility whenever possible; often I receive e-mails including the solution (and any alternatives) and a statement indicating their intention to proceed unless they hear differently from me by a certain date.

5. *Quality Assurance*

We perform quality assurance on all aspects of our cataloging work, but what I am referring to here is quality assurance on management practices: feedback and testing assumptions. From time to time, I will ask team members to anonymously submit to me their thoughts on "the state of the union," which we then discuss as a group. The survey requests responses to phrases such as "Three things I really like about my work environment are . . . " and "Three things I would like to see change about my work environment are. . . ." I deliberately avoid the extremes of "best" and "worst" and caution them to focus on feasible changes rather than unrealistic ones. Additionally (at individual meetings), I ask them to consider statements such as "Specific things I do to help my job performance are . . . " and "Specific things I could do to help improve my job performance are. . . ."

More importantly for me, though, are corollary phrases I pose to them: "Specific things my manager does to help my job performance are . . . " and "Specific things my manager could do to help improve my job performance are. . . ." It is clear from these types of vulnerable questions that a deep level of trust must exist between not only the manager and each staff member but also between the manager and the team as a whole. I have been both pleased and surprised at some of the responses I have received. And, as with all survey questions, if you're not willing and able to make changes as discussed, it is of little value to reinforce what is lacking in your work environment. Some of the improvements are quite simple and were not previously in place due only to typical human miscommunication–or more correctly, lack of bringing attention of the issues to appropriate parties. While I believe that I have a good relationship with each of my team members and feel that they are generally confident that I will listen with an open mind to any ideas they might have (and implement changes as warranted), there will never be any way of getting around the fact that we are not peers. No matter how comfortable a staff member feels with his or her manager, there is always an emotional risk (however hopefully small) in making suggestions to the manager about the *manager's* work style.

In addition to the above overall checks and balances of how things are going, situations sometimes arise that cause us to rethink our current workflow and/or cataloging production. I have found that describing the problem to the team, along with the information we need, is usually the most effective way to glean solutions to these challenges. They are, after all, the ones who own knowledge of the details of "how things work" and are in the best position to suggest options for solutions. Additionally, it is an important part of empowering staff to have a say in their own work. (How often do we hear of staff feeling alienated by merely being told by the "higher-ups" about a new policy or procedure?) I usually ask for at least two solutions, outlining any pertinent parameters, with pros and cons of each. The team and I agree on a deadline; and they then manage assignments of gathering the data, setting team meetings related to the issue, writing the report, etc. I do ask them to try to rotate similar tasks when possible on different projects; many people don't enjoy always writing reports, for example. They have indicated to me that they are comfortable with this method and prefer this over my assigning specific tasks within a project.

We have documented lists of tasks performed by each individual: charts showing each name and what they perform and each task and who performs it. In addition to usual work related to cataloging, we include teamwork, ongoing projects, monitoring and updating the team on pertinent information from electronic bulletin boards (such as AUTOCAT), tools (such as Cataloger's Desktop), and systems related to our work (our local system, OCLC, etc.). Reviewing these tasks annually enables us to always be as prepared as possible for unforeseen contingencies (emergency medical leave, etc.). When a team member resigns, the team reviews his or her task assignments; and together we determine if changes should be made, sometimes including a mere desire to switch some tasks with that position. (Note: Because the team dynamics are so critical to making team responsibility work and in part because we are a small team, once I vet candidates, the team always meets as a group with the top two or three.)

Periodically and when new situations warrant, the team reviews their individual and team production to determine if changes are necessary. Specific examples needing a shift in priority include an upcoming systems migration, a team member's maternity leave (three months at Tufts), or an unexpected short-term increase in a specific format. This exercise proves to be a good test of our assumptions–as individual team members and manager and as a group. When more and particularly unexpected work is added, the general thought is that more staff should be added. We have found, though, that the team often determines as a group that this is not the best option. We carefully review what impact the new work will have and for how long, as well as the advantages and disadvantages of deliberately backlogging it or other work (i.e., spreading out the work over an extended time), adding temporary or permanent staff, or outsourcing specific projects.

CONCLUSION

I will summarize by concluding that while I feel very fortunate working with the current team and that indeed, the more cohesive a particular team is, the higher the likelihood of success of any work environment and performance, I also have become convinced that adults in any work place are entitled to and should be expected to own and manage as much of their work life as possible–self-responsibility. This requires working closely with each individual (particularly new staff members) to determine if there is a need for improvement in specific competencies (delineated by the University or not). And less experienced staff usually do need to be more closely monitored and assisted at first. But, overall, self-responsibility just plain works and results in a higher quality of performance and satisfaction in individual staff members, the team as a group, and the manager.

Finally, an explanation of the title. A couple of years ago, my then-4-year-old niece, Molly, and I were playing a game in which players were to complete a common phrase with more "difficult" ones for older players. I drew a card that read, "When you come to a fork in the road, what do you do?" Trying to engage Molly in the older players' turns, I posed the card's question to her. In that pure logic that only young children possess, she immediately responded, "Pick it up" (of course–what else would you do with it!). When the adults all laughed, she added, puzzled at our glee, "You don't want to run over it, do you?" Her literal yet profound reasoning meshes well with my fundamental management philosophy of getting back to basics–expecting, encouraging, and empowering staff to take responsibility for as many aspects of their working lives as possible.

doi:10.1300/J104v44n03_13

Index

AACR (Anglo-American Cataloging Rules)
　annotation in cataloging, 107-108
　bibliographic control research, 123
　comparison of cataloging and other information retrieval services, 308-309,312
　future of cataloging, 274
　and Italian cataloging rules, 137,143-146
　practical decisions in digital environment, 290
　review of CCQ, 42,47
　unique identity of entities, 347,354
　video cataloging, 235,240
AAUP (American Association of University Professors), 152,171
Abbreviations, Italian cataloging rules, 142
Abridgements of best-selling books, 187
Abstracting and indexing services compared to catalogs, 316-319
　authority control, 317-318
　contributors to creation, 317
　descriptions, detail in, 318
　discoverability function, 316
　function, 316
　granularity of description, 316
　in-house vs. outside standards, 317
　metadata, abstracts and indexes as, 319
　numerical identifiers, dependence on, 316
　permanency of, 318-319
　speed of publication, 317
　style manuals, use of, 318
　thesauri, use of, 318
　transiency of, 318-319
Accented characters and bibliographic control, 125
Access 2005, 284
Access vs. ownership decisions in cataloging, 274
Accompanying material for best-selling books, 187
Accuracy in cataloging. *See* Quality control
ACRL (Association of College and Research Libraries)
　audiences for papers, 259
　conferences, 259-269
　　and ALCTS, 259-265
　　attendance, 266
　　audiences for papers, 259-260
　　bibliography of ACRL national conferences, 267-268
　　niche topics, 266
　　perceptions based on lack of technical services papers, 266
　　reasons for lack of cataloging and technical services papers, 265-266
　　stereotypes about catalogers, 267
　holistic view of academic librarians due to of Internet growth, 260
　special format catalogers, ACRL Delaware Valley Chapter, 224
　stereotypes about catalogers, 267
　tenure issues for technical services librarians, 152,155,171,174

underrepresentation of topics of
interest to technical services
librarians, 259-269
Adaptations of best-selling books, 187
Adjutant General's Office, Ruth Carter
at, 8
ADONIS (Article Delivery Over
Network Information
Systems), 120-121
Advertisements for cataloger positions,
251
AGRICOLA, 340
AIB (Associazione italiana
biblioteche), 142-146
AIDS Treatment Thesaurus, 337
ALCTS (Association for Library
Collections and Technical
Services)
and ACRL national conferences,
259-265
Ruth's work with, 35
special format catalogers, 227,230
Allison, D. A., 239
Almanacs, 56
Alumna distinguished, Graduate
School of Library and
Information Science,
University of Illinois at
Urbana-Champaign, 15
Amazon.com
blurring of catalogs and web
searches, illustration, 291
comparison of cataloging and other
information retrieval
services, 308,320,322
structure and function in
information systems, 291
American Almanacs, 56
American Association of University
Professors, 152,171
American Association of University
Professors (AAUP), 152,171
American Film Institute, 316
American National Standards Institute,
ANSI/NISO Z39.19, 335

American Sunday School Union, 73
Analytical skills and analytical work,
24,31
Ruth's Perry Mason syndrome, 9
Anderson, D., 349
Anglo-American
cataloging rules. *See* AACR
see also British
Annotated Guide to Current National
Bibliographies, 353
Annotations in cataloging, 95-111
1883 Library Association
cataloging rules, 97
ambiguity of titles, 96
class-lists, 100
closed vs. open access systems, 96
cooperation among catalogers, 100
critical vs. descriptive evaluation,
98-99
decline in printed catalogues after
WWI, 104
delegation of work, 102-103
dictionary catalogues, 97-98,101
evaluing content, 97-98
inducements to read, annotations as,
101,105
quality and standards in cataloging
practice, 107
reading
inducing people to read what
they would not have thought
of reading, 101,105
reader requirements, 100
recommendations, annotations as,
101,105
reference books, 99
revision of, 105
scholarly libraries, 101
standardization, 107
Subject Access Project, adding
indexes and tables of contents
to catalog records, 108
systematic exposition of annotation
requirements, 96
time and expense considerations,
100, 106

Index

ANSI/NISO Z39.19, 335
ANSI/NISO Z39.50, 122,126-127
Antarctica Systems, 298
Antelman, K., 354-355
Antipopes, Italian cataloging tradition, 135
Aquatic Sciences and Fisheries Abstracts (ASFA) thesaurus, 336
Archives and archival organization
   contributions and participation by Ruth. *See* Carter, Ruth C.
   images of archival resources, placing online, 26
   unique identifiers of information, 345,354
ARL (Association of Research Libraries)
   and ACRL national conferences, 260,263
   developments in 1960s and 1970s, 273
   knowledge structures and the Internet, 338,340
   special format catalogers, 223
   technical services librarians and tenure issues, 153,159
Army. *See* United States Army
Article Delivery Over Network Information Systems (ADONIS), 120-121
ASFA (Aquatic Sciences and Fisheries Abstracts) thesaurus, 336
Association for Library Collections and Technical Services. *See* ALCTS
Association of American Colleges, 152
Association of College and Research Libraries. *See* ACRL
Associazione italiana biblioteche (AIB), 142-146
Assumptions testing and self-responsibility, 374
Athens University of Economics and Business, 116
Audiences
   ACRL conference papers, 259-260
   see also Users
Audiovisual catalogers
   OLAC, 225,227,230
   review of CCQ, 51
   see also Video cataloging
Aulik, J. L., 224
Authority control
   abstracting and indexing services compared to catalogs, 317-318
   CCQ review, 51
   descriptive bibliographies compared to catalogs, 311-312
   entity identification. *See* Unique identifiers of entities
   enumerative bibliographies compared to catalogs, 317-318
   Functional Requirements for Bibliographic Records. *See* FRBR
   GARE (Guidelines for Authority and Reference Entries), 352
   GARR (Guidelines for Authority Records and References), 141,352
   GSARE (Guidelines for Subject Authority and Reference Entries), 352
   MLAR (Minimal Level Authority Record), 349-351,356
   numbers as unique identifiers. *See* Unique identifiers of entities
   principia bibliographica, balancing principles, practice, and pragmatics in digital environments, 281-305
   RDA (Resource Description and Access), 286,296,308,347
   union lists and union catalogs, 311
   University of Bradford research projects on bibliographic control, 123,127-128
   VIAF, 348,356,358-359
   Wiki model, 283-290

see also Bibliographic control; Catalog librarians and cataloging
Authority data clusters, 348,357-358
Authors
 books of Monroe County, Indiana, 88-89
 CCQ (Cataloging & Classification Quarterly), 40-42
AUTOCAT, 128,159,162,169,225
AUTOMATCH, 123-124
Awards bestowed on Ruth
 Bowker/Ulrich Award, 11,16
 Distinguished Alumna Award, Graduate School of Library and Information Science, University of Illinois at Urbana-Champaign, 15
Ayres, F. H., 113

Bachelor of Science degree, 8
Baker, E. A., 100
Baking, 37
Balancing quantity (bottom line) and quality (user needs), 234-235,276,278
Balancing search technology and bibliographic control, 282-283
Ballard, C. G., 58
Battersea, 106
Beale, D. D., 115
Beall, J., 198
Beaudiquez, M., 347
Bélaire, J., 355
Ben Franklin, 61
Benemann, W. E., 250
Best-selling books, instantiations, 179-195
 accompanying material relationship, 187
 age of progenitor work, 186
 American marketplace, 183
 "bibliographic families," 181
 canonicity, 189
 characteristics of, 184
 codification of bibliographic records, 183
 cookbooks, 184
 copyright issues, 192
 cowboy fiction, 184
 cultural issues
  books as mirror of culture, 184-185
  impact of deviations and mutations, 189-191
  marketplace, 191
 depression, stories of, 184
 derivation patterns, 185
 digital environment, effect of multiple instantiations in, 191
 evolution of instantiation networks, 184-185,190
 fiction, sample of 20th-century best-sellers, 185,194-195
 films, screenplays, and television adaptations, 190-191
 FRBR, "work" entity in, 180
 information retrieval and linkage of relationships among works, 179,181
 "instantiation networks," 181,184-185,190
 instantiations, defined, 180
 Internet searches, 191
 Kinsey report, 184
 lunchboxes and similar paraphernalia, 190-191
 maps as accompanying material, 187
 methodology for determining patterns of derivation and mutation, 183
 nonfiction, sample of 20th-century best-sellers, 185,194-195
 online searching, 191
 paraphernalia related to, 190
 persistence, 189

Index

pockets containing accompanying material, 187
predecessor relationship, 187
Publisher's Weekly's list, 183
romantic fiction, 184
rural life, tales of, 184
sample of 20th-century best-sellers, 194-195
science fiction, 184
searching online for, 191
sequels, 184
serials, 184
simultaneous editions, 189
size of instantiation networks, 185-186
sound recordings as accompanying material, 187
suffrage topics, 184
taxonomical categories describing evolution, 186-187,190
urban life, tales of, 184
war, stories of, 184
Watergate affair, 184
web-searching, 191
women's issues, 184
the "works" phenomenon and, 179-195
World Wide Web instantiations, 183
Bethnal Green, 105-106
Biagi, G., 133,136
Bianchini, C., 131
BIBCO, 275,277
Bibles, history of books in Monroe County, Indiana, 62-63,67,73-74
Bibliographic control
annotations, 95-111
bibliometrics, 290-298
catalog librarians and cataloging. See Bibliographic control
cataloging compared to descriptive bibliography, abstracting and indexing services, and metadata, 307-327
entity identification. See Unique identifiers of entities
Functional Requirements for Bibliographic Records. See FRBR
ISBD, 138,141,143,237,241,297
RDA (Resource Description and Access), 286,296,308,347
recasting for digital environment, 281-305
Ruth's work, 9,28-31
self-responsibility, bibliographic access theory at Tisch Library, 366
showcasing technical services librarians' portfolio, 172
VIAF, 348,356,358-359
see also Authority control; Catalog librarians and cataloging; University of Bradford research projects on bibliographic control
"Bibliographic families," best-selling book instantiations, 181
Bibliographic work by Ruth, 9,11,20
Bibliometrics, flexibility of bibliographic data elements, 290-298
"Big Brother" concerns, unique identifiers of entities, 355
Bio-bibliographies and Italian cataloging rules, 133
Biographical and Genealogical Master Index, 296
Bishopsgate Institute, 101
BL (British Library), 119,122
Bibliographic Services Division, 118
BLCMP, 117,119,121
Document Supply Centre, 120
early 20th-century catalog, 95-111
Name Authority File, 123
Research and Development Department, 116

University of Bradford research projects on bibliographic control, 118-119
Blackstone's Commentary in early Monroe County, Indiana, book collections, 59-60
Blackwell Publishing, 108
Blairs Lectures, in early Monroe County, Indiana, book collections, 59
Blanchard, C., 58,61,63,72-73
Bland, R., 234,237
BLCMP, 117,119,121
Bloomington, Indiana, newspapers, 61
BNB (British National Bibliography), 95,106-107,115-118,122
BNI (Italian National Bibliography), 137-138
Boehr, D. L., 234
Bolin, M. K., 235
Bolivian pamphlet collection, 30
Bonazzi, G., 133-134
Books
    Ruth as enjoying books and libraries more than computers, 21
    history of books in Monroe County, Indiana. *See* Monroe County, Indiana, history of books in
    Nietz collection of early American school textbooks, 30
BOPAC (Bradford OPAC), 113,126-128
Boston Globe, 296
Botanics, 61
Bothmann, R. L., 221
Bourdon, F., 344,346-347,351,355-356
Bowers, F., 312
Bowker/Ulrich Award, 11,16
Bowman, J. H., 95
Boydston, J. M. K., 223
Bradford University, 113,118,120
    Bradford OPAC (BOPAC), 113,126,126-128
Bredderman, P., 250
Brisson, R., 35

British
    BNB (British National Bibliography), 95,106-107,115,115-118,122
    British Library. *See* BL
    British Museum, 133
    BSI (British Standards Institution) and BSI standards, 335-336
    cataloging rules. *See* AACR (Anglo-American Cataloging Rules)
    Voyager Catalogue, 299
Broadening searches, descriptive bibliographies compared to catalogs, 312
Bromley, 100
Brown, J. D., 96-98,100,105
Browsability and browse functionality
    interview with Ruth, 26-27
    knowledge structures online, 330,332-333,336,338-339
    metalogs, browsable keyword indexes, 286
    search technology, 286,290
    structure and function in information systems, 290-293
Browsability of collections, 26-27
Brunet, J. C. (French bibliographer), 133
Bryant, P., 123
BSI (British Standards Institution) and BSI standards, 335-336
Budget and staffing constraints in cataloging, 234-235,238,277, 374
Buley, R. C., 56,61-62
Business case
    balancing quantity (bottom line) and quality (user needs), 234-235,276,278
    balancing search technology and bibliographic control, 282-283
    labor intensive practice of cataloging, 249,272-274,276

staffing constraints, 234-235,238, 277,374
and unique identifiers of entities, 344,350,354-355
Butler, P., 309
Buttlar, L., 224

Campbell, D., 239,320
Canadian AIDS Treatment Information Exchange (CATIE) HIV/AIDS Treatment Thesaurus, 337
Carnegie classification of institutions, 153
Carnegie Mellon University, 27
Carnegie Museum of Natural History, 11,20
Carter, Ruth C.
  acquisition of research materials for future historians, 27-28
  Adjutant General's Office, work in, 8
  American Memory Project, 26
  analytical skills and analytical work, 8
  archives and archival organization, 15
    archival finding aids, 26
    bridging of history and libraries, 25
    cataloging, similarities and differences, 26-27
    interview with Ruth, 20-21,23, 25-27
  awards
    Bowker/Ulrich Award, 11,16
    Distinguished Alumna Award, Graduate School of Library and Information Science, University of Illinois at Urbana-Champaign, 15
  Bolivian pamphlet collection, 30
  cataloging, work in, 9-10
    archival organization, similarities and differences, 26-27
    card catalogs vs. online catalogs, 27
    cooperative cataloging plans and programs, 29-31
    devaluing and deprofessionalizing, 30-31
    improving user's ability to connect with desired information, 27
    indexing terms reflecting changes in cataloging profession and world at large, 50
    interview with Ruth, 21,23,26-27
    poetry on Ruth's cataloging service, 53
    resource type, importance as basic qualifier, 28-29
    retrospective conversion of print catalogs to online, 12
    series cataloging, 10
    term usage reflecting changes in profession and world, 50
    University of Pittsburgh, head of cataloging, 29-30
  cats in Ruth's life, 37
  Charleston, life in, 37-38
  Cincinnati, life in, 8-9,20
  Civil Service exam, 8
  Clifton Avenue, 20
  CONSER policy committee, 11
  consultations, 14-15
  cooperation, Ruth's example, 280
  Cuba experience, 36
  Curator of Manuscripts, Cincinnati Historical Society, 8
  Curator of Manuscripts and Reference Assistant, Ohio Historical and Philosophical Society, 20
  dissertation, 23,27,38

Distinguished Alumna Award,
  Graduate School of Library
  and Information Science,
  University of Illinois at
  Urbana-Champaign, 15
editing journals
  interview with Ruth, 25
editorship at CCQ, 39-52
  authors, relationship with, 34
  changes in CCQ, 32-33,39-52
  choices, 13
  choices for, 12
  contemporary content, 46
  controversial articles, 34
  editorials, 34
  examination of contributors,
    articles, and changes,
    13,39-52
  history of, 39-52
  internationalization, 32,34,40-42
  interview with Ruth, 32-35
  online presence, 33
  poetry about, 54
  practical content, 46
  subject indexing, 46-50
  success of, 12-13
  term usage reflecting changes in
    profession and world, 50
  theme issues, 40-41,43-45
  theoretical content, 46
education
  Bachelor of Science degree, 8,20
  education degree, 20
  history degrees, 8,20,25
  library science degree, 20
  Master of Arts degree, 8
  PhD, 25
  primary and secondary, 8
elections, political junkie, 36
Encoded Archival Description, 26
flexibility, Ruth's example, 280
fun factor in Ruth's work, 16
geography teacher, 8
Golden Era of Cataloging, 272
historians of the future, providing
  access to, 27-28

historical studies and work in history
  Cincinnati Historical Society, 8
  interview with Ruth, 20,22
  Ph.D. in History, University of
    Pittsburgh, 15
  retirement plans, 38
  teaching positions, 8
hobbies, 37
honors, 15
IFLA, 11
images of archival resources, 26
innovation, Ruth's example, 279
interlibrary loans, 26
Internet resources and physical
    library materials, differences
    in bibliographic control, 28-29
interview, 19-37
JOIC, 54
library automation, 10-11
  interview with Ruth, 21,23,30
library school and library science
  degree, 9,20
mentorships, 14
  Ruth's mentors, 22-24
metadata, 31
metadiscussions and metadebates,
  54
monograph publications, 12-13,
  15-16
mysteries (literary genre), 8
newspaper preservation, 11
Nietz collection of early American
  school textbooks, 30
OCLC, 10-11,23,29-30
Ohio Historical and Philosophical
  Society, 20
OPAC, music under Ruth's baton,
  53
Parkland Junior College, 20,23
PaULS (Pennsylvania Union List of
  Serials), 30
Pennsylvania Newspaper Project, 11
Pentagon work. See United States
  Army, below in this heading
perseverance, Ruth's example, 280

pets, 37
PhD in history, 15,25
    dissertation, 23,27,38
    interview with Ruth, 21-23
photographs of archival resources, 26
Pittsburgh, life in, 11-12
political junkie, 36
problem-solving skills, 8,31
professional organizations, 14-15
    interview with Ruth regarding, 35-36
public school education, 8
publishing experience, 25
    CCQ. *See* Editorship at CCQ, above in this heading
    monograph publications, 12-13,15-16
reading, 21
    mysteries (literary genre), 8
    retirement plans, 37
reference assistant, Cincinnati Historical Society, 8
reference librarianship, 9
resource type, importance as basic qualifier, 28-29
retirement, 37-38
search engine design, 31
search technology
    cataloging and archival organization, similarities and differences, 27
    devaluing and deprofessionalizing cataloging, 30-31
    historians' full-text search needs, 28
serials librarianship
    Bowker/Ulrich Award, 11,16
    interview with Ruth, 21,29
    serials control activities, 11
    series cataloging, 10
South Carolina retirement, 37-38
Soviet Union experience, 36
systems analyst work
    early days, 8-9
    interview with Ruth, 20
    University of Pittsburgh, 11,29-30
systems and technology
    change in specialization, 10
    early days, 8-9
    interview with Ruth, 21-22,24
    Parkland College, 10
    poetry on Ruth's service, 53
    University of Pittsburgh Library, head of technical services at, 29-30
teaching positions
    Greenhills High School, 8
    interview with Ruth, 20
    librarians as teachers, 8
technology and electronic solutions
    archival access, 26-27
    bibliographic control differences between online resources and physical materials, 28-29
    catalogers as necessary link between information and users, 31
    CCQ, reflection of changes in cataloging profession and world at large, 50
    improving user's ability to connect with desired information, 27
    in-depth coverage in CCQ, 33
    retrospective conversion of print catalogs to online, 12
travels, 36
union list work, 11-13,29-30
United States Army
    Adjutant General's Office, 8
    interview with Ruth, 20
    Office of Chief of Staff, 9
University of Pittsburgh
    cataloging, head of, 29-30
    PhD in history, 15,21-23
    systems analyst, 11
U.S. Newspaper Program, 11

user focus, 14,21,27
    catalogers as necessary link between information and users, 31
    CCQ, 32-33
    improving user's ability to connect with desired information, 27
    Internet resources and physical library materials, differences in bibliographic control, 29
Vietnam War, 20
zoology classes, 9
Catalog librarians and cataloging
    AACR. *See* AACR (Anglo-American Cataloging Rules)
    abstracting compared to cataloging. *See* Abstracting and indexing services compared to catalogs
    access vs. ownership decisions, 274
    and ACRL. *See* ACRL
    annotations. *See* Annotations in cataloging
    and ARL. *See* ARL
    balancing quantity (bottom line) and quality (user needs), 234-235,276,278
    balancing search technology and bibliographic control, 282-283
    bibliographic control. *See* Bibliographic control
    blurring of catalogs and web searches, illustrations, 291-293
    browsing as catalog emphasis, 290
    budget and staffing constraints, 234-235,238,277,374
    cataloghi di biblioteche e indici bibliografici, 133,140
    CataWiki, 284
    CCQ. *See* CCQ
    challenges in cataloging, 271-279
    compared to other information access services, 307-327
    compensation for cataloging records, 277,279
    contributions and participation by Ruth. *See* Carter, Ruth C.
    cooperative activities, 273-274
    dates for web pages, 293-294
    decline in cataloging and classification course work, 224-225
    definitions of terms, 308-309
    descriptive bibliographies. *See* Descriptive bibliographies compared to catalogs
    education and training of catalogers as essential to library viability, 222-223
    electronic solutions, 273
    enriched catalog entries, example of, 287-289
    entity identification. *See* Unique identifiers of entities
    enumerative bibliographies. *See* Enumerative bibliographies compared to catalogs
    errors. *See* Errors and errata
    explicit links and differentiations, 181
    exposure of work to public, 273
    fair compensation for cataloging records, 277,279
    film. *See* Video cataloging
    flexibility of bibliographic data elements, 290-298
    focused browsing of library bookstacks, 275
    Functional Requirements for Bibliographic Records. *See* FRBR
    future of, 128,223-224,271-279
    Google's recognition of value, 304
    identification of entities. *See* Unique identifiers of entities
    image. *See* Perceptions and stereotypes, below under this heading
    IME ICC, 141,144

indexing compared to cataloging.
    See Abstracting and indexing
    services compared to catalogs
Italian rules. *See* Italian cataloging
    rules and international
    tradition
keyword searching, effect of, 280
labor intensive practice, 249,
    272-274,276
lagging terminology because of
    publication process, 290
library school coursework and
    offerings, 223,277
managing staff. *See*
    Self-responsibility
mentorships, 224,230
metadata
    cataloging as type of metadata,
        319
    human-created metadata
        compared to cataloging. *See*
        Metadata
    "metalogs," 283-290
mistakes. *See* Errors and errata
national databases, contributions to,
    273
nonalphabetical clustering, 180-181
non-print catalogers. *See* Special
    formats catalogers
OLAC, 225,227,230
OPAC. *See* OPAC
open catalogs and directories,
    283-284,332
outsourcing, 275, 277-278
    errors. *See* Error rates in
        monograph copy cataloging
        bibliographic records before
        and after outsourcing at
        University of Saskatchewan
        library
perceptions and stereotypes,
    225,267,273-275,324
    see also Value perception, below
        under this heading

permanency of catalogs compared
    to other information retrieval
    services, 313,318-319
Pléiade, catalog entry vs. Wikipedia
    entry, 285-290
public exposure of work, 273
punctuation concerns, 237,241,
    278-279,313,366
quality. *See* Quality and standards
    in cataloging practice
quo vadis (where are you going?),
    cataloging, 271-279
ratio of catalogers to resources, 223
RDA (Resource Description and
    Access), 286,296,308,347
recasting for digital environment,
    281-305
reluctance to go beyond traditional,
    286
responsibility. *See* Self-responsibility
retirement of catalogers, 223-224,
    230,274,276
RICA (regole italiane di
    catalogazione per autori). *See*
    Italian cataloging rules and
    international tradition
search engines
    blurring of catalogs and web
        searches, illustrations,
        291-293
    effect of, 275
    see also Search technology
self-responsibility. *See*
    Self-responsibility
special formats. *See* Special formats
    catalogers
standards. *See* Quality and
    standards in cataloging
    practice
stereotypes. *See* Perceptions and
    stereotypes, above under this
    heading
structure and function. *See*
    Structure and function in
    information systems

technology-driven, 280
tensions between local and national/international needs, 309
Tisch Library at Tufts University, management style. *See* Self-responsibility
trends and challenges in cataloging, 271-279
undated web pages, 293-294
union catalogs. *See* Union lists and catalogs
users and catalogs, 280,309,324
    balancing quantity (bottom line) and quality (user needs), 234-235,276,278
    generation of citations from bibliographic records, 286
value and value perception, 273-275,324
    adding value to catalog entries, 286
    Google recognition of value, 304
    quality. *See* Quality and standards in cataloging practice
vendors providing catalog entries, 234-235,242,273,277
videos. *See* Video cataloging
vocabulary control. *See* Vocabulary control
Voyager Catalogue, 299
where are you going? (quo vadis), cataloging, 271-279
Wiki model. *See* Wiki model of cataloging
works, clustering, 180
workshops by professional organizations, 277
see also Carter, Ruth C.
Catalogazione verso il futuro, 141
Cataloghi di biblioteche e indici bibliografici, 133,140
Cataloging & Classification Quarterly. *See* CCQ

CataWiki, 284
see also Wiki model of cataloging
Categorized clusters of potential matches, unique identifiers and, 358
CATIE (Canadian AIDS Treatment Information Exchange) HIV/AIDS Treatment Thesaurus, 337
Cats in Ruth's future, 37
CCQ (Cataloging & Classification Quarterly), 13,39-52
    AACR, 42,47
    audiovisual materials, 51
    authority control, 51
    authors, 40-42
    CDS/ISIS, 51
    changes in CCQ, 39-52
    contemporary content, 46
    Cook, C. D., 39-40
    data mining, 51
    Edgar, N. L., 42
    editorship of Ruth. *See* Carter, Ruth C.
    examination of contributors, articles, and changes, 39-52
    Gibbs, G. E., 39
    H. W. Wilson, 46,48
    historical analysis of content, 39-52
    historical content, 46
    Holzberlein, D., 42
    indexing
        content related to, 51
        subject indexing of CCQ articles, 46-50
        terms reflecting changes in cataloging profession and world at large, 50
    internationalization, 40-42
    Kascus, M., 40,46
    Library Literature & Information Science Full Text, 46
    Library of Congress Subject Headings, 47-48
    metadata, 51

practical content, 46
review of, 39-52
semantic web, 51
term usage reflecting changes in profession and world, 50
theme issues, 40-41,43-45
theoretical content, 46
thesauri, 51
union catalogs, 42
XML, 51
CDS/ISIS (computer language), changes in library profession, 51
Chait, R. P., 155
Chambers, S., 233
Chaplin, A, 136
Chapman, A., 236,241,243
Charleston, Ruth's life in, 37-38
Chelmsford, 106
Chicago Manual of Style, 318
Childers, S., 239
Chilovi, D., 135
Chisman, J., 239
Chronicle Careers, 251
Cincinnati, Ruth's life in, 8-9,20
Cincinnati Historical Society, 20,27
Circulation, and flexibility of bibliographic data elements, 290-298
"Circumsumption," vocabulary control, 303
Citation practice
  hampered by online publishing practices, 294
  users, generation of citations from bibliographic records, 286
Classical books in early Monroe County, Indiana, 57
Classification of Library Personnel, ALA Committee, 152
Class-lists and catalog annotations, 100
"Cleaning of database records" and bibliographic control research, 117,121-122
Clergymen's books in early Monroe County, Indiana, 63

Clients
  knowledge structures online, client-oriented gateways and portals, 338
  see also Users
Clifton Avenue, Ruth's residence, 20
Cluster. See Data clusters
CMDS (Collection Management and Development Section), 262
Cochrane, P. A., 108,338
CODES (Collection Development and Evaluation Section), 262
Cohen, B., 35
Collection Development and Evaluation Section (CODES), 262
Collection Management and Development Section (CMDS), 262
College libraries. See ACRL (Association of College and Research Libraries) conferences
Collison, R. L. W., 105
Colonial Twins of Virginia, 21
Commentaries on best-selling books, 187
Commissione Cibrario, 132-133
Commissione RICA, 140-146
Common vs. uncommon words (word frequency). See Typographical errors, impact on information retrieval
Compensation for cataloging records, 277,279
Competency management and self-responsibility, 369-370
Completeness of catalog records, case study, 233-257
Complexity
  Italian cataloging rules and international tradition, 141
  University of Bradford research projects on bibliographic control, 117-118,120

Computer systems. *See* Systems and technology
Concatenations of evolving intellectual entities instantiations, 180
Concordances and best-selling books, 187
Condensations and best-selling books, 187
CONSER (Cooperative Online Serials), 11,29-30,171-172,275
Control numbers. *See* Unique identifiers of entities
Controlled vocabularies. *See* Vocabulary control
Cook, C. D., 39-40
Cookbooks as best-selling books, 184
Cook's Thesaurus, 334
Cooperative Online Serials (CONSER), 11,29-30,171-172,275
Copyright issues and best-selling books, 192
Corporate bodies, Italian cataloging rules, 135,138-139,142
Cost considerations
  annotations in cataloging, 100,106
  balancing quantity (bottom line) and quality (user needs), 234-235,276,278
  balancing search technology and bibliographic control, 282-283
  labor intensive practice of cataloging, 249,272-274,276
  staffing constraints, 234-235,238, 277,374
  unique identifiers of entities, 344,350-351,353-355
  University of Bradford research projects on bibliographic control, cost of merging databases, 119
Cowboy fiction as best-selling books, 184

Critical essays, Italian cataloging rules, 135
Critical vs. descriptive evaluation, annotations in cataloging, 98-99
Criticisms of best-selling books, 187
Cross-reference structures, University of Bradford research projects on bibliographic control, 128
Croydon, 97, 105
Croydon-Savage, 105
CSA Illumina, 339-340
Culbertson, R., 39
Culture and cultural concerns
  best-selling books. *See* Best-selling books, instantiations
  cataloging departments, cultural shifts by management and staff. *See* Self-responsibility
  documentations of cultural record, 180,184-185,313,323
  entity identification, cultural differences within same language, 355
  Italian cataloging rules and international tradition, 136
Customization of displayed forms of names and terms, 346
Cutter, C. A., 133,237,272

Data clusters
  authority data clusters, 348,357-358
  entity identification. *See* Unique identifiers of entities
  nonalphabetical clustering, 180-181
  works, clustering, 180
Data mining, changes in library profession, 51
Data processing. *See* Systems and technology
Dates, typos in, 200
De Pinedo, I., 144
Deadlines and schedules
  meetings, 368

production schedules, 367
review and adjustment, 368-369
DELOS/NSF Working Group on Actors and Roles, 348
Delsey, T., 351-353
Dent, R., 96-97
DePew, J. N., 153
Depression, best-selling stories, 184
Derivation patterns. *See* Best-selling books
"Derivative bibliographic relationships," 180
Descriptive bibliographies compared to catalogs, 309-315
  array of evidence, 312
  authority control, 311-312
  broadening and narrowing searches, 312
  contributors to creation, 310-311
  detail in description, amount of, 312
  differences among multiple editions or expressions, 313
  evaluation, 314
  functional differences, 314-315
  inconsistencies, 311
  local vs. national/international needs, 309
  object of description as essential difference, 310
  permanence of documentation, 313
  predictability, 311
  quality and standards in cataloging practice, 311
  scope differences, 310
  selection process, 314
  standardization, 311
  uniformity and predictability, 310-311
  union catalogs, 311
  variations in extant copies, identification, 310
Design of online knowledge structures, user behavior and, 335
Dewey standard, Italian cataloging rules and, 143-144

Dictionaries
  dictionary catalogs, 97-98,101
  Dictionary of Phrase and Fable, 287
  as metadata, 319
  Monroe County, Indiana, history of books in, 73-75
Digital environments. *See* Electronic environments
Diller, K., 239
Directories as online knowledge structures, 332-333
  open catalogs and directories, 283-284,332
Discoverability function
  comparison of cataloging and other information retrieval services, 316
  see also Search technology
Discussion-group contributions in support of
  tenure for technical services librarians, 171
Distinguished Alumna Award, Graduate School of Library and Information Science, University of Illinois at Urbana-Champaign, 15
DLC copy "cataloging" and self-responsibility, 366
DOCMATCH projects, 118,120-121
Document Supply Centre (DSC), 123
Documentations of cultural record, 180,184-185,313,323
Dominican University, 224
Doubleday, W. E., 100
Doyle, L., 338
DSC (Document Supply Centre), 123
Duckett, B., 108
Duxbury, A., 107
Dynamic thesauri as online knowledge structures, 334,336

Eastern Washington University (EWU), 233-257
EBay, 285

Edgar, N. L., 42
Editing
   case study of editing required for accuracy and completeness, 233-257
   Cataloging & Classification Quarterly. *See* CCQ
   method of quality measurement, 241-248
   self-responsibility, editing decisions at Tisch library, 367
Editions as instantiations, 180
Education and training
   library viability, catalogers' training as essential to, 222-223
   Ruth's education, 8,20,25
   special formats catalogers, 228-230
   tenure for technical services librarians, training, workshops, and instructional presentations as teaching, 170
   see also Teaching
Education Resources Information Center (ERIC), 339-340
Edwards, Edward, 133
EEC funding of bibliographic control research, 120,125
Elections, Ruth as political junkie, 36
Electronic environments
   best-selling books, effect of multiple instantiations in digital environment, 191
   scanned library books, structure and function in information systems, 291
   uncataloged work, 273
   see also Online; Systems and technology
Encyclopedias
   as metadata, 319
   Nicholsons encyclopedia, sale in Monroe County, Indiana, 59
   Wikipedia, 283,287,289-290, 295-296,304

Enriched catalog entries, example of, 287-289
Enriched search requests, 285
Entity identification. *See* Unique identifiers of entities
Enumerative bibliographies compared to catalogs, 316-319
   authority control, 317-318
   contributors to creation, 317
   descriptions, detail in, 318
   discoverability function, 316
   function, 316
   granularity of description, 316
   in-house vs. outside standards, 317
   numerical identifiers, dependence on, 316
   permanency of, 318-319
   quality and standards in cataloging practice, 317
   speed of publication, 317
   style manuals, use of, 318
   thesauri, use of, 318
   transiency of, 318-319
Equitability. *See* Tenure for technical services librarians
ERIC (Education Resources Information Center), 339-340
Errors and errata
   impact on information retrieval. *See* Typographical errors, impact on information retrieval
   outsourcing of bibliographic records at University of Saskatchewan library, 213-219
      definition of major errors, 218
      definition of quality, 214
      error rate calculation as number of errors per number of key fields, 215
      in-house survey, 214
      LC records in outsourced sample, 217
      location distribution of cataloged materials, 215

NLC records in outsourced
    material, 217
subject distribution of cataloged
    materials, 216
types of errors, 217
structure and function in
    information systems, 295-296
University of Bradford research
    projects on bibliographic
    control, human error and
    allocated codes, 114,117
wiki model of cataloging, 284,
    295-296
Estate records in Monroe County,
    Indiana, early book
    collections, 75
Evaluation and evaluative practices
    annotations in cataloging, evaluing
        content, 97-98
    descriptive bibliographies
        compared to catalogs, 314
    tenure for technical services
        librarians, 168
Evans, A. F., 162
Eversberg, B., 320-321
EWU (Eastern Washington
    University), 233-257
Excerpts of best-selling books, 187
Expert system approach, University of
    Bradford research projects on
    bibliographic control, 117,122
Extensible relationships in information
    systems, 296-298
Extractions of best-selling books, 187

Faculty status for technical services
    librarians. *See* Tenure for
    technical services librarians
Fairness
    compensation for cataloging
        records, 277,279
    tenure. *See* Tenure for technical
        services librarians
Fast, K. V., 239

Federal service entrance exam, 8
Fiction
    librarians' encouragement,
        19th-century debate, 101
    sample of 20th-century best-sellers,
        185,194-195
Film
    best-selling books, instantiations,
        187,190-191
    cataloging. *See* Video cataloging
Filtering of duplicates
    University of Bradford research
        projects on bibliographic
        control, 119
"Find in a Library," 293
Fire, variance in count of books in
    Monroe County, Indiana, 58
FirstSearch, 207, 214
Flexibility
    bibliographic data elements, 290-298
    Ruth's example, 280
    self-responsibility, flextime, 371
Foley Center Library project, 233-257
Foreign users and Italian cataloging
    rules, 134
FRBR (Functional Requirements for
    Bibliographic Records)
    best selling books and the "works"
        phenomenon, 180
    bibliographic control research, 126
    comparison of cataloging and other
        information retrieval
        services, 308-309
    future of cataloging, 277,279-280
    interview with Ruth, 30-31
    Italian cataloging rules, 141,144
    measuring quality of cataloging,
        237
    practical decisions in digital
        environment, 284,296
    wiki model of cataloging, 284
    "work" entity in, 180
Frequency distribution of English
    alphabet, 114
Frusciano, T. J., 35

Fumagalli, G., 132-133,135,140
Fun factor in Ruth's work, 16
Function
    abstracting and indexing services compared to catalogs, 316
    enumerative bibliographies compared to catalogs, 316
Functional differences
    descriptive bibliographies compared to catalogs, 314-315
Functional Requirements for Bibliographic Records. *See* FRBR
Future of catalog librarians and cataloging, 128,223-224, 271-279
Fuzzy matches, entity identification, 354

Gar, T., 133
Garcha, R., 224
GARE (Guidelines for Authority and Reference Entries), 352
GARR (Guidelines for Authority Records and References), 141,352
Gateways and portals as online knowledge structures, 338-339
Genealogical records, Monroe County, Indiana, 73
Generic Everylibrarian, 154
Geography teacher, Ruth as, 8
Georgetown University, 191,193
Getty Union List of Artist Names, 357
Gibbs, G. E., 39
Gilchrist, A., 332
Goals and goal setting, self-responsibility, 367,369-370
Golden Era of Cataloging, 272
Gonzaga University, 233-257
Google
    best selling books and the "works" phenomenon, 193
    comparison of cataloging and other information retrieval services, 304,308,317,319,321,323
    future of cataloging, 275
    interview with Ruth, 31
    knowledge structures and the Internet, 340
    practical decisions in digital environment, 284-287, 291-293,295,304
    recognition of value of catalog librarians and cataloging, 304
Google Book Search, 193,284,291-292
Google Books, 286
Google Print, 275
Google Scholar, 286
Gorman, M., 278,282
Graesse catalog, 133
Graham, P. S., 236
Granularity of description, abstracting and indexing services compared to catalogs, 316
Greek language experiment, University of Bradford research projects on bibliographic control, 125-126
Greg, W. W., 313
GSARE (Guidelines for Subject Authority and Reference Entries), 352
Guerrini, M., 132
Guidelines for Authority and Reference Entries (GARE), 352
Guidelines for Authority Records and References (GARR), 141,352
Guidelines for Subject Authority and Reference Entries (GSARE), 352

H. W. Wilson, 46,48
Hampstead Public Library, 101
Hanson, M. E., 271
Harris, M. H., 73
Harrison, K. C., 104

Haworth Press, 35,340
Heinz, Senator John, 27
Heirlooms, Monroe County, Indiana, 73
Helen Project, 125-126
Henderson, K., 20,22-23
Henderson, W. T., 23
Hierarchical structures in controlled vocabularies, 300
Hill, J. S., 151,178
Hiring decisions, self-responsibility, 374
Historical analysis of CCQ content, 39-52
History and historical work, 55-149
  annotation in cataloging, history of. *See* Annotations in cataloging
  archival work. *See* Archives and archival organization
  bibliographic control research. *See* University of Bradford research projects on bibliographic control
  CCQ historical content, 46
  contributions and participation by Ruth. *See* Carter, Ruth C.
  documentations of cultural record, 180,184-185,313,323
  Italian cataloging rules. *See* Italian cataloging rules and international tradition
  Monroe County, Indiana. *See* Monroe County, Indiana, history of books in
  providing access to historians of the future, 27-28
Hitchcock, L. A., 108
HIV/AIDS Treatment Thesaurus, 337
Ho, J., 238
Hobbies of Ruth Carter, 37
Holistic view of academic librarians due to of Internet growth, 260,263
Holley, R. P., 259,355
Holzberlein, D., 42

Honors awarded to Ruth. *See* Awards
Horan, M. L., 234
Hot Jobs Online, 251
Howarth, L. C., 235,321
HSS database in bibliographic control research, 122
Huggill, J. A. W., 115
Human-generated metadata, 320
Hume, M., 239
H. W. Wilson, 46,48
Hyperglossary, Virtual, 336

ICCP (Paris International Conference on Cataloging Principles), 132-145
ICCU (Instituto Centrale per il Catalogo Unico), 141-142,144
Identification of entities. *See* Unique identifiers of entities
IFLA (International Federation of Library Associations and Institutions)
  contributions and participation by Ruth, 11,35-36
  FRANAR, 353
  GARE, 352
  GARR, 141,352
  GSARE, 352
  IME ICC, 141,144
  and Italian cataloging rules, 136,138,143-146
  unique identity of entities, 344,347,349,351-353,356
  video cataloging, 237
Il codice desiderato, "The wished for code," 143
Illiteracy in early Monroe County, Indiana, 63
Illustrated texts as best-selling books, 187
Image of catalog librarians and cataloging, perceptions and stereotypes, 225,267, 273-275,324

Images of archival resources, placing online, 26
IMDb (Internet Movie Database), 240
IME ICC (International Meeting of Experts on International Cataloguing Code), 141,144
Indexes and indexing
   CCQ. *See* CCQ (Cataloging & Classification Quarterly)
   comparison of indexes and catalogs. *See* Abstracting and indexing services compared to catalogs
   contributions and participation by Ruth, 9,32
   knowledge structures online, 337,341
   Librarians' Internet Index (LII), 332-333,339
   metadata, indexes as, 319
   search technology and browsable keyword indexes, 286
Indiana. *See* Monroe County, Indiana, history of books in
InfoMine, 332-333,339
Information technology. *See* Systems and technology
Innovation
   following Ruth's example, 279
   showcasing for technical services portfolio, 172
Input errors. *See* Typographical errors, impact on information retrieval
INSPEC Thesaurus, 338
Instantiations
   concatenations of evolving intellectual entities, 180
   defined, 180
   "derivative bibliographic relationships," 180
   editions as, 180
   "instantiation networks," 181,184-185,190
   see also Best-selling books, instantiations

Institute of Politics, oral history project, 24
Instituto Centrale per il Catalogo Unico (ICCU), 141-142,144
Insubordinate headings in controlled vocabularies, 299
"Intelligent numbers." *See* Unique identifiers of entries
Inter-library lending, 26,123-124
International conference on cataloging principles. *See* Paris International Conference on Cataloging Principles (ICCP)
International Federation of Library Associations and Institutions. *See* IFLA
International Meeting of Experts on International Cataloguing Code (IME ICC), 141,144
International numbering systems
   entity identification. *See* Unique identifiers of entities
   ISBD, 138,141,143,237,241,297
   linking from abstracting and indexing services to electronic resources, 316
International Standard Bibliographic Description (ISBD), 138,141,143,237,241,297
Internationalization of CCQ (Cataloging & Classification Quarterly), 40-42
Internet
   cultural record, as keeper of permanent documentations of, 323
   holistic view of academic librarians due to of Internet growth, 260,263
   Librarians' Internet Index (LII), 332-333,339
   wiki model. *See* Wiki model of cataloging
   see also Online environment and online resources; Web sites and web displays

InterParty, 348,352
Interview with Ruth, 19-37
Intner, S. S., 53,236
ISBD (International Standard Bibliographic Description), 138,141,143,237,241,297
ISO standards and norms, 141,335,352
Italian cataloging rules and international tradition, 131-149
  AACR2, 143,145
  abbreviations, 142
  AIB cataloging and Indexing Commission, 145
  ALA code, 136
  Anglo-American code, 143
  Anglo-American code as model, 133,138
  antipopes, 135
  authors' names, 137
  author/title catalogues, 133
  bio-bibliographies, 133
  BNI model, 137
  collective publications, 135
  Commissione Cibrario, 132
  Commissione RICA, 140-146
  complexity of cataloging levels, 141
  controversial issues, 142
  corporate bodies, 135,138,142
  "corporate body author," 139
  critical essays, 135
  cultural concerns, 136
  descriptions, 137
  Dewey standard, 143
  dissimilarities and contradictions, 134
  electronic catalog and electronic media, 145
  electronic environments, 141
  entities and data structions, relationships, 145
  form of access, 142
  FRANAR/FRAR, 141
  FRBR, 141
  Guidelines for Authority Records and References, 141
  harmonization of rules, 141
  headings, choice and form of, 137
  and IFLA, 136,138,143-146
  intellectual responsibility, 142
  International Conference on cataloging Principles (ICCP), 132
  International Meetings of Experts for an International cataloging Code (IME-ICC), 144
  ISBD, 141
  ISO norms, 141
  jurisdictions, 137
  Library of Congress model, 137
  new access modes, 141
  new physical formats, 141
  obsolescence of new code, 145
  online environment, 145
  opera liberettos, 135
  Panizzi's rules for printed cataloge of British Museum, 133
  Paris International Conference on Cataloging Principles (ICCP), 132-133,135,137-141,144-145
  participation in international events, 144
  patriarchs, 135
  problems with 1922 rules, 134
  Regole per la compilazione del catalogo alfabetico, 133
  Renaissance rulers, 135
  retrieval function vs. bibliographic function, 142
  RICA, 135,138-141,143,145
  Roman emperors, 135
  shared cataloging, 141
  sharing and harmonization of multiple countries' codes, 132,136
  subject catalogues, 133
  translations, 135
  transliterated names, form of, 142
  unification of Italy, 132

union cataloge of Italian libraries, 134
users' needs, 132
Vatican Library rules, 134
Italian National Bibliography (BNI), 137-138

JAO (Journal of Archival Organization), 35
Jargon in job descriptions, 173
Jast, L. S., 96-97,100
Java applets, 126-127
Jewett, C. C., 58
JIC (Journal of Internet Cataloging), 35
Jizba, L., 39
Joachim, M. D., 22,55
Job descriptions, tenure for technical services librarians, 173
Job satisfaction. *See* Self-responsibility
Jobs Online, 251
Johnson, E., 338
JOIC (Joint Operational Information Concept), 54
Joint Operational Information Concept (JOIC), 54
Journal editorship. *See* CCQ (Cataloging & Classification Quarterly)
Journal of Archival Organization (JAO), 35
Journal of Internet Cataloging (JIC), 35
JUMBO code, 117-118,120

Kafadar, K., 199
KartOO, 298
Kascus, M., 32,40,46
Kent, R. D., 97
Keyword searching, 280,286
  see also Search technology
King's College, London, 125
Kinsey Report as best-selling book, 184

Knowledge structures online, 329-342
  advanced visual and graphic interfaces, 336,338
  alphabetical access, 338
  ANSI/NISO Z39.19, 335
  ARL (Association of Research Libraries), 340
  browse functionality, 330
  browsing requirements and functionality, 330,332-333, 336,338-339
  client-oriented gateways and portals, 338
  constraining or supporting search technology, 332
  CSA Illumina, 340
  databases, integration of thesauri with, 336
  design of, and user behavior, 335
  directories, 332-333
  dynamic thesauri, 334,336
  gateways and portals, 338-339
  indexes, 337,341
  interfaces, 336
  Internet, 329-341
  machine-aided indexing, 334
  metadata, 341
  multiple vocabularies, interoperation, 335
  navigation of search results, 332
  "purity" of categories, 333
  revision and resorting of web directories, 333
  Scholars' Portal, 340
  specialized directories, 332-333
  spelling concerns, 336
  static thesauri, 334,336
  structure, defined, 331
  subject directories, 332-333
  subject-oriented gateways and portals, 338-339
  tables of contents, 341
  "taxonomies," 332-333
  thesauri, 334-338
  truncation, 336

users' fundamental needs, 330
"virtual libraries," 339
vocabulary control, 334,339
web-based OPAC, 341
XML, 336
Koch, T., 339

Labor intensive practice of cataloging, 249,272-274,276
Lagging terminology because of publication process, 290
Lam, V., 214,236
Lancaster, F. W., 339
Lane, L. C., 282,304
Language books in early Monroe County, Indiana, 74
Language transliteration, University of Bradford research projects on bibliographic control, 125
Language variations and unique identifiers of entities, 344,346,349,356
LASER database, 120
Latin American materials, SALALM, 274
Latin vs. Greek alphabet, University of Bradford research projects on bibliographic control, 125
Law books in early Monroe County, Indiana, 56,59,67
LC (Library of Congress)
  American Memory Project, 25-26
  annotation in cataloging, 103
  bibliographic control research, 119,126,128
  comparison of cataloging and other information retrieval services, 318
  error rates in monograph copy cataloging, LC records and, 217
  future of cataloging, 272-273
  interview with Ruth, 25-26,47-48
  and Italian cataloging rules, 137-138
  knowledge structures and the Internet, 333
  LC OPAC, University of Bradford research projects on bibliographic control, 128
  LCC (Library of Congress Classification), 240,333
  LCSH (Library of Congress Subject Headings), 47-48,299,318, 333,355
  outsourcing and error rates in cataloging, 217
  PCC (Program for Cooperative Cataloging), 172
  practical decisions in digital environment, 283,286,288, 296,299
  review of CCQ, 40
  SACO (subject authority program), 172
  technical services librarians and tenure issues, 172
  unique identity of entities, 355
  video cataloging, 234,238,240,242, 246,274-275
LEAF Project, 348
Leazer, G. H., 183,191
Letters in support of tenure for technical services librarians, 170-171
Letture di Bibliologia, 133
Lewisham Public Libraries, 97
Leysen, J. M., 223
"Librarian," defined, 177
Librarians' Internet Index (LII), 332-333,339
Librarians' personal responsibility for missing books in early Monroe County, Indiana, 60
Librarians' tenure. See Tenure for technical services librarians
Library and Information Technology Association (LITA), 35,282
Library management. See Self-responsibility

Library of Congress. *See* LC (Library of Congress)
Library schools
   cataloging coursework and offerings, 223-225,230,277
   Ruth's, 9,20
   special formats catalogers, 221-231
Librettos and best-selling books, patterns of derivation and mutation, 187
LII (Librarians' Internet Index), 332-333,339
Lilly Library, 70
LISA database, 340
LITA (Library and Information Technology Association), 35,282
Literary Register, 61
Literature
   Monroe County, Indiana, history of books in, 74-75
   mysteries, 8
   "The Appraisal of Literature," 98
   see also Poems; Reading
Liu, Y. Q., 235
Local vs. national/international needs, descriptive bibliographies compared to catalogs, 309
London University, 119
Look Smart, 332
Lowery, C. B., 153
Lubetzky, S., 136-137,309-310
Lunchboxes and other paraphernalia, instantiations of best-selling books, 190-191
Lynch, C., 346
Lynch, M. F., 115
Lytle, Brig. Gen William, 16,27,38

Ma, Y., 235
MacArthur Foundation, 295
MacEwan, A., 352
Machine-aided indexing, 334
Machine-generated record control numbers. *See* Unique identifiers of entities

MACS, 356
Madan, F., 313
Madison Museum, 61
"Magic" in search technology, 304
Majority library culture (reference, bibliographic instruction, collection building), 164,168,170,174
Maltby, A., 107
Maltese, D., 135-137
Managing cataloging staff. *See* Self-responsibility
Mann, T., 275,321-322
Mapping XML structures to MARC structures, 300-302
Maps as accompanying material to best-selling books, 187
MARAC (Mid Atlantic Regional Archives Conference), 36
MARS, 122
Massey, O., 236-237,241,243
McGarry, D., 237
Medical Subject Headings (MeSH), 298-303,333,336
MELVYL, 128
Memoir of the Geological Society of America, 20
Mentoring and mentorships, 14
   catalog librarians and cataloging, 224,230
   Ruth's mentors, 22-24
   special formats catalogers, 230
   tenure for technical services librarians, 173
MeSH (Medical Subject Headings), 298-303,333,336
Metadata
   abstracts and indexes as, 319
   cataloging as type of metadata, 319-324
      Amazon.com, 320-321
      authenticity and reliability, 321
      authority control, 321
      context, loss of, 320-321
      contributors to creation, 321

Index 401

economy of attention, 320
object of description, 320
permanency of, 323
standardization, 321
value, 323
CCQ (Cataloging & Classification Quarterly), 51
changes in library profession, 51
definitions, 319-320
dictionaries as, 319
encyclopedias as, 319
human-generated metadata, 320
knowledge structures online, 341
metadiscussions and metadebates, 54
metalogs, 283-290
plethora of metadata schemes, 282
professional creation of, 320
reinventing the wheel, 283
relevance ranking, 323
search technology, metadata generated by, 319-320
telephone books as, 319
use of term, 308
users, transition from catalog to search engines, 322
value-added, 285-290
wiki model, 283-290
Metadiscussions and metadebates, 54
Metalogs, 283-290,319-324
cataloging as type of metadata
Amazon.com, 320-321
authenticity and reliability, 321
authority control, 321
context, loss of, 320-321
contributors to creation, 321
economy of attention, 320
object of description, 320
permanency of, 323
standardization, 321
value, 323
online resources, 283-290
wiki model, 283-290
Mid Atlantic Regional Archives Conference (MARAC), 36

Military. *See* United States Army
Miller, D. R., 281
Miller, S. J., 235
Milstead, J., 334,336
Miltons Work in early Monroe County, Indiana books, 59
Mingam, M., 355
Minimal Level Authority Record (MLAR), 349-351,356
Minority library culture (technical services, circulation, systems, administration), 164,168,174
Mistakes. *See* Errors and errata
MLA (Music Library Association), 227
MLAR (Minimal Level Authority Record), 349-351,356
Monroe County, Indiana, history of books in, 55-77
authors and titles, list of, 88-89
Bibles, 62-63,67,73-74
Blackston, 60
Blackstone's Commentary, 59
Blairs Lectures, 59
buying books, 67-73
itemization of merchants' book sales, 72
cataloge dating from 1850, 58
Chataubriands Travels, 59
Chitty's Pleadings, 59
classical books, 57
clergymen's books, 63
county press, 61
estate records, 75
fire, variance in count of books, 58
heirlooms and genealogical records, 73
Indiana University Library, 56-57
language books, 74
law books, 56,59,67
Lewis & Clarks' travels, 59
librarians' personal responsibility for missing books, 60
literary magazine, 61
literature, 74-75

lost and destroyed records, 58
Lyric Poems, 59
medical magazine, 61
Miltons Work, 59
Monroe County Library, 57-58
  itemization of books in, 90-93
  newspaper advertisements for sale and purchase, 74
  newspaper publication, 61
  Nicholsons encyclopedia, sale of, 59
  periodicals, 61
  population growth, 75
  private ownership, 58,61-67,75
  public libraries, 57-58,90-93
  purchases of books, 67-73
  reading tastes, 73-75
  religious books, 62-63,67,73-74,76
  sales of books, 67-73
  Salmagundi, 59
  science books, 74
  settling accounts with former librarians, 59-60
  Shakespeair, 59
  specific titles and authors, 88-89
  State Seminary, 57
  stolen and unreturned library books, 59-61
  tastes in reading, 73-75
    itemization of merchants' book sales, 71-72
  titles and authors, list of, 88-89
  university libraries, 56-57
  Vicar of Wakefield, 59
  Volnie's Ruins, 59
  wills and probate records, 63,67
Monroe County Library, 60,66
Monthly goals
  self-responsibility, 368
Movies
  best-selling books, video recordings of, 187,190-191
  cataloging. See Video cataloging
  Internet Movie Database (IMDb), 240

Moynahan, S. A., 271
Muller, E., 23-24
Multiple entities assigned one identifying number, 357
Multiple vocabularies, interoperation, 335
Museums' requirements vs. libraries' requirements, unique identifiers of entities, 345,354
Music Library Association (MLA), 227
Musical adaptations of best-selling books, 187
Mutation patterns. See Best-selling books
Myall, C., 233
Mysteries (literary genre), 8

Name authority
  entity identification. See Unique identifiers of entities
  Getty Union List of Artist Names, 357
  NACO, 30,172,179,275,277
  NASA (National Aeronautics and Space Administration) Thesaurus, 336-337
  National bibliographic agencies (NBAs), 347,351
  National Central Library in Florence, 139
  National conferences. See ACRL (Association of College and Research Libraries) conferences
  National Information Standards Organization (NISO), 122,126-127,335-336
  National Library of Medicine (NLM), 294,300-304,339
  National Library Service (SBN), 144
  Navigation of information

browsability. *See* Browsability and browse functionality
knowledge structures online, navigation of search results, 332
unique identifiers of entities, navigation of data, 346
NBAs (national bibliographic agencies), 347,351
New York State Library School, 103
Newnes Ltd, 98
Newspapers
  Monroe County, Indiana, history of books, 61,74
  preservation, 11
Nietz collection of early American school textbooks, 30
NISO (National Information Standards Organization), 122,126-127,335-336
NLM (National Library of Medicine), 294,300-304,339
Nonalphabetical clustering, 180-181
Nonfiction, sample of 20th-century best-sellers
  best-selling books, instantiations, 194-195
Non-print catalogers. *See* Special formats catalogers
Norris, D. M., 105
Notess, G. R., 332-333
Novotny, E., 239
Numbers
  comparison of catalogs to other information retrieval services, dependence on numerical identifiers, 316
  typos in, 200
  as unique identifiers. *See* Unique identifiers of entities

Obsolescence
  controlled vocabularies, 298-299
  Italian cataloging rules and international tradition, 145

OCLC
  best selling books and the "works" phenomenon, 179,183
  comparison of cataloging and other information retrieval services, 311
  contributions and participation by Ruth, 10-11,23,29-30
  Enhance program, 30
  future of cataloging, 272-273,278
  OCLC-CAT, 225
  OCLC/LTS, 217,219
  practical decisions in digital environment, 283,293
  technical services librarians and tenure issues, 168
  video cataloging, 233-234,240-241, 244
  WorldCat, 185,187,193,197, 200-201,207,213,249,283
Office space for scholarly work, tenure for technical services librarians, 169
Ohio Historical and Philosophical Society, 20
OLAC (Online Audiovisual Catalogers), 225,227,230
Online environment and online resources
  bibliographic control differences between online resources and physical materials, 28-29
  errata in online catalogs. *See* Typographical errors, impact on information retrieval
  images of archival resources, placing online, 26
  Internet resources and physical library materials, differences in bibliographic control Ruth C. Carter, 28-29
  Italian cataloging rules and international tradition, 141,145

knowledge structures. *See* Knowledge structures online
metalogs, 283-290
numbering systems linking abstracting and indexing services to electronic resources, 316
Virtual Hyperglossary, 336
wikis. *See* Wiki model of cataloging
see also Internet; Search technology; Semantic web; Web sites and web displays
OPAC (Online Public Access Catalog), 95,125-126,142,238-240,275
music under Ruth's baton, 53
Open catalogs and directories, 283-284,332
union lists and union catalogs, 283-285
Voyager Catalogue, 299
see also Wiki model of cataloging
Opera liberettos, Italian cataloging rules, 135
Osborn, A. D., 137
Outsourcing, 275,277-278
catalog librarians and cataloging, 277-278
error rates before and after outsourcing at University of Saskatchewan library, 213-219
self-responsibility, 374
Ovid gateway, 339

Panizzi, Sir Anthony, 133
Paraphernalia related to best-selling books, 190
Paris International Conference on Cataloging Principles (ICCP), 132-145
Park, B., 153
Parkland College, 20,23

Patriarchs and Italian cataloging rules, 135
Patrons. *See* Users
PaULS (Pennsylvania Union List of Serials), 30
PCC (Program for Cooperative Cataloging), 237,252,277
Peckham, H. H., 68
Pennsylvania Library Association, 36
Pennsylvania Newspaper Project, 11
Pennsylvania Union List of Serials (PaULS), 30
Pentagon work by Ruth. *See* Carter, Ruth C.
Perceptions and stereotypes. *See* Catalog librarians and cataloging
Performance reviews and self-responsibility, 369-370
Pering, C., 56
Periodicals in early Monroe County, Indiana, 61
Permanency of catalogs compared to other information retrieval services, 313,318-319
Perseverance, Ruth's example, 280
"Persona," unique identifiers of entities, 354
Petrucciani, A., 138,144
Petzholdt, Julius, 133
Photos of archival resources, placing online, 26
Piggott, M., 106
Pittsburgh, Ruth's life in, 11-12
Pittsburgh Regional Library Center, 29
Pléiade, catalog entry vs. Wikipedia entry, 285-290
Plumb Design Visual Thesaurus, 336
Pockets containing accompanying material, best-selling books and, 187
Poems
in honor of Ruth, 53-54
Lyric Poems in early Monroe County, Indiana, 59

Politics, Ruth as political junkie, 36
Popular books. *See* Best-selling books
Porter, G., 250
Portfolio development. *See* Tenure for technical services librarians
Pratt Institute Library School, 103
Preservation
    cultural record, documentation of, 180,184-185,313,323
    see also Archives and archival organization
Principi di catalogazione e regole italiane, 136
Principia bibliographica, balancing principles, practice, and pragmatics in digital environments, 281-305
Privacy concerns
    "Big Brother," unique identifiers of entities, 355
    self-responsibility, 372
Private book ownership in early Monroe County, Indiana, 61-67,75
Probate records in Monroe County, Indiana, 63,67
Problem-solving
    Ruth's skills, 8,31
    self-responsibility, 373
Productivity. *See* Self-responsibility
Professional creation of metadata, 320
Professional organization participation
    Ruth C. Carter, 15
    special formats catalogers, 228,230
Program for Cooperative Cataloging (PCC), 237,252,277
Project AUTHOR, 348
Project Helen, 125-126
Project MACS, 348
Project Muse, 294
ProQuest, 340
Public libraries
    Monroe County, Indiana, history of books in, 90-93
Publisher's Weekly's list, best-selling books, 183

Publishing
    bibliographic control, publishers' role in, 114-115
    Ruth's experience. *See* Carter, Ruth C.
    unique identifiers of entities, publishers' needs, 345,354,357,359
    see also Editing
PubMed, 300,303-304
Punctuation concerns, quality and standards in cataloging practice, 237,241,278-279, 313,366
"Purity" of categories, knowledge structures online, 333

QUALCAT project, 122-123
Quality and standards in cataloging practice, 233-257,271-279
    adding value to catalog entries, 286
    annotations in cataloging, 107
    balancing bottom line and user needs, 234-235,278
    balancing quality and quantity, 276
    budget and staffing constraints, 234-235,238,277
    contradictions in literature, 236
    definitions of quality, 236-237,239
    descriptive bibliographies compared to catalogs, 311
    Eastern Washington University project, 233-257
    editing changes, as method of quality measurement, 241-248
    enriched catalog entries, example of, 287-289
    entity identification, ISO standard, 352
    enumerative bibliographies compared to catalogs, 317
    errors. *See* Errors and errata
    Foley Center Library project, 240-248

Gonzaga University project, 233-257
in-house vs. outside standards, 317
Italian cataloging rules, 143
labor intensive practice, 249,272-274
lagging terminology because of publication process, 290
metadata, cataloging as type of, 321
national and international standards, 276
outsourcing, 275
   error rates in monograph copy cataloging bibliographic records before and after outsourcing at University of Saskatchewan library, 213-219
Pléiade, catalog entry vs. Wikipedia entry, 285-290
punctuation concerns, 237,241, 278-279,313,366
QUALCAT project, 122-123
richness of content and links, 287
self-responsibility, 372-373
simplification of codes and standards, 278
tracking errors, 241-242
University of Bradford research projects on bibliographic control, 114-115,122-123
value perception, 273-275,324
   adding value to catalog entries, 286
vendors providing catalog entries, 234-235,242,273,277
video cataloging, 235-236,238-240, 243-252
vocabulary control, 280
"white list" of preferred record sources, 250
Wiki model, 281-305
Quinn, J. H., 97,101
Quo vadis (where are you going?), cataloging, 271-279
Quotas, and tenure for technical services librarians, 161,169

Randal, B. N., 200
Ratio of catalogers to resources, 223
RDA (Resource Description and Access), 286,296,308,347
RDN (Resource Discovery Network), 332-333
Reading
   Ruth's excessive enjoyment (poor choice for librarian), 21
   annotated catalog entries
      inducing people to read what they would not have thought of reading, 101,105
      reader requirements, 100
   Monroe County, Indiana
      illiteracy, 63
      reading tastes, 73-75
      see also Monroe County, Indiana, history of books in
   mysteries (literary genre), 8
   retirement plans of Ruth, 37
Record control numbers. *See* Unique identifiers of entities
Recorded knowledge of culture, 180,184-185,313,323
Reference bibliographies. *See* Enumerative bibliographies
Reference books, annotations in cataloging, 99
Reference librarianship
   contributions and participation by Ruth, 8-9
   RUSA (Reference and User Services Association), 262
Regole italiane di catalogazione per autori (RICA), 132-135, 138-141,143,145
Relevance ranking and metadata, 323
Religious books in early Monroe County, Indiana, 62-63,67, 73-74,76
Renaissance rulers, Italian cataloging rules, 135
Research libraries

ACRL. *See* ACRL (Association of College and Research Libraries) conferences
RLIN (Research Libraries' Information Network), 180,185,273,278,283,303
Research studies, 151-269
Resource Description and Access (RDA), 286,296,308,347
Resource Discovery Network (RDN), 332-333
Responsibility among team members. *See* Self-responsibility
Retirement
  impending retirement of catalogers, 223-224,230,274,276
  Ruth's plans, 37-38
  special formats catalogers, 223-224,230
Retractions, wiki model of cataloging, 294
Retrieval function vs. bibliographic function, Italian cataloging rules, 142
Revelli, C., 136-137
Revie, C., 336
RICA (regole italiane di catalogazione per autori), 132-135,138-141, 143,145
Ridley, J. M., 113
Riggs, R., 153
Rights management agencies' needs related to entity identification, 345,354,357,359
RLIN (Research Libraries' Information Network), 180,185,273,278, 283,303
Roe, S. K., 23,39
Roget's, 285
Roman emperors and Italian cataloging rules, 135

SACO (subject authority program), 172,179
SALALM (Seminar on the Acquisition of Latin American Library Materials), 274
Sales of books in early Monroe County, Indiana, 67-73
Sample of 20th-century best-sellers, 194
Savage, E., 98,100-103,105
Sayers, W. C. B., 103-105
SBN (National Library Service), 144
Scanned library books, structure and function in information systems, 291
Schedules. *See* Deadlines and schedules
Schneider, G., 312
Scholars' Portal, 339-340
Science books in early Monroe County, Indiana, 74
Science fiction as best-selling books, 184
SCOLCAP database, 119
Scopus, 304
Screenplays from best-selling books, patterns of derivation and mutation, 187,190
Search technology
  archival organization and cataloging, similarities and differences, 27
  bibliographic control, balancing with, 282-283
  blurring of catalogs and web searches, illustrations, 291-293
  browsability, 286,290
  cluster approach, unique identifiers of entities, 358-359
  devaluing and deprofessionalizing cataloging, 30-31
  enriched search requests, 285
  future of cataloging, 275
  Google. *See* Google
  historians' full-text search needs, 28
  IMDb popularity, 240

input errors. *See* Typographical errors, impact on information retrieval
knowledge structures, effect on. *See* Knowledge structures online
"magic," 304
metadata generated by, 319-320
reinventing the wheel, 283
semantic web. *See* Semantic web
thesaural relationships in, 285
University of Bradford research projects on bibliographic control
    search engines, criticism of, 128-129
    search options, 127
Searching online for best-selling books, 191
Self-confidence of cataloging staff, 365
Self-responsibility, 363-375
    assumptions, testing, 374
    backlogs, 374
    bibliographic access theory at Tisch Library, 366
    calendar responsibilities, 368
    case study, 370-371
    cataloging for users vs. cataloging for catalogers, 366-367
    competency management, 369-370
    deadlines, 368-369
    DLC copy "cataloging," 366
    editing decisions at Tisch library, 367
    flex time, 371
    followup of unresolved issues, 372
    goals and goal setting, 367,369-370
    hiring decisions, 374
    manager, defined, 366
    missed work, 371
    monthly goals, 367-368
    outsourcing, 374
    performance reviews, 369-370
    privacy concerns, 372
    problem-solving, 373
    projecting production numbers, 367
    quality assurance, 372-373
    resignations and replacements, 374
    resource investment by managers, 365
    schedules, 365,367-368
    self-confidence of staff, 365
    SMART goals, 370
    soft skills, 370
    staff, defined, 366
    supervisor, defined, 366
    task rotation, 373
    team, defined, 366
    temporary hires for new work, 374
    trust, 365,372-373
    unresolved issues, followup, 372
Semantic web
    changes in library profession, 51
    unique identifiers of entities, 347
Seminar on the Acquisition of Latin American Library Materials (SALALM), 274
Sequels to best-selling books, instantiations, 184
Serial shelf marks, University of Bradford research projects on bibliographic control, 123
Serials and serials librarianship
    best-selling books, instantiations, 184
    Bowker/Ulrich Award, 11,16
    CONSER (Cooperative Online Serials), 11,29-30,172,275
    contributions and participation by Ruth, 10-12,21,24,29-30, 35-36
    ISSN (International Standard Serial Number), 316,344
Serialist, 225-226
"Shadow" error theory, confirmation of, 198
Shakespeair in early Monroe County, Indiana, 59
Sharp, H., 105
Sheffield Public Libraries, 104

Shin, H., 236
Shiri, A. A., 336
Shoenung, J. G., 236
Simmons College Symposium, 224
Simpson, F. K., 236
SMART goals and self-responsibility, 370
Smiraglia, R. P., 179
Smithsonian, 20
Snaith, S., 104
Sound performances and best-selling books, patterns of derivation and mutation, 187,190
Special formats catalogers, 221-231
　advertisements for cataloger positions, 251
　education and training, 228-230
　ideas for organizations, schools, and catalogers, 230
　impending retirements, 230
　increase in responsibilities, 224
　library schools, 221-231
　mentorships, 230
　national cooperative programs for, 252
　professional organization participation, 227-228,230
　professional organizations, 221-231
　skills sets, 251
　survey findings, 226-227
　video cataloging, 235-236,238-240, 243-252
Specialized directories, knowledge structures online, 332-333
Spelling concerns
　errata. *See* Typographical errors, impact on information retrieval
　knowledge structures online, 336
　unique identifiers of entities, spelling variations, 355
Staff management. *See* Self-responsibility
Standards and standardization
　annotations in cataloging, 107
　descriptive bibliographies compared to catalogs, 311
　identification of entities. *See* Unique identifiers of entities
　see also Quality and standards in cataloging practice
State Library of Pennsylvania, 30
Statement of International Cataloging Principles, 132,347,354-355
Statistical analysis of conference papers. *See* ACRL (Association of College and Research Libraries) conferences
Steinhagen, E. N., 271
Stereotypes. *See* Catalog librarians and cataloging
Stevens, R. E., 22
Stevenson, R., 98
Stolen and unreturned library books in early Monroe County, Indiana, 59-61
Structure and function in information systems, 290-298
　Amazon.com, 291
　blurring of catalogs and web searches, 291
　browsing or sequential access to controlled data elements, 290-293
　definition of structure, 331
　errors, 295-296
　extensible relationships, 296-298
　"Find in a Library," 293
　flexibility of bibliographic data elements, 290-298
　Google Book Search, 291-292
　scanned library books, 291
　simplicity in structuring bibliographic linking, 297-298
Stuhlman, D., 172
Style manuals, use of, 318
Subject Access Project, 108
Subject authority

entity identification. *See* Unique
identifiers of entities
indexes. *See* Indexes and indexing
Italian cataloging rules and
international tradition, 133
knowledge structures online,
332-333
SACO, 172,179
Subject-oriented gateways and portals,
338-339
Superstructure necessary for
administering unique
identifiers of entities, 345
Supervision styles. *See*
Self-responsibility
"Suprasumption," vocabulary control,
303
Svenonius, E., 237
SWALCAP database, 119
System independence, unique
identifiers of entities, 349
Systematic bibliographies. *See*
Enumerative bibliographies
Systems and technology
Ruth as enjoying books and
libraries more than
computers, 21
ACRL topics of interest to technical
services librarians. *See*
ACRL (Association of
College and Research
Libraries) conferences
analyst positions. *See* Systems
analyst work
contributions and participation by
Ruth. *See* Carter, Ruth C.
librarians' tenure. *See* Tenure for
technical services librarians
principia bibliographica, balancing
principles, practice, and
pragmatics in digital
environments, 281-305
systems analyst. *See* Systems
analyst work

technical services, underrepresentation
in papers at acrl national
conferences, 233-257
tenure. *See* Tenure for technical
services librarians
tenure for technical services
librarians, 151-177

Tables of contents, knowledge
structures online, 341
Tanselle, G. T., 309-310,312,315
Task rotation, self-responsibility, 373
Tate, E., 313
Taxonomies
best-selling books, taxonomical
categories describing
evolution, 186-187,190
jargon in descriptions of jobs, 173
knowledge structures online,
332-333
Taylor, M. S., 105
Teaching
contributions and participation by
Ruth. *See* Carter, Ruth C.
instructional materials, showcasing
for portfolio tenure for
technical services librarians,
172
tenure for technical services
librarians, 154,161-162,
169-170
Team, defined, 366
Teamwork. *See* Self-responsibility
Technical services. *See* Systems and
technology
Telephone books as metadata, 319
Television and best-selling books, 190
Temporary hires for new work
self-responsibility, 374
Tenure for technical services
librarians, 151-178
ACRL (Association of College and
Research Libraries), 174

bibliographic or authority records, showcasing for portfolio, 172
cross-departmental projects and committees, involvement in, 171-172
electronic discussion-group contributions in support of, 171
equal access to tenure track positions, 168
evaluative practices, equitability, 168
external comment on scholarly and service contributions, 171
generic Everylibrarian, 154
innovation, showcasing for portfolio, 172
input from librarians regarding tenure standards and processes, 173
instructional materials, showcasing for portfolio, 172
interaction with and exposure to academic faculty, 163
invisibility, 163
invisibility, interaction with and exposure to academic faculty, 163
jargon as impediment, 173
language and jargon in descriptions of jobs, 173
letters and dossiers in support of, 170-171
"librarian," defined, 177
majority library culture (reference, bibliographic instruction, collection building), 164,168,170,174
mentoring programs, 173
minority library culture (technical services, circulation, systems, administration), 164,168,174
NACO, CONSER, etc., programs, letters from reviewers, 171

NACO/SACO contributions, showcasing for portfolio, 172
national and international cooperative work, 173
numeric quotas, 161,169
observation reports, 170
office space for scholarly work, 169
portfolio development
    difficulty, 154
    strategies for, 172
power of word choices, 169
priorities, alteration, 169
SACO (subject authority program). *See* SACO (subject authority program)
sample questionnaire, 177-178
scholarly and service pursuits, 169
separation of scholarly work, 169
systems and technology, 151-177
taxonomy development, language and jargon in descriptions of jobs, 173
teaching issue, strategies for, 169-170
teaching vs. contributions to teaching enterprise, 154,161-162
time-management, 160,169
training, workshops, and instructional presentations as teaching, 170
trivialization of library management, 162,170
"unique contributions to academic community and to higher education itself," 169
user services, language and jargon in descriptions of jobs, 173
visibility, interaction with and exposure to academic faculty, 163
web pages, showcasing for portfolio, 172
workload concerns, 160
workload issues, 169

Term usage
   CCQ, reflecting changes in
      profession and world, 50
   jargon in job descriptions, 173
Text string identification, unique
      identifiers of entities,
      346,348-349
Thesauri
   abstracting and indexing services
      compared to catalogs, 318
   ASFA, 336
   CATIE HIV/AIDS Treatment
      Thesaurus, 337
   CCQ (Cataloging & Classification
      Quarterly), 51
   enumerative bibliographies
      compared to catalogs, 318
   knowledge structures online,
      334-338
   NASA, 336-337
   search technology, thesaural
      relationships in, 285
   UNESCO, 336-337,351
Think Map, 338
Thomas, D., 239
Thomas, S., 238
Tillett, B., 238,343
Tisch Library at Tufts University,
      management style
   catalog librarians and cataloging.
      See Self-responsibility
Toronto Conference on the Future of
      AACR2, 126
Translations
   best-selling books, patterns of
      derivation and mutation,
      187,190
   Italian cataloging rules and
      international tradition, 135
Transliteration
   Italian cataloging rules,
      transliterated names, 142
   University of Bradford research
      projects on bibliographic
      control, 125-126

Truncation
   knowledge structures online, 336
   typographical errors, impact on
      information retrieval, 200-201
Tsao, J., 234
Typographical errors, impact on
      information retrieval,
      197-211
   numbers and dates, typos in, 200
   "shadow" error theory,
      confirmation of, 198
   truncations, 200-201
   typo frequency, 199-201
      statistical tables, 202-203,
         205-206
   unqualified keyword searches, 201
   weighted and unweighted averages,
      207-208,210-211
   word frequency (common vs.
      uncommon words), 199
      statistical tables, 202-203,
         205-206

UBC (Universal Bibliographic
      Control), 347,349,352
UNESCO Thesaurus, 336-337,351
Union lists and union catalogs
   authority control, 311
   CCQ content, 42
   descriptive bibliographies
      compared to catalogs, 311
   Getty Union List of Artist Names,
      357
   inconsistencies in collective
      creation of, 311
   Italian libraries, 134
   PaULS (Pennsylvania Union List of
      Serials), 30
   wiki model, 283-285
   work by Ruth, 11-13,29-30
"Unique contributions to academic
      community and to higher
      education itself," 169
Unique identifiers of entities, 343-361
   administration concerns, 345

administration issues, 351,358
archives' requirements vs. libraries' requirements, 345,354
authority data clusters, 348,357-358
benefits of, 344,350
"Big Brother" concerns, 355
business need and business case, 344,350,354-355
categorized clusters of potential matches, 358
centralized vs. decentralized model, 347
cluster approach, 348,357-358
controlled vocabularies, 345-346
cost considerations, 350-351,353
cultural differences within same language, 355
customization of displayed forms of names and terms, 346
data clusters, 348,357-358
data manipulation, 346
de facto universal characters for numbering, 349
duplication concerns, 344
duplication issues, 346,357
fuzzy matches, 354
IFLA Statement of International cataloging Principles, 347
IFLA Working Group on International Authority System, 351
IFLA's FRANAR (Functional Requirements and Numbering for Authority Records), 353
IFLA's Guidelines for Authority and Reference Entries (GARE), 352
IFLA's Guidelines for Authority Records and References (GARR), 352
"intelligent numbers," 356
international cooperation efforts, 346-347
internationalization concerns, 344
internationalization issues, 346
ISO standard, 352
language variations, 344,346,349, 356
multiple entities assigned one number, 357
museums' requirements vs. libraries' requirements, 345,354
name changes, 354
national bibliographic agencies (NBAs), 347
navigation of data, 346
"persona," 354
publishers' needs, 345,354,357,359
quality and standards in cataloging practice. *See* Quality and standards in cataloging practice
RDA (Resource Description and Access), 347
recent initiatives, 348
redundant international work, 348
rights management agencies' needs, 345,354,357,359
same language using different words, 355
scope of entity identification, 345,350,353
search engines, cluster approach, 358-359
Semantic Web issues, 347
spelling variations, 355
superstructure necessary for administering, 345
system independence, 349
text string identification, 346,348-349
UBC (Universal Bibliographic Control), 347
VIAF (Virtual International Authority File), 348,356,358-359
Virtual International Authority File (VIAF) model, 356,358-359
word order conventions, 356

Unique identity of entities
   IFLA (International Federation of Library Associations and Institutions), 344,347,349, 351-353,356
Uniqueness of bibliographic identifiers, University of Bradford research projects on bibliographic control, 115-116
United States Army
   Adjutant General's Office, 8
   interview with Ruth, 20
   Office of Chief of Staff, 9
Universal Bibliographic Control (UBC), 347,349,352
Universal Standard Bibliographic Code (USBC), 113,115-123, 123-124
Universal Standard Book Number (USBN), 114
University libraries
   ACRL. *See* ACRL (Association of College and Research Libraries) conferences
   Monroe County, Indiana, history of books in, 56-57
University of Bath, 122
University of Bradford research projects on bibliographic control, 113-130
   accented characters, 125
   ANSI/NISO Z39.50, 122,126-127
   authority control, 123,127-128
   AUTOCAT discussion list, 128
   AUTOMATCH, 123-124
   bilateral agreements, 120
   BOPAC Projects, 126-128
   British Library (BL), 118-119
   British National Bibliography (BNB), 115-117
   "cleaning of database records," 117,121-122
   complex codes, 117-118,120
   cost of merging databases, 119
   cross-reference structures, 128
   databases in, 113-130
   derived (allocated) codes vs. manual codes, 114,116
   DOCMATCH projects, 120-121
   EEC funding, 120
   expert system approach, 117,122
   filtering, 118-119,124
   frequency distribution of English alphabet, 114
   Functional Requirements for Bibliographical Records, 126
   future of cataloging, 128
   Greek language experiment, 125-126
   Helen Project, 125-126
   human error and allocated codes, 114,117
   important but small differences, 117
   index linking USBC's to ADONIS numbers, 121
   interface problems, 122,126
   inter-library lending, USBC in, 123-124
   Internet growth, 126
   ISBN (International Standard Book Number) in history of bibliographic control, 114,122
   Java applets, 126-127
   journal articles, 121
   JUMBO codes, 117-118,120
   language transliteration, 125
   Latin vs. Greek alphabet, 125
   LC OPAC, 128
   major classification schemes, 129
   master index linking USBC's to ADONIS numbers, 121
   merging databases, 117-119
   mixed alphanumeric codes, 114
   national database creation, 120
   OPACs, 125-126
   programming languages, 121
   Project Helen, 125-126
   publishers' role in bibliographic control, 114-115

QUALCAT project, 122-123
quality and standards in cataloging practice. *See* Quality and standards in cataloging practice
quality control, 122-123
   search engines, criticism of, 128-129
   search options, 127
   serial shelf marks, 123
   small but important differences, 117
   testing, 115-116
   transliteration project, 125-126
   UKLDS (United Kingdom Library Database System), 118,120
   uniqueness of bibliographic identifiers, 115-116
   USBC (Universal Standard Bibliographic Code), 115-117,122-124
   USBN (Universal Standard Book Number), 114
   user interface problems, 122,126
   volume of requests, 123
   weighting methods, 118
   World Wide Web, growth of, 126
University of Cincinnati, 20
University of Colorado, 200
University of Crete, 125
University of Illinois, 20,22,152
University of Leeds, 118
University of Pittsburgh, 21,23-24,29
University of Saskatchewan, 213-219
University of Sheffield, 115
University of Toronto, 340
USBC (Universal Standard Bibliographic Code), 113,115-124
USBN (Universal Standard Book Number), 114
Users
   Ruth as intensive library user, 21,27
   balancing quantity (bottom line) and quality (user needs), 234-235,276,278

   and catalogs, 280, 309, 324
   contributions and participation by Ruth. *See* Carter, Ruth C.
   foreign users and Italian cataloging rules, 134
   Italian cataloging rules, users' needs, 132
   jargon in descriptions of jobs, 173
   knowledge structures online, users' fundamental needs, 330
   metadata, transition from catalog to search engines, 322
   University of Bradford research projects on bibliographic control, user interface problems, 122,126
   user needs vs. user wants, 324

Value
   cataloging. *See* Catalog librarians and cataloging
   metadata, 285-290
Van Orden, R., 108
Vatican Library rules, 134
Vendors providing catalog entries, 234-235,242,273,277
VIAF (Virtual International Authority File), 348,356,358-359
Video cataloging
   case study of editing required for accuracy and completeness, 233-257
   quality and standards in cataloging practice, 238-240,243-252
   special formats catalogers, 236,238-240,243-252
Video recordings of best-selling books, 187,190-191
Virtual Hyperglossary, 336
Virtual International Authority File (VIAF), 348,356,358-359
"Virtual libraries," 339
Visual thesaurus, 336

Vocabulary control, 280,298-303
   hierarchical structures, 300
   insubordinate headings, 299
   interoperation of multiple vocabularies, 335
   knowledge structures online, 334,339
   lagging terminology because of publication process, 290
   mapping XML structures to MARC structures, 300-302
   obsolescence, 298-299
   quality and standards in cataloging practice, 280
   unique identifiers of entities, 345-346
Voyager Catalogue, 299

Walbridge, S., 239
War stories as best-selling books, 184
Ward, P., 106-107
Web sites and web displays
   best-selling books, instantiations, 183
   flexibility of bibliographic data elements, 290-298
   searching. *See* Search technology
   showcasing for technical services portfolio, 172
   and University of Bradford research projects on bibliographic control, 126
   see also Online environment and online resources; Semantic web
Weihs, J., 235
Weitz, J., 235
Where are you going? (quo vadis), cataloging, 271-279
"White list" of preferred record sources, 250
Wiki model of cataloging, 281-305
   enriched catalog entries, example of, 287-289

   errors and edits, 284,295-296
   FRBR relationships, 284
   metadata, 283-290
   Pléiade, catalog entry vs. Wikipedia entry, 285-290
   retractions, 294
   union lists and union catalogs, 283-285
   see also Open catalogs and directories
Wikipedia, 283,287,289-290,295-296, 304
Will, L., 335
Williamson, N., 329-331
Wills and probate records in Monroe County, Indiana, 63,67
Wilson, H. W., 46,48
Women's issues in best-selling books, 184
Word frequency (common vs. uncommon words). *See* Typographical errors, impact on information retrieval
Word order conventions, 356
"Work"
   and best-sellers. *See* Best-selling books
   clustering, 180
   defined as entities for information retrieval, 181
   FRBR (Functional Requirements for Bibliographic Records), 180
   as key entities of recorded knowledge, 180
Work schedules and workloads
   self-responsibility, 365
   tenure for technical services librarians, 160,169
WorldCat database, 185,193,197, 200-201,207,213,249,283

XML
   benefits and pitfalls, 284
   changes in library profession, 51

flexibility of bibliographic data elements, 290-298
hampered schema development, 290
knowledge structures online, 336
mapping XML structures to MARC structures, 300-302
practical decisions in digital environment, 284,290-298, 300
review of CCQ, 51
"suprasumption" and "circumsumption" relationships, 303

Yahoo, 332-333
Yannakoudakis, E. J., 115
Yee, M. M., 290,307

Z39.19, ANSI/NISO standard, 335
Z39.50, ANSI/NISO standard, 122,126-127
Zeng, L., 236
Zoology study by Ruth, 9
Zoomerang, 155,169